The Writer's World: Sentences and Paragraphs

Lynne Gaetz
Lionel Groulx College

Suneeti Phadke
St. Jerome College

PEARSON

Prentice Hall

Upper Saddle River, New Jersey 07458

Library of Congress Cataloging-in-Publication Data

Gaetz, Lynne
  The Writer's World: sentences and paragraphs / Lynne Gaetz, Suneeti Phadke.
    p. cm.
  Includes index.
  ISBN 0-13-183041-4
  1. English language—Sentences—Problems, exercises, etc.   2. English
language—Paragraphs—Problems, exercises, etc.   I. Phadke, Suneeti   II. Title.

PE1441.G34 2005
808'.042—dc22   2005044769

Editorial Director: Leah Jewell
Executive Editor: Craig Campanella
Acquisitions Assistant: Joan Polk
VP/Director, Production and Manufacturing: Barbara Kittle
Production Editor: Joan E. Foley
Production Assistant: Marlene Gassler
Copyeditor: Kathryn Graehl
Text Permissions Specialist: Jane Scelta
Development Editor in Chief: Rochelle Diogenes
Development Editor: Veronica Tomaiuolo
Manufacturing Manager: Nick Sklitsis
Prepress and Manufacturing Buyer: Benjamin Smith
VP/Director, Marketing: Brandy Dawson
Marketing Manager: Kate Mitchell
Marketing Assistant: Anthony DeCosta

Media Project Manager: Alison Lorber
Director, Image Resource Center: Melinda Reo
Manager, Image Rights and Permissions: Zina Arabia
Manager, Visual Research: Beth Brenzel
Image Permissions Coordinator: Vickie Menanteaux
Manager, Cover Visual Research & Permissions: Karen Sanatar
Director, Creative Design: Leslie Osher
Art Director, Interior Design: Laura Gardner
Cover Design: Anne DeMarinis
Cover Art: (front) Judith Miller Archive/Dorling Kindersley Media Library; (rear) Photodisc Green/Getty Images, Inc.; Brand X Pictures/Getty Images, Inc.; Royalty Free/CORBIS; Stockdisc Classice/Getty Images, Inc.

This book was set in 11/13 Janson by Pine Tree Composition, Inc., and was printed and bound by Courier Companies, Inc. Covers were printed by Phoenix Color Corp.

For permission to use copyrighted material, grateful acknowledgment is made to the copyright holders on page 473, which is considered an extension of this copyright page.

PEARSON EDUCATION LTD.
PEARSON EDUCATION SINGAPORE, PTE. LTD
PEARSON EDUCATION, CANADA, LTD
PEARSON EDUCATION–JAPAN
PEARSON EDUCATION AUSTRALIA PTY, LIMITED

PEARSON EDUCATION NORTH ASIA LTD
PEARSON EDUCACIÓN DE MEXICO, S.A. DE C.V.
PEARSON EDUCATION MALAYSIA, PTE. LTD
PEARSON EDUCATION, UPPER SADDLE RIVER, NJ

10   9   8   7   6   5   4   3   2

ISBN 0-13-183041-4

Contents

Inside Front Cover
Sentences Checklist
Revising and Editing Symbols

Preface   viii

 The Writing Process   2

 Exploring   3

What Is Exploring?   3
Topic   4
Audience   4
Purpose   5
Exploring Strategies   5
Journal and Portfolio Writing   10

 Developing   12

What Is Developing?   12
Narrow the Topic   14
The Topic Sentence   15
The Supporting Ideas   20
The Paragraph Plan   28
The First Draft   29

 Revising and Editing   32

What Is Revising and Editing?   32
Revise for Unity   33
Revise for Adequate Support   34
Revise for Coherence   36
Revise for Style   38
Edit for Errors   38
The Final Draft   41

 Paragraph Patterns   43

What Are Paragraph Patterns?   43
A) The Illustration Paragraph   44
B) The Narrative Paragraph   49
C) The Descriptive Paragraph   54
D) The Process Paragraph   60
E) The Definition Paragraph   65
F) The Comparison and Contrast Paragraph   70
G) The Cause and Effect Paragraph   75
H) The Argument Paragraph   81

 Writing the Essay   89

Exploring the Essay   89
Explore Topics   92
The Thesis Statement   93
The Supporting Ideas   96
The Essay Plan   97
The Introduction   98
The Conclusion   100
The First Draft   102
Revising and Editing the Essay   102
The Final Draft   103

PART II — The Editing Handbook   106

GRAMMAR SECTION 1: Some Parts of Speech   108

 Nouns, Determiners, and Prepositions   108

Nouns   109
Count Nouns and Noncount Nouns   114
Determiners   116
Prepositions   120

 Pronouns   127

Pronoun-Antecedent Agreement   128
Indefinite Pronouns   130
Vague Pronouns   132
Pronoun Shifts   133
Pronoun Case   134
Problems with Possessive Pronouns   136
Relative Pronouns   140
Reflexive Pronouns (-self, -selves)   142

GRAMMAR SECTION 2: Problems with Verbs   147

 Subjects and Verbs   147

Identifying Subjects   148
Identifying Prepositional Phrases   151
Identifying Verbs   153

The Past Perfect Tense: Had
  & Past Participle   187
The Past Participle as an Adjective   190
The Passive Voice: Be & Past Participle   190

 Present and Past Tenses   159

Understanding Verb Tense   160
The Simple Present Tense   160
The Simple Past Tense   166
Avoiding Double Negatives   174

 Progressive Tenses   197

Understanding Progressive Tenses   198
Present Progressive   198
Past Progressive   200
Using Complete Verbs   202
Other Progressive Forms   203

 Past Participles   178

Past Participles   179
The Present Perfect Tense: Have/Has
  & Past Participle   183

 Other Verb Forms   208

Modals   209
Nonstandard Forms: Gonna, Gotta, Wanna   213
Conditional Forms   214
Gerunds and Infinitives   218

GRAMMAR SECTION 3: Verb Agreement and Consistency 224

 Subject-Verb Agreement 224

Basic Subject-Verb Agreement Rules 225
Verb Before the Subject 229
More Than One Subject 231
Special Subject Forms 231
Interrupting Words and Phrases 234

 Tense Consistency 240

Consistent Verb Tense 241

GRAMMAR SECTION 4: Effective Sentences 248

 Sentence Combining 1 248

Comparing Simple and Compound
  Sentences 249
Combining Sentences Using Coordinating
  Conjunctions 249
Combining Sentences Using
  Semicolons 253
Combining Sentences Using Transitional
  Expressions 255

 Sentence Combining 2 261

Understanding Complex Sentences 262
Using Subordinating Conjunctions 262
Using Relative Pronouns 267
Combining Questions 270

 Sentence Variety and Exact Language 275

Achieving Sentence Variety 276
Using Specific Vocabulary 279
Avoiding Clichés 281
Slang versus Standard English 283

GRAMMAR SECTION 5: Common Sentence Errors 288

 Fragments 288

Understanding Fragments 289
Phrase Fragments 289
Explanatory Fragments 290
Dependent-Clause Fragments 292

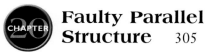 **Run-Ons** 298

Understanding Run-Ons 299

Faulty Parallel Structure 305

Identifying Parallel Structure 306
Correcting Faulty Parallel Structure 307

GRAMMAR SECTION 6: Modifiers   316

 CHAPTER **Adjectives and Adverbs**   316

Adjectives   317
Adverbs   321
Comparative and Superlative Forms   325

 CHAPTER **Mistakes with Modifiers**   333

Misplaced Modifiers   334
Dangling Modifiers   338

 GRAMMAR SECTION 7: Word Use and Spelling   344

 CHAPTER **Spelling**   344

Improving Your Spelling   345
Writing *ie* or *ei*   345
Adding Prefixes and Suffixes   347
Writing Two-Part Words   352
Commonly Misspelled Words   353

 CHAPTER **Commonly Confused Words**   359

Commonly Confused Words   360

 GRAMMAR SECTION 8: Punctuation and Mechanics   369

 CHAPTER **Commas**   369

Understanding Commas   370
Commas in a Series   370
Commas After Introductory Words
   and Phrases   371
Commas Around Interrupting Words
   and Phrases   371
Commas in Compound
   Sentences   374
Commas in Complex Sentences   375
Commas in Business Letters   378

 CHAPTER **The Apostrophe**   383

Understanding Apostrophes   384
Using Apostrophes in Contractions   384
Using Apostrophes to Show Ownership   387
Using Apostrophes in Expressions
   of Time   389

 CHAPTER **Quotation Marks and Capitalization**   394

Direct and Indirect Quotations   395
Quotation Marks   395
Capitalization   400
Titles   402

GRAMMAR SECTION 9: Editing   406

 CHAPTER **Editing Practice**   406

 PART III — Reading Strategies and Selections   416

 CHAPTER 29 **Reading Strategies and Selections**   417

Reading Strategies   417

Reading Selections   421

- Reading 1: **"Fish Cheeks,"** by Amy Tan   421
- Reading 2: **"The Hijab,"** by Naheed Mustafa   423
- Reading 3: **"A Conversation with John E. Smelcer,"** by Dale E. Seeds   425
- Reading 4: **"The Point Is?"** by John G. Tufts   428
- Reading 5: **"Sports and Life: Lessons to Be Learned,"** by Jeff Kemp   430
- Reading 6: **"Birth,"** by Maya Angelou   433
- Reading 7: **"For Marriage,"** by Kirsteen Macleod   435
- Reading 8: **"Against Marriage,"** by Winston Murray   436
- Reading 9: **"The Appalling Truth,"** by Dorothy Nixon   438
- Reading 10: **"The New Addiction,"** by Josh Freed   442
- Reading 11: **"The Culture War,"** by Linda Chavez   444
- Reading 12: **"Going Thin in Fiji,"** by Ellen Goodman   447
- Reading 13: **"What It Feels Like to Walk on the Moon,"** by Buzz Aldrin   449
- Reading 14: **"The Zoo Life,"** by Yann Martel   452
- Reading 15: **"Political Activism,"** by Craig Stern   454
- Reading 16: **"How to Handle Conflict,"** by P. Gregory Smith   457
- Reading 17: **"The Rewards of 'Dirty Work,'"** by Linda L. Lindsey and Stephen Beach   459

Appendices

- Appendix 1: Grammar Glossary   462
- Appendix 2: Verb Tenses   464
- Appendix 3: Combining Ideas in Sentences   465
- Appendix 4: Punctuation and Mechanics   466
- Appendix 5: Spelling, Grammar, and Vocabulary Logs   469

Credits   473

Index   475

Inside Back Cover
Paragraph and Essay Checklists

About the First Edition of *The Writer's World: Sentences and Paragraphs*

Whether your students enroll in the course with varying skill levels, whether they are native or nonnative speakers of English, or whether they learn better through the use of visuals, *The Writer's World* can help students produce writing that is technically correct and rich in content. It is our goal for this preface to give you a deeper understanding of how we arranged the text and the key components found in *The Writer's World: Sentences and Paragraphs*.

A Research-Based Approach

From the onset of the development process, we have comprehensively researched the needs and desires of current developmental writing instructors. We met with more than 45 instructors from around the country, asking for their opinions and insights regarding (1) the challenges posed by the course, (2) the needs of today's ever-changing student population, and (3) the ideas and features we were proposing to provide them and you with a more effective learning and teaching tool. Prentice Hall also commissioned dozens of detailed manuscript reviews from instructors, asking them to analyze and evaluate each draft of the manuscript. These reviewers identified numerous ways in which we could refine and enhance our key features. Their invaluable feedback was incorporated throughout *The Writer's World*. The text you are seeing is truly the product of a successful partnership between the authors, publisher, and well over 100 developmental writing instructors.

How We Organized *The Writer's World*

The Writer's World is separated into three parts for ease of use and convenience.

Part I: The Writing Process teaches students how to formulate ideas (Exploring); how to expand, organize, and present those ideas in a piece of writing (Developing); and how to polish writing so

that they convey their message as clearly as possible (Revising and Editing). The result is that writing becomes far less daunting because students have specific steps to follow.

Chapter 4 of Part I gives students an overview of 8 patterns of development. As they work through the practices and write their own paragraphs, students begin to see how using a writing pattern can help them fulfill their purpose for writing.

Chapter 5 of Part I covers the parts of the essay and explains how students can apply what they have learned about paragraph development to essay writing.

Part II: The Editing Handbook is a thematic grammar handbook. In each chapter, the examples correspond to a section theme, such as Social Science or Entertainment and Culture. As students work through the chapters, they hone their grammar and editing skills while gaining knowledge about a variety of topics. In addition to helping retain interest in the grammar practices, the thematic material provides sparks that ignite new ideas that students can apply to their writing.

Part III: Reading Strategies and Selections offers tips, readings, and follow-up questions. Students learn how to write by observing and dissecting what they read. The readings contain themes that are found in Part II: The Editing Handbook, thereby providing more fodder for generating writing ideas.

How *The Writer's World* Meets Students' Diverse Needs

We created *The Writer's World* to meet your students' diverse needs. To accomplish this, we asked both the instructors in our focus groups and the reviewers at every stage not only to critique our ideas but to offer their suggestions and recommendations for features that would enhance the learning process of their students. The result has been the integration of many elements that are not found in other textbooks, including our visual program, coverage of nonnative speaker material, and strategies for addressing the varying skill levels students bring to the course.

The Visual Program

A stimulating, full-color book, *The Writer's World* recognizes that today's world is a visual one, and it encourages students to become better communicators by responding to images. Chapter opening visuals in Part I help students to think about the chapters' key concepts in new ways. For example, in the Chapter 5 opener, a photograph of a suspension bridge sets the stage for essay writing. Both the bridge and an essay need specific types of support to make them sturdy structures.

In Part II, **photos on the part-opening page** give students additional visual cues highlighting the importance of correct grammar and mechanics. These nine photos are carried through each section, and even serve as a visual tabbing guide for Part II. In addition, **each chapter in Part II opens with another photo** to help illustrate the theme of the examples and exercises in that chapter and section. These visual aids can also serve as sources for writing prompts.

Finally, each copy of *The Writer's World* includes a free **Visualizing Writing CD-ROM** with 52 audio and animated "mini-lectures" to help students understand key concepts. These lectures, taken from the Prentice Hall library of animations, offer more support to visual and auditory learners, and can be accessed on any computer. The audio portion of the grammar lectures can also be heard on a home or car CD player.

Seamless Coverage for Nonnative Speakers

Instructors in our focus groups noted the growing number of nonnative/ESL speakers enrolling in the developmental writing courses. Although some of these students have special needs relating to the writing process, many of you still have a large portion of native speakers in your courses whose more traditional needs must also be satisfied. To meet the challenge of this rapidly changing dynamic, we have carefully implemented and integrated content throughout to assist these students. *The Writer's World* does not have separate ESL boxes, ESL chapters, or tacked-on ESL appendices. Instead, information that traditionally poses challenges to nonnative speakers is woven seamlessly throughout the book. In our extensive experience teaching writing to both native and nonnative speakers of English, we have learned that both groups learn best when they are not distracted by ESL labels. With the seamless approach, nonnative speakers do not feel self-conscious and segregated, and native speakers do not tune out to detailed explanations that may also benefit them. Many of these traditional problem areas receive more coverage than you would find in other textbooks, arming the instructor with the material to effectively meet the needs of nonnative speakers. Moreover, the Annotated Instructor's Edition provides over 75 ESL Teaching Tips designed specifically to help instructors better meet the needs of their nonnative speakers.

Issue-Focused Thematic Grammar

In our survey of the marketplace, many of you indicated that one of the primary challenges in teaching your course is finding materials that are engaging to students in a contemporary context. This is especially true in grammar instruction. **Students come to the course with varying skill levels,** and many students are simply not interested in grammar. To address this challenge, we have introduced **issue-focused thematic grammar** in *The Writer's World*.

Each section in Part II revolves around a common theme. These themes include Social Sciences, Entertainment and Culture, Beliefs, Politics, Science, Relationships, Zoology, and the Business World. Each chapter within the sections includes issues related to the theme. The thematic approach enables students to broaden their awareness of important subjects, allowing them to infuse their writing with reflection and insight. Also, we believe (and our reviewers concurred) that it makes grammar more engaging. And the more engaging grammar is, the more likely students will retain key concepts—raising their skill level in these important building blocks of writing.

We also feel that it is important not to isolate grammar from the writing process. Therefore, the Writer's Room at the end of each grammar section contains paragraph writing topics that are related to the theme of the section and that follow different writing patterns. To help students appreciate the relevance of their writing tasks, each grammar chapter begins with a grammar snapshot—a sample taken from an authentic piece of writing that highlights the grammar concept. There is also an editing checklist that is specific to the grammar concepts covered in that chapter. Finally, at the end of each grammar section, there is The Writers' Circle, a collaborative activity that is particularly helpful to nonnative speakers.

What Tools Can Help Students Get the Most from *The Writer's World*?

Overwhelmingly, focus group participants and reviewers asked that both a larger number and a greater diversity of exercises and activities be incorporated into a new text. In response to this feedback, we have developed and tested the following items in *The Writer's World*. These tools form the pedagogical backbone of the book, and we are confident they will help your students become better writers.

Hints

In each chapter, **Hint** boxes highlight important writing and grammar points. Hints are useful for all students, but many will be particularly helpful for nonnative speakers. For example, in Chapter 3 there is a hint about being direct and avoiding circular reasoning, and in Chapter 12 there is one about using the past conditional correctly.

The Writer's Desk

Part I includes **The Writer's Desk** exercises that help students get used to practicing all stages and steps of the writing process. Students begin with prewriting and then progress to developing, organizing (using paragraph plans), drafting, and finally, revising and editing to create a final draft.

Checklists

Each end-of-chapter checklist is a chapter review exercise. Questions prompt students to recall and review what they have learned in the chapter.

The Writer's Room

The Writer's Room contains writing activities that correspond to general, college, and workplace topics. Some prompts are brief to allow students to freely form ideas while others are expanded to give students more direction.

There is literally something for every student writer in this end-of-chapter feature. Students who respond well to visual cues will appreciate the photo writing exercises in **The Writer's Room** in Part II. Students who learn best by hearing through collaboration will appreciate the discussion and group work prompts in **The Writers' Circle** section of selected **The Writer's Rooms**. To help students see how grammar is not isolated from the writing process, there are also **The Writer's Room** activities at the end of sections 1 to 8 in Part II: The Editing Handbook.

Acknowledgments

Many people have helped us produce *The Writer's World*. First and foremost, we would like to thank our students for inspiring us and providing us with extraordinary feedback. Their words and insights pervade this book.

We also benefited greatly from the insightful comments and suggestions from over 100 instructors across the nation, all of whom are listed in the opening pages of the Annotated Instructor's Edition. Our colleagues' feedback was invaluable and helped shape *The Writer's World* series content, focus, and organization.

We are indebted to the team of dedicated professionals at Prentice Hall who have helped make this project a reality. They have boosted our spirits and have believed in us every step of the way. Special thanks to Veronica Tomaiuolo for her magnificent job in polishing this book and to Craig Companella for trusting our instincts and enthusiastically propelling us forward. Kate Mitchell worked tirelessly to ensure we were always meeting the needs of instructors. We owe a deep debt of gratitude to Yolanda de Rooy, whose encouraging words helped ignite this project. Joan Foley's attention to detail in the production process kept us motivated and on task and made *The Writer's World* a much better resource for both instructors and students. We would also like to thank Laura Gardner for her brilliant design, which helped keep the visual learner in all of us engaged.

Finally, we would like to dedicate this book to our husbands and children who supported us and who patiently put up with our long hours on the computer. Manu, Octavio, and Natalia continually encouraged us. We especially appreciate the help and sacrifices of Diego, Becky, Kiran, and Meghana.

A Note to Students

Your knowledge, ideas, and opinions are important. The ability to clearly communicate those ideas is invaluable in your personal, academic, and professional life. When your writing is error-free, readers will focus on your message, and you will be able to persuade, inform, entertain, or inspire them. *The Writer's World* includes strategies that will help you improve your written communication. Quite simply, when you become a better writer, you become a better communicator. It is our greatest wish for *The Writer's World* to make you excited about writing, communicating, and learning.

Enjoy!
Lynne Gaetz and Suneeti Phadke
TheWritersWorld@hotmail.com

Lynne Gaetz and family in Mexico

Suneeti Phadke and family in Quebec, Canada

The Writing Process

The ability to express your ideas in written form is very useful in your personal, academic, and professional life. It does not take a special talent to write well. If you are willing to practice the writing process, you will be able to produce well-written sentences, paragraphs, and essays.

The Writing Process

The writing process involves exploring, expanding, and organizing ideas and then bringing them all together in sentences and paragraphs. Before you begin working through the chapters in Part I, review the main steps in the writing process.

Exploring

Step 1: Consider your topic.

Step 2: Consider your audience.

Step 3: Consider your purpose.

Step 4: Try exploring strategies.

Developing

Step 1: Narrow your topic.

Step 2: Express your main idea.

Step 3: Develop your supporting ideas.

Step 4: Make a plan or an outline.

Step 5: Write your first draft.

Revising and Editing

Step 1: Revise for unity.

Step 2: Revise for adequate support.

Step 3: Revise for coherence.

Step 4: Revise for style.

Step 5: Edit for technical errors.

Exploring

> *The greatest mistake you can make in life is to be continually fearing you will make one.*
>
> —ELBERT HUBBARD (1856–1915)
> *American author*

CONTENTS

- What Is Exploring?
- Topic
- Audience
- Purpose
- Exploring Strategies
- Journal and Portfolio Writing

The exploring stage of the writing process is like arriving on a new shore. You fearlessly move ahead making new discoveries.

What Is Exploring?

An explorer investigates a place to find new and interesting information. **Exploring** is also useful during the writing process. Whenever you have trouble finding a topic, you can use specific techniques to generate ideas.

There are four steps in the exploring stage of the writing process.

ESSAY LINK

When you plan an essay, you should also follow the four exploring steps.

EXPLORING

STEP 1	**Consider your topic.** Think about who or what you will write about.
STEP 2	**Consider your audience.** Determine who your intended readers will be.
STEP 3	**Consider your purpose.** Think about your reasons for writing.
STEP 4	**Try exploring strategies.** Practice using various techniques to find ideas.

Understanding Your Assignment

As soon as you are given an assignment, make sure that you understand your task. Answer the following questions about the assignment.

- How many words or pages should I write?
- What is the due date for the assignment?
- Are there any special qualities my writing should include?
- Will I write in class or at home?

After you have considered your task, think about your topic, purpose, and audience.

Topic

Your **topic** is what you are writing about. When your instructor gives you a topic for your writing, you can narrow it to suit your interests. For example, if your instructor asks you to write about relationships, you could write about marriage, divorce, children, family responsibilities, or traditions. You could focus on an aspect of the topic that you know about and find interesting.

When you think about the topic, ask yourself the following questions.

- What about the topic interests me?
- Do I have special knowledge about the topic?
- Does anything about the topic arouse my emotions?

Audience

Your **audience** is your intended reader. The reader might be your instructor, other students, your boss, your co-workers, and so on. When you write, remember to adapt your language and vocabulary for each specific audience. For example, in a formal report written for your business class, you might use specialized accounting terms.

When you consider your audience, ask yourself the following questions.

- Who will read my assignment? Will it be my instructor, other students, or people outside my classroom?
- What do my readers probably know about the subject?
- What information will my readers expect?

 **Your Instructor as Your Audience**

For many college assignments, your audience is your instructor. When you write for him or her, use standard English. In other words, try to use correct grammar, sentence structure, and vocabulary.

Do not leave out information because you assume that your instructor knows a lot about the topic. When your instructor reads your work, he or she will expect you to reveal what you have learned or what you have understood about the topic.

Purpose

Your **purpose** is your reason for writing. Sometimes you may have more than one purpose. When you consider your purpose, ask yourself the following questions.

- Do I want to **entertain?** Is my goal to tell a story?
- Do I want to **persuade?** Is my goal to convince the reader that my point of view is the correct one?
- Do I want to **inform?** Is my goal to explain something or give information about a topic?

 **Purposes May Overlap**

Sometimes you may have more than one purpose. For example, in a paragraph about a childhood memory, your purpose could be to tell a story about your first trip to a new place. At the same time, you could inform your readers about the things to see in that area, or you could persuade readers that traveling is, or is not, worthwhile.

Exploring Strategies

After you determine your topic, audience, and purpose, try some **exploring strategies**—also known as **prewriting strategies**—to help get your ideas flowing. The three most common strategies are *freewriting*, *brainstorming*, and *clustering*. It is not necessary to do all of the strategies explained in this chapter. Find the strategy that works best for you.

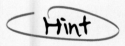 **When to Use Exploring Strategies**

You can use the exploring strategies at any stage of the writing process.

- To find a topic
- To narrow a broad topic
- To generate ideas about your topic
- To generate supporting details

Freewriting

When you **freewrite,** you write without stopping for a limited period of time. You record whatever thoughts come into your mind without worrying about them. Even if you run out of ideas, you can just repeat a word or phrase, or you can write "I don't know what to say."

During freewriting, do not be concerned with your grammar or spelling. If you use a computer, let your ideas flow and do not worry about typing mistakes. Remember that the point is to generate ideas and not to create a perfect sample of writing.

MANUEL'S FREEWRITING

College student Manuel Figuera jotted down some of his thoughts about fears. He wrote for five minutes without stopping.

What do I think about fears? I don't know. I'm not afraid of anything. No, that's not true. I had a lot of fears when I was a kid. I was sure a monster lived under the bed. I would check under the bed every night and when I got out of bed I'd jump a few feet so the monster couldn't grab my leg. What else? Think, think, think. . . . Probably everybody is afraid of something. My sister hates spiders and other bugs. I guess I still have some fears. I don't like to speak in public. I get nervous when I have to read out loud too. There are ways to get over fears, though. I learned some techniques about public speaking.

PRACTICE I

Underline topics from Manuel's freewriting that could be expanded into complete paragraphs.

The Writer's Desk **Freewriting**

Choose one of the following topics and do some freewriting. Remember to write without stopping.

TOPICS: Children   Kindness   Work

_____

_____

_____

_____

_____

_____

_____

Brainstorming

When you **brainstorm,** you create a list of ideas. You can include opinions, details, images, questions, or anything else that comes to mind. If you need to, you can stop and think while you are creating your list. Do not worry about grammar or spelling. Remember that the point is to generate ideas.

MADHURI'S BRAINSTORMING

College student Madhuri Desai brainstormed about the topic "moving away from home." Her audience was her instructor and other students, and her purpose was to entertain.

- moved out of my family home three years ago
- hard to get an apartment
- first roommate: terrible!
- rude, selfish, messy, never talked to me, annoying boyfriend
- hard to pay the rent and go to school
- lessons I learned about finding a roommate
- bad experience with truck I borrowed
- some boxes fell off while driving
- sometimes miss my family

PRACTICE 2

Read Madhuri's list about moving, and underline ideas that could be developed into complete paragraphs.

The Writer's Desk **Brainstorming**

Choose one of the following topics and brainstorm. Let your ideas flow when you create your list.

TOPICS: Traditions   College   Fashion trends

_____

_____

_____

_____

_____

_____

_____

_____

_____

_____

Clustering

When you **cluster,** you draw a word map. To begin, write your topic in the middle of the page. Then, think of ideas that relate to the topic. Using lines or arrows, connect each idea to the central topic or to other ideas. Keep writing, circling, and connecting ideas until you have groups or "clusters" of them on your page. When you finish, you will have a visual image of your ideas.

ANTON'S CLUSTERING

College student Anton Gromyko used clustering to explore ideas about movies.

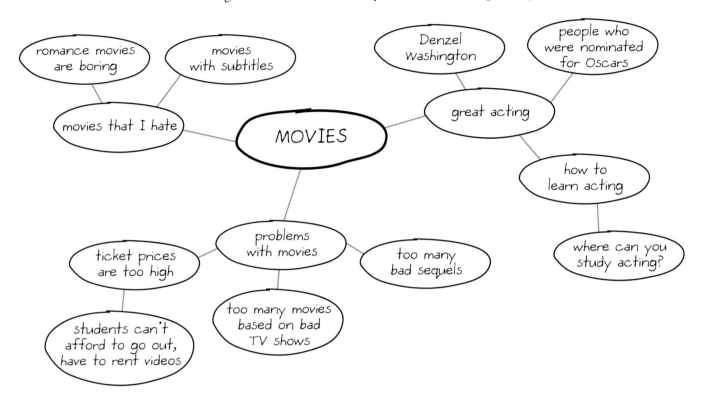

PRACTICE 3

Look at Anton's clustering. Circle one or more clusters that would make a good paragraph.

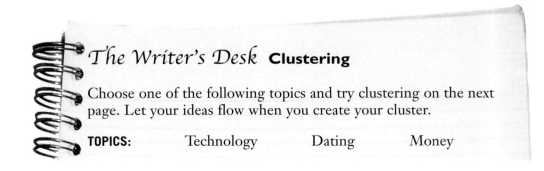

The Writer's Desk **Clustering**

Choose one of the following topics and try clustering on the next page. Let your ideas flow when you create your cluster.

TOPICS: Technology Dating Money

_____

_____

_____

_____

_____

_____

_____

_____

_____

_____

_____

_____

_____

_____

_____

_____

_____

_____

_____

_____

_____

_____

_____

 **Questioning**

Another way to generate ideas about a topic is to ask yourself a series of questions and write responses to them. The questions can help you define and narrow your topic. One common way to do this is to ask yourself *who, what, when, where, why,* and *how* questions.

Question	Possible Answers
Why do people travel?	To escape, to learn about other cultures, to get good weather
How can they travel?	Flying, taking a train or bus, walking tours, hiking, sailing, cycling
What are inexpensive ways to travel?	Find last-minute deals, go backpacking, stay with friends or in youth hostels, share gas

Journal and Portfolio Writing

Keeping a Journal

American educator and writer Christina Baldwin once said, "Journal writing is like a voyage to the interior." One good way to practice your writing is to keep a journal. In a journal, you record your thoughts, opinions, ideas, and impressions. Journal writing provides you with a chance to practice your writing without worrying about the audience. It also gives you a source of material when you are asked to write about a topic of your choice.

You can write about any topic that appeals to you. Here are some suggestions.

- **College**   You can describe new things you have learned, express opinions about your courses, and list ideas for assignments.
- **Your Personal Life**   You can describe your feelings about your career goals. You can also write about personal problems and solutions, reflect about past and future decisions, express feelings about your job, and so on.
- **Controversial Issues**   You can write about your reactions to controversies in the world, in your country, in your state, in your city, in your college, or even within your own family.
- **Interesting Facts**   Perhaps you have discovered new and interesting information in a course, in a newspaper, or in some other way. You can record information about any interesting facts in your journal.

Keeping a Portfolio

A **writing portfolio** is a place where you keep samples of all of your writing. It could be in a binder or an electronic file folder. The purpose of keeping a portfolio is to have a record of your writing progress.

In your portfolio, keep all drafts of your writing assignments. When you work on new assignments, review your previous work in your portfolio. Identify your main problems, and try not to repeat the same errors.

 The Writer's Room   **Topics to Explore**

Writing Activity 1

Choose one of the following topics, or choose your own topic. Then generate ideas about the topic. You may want to try the suggested exploring strategy.

General Topics

1. Try freewriting about friendship. Jot down any ideas that come to mind.
2. Try brainstorming about important ceremonies. List the first ideas that come to mind.
3. Try clustering about the idea of luck. First, write the word *luck* in the middle of the page. Then create clusters of ideas that relate to the topic.

College or Work-Related Topics

4. Try freewriting to come up with ideas about workplace environments.

5. Brainstorm about time. To get ideas, list anything that comes to mind when you think about time.

6. Try clustering about stress. Write the word *stress* in the center of the page, and then create clusters of ideas about the topic.

EXPLORING CHECKLIST

When you explore a topic, ask yourself the following questions.

What is my **topic?** Consider what you will write about.

Who is my **audience?** Think about your intended reader.

What is my **purpose?** Determine your reason for writing.

Which exploring strategy will I use? You could try one of the next strategies or a combination of strategies.

> **Freewriting** is writing without stopping for a limited period of time.
>
> **Brainstorming** is making a list.
>
> **Clustering** is drawing a word map.
>
> **Questioning** is asking and answering questions.

See Chapter 1 on the Visualizing Writing CD-ROM for additional audio and mini-lectures on **Brainstorming, Clustering, Freewriting, Questioning,** and **Keeping a Journal**.

CHAPTER 2

Developing

> *Inspiration is wonderful when it happens, but the writer must develop an approach for the rest of the time.*
>
> —LEONARD BERNSTEIN (1918–1990)
> *American composer*

CONTENTS

- What Is Developing?
- Narrow the Topic
- The Topic Sentence
- The Supporting Ideas
- The Paragraph Plan
- The First Draft

The developing stage of the writing process is like creating a sand castle. Using a variety of tools, you develop your structure.

ESSAY LINK

You can follow similar steps when you develop an essay. See Chapter 5 for more details about essay writing.

What Is Developing?

Chapter 1 explained how you can explore ideas for writing. This chapter will take you, step by step, through the development of a paragraph. There are five key steps in the developing stage.

DEVELOPING

STEP 1	**Narrow your topic.** Find an aspect of the topic that interests you.
STEP 2	**Express your main idea.** Write a topic sentence that expresses the main idea of the piece of writing.
STEP 3	**Develop your supporting ideas.** Generate ideas that support your topic sentence.
STEP 4	**Make a plan.** Organize your main and supporting ideas, and place your ideas in a plan.
STEP 5	**Write your first draft.** Communicate your ideas in a single written piece.

Reviewing Paragraph Structure

A **paragraph** is a group of sentences focusing on one central idea. Paragraphs can stand alone, or they can be part of a longer work such as an essay, a letter, or a report.

The **topic sentence** expresses the main point of the paragraph and shows the writer's attitude toward the subject.

The **body sentences** provide details that support the main point.

The **concluding sentence** brings the paragraph to a satisfactory close.

```
Topic sentence _____
_____ . Supporting detail _____
_____ . Supporting detail _____
_____ . Supporting detail _____
Concluding sentence _____
```

VEENA'S PARAGRAPH

College student Veena Thomas wrote the following paragraph. Read her paragraph and then answer the questions.

> **As college students, we have a completely different culture than anyone else.** A few thousand students live together in what amounts to our own little city. Crowded into doubles and triples, we are brought together by our physical closeness, our similarities, and our differences. We share the bathrooms with strangers who soon become friends. We laugh together, cry together, and sleep through class together. Our dorm room becomes our refuge with its unmade beds, posters on the wall, and inflatable chairs. Money is a problem because we never have enough of it. When we get sick of cafeteria food, we subsist on 25-cent ramen noodles and boxes of oatmeal. We drink way too much coffee, and we order pizza at 1 a.m. We live on College Standard Time, which is about four hours behind everyone else. So while everyone else sleeps, we hang out with our music playing until the early hours of the morning. It's a different life, but it's our life, and we love it.

PRACTICE 1

Look at the structure of Veena's paragraph. The topic sentence (a statement of a main idea) is in bold. List Veena's supporting ideas. The first one has been done for you.

City of students crowded together

_____

_____

_____

_____

_____

Paragraph Form

Your paragraphs should have the following form.

- Always indent the first word of a paragraph. Move it about one inch, or five spaces, from the left-hand margin.
- Leave a 1- to 1½-inch margin on each side of your paragraph.
- Begin every sentence with a capital letter, and end each sentence with the proper punctuation.

It is important to spend time with your children.

Narrow the Topic

Sometimes you may be given a topic that is too broad for one paragraph. In those situations, you need to make your topic fit the size of the assignment. When you **narrow your topic,** you make it more specific. To narrow your topic, you can use the exploring strategies (freewriting, brainstorming, or clustering) that you learned in Chapter 1.

DONOVAN'S LIST TO NARROW THE TOPIC

College student Donovan Lynch used brainstorming to narrow his broad topic, "food."

- good restaurants
- when I ate too much junk food
- labeling genetically modified food

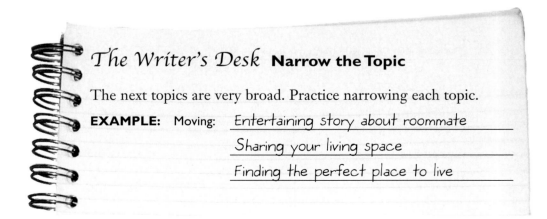

The Writer's Desk **Narrow the Topic**

The next topics are very broad. Practice narrowing each topic.

EXAMPLE: Moving: Entertaining story about roommate

Sharing your living space

Finding the perfect place to live

1. College: _____

_____

_____

2. Money: _____

_____

_____

3. Technology: _____

_____

_____

4. Children: _____

_____

_____

5. Work: _____

_____

_____

The Topic Sentence

The next step in the writing process is to write a sentence that expresses the main idea. In a paragraph, the statement of the main idea is called the **topic sentence.** The topic sentence of a paragraph has several features.

- It introduces the topic.
- It states the main (or controlling) idea.
- It is the most general sentence.
- It is supported by other sentences.

The **controlling idea** is an essential part of the topic sentence because it makes a point about the topic. The controlling idea expresses the writer's opinion, attitude, or feeling. You can express different controlling ideas about the same topic. For example, the following topic sentences are about leaving the family home, but each sentence makes a different point about the topic.

narrowed topic   controlling idea
Leaving the family home is a traumatic experience for some college students.

controlling idea   narrowed topic
The most exciting and important part of a youth's life is **leaving the family home.**

PRACTICE 2

Read each topic sentence. Underline the topic once and the controlling idea twice. To find the topic, ask yourself what the paragraph is about.

EXAMPLE:

<u>College students</u> <u><u>should take their studies seriously</u></u>.

1. Several interesting things happened when the probe landed on Mars.

2. Children without siblings tend to be self-reliant.

3. The Halloween costume was truly original.

4. On my eleventh birthday, I did a silly thing.

5. There should not be a mandatory retirement age.

6. Our vacation was filled with exciting experiences.

7. Three strategies can help you speak with strangers.

8. The dorm room was an uncontrollable mess.

9. Smoking should be permitted in bars and restaurants.

Writing an Effective Topic Sentence

When you develop your topic sentence, avoid some common errors by asking yourself these four questions.

ESSAY LINK

When you write a thesis statement for an essay, ask yourself questions 1 to 3 to ensure that your thesis statement is complete and valid.

1. **Is my topic sentence a complete sentence?**
   Your topic sentence should always be a complete sentence that reveals a complete thought.

Incomplete:	Living in student housing.
	(This is a topic but *not* a topic sentence. It does not express a complete thought.)
Topic sentence:	Because some college students do not take their studies seriously, it can be difficult to live in student housing.

2. **Does my topic sentence have a controlling idea?**
   Your topic sentence should make a point about your paragraph's topic. It should not announce the topic.

Announcement:	I will write about nursing.
	(This sentence announces the topic but says nothing relevant about it. Do not use expressions such as *My topic is* or *I will write about*.)
Topic sentence:	Nurses need to be in good physical and psychological health.

3. **Does my topic sentence make a valid and supportable point?**
Your topic sentence should express a valid point that you can support with details and examples. It should not be a vaguely worded statement, and it should not be a highly questionable generalization.

Vague:	Today's students are too weak.
	(How are they weak?)
Invalid point:	Today's students have more responsibilities than those in the past.
	(Is this really true? This might be a hard assertion to prove.)
Topic sentence:	With a little organization, it is possible to juggle school work, raise a child, and hold a part-time job.

4. **Can I support my topic sentence in a single paragraph?**
Your topic sentence should express an idea that you can support in a paragraph. It should not be too broad or too narrow.

Too broad:	There are many good libraries.
	(It would be difficult to write only one paragraph about this topic.)
Too narrow:	The college library is located beside the student center.
	(What more is there to say?)
Topic sentence:	The college library, which is beside the student center, contains valuable resources for students.

PRACTICE 3

Identify why each of the following topic sentences is not effective. Then, choose the word or words from the list that best describe the problem with each topic sentence. (A topic sentence may have more than one problem.) Finally, correct the problem by revising each sentence.

Incomplete	Vague	Announces
Invalid	Broad	Narrow

EXAMPLE:

I am going to write about athletes.

Problem: _Announces; broad_

Revised sentence: _The salaries in professional basketball are too high._

1. Using innocent animals to test beauty products.

Problem: _____

Revised statement: _____

_____

2. Everybody likes reality television.

    Problem: _____

    Revised statement: _____

    _____

3. In this paper, I will give my opinion about the legal driving age.

    Problem: _____

    Revised statement: _____

    _____

4. Adolescents are more reckless.

    Problem: _____

    Revised statement: _____

    _____

5. Having a part-time job.

    Problem: _____

    Revised statement: _____

    _____

6. Money is important.

    Problem: _____

    Revised statement: _____

    _____

 **Placement of the Topic Sentence**

Because you are developing your writing skills, it is a good idea to place your topic sentence at the beginning of your paragraph. Then, follow it with supporting details. Opening your paragraph with a topic sentence helps your readers immediately identify what your paragraph is about.

PRACTICE 4

Choose the best topic sentence for each paragraph.

1. When a person undergoes a period of high stress, he or she may experience sleep problems. Insomnia can also be caused by high alcohol consumption; although alcohol makes it easier to fall asleep,

the quality of the sleep is reduced. Furthermore, irregular sleeping and waking times can provoke insomnia.

Possible topic sentences:

_____ Many people in the world get insomnia.

_____ Insomnia, the inability to have prolonged deep sleep, is caused by several factors.

_____ Insomnia is the inability to have prolonged deep sleep.

2. After a marital breakup, boys are more likely to have external behavior problems. For example, they may become more impulsive, aggressive, and antisocial. After divorce, girls generally internalize their anger and frustration. They may become anxious and depressed.

Possible topic sentences:

_____ Girls often become withdrawn after a divorce.

_____ Divorce is common in North America.

_____ Research suggests that male and female children react to divorce in different ways.

3. We expect our lives to follow the pattern of such stories. We grow up believing that love will just happen, without effort. We become convinced that we will only find happiness once we find a soul mate, and we expect this soul mate to fulfill all of our needs and to feel eternally lustful toward us.

Possible topic sentences:

_____ Fairy tales give us unrealistic expectations about love.

_____ Through stories, we learn that love never dies.

_____ Love is a great thing.

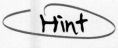 **Write an Interesting Topic Sentence**

Your topic sentence should not express an obvious or well-known fact. Write something that will interest your readers and make them want to continue reading.

Obvious: People need to work to earn a good salary.
          (Everybody knows this.)

Better: When looking for a job, remember that some things are more important than having a good salary.

The Writer's Desk Write Topic Sentences

Narrow each topic. Then, write a topic sentence that contains a controlling idea. (You could refer to your ideas in The Writer's Desk: Narrow the Topic on page 14.)

EXAMPLE: Moving

Narrowed topic: _Living with a roommate_

Topic sentence: _My first experience of living with a roommate turned out to be a disaster._

1. College

   Narrowed topic: _____

   Topic sentence: _____
   _____

2. Money

   Narrowed topic: _____

   Topic sentence: _____
   _____

3. Technology

   Narrowed topic: _____

   Topic sentence: _____
   _____

4. Children

   Narrowed topic: _____

   Topic sentence: _____
   _____

5. Work

   Narrowed topic: _____

   Topic sentence: _____
   _____

ESSAY LINK

In an essay, you place the thesis statement in the introduction. Then each supporting idea becomes a distinct paragraph with its own topic sentence.

The Supporting Ideas

After you have written a clear topic sentence, you can focus on **supporting details**—the facts and examples that provide the reader with interesting information about the subject matter. There are three steps you can take to determine your paragraph's supporting details.

1. Generate supporting ideas.
2. Choose the best supporting ideas.
3. Organize your ideas.

Generating Supporting Ideas

You can use an exploring strategy—freewriting, brainstorming, or clustering—to generate supporting ideas.

MADHURI'S SUPPORTING IDEAS

Madhuri Desai chose one of her narrowed topics related to "moving" and wrote her topic sentence. Then she listed ideas that could support her topic sentence.

TOPIC SENTENCE: **My first experience of living with a roommate turned out to be a disaster.**

- "Kate" and boyfriend never talked to me.
- She is a totally messy person!
- She left dirty dishes in the living room.
- Her dirty laundry was all over the apt.
- She never bought toilet paper, detergent, etc.
- Her boyfriend was at the apt. too much.
- He ate my food without asking.
- He hogged the remote control.
- She used my makeup, shampoo, soap, etc.
- She rarely paid her share of bills.

> **TECHNOLOGY LINK**
>
> If you write your paragraph on a computer, put your topic sentence in bold. Then you (and your instructor) can easily identify it.

The Writer's Desk **List Supporting Ideas**

Choose one of your topic sentences from The Writer's Desk: Write Topic Sentences on page 20 and make a list of ideas that could support it.

Topic sentence: _____

Supporting ideas: _____

_____

_____

_____

_____

_____

_____

_____

_____

Choosing the Best Ideas

A paragraph should have **unity**, which means that all of its sentences must relate directly to its topic sentence. To achieve unity, examine your prewriting carefully and then choose three or four ideas that are most compelling and that clearly support your topic sentence. You may notice that several items in your list are similar; therefore, you can group them together. Remove any ideas that do not support your topic sentence.

MADHURI'S SUPPORTING IDEAS

First, Madhuri crossed out ideas that she did not want to develop. Then, she highlighted three of her most appealing ideas and labeled them A, B, or C. Finally, she regrouped other supporting details from her list.

TOPIC SENTENCE: <u>My first experience of living with a roommate turned out to be a disaster.</u>

- "Kate" and boyfriend never talked to me.
- She is a totally messy person! ⎫
- She left dirty dishes in the living room. ⎬ A
- Her dirty laundry all was over the apt. ⎭
- She never bought toilet paper, detergent, etc.
- Her boyfriend was at the apt. too much. ⎫
- He ate my food without asking. ⎬ B
- He hogged the remote control. ⎭
- She used my makeup, shampoo, soap, etc.
- She rarely paid her share of bills.   C

TECHNOLOGY LINK

On a computer, you can cut (ctrl X) and paste (ctrl V) similar ideas together.

 **Identifying the Best Ideas**

There are many ways to highlight your best ideas. You can circle the best supporting points and then use lines or arrows to link them with secondary ideas. You could also use highlighter pens or asterisks to identify the best supporting points.

The Writer's Desk **Choose the Best Ideas**

For the Writer's Desk on page 21, you produced ideas to support your topic sentence. Identify ideas that clearly support the topic sentence. If there are any related ideas, group them. You can cross out ideas that you do not want to develop.

Organizing Your Ideas

The next step is to organize your ideas in a logical manner. There are three common organizational methods: time order, emphatic order, and space order. You can use **transitions**—words such as *first, then,* and *furthermore*—to guide readers from one idea to the next. You can find a more complete list of transitions on pages 36 and 37 in Chapter 3, "Revising and Editing."

ESSAY LINK

In an essay, you can also use time, space, or emphatic order to organize your ideas.

Time Order

When you use **time order,** you arrange the details according to the sequence in which they have occurred. Use time order to narrate a story, explain how to do something, or describe a historical event.

before   now   after

Here are some transitional expressions you can use in time order paragraphs.

after that	first	later	next
eventually	in the beginning	meanwhile	then
finally	last	months after	while

The next paragraph uses time order.

> Throughout the history of music, financial backing has been needed to support the composition and production of musical performances. In Europe during the Middle Ages, the greatest patron of music was the church. Then, in the Renaissance, Baroque, and Classic eras, the foremost patrons were wealthy aristocrats who employed composers and performers in their courts. Later, in the nineteenth century, the main support for music gradually spread to the middle classes. Public concerts became common, and music was funded by ticket sales and by the sale of printed music for amateurs to perform at home. Finally, during the twentieth century, this reliance on wider support has continued to grow. Now, the central driving force behind the production of most popular music is commercial gain. The profits are enormous.
>
> —Jeremy Yudkin, *Understanding Music*

PRACTICE 5

Use time order to organize the supporting details beneath each of the topic sentences. Number the details from 1 to 5.

1. If you win a large amount of money in a lottery, there are some things you should do to maintain your sanity.

    _____ Take a leave of absence from your job.

    _____ Keep enough money in your bank account to take a vacation.

_____ Take a long vacation.

_____ Collect the money and immediately deposit it in a safe bank fund.

_____ Stay away until the publicity about your win dies down.

2. In 1897, a tragic event occurred to a young Inuit boy from Greenland named Minik.

_____ The Inuit had no immunity to the diseases that were common in North America.

_____ Through a window, museum visitors watched the Inuit interact.

_____ Minik ended up alone in America and was raised by the museum director.

_____ Explorer Robert Peary decided to bring six Inuit, including seven-year-old Minik, to New York.

_____ The six Inuit were put on display in the American Museum of Natural History.

_____ Minik's father was the first to die, followed by most of the others.

Emphatic Order

When you use **emphatic order,** you organize supporting details in a logical sequence. For example, you can arrange details from least to most important, from best to worst, from least appealing to most appealing, from general to specific, and so on. How you order the details often depends on your purpose for writing.

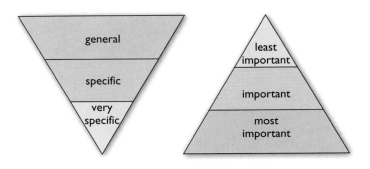

Here are some transitional expressions you can use in emphatic order paragraphs.

above all	first	moreover	particularly
clearly	furthermore	most important	principally
especially	least of all	most of all	therefore

The following paragraph uses emphatic order. The writer presents characteristics from the least to the most important.

Psychologists have determined that people facing difficult circumstances have no single source of resilience. Rather, many factors come into play. First, those with developed social skills tend to be more resilient. Furthermore, some people have a genetic predisposition toward higher self-esteem. But one character trait, above all others, seems to help people cope, and that is the ability to maintain an optimistic attitude. According to author Martin Seligman, positive thinkers tend to believe that problems are outside themselves and not permanent, and they generally rise above failure.

—Suzanne Moreau, student

 **Using Emphatic Order**

When you organize details using emphatic order, use your own values and opinions to determine what is most or least important, upsetting, remarkable, and so on. Another writer may organize the same ideas in a different way.

PRACTICE 6

Use emphatic order to organize the supporting details beneath each topic sentence. Number them in order from most important (1) to least important (5).

1. High school students should get part-time jobs.

   _____ They have spending money for social activities.

   _____ They learn to be more independent and more organized.

   _____ They learn the value of money and what the working world is really like.

   _____ They can buy more fashionable clothes.

   _____ They should not depend on parents for money.

2. My friend Kiran is extremely responsible.

   _____ He is a member of a rock band, and he practices his music every weekend.

   _____ He studies hard because he wants to go to medical school.

   _____ He helps take care of his sister.

   _____ He takes very good care of his car.

   _____ He has a part-time job.

Space Order

When you use **space order,** you describe an image in the sequence in which you see it. For example, you could describe something or someone from top to bottom or bottom to top, from left to right or right to left, or from far to near or near to far.

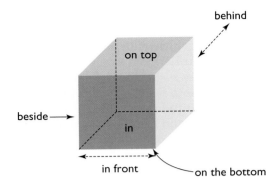

Here are some transitional expressions you can use in space order paragraphs.

above	closer in	near	next to
at the back	farther out	on the bottom	to the left
behind	in front	on the top	under

In the next paragraph, by taking the reader on a visual tour around his home, the writer describes the effects of a tornado.

> We jumped out of bed and did not know what we would find. We ran to the back of the house. What we found was our oldest daughter still asleep in a completely undisturbed room. We discovered our other two daughters also still asleep in another intact room. The storm did not touch the back portion of the house. Our section in the front of the home was less fortunate. The roof was in a tree. The rain was coming in and bringing globs of wet insulation with it. My wife began running around putting pots under the leaks, but I told her to forget it because the roof was gone.
>
> —Louis M. Tursi, *The Night Crawler*

PRACTICE 7

Read the next paragraph and answer the questions that follow.

> Patrick was my mate, and, as he was the first tramp I had known at all well, I want to give an account of him. He was a tallish man, aged about thirty-five, with fair hair going grizzled and watery blue eyes. His features were good, but his cheeks had that grayish look that comes of a bread and margarine diet. He was dressed, rather better than most tramps, in a tweed jacket and a pair of old evening trousers with the braid still on them. Evidently the braid figured in his mind as a lingering scrap of respectability, and he took care to sew it on again when it came loose.
>
> —Adapted from George Orwell, *Down and Out in London and Paris*

1. The writer uses spatial order to organize this paragraph. What main physical characteristics of the tramp does Orwell describe? List five characteristics.

a. _____   b. _____

c. _____   d. _____

e. _____

2. In what order does the writer describe these characteristics? Choose the best answer.

   a. From top to bottom   b. From bottom to top

PRACTICE 8

Use space order to organize the supporting details beneath the topic sentence. Starting from the bottom and ending with the top, number the sentences from 1 to 5.

> Tourists and architectural students gasp in delight when they see the Casa Mila, the last completed avant-garde architectural work of Antoni Gaudí.

_____ Chimneys made of broken ceramic tiles rise from the roof and seem to touch the sky.

_____ The sidewalk in front of the building is decorated with blue and green ceramic tiles designed in the form of starfish.

_____ The walls of the building are not straight but are in the shape of a gigantic wave.

_____ The roof, dotted with small windows, is sand-colored.

_____ Each balcony has curved black railings giving a further impression of waves on the ocean.

PRACTICE 9

Read the following topic sentences. Decide what type of order you could use to develop the paragraph details. Choose time, space, or emphatic order.

EXAMPLE:

College students should take their studies seriously. _____*Emphatic*_____

1. Several interesting things happened when the probe landed on Mars. _____

2. Children without siblings tend to be self-reliant. _____

3. The Halloween costume was truly original. _____

4. On my eleventh birthday, I did a silly thing. _____

5. The dorm room was an uncontrollable mess. _____

6. Smoking should be permitted in public bars and restaurants. _____

The Writer's Desk **Organize Your Ideas**

Look at the list of ideas that you wrote for the Writer's Desk on page 21. Organize your ideas using space, time, or emphatic order by placing numbers beside the ideas.

The Paragraph Plan

A **paragraph plan,** or **outline,** is a map that shows the paragraph's main and supporting ideas. To make a plan, write your topic sentence, and then list supporting points and details in the order you wish to present them. You can use time, space, or emphatic order to organize the supporting points.

 **Adding Specific Details**

When you prepare your paragraph plan, ask yourself whether your supporting ideas are detailed enough. If not, then you could add details to make that supporting idea stronger. For example, in Madhuri's list about her roommate, one of her points is that her friend was irresponsible about bill payments. She added the following details to make that point stronger and more complete.

She rarely paid her share of the bills.

— never bought supplies like toilet paper or detergent

Added: — never paid the phone bill

— often borrowed money from me to pay the rent

MADHURI'S PARAGRAPH PLAN

After she chose her best ideas and organized them, Madhuri wrote a paragraph plan.

TOPIC SENTENCE:	My first experience of living with a roommate turned out to be a disaster.
Support 1:	Kate rarely paid her share of the bills.
Details:	— never paid the phone bill
	— often borrowed money from me to pay the rent
	— never bought supplies like toilet paper or detergent
Support 2:	She was such a messy person.
Details:	— left her dirty laundry lying around
	— dirty dishes, bowls, cups all over the apartment
Support 3:	Her annoying boyfriend was at the apt. too much.
Details:	— ate my food without asking
	— hogged the remote control
	— left cigarette butts in beer bottles around the apt.
Conclusion:	I was so happy when my landlord let me break my lease.

The Writer's Desk **Write a Paragraph Plan**

Look at the topic sentence and the organized list of supporting ideas that you created for the previous Writer's Desks. Now, fill in the following paragraph plan. Remember to include details for each supporting idea.

Topic sentence: _____

_____

Support 1: _____

Details: _____

_____

Support 2: _____

Details: _____

_____

Support 3: _____

Details: _____

_____

The First Draft

The next step is to write the first draft. Take information from your paragraph plan and, using complete sentences, write a paragraph. Your first draft includes your topic sentence and supporting details.

MADHURI'S FIRST DRAFT

Madhuri wrote the first draft of her paragraph about her roommate. You may notice that her paragraph contains mistakes. In Chapter 3, you will see how she revises and edits her paragraph.

My first experience of living with a roommate turned out to be a disaster. Kate rarely paid her share of the bills. She never paid the phone bill. She often borrowed money from me to pay the rent. She never bought supplies like toilet paper or detergent. She was an incredibly messy person, she left her dirty laundry and dirty dishes all over the apartment. Her annoying boyfriend was at our place way to much. He ate my food without asking. When we watch TV, he hogged the remote. Sometimes both of them left cigarette butts in beer bottles. I was so happy when my landlord finally aloud me to break my lease.

ESSAY LINK

Essays end with a concluding paragraph. For more information about essay conclusions, see page 100.

 **Writing the Concluding Sentence**

Some paragraphs end with a **concluding sentence,** which brings the paragraph to a satisfactory close. If you want to write a concluding sentence for your paragraph, here are three suggestions.

• Restate the topic sentence in a new, fresh way.

• Make an interesting final observation.

• End with a prediction, suggestion, or quotation.

The Writer's Desk **Write Your First Draft**

In the previous Writer's Desk on page 29, you created a paragraph plan. Now, on a separate sheet of paper, write your first draft of that paragraph.

 The Writer's Room   **Topics to Develop**

Writing Activity 1

In the Writer's Room in Chapter 1, "Exploring," you used various strategies to find ideas about the following topics. Select one of the topics and write a paragraph. Remember to follow the writing process.

General Topics

1. friendship
2. ceremonies
3. luck

College or Work-Related Topics

4. work environment
5. time
6. stress

Writing Activity 2

Describe your neighborhood. You could describe a person you frequently see or a place such as a park or building.

DEVELOPING CHECKLIST

When you develop a paragraph, ask yourself the following questions.

Does my **topic sentence** introduce the topic and state the controlling idea?

Do I **support the topic sentence** with facts and examples?

Do I **organize the details** using time, space, or emphatic order?

Does my **paragraph plan** help me visualize the main and supporting ideas?

Does my **first draft** use complete sentences?

See Chapter 2 on the Visualizing Writing CD-ROM for additional audio and animated mini-lectures on **How to Write a Paragraph**, **Topic Sentence**, **Developing the Paragraph**, and **Drafting the Paragraph**.

CHAPTER 3

Revising and Editing

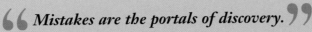

" Mistakes are the portals of discovery. "
—JAMES JOYCE (1882–1941)
Irish author

CONTENTS

- What Is Revising and Editing?
- Revise for Unity
- Revise for Adequate Support
- Revise for Coherence
- Revise for Style
- Edit for Errors
- The Final Draft

The revising and editing stage of the writing process is like adding the finishing touches to a sand castle. Small improvements can make the difference between a stable or an unstable structure.

What Is Revising and Editing?

Revising and editing are effective ways to improve your writing. When you **revise,** you modify your writing to make it more convincing and precise. You do this by looking for inadequate development and poor organization, and then you make any necessary changes. When you **edit,** you proofread your final draft. You look for errors in grammar, spelling, punctuation, and mechanics.

There are five key steps in the revising and editing stage.

REVISING AND EDITING

STEP 1 → **Revise for unity.** Make sure that all parts of your work relate to the main idea.

STEP 2 → **Revise for adequate support.** Ensure that you have enough details to effectively support the main idea.

STEP 3 → **Revise for coherence.** Verify that your ideas flow smoothly and are logically linked.

STEP 4 ➤ **Revise for style.** Make sure that your sentences are varied and interesting.

STEP 5 ➤ **Edit for technical errors.** Proofread your work and correct errors in grammar, spelling, mechanics, and punctuation.

Revise for Unity

When a paragraph has **unity,** all of the sentences support the topic sentence. If a paragraph lacks unity, then it is difficult for the reader to understand the main point. To check for unity, verify that every sentence relates to the main idea.

> **ESSAY LINK**
>
> When revising an essay, ensure that each body paragraph has unity.

Ernesto's Paragraph Without Unity

College student Ernesto Garcia wrote the following paragraph. As he wrote, he accidentally drifted away from his main idea. Some sentences do not relate to the topic sentence. If Ernesto removed the highlighted sentences, then his paragraph would have unity.

> **My father has always spent far too much time in front of the television.** When I was a child, each day my dad got home from work, took off his coat, and then went to the television to see what was on. Later, while the rest of us were eating supper in the kitchen, he would take his plate to the living room and watch the news. On weekends, he watched sports, and we would hear him yelling every time his team's players made a mistake. Growing up, we missed his conversation and company. Because of my father's influence, I became a television addict, too. After work, when my friends invited me out, I would find excuses to turn them down because I wanted to watch the latest episode of some television program. Today my father is an old man, and the television is still his constant companion.

PRACTICE I

Read paragraphs A, B, and C. For each one, underline the topic sentence. Then indicate whether the paragraph has unity. If the paragraph lacks unity, remove the sentences that do not relate to the topic sentence.

A. If you want to improve your writing, diary keeping is an ideal way to exercise your craft. Because diary writing is not meant for an audience, it frees your creativity. Daily writing is like practicing the scales on a piano: you express yourself in your given art without worrying about the final product. In fact, many well-known writers keep a diary. However, some writers are tormented and have unhealthy lifestyles. William Burroughs had a drug habit. Other writers, such as Jack Kerouac and F. Scott Fitzgerald, were alcoholics. The best writers practice their craft every day. According to Henry Miller, "to write each day is the thing, not to turn out masterpieces."

Is the paragraph unified?

a. Has unity   b. Lacks unity

B. To minimize the problems associated with divorce, parents need to maintain a stable environment for their children. For example, any fighting over finances or child visitation should not occur in front of the children. Parents should try to live near each other so that the kids have easy access to both parents. To further stabilize children's lives after a divorce, many parents now opt for the "family home." The kids don't have to change houses to visit each parent; instead, the parents take turns living in the family home. If parents just remember to put children first, then the effects of divorce on the children can be minimized.

Is the paragraph unified?

a. Has unity   b. Lacks unity

C. When people watch movies, they rarely appreciate a very important part of the filmmaking process. Foley artists make movies come alive by using simple, everyday objects to create sound effects. For example, to reproduce the sound of crickets, a foley artist can simply run a fingernail along the teeth of a comb. The sounds of a fight can be created by hitting watermelons and breaking pieces of bamboo. Twisting cellophane resembles the crackling of a fire. *The Lord of Rings* had many astounding visual effects, including computer-generated characters such as orcs. The filmmakers also used clever camera angles to make Frodo, the main hobbit, look very small. Even though technology has become more sophisticated and libraries of recorded sound effects exist, most directors still prefer the involvement of foley artists.

Is the paragraph unified?

a. Has unity   b. Lacks unity

ESSAY LINK

When you revise an essay, ensure that you have adequately supported the thesis statement. Also, verify that each body paragraph has sufficient supporting details.

Revise for Adequate Support

When you revise for **adequate support,** ensure that your paragraph contains strong and convincing supporting details. The following paragraph attempts to persuade, but it does not have any specific details that make strong points.

Advertising companies work hard to get our attention. Some corporations spend a fortune on music for their television commercials. Advertisers also pay celebrities to endorse their products. Also, many marketing firms work on making the consumer laugh, so some commercials are very funny. There are some great commercials on television.

PRACTICE 2

When the preceding paragraph about advertising is expanded with specific details and examples, it becomes more convincing. Try adding details on the lines provided.

Advertising companies work hard to get our attention. Some corporations spend a fortune on music for their television commercials. For example, _____

_____

_____

Advertisers also pay celebrities to endorse their products. _____

_____

_____

Also, many marketing firms work on making the consumer laugh, so some commercials are very funny. _____

_____

_____

There are some great commercials on television.

 **Avoiding Circular Reasoning**

Circular reasoning means that a writer restates his or her main point in various ways but does not provide supporting details. The main idea goes in circles and never progresses—kind of like a dog chasing its tail. Avoid using circular reasoning by writing a concise topic sentence and by supporting the topic sentence with facts, examples, or anecdotes.

For example, the following paragraph has circular reasoning.

> Young people advertise for companies by wearing too many logos on their clothing. A lot of their clothing contains pictures from large corporations. These "walking billboards" are unconsciously promoting huge companies.

PRACTICE 3

The next passages do not have sufficient supporting examples. List examples for each topic.

EXAMPLE:

Legalized gambling has negative effects on our society. First, gambling attracts criminals. Loan sharks, who charge high interest rates, often conduct business inside casinos. Also, governments rely too heavily on the revenue that legalized gambling generates.

Add examples: Encourages addiction to gambling

Gives people false hope about getting rich quickly

Attracts people who can least afford to lose money

1. Young people advertise for companies by wearing too many logos on their clothing. A lot of their clothing displays pictures

from large corporations. These "walking billboards" are unconsciously promoting huge companies.

Add examples: _____

_____

_____

2.   When you prepare for a test, there are a few things that you should do. You should find out exactly what you are supposed to study. What else should you do?

Add examples: _____

_____

_____

3.   Since 2000, reality television has invaded our homes. There are many types of reality shows. They all include ordinary people who participate in unusual contests.

Add examples: _____

_____

_____

Revise for Coherence

Think of reading as if it were a sailing trip. It is much more comfortable to sail if the water is calm. When you revise for coherence, you ensure that your reader has a smooth voyage through your paragraph. **Coherence** means that the sentences flow smoothly and are logically organized.

Transitional Expressions

Transitional expressions are linking words or phrases, and they show the reader the connections between ideas in paragraphs and essays. Here are some common transitional expressions.

ESSAY LINK

To create coherence in an essay, you can place transitional expressions at the beginning of each body paragraph.

Function	Transitional Word or Expression
Addition	again, also, besides, first (second, third), for one thing, furthermore, in addition, in fact, moreover, next, then
Concession of a point	certainly, indeed, no doubt, of course, to be sure
Comparison	as well, equally, likewise, similarly
Contrast	however, in contrast, instead, nevertheless, on the contrary, on the other hand
Effect or result	as a result, consequently, then, therefore, thus

Function	Transitional Word or Expression
Example	for example, for instance, in other words, namely, specifically, to illustrate
Emphasis	above all, clearly, in fact, in particular, indeed, least of all, most important, most of all, of course, undoubtedly
Space	above, at the back, behind, below, beside, closer in, farther out, in front, in the middle, inside, nearby, on the bottom, on the left/right, on top, outside, under
Summary or conclusion	generally, in conclusion, in other words, in short, on the whole, therefore, thus, to conclude, to summarize
Time	after that, at that time, at the moment, currently, earlier, eventually, first (second, etc.), gradually, immediately, in the future, in the past, later, meanwhile, now, one day, presently, so far, subsequently, suddenly, then, these days

 **Hint** **Use Transitional Expressions with Complete Sentences**

When you add a transitional expression to a sentence, ensure that your sentence is complete. Your sentence must have a subject and a verb, and it must express a complete thought.

Incomplete: First, the price of movie tickets.

Complete: First, the price of movie tickets <u>is too high</u>.

PRACTICE 4

Add the following transitional expressions to the next paragraph. Use each transitional word once. There may be more than one correct answer for each space.

also	furthermore	undoubtedly
first	however	

When you go backpacking in a foreign country, there are a few simple things you should pack for the trip. _____, bring clothing that is easy to wash. Leave items that need ironing or dry cleaning at home. _____, make sure you pack a small medical kit. It could be difficult and expensive to find things such as aspirin and bandages if you're on a beach in Thailand. _____, bring a comfortable money belt that you can wear under your clothing. _____, try not to overpack. After you've packed your bag, remove things so that there is a small empty space in your pack. _____, you will find and buy items during your trip.

ESSAY LINK

Revise your essays for style, ensuring that sentences are varied and that your language is exact. To learn more about sentence variety and exact language, see Chapter 17.

Revise for Style

Another important step in the revision process is to ensure that you have varied your sentences and that you have used concise wording. When you revise for sentence style, ask yourself the following questions.

- Have I used a variety of sentence patterns?
- Have I used exact language?
- Have I avoided using repetitious or vague language?

MADHURI'S REVISION

College student Madhuri Desai wrote a paragraph about moving out of her home. Read the revisions that she made to her paragraph. She revised for unity, support, and coherence. She also looked at style and decided to combine some sentences.

Added a transition ➤
Added exact language ➤

Combined sentences ➤

Removed a sentence ➤
Added a transition ➤
Exact language ➤
Added a transition ➤

Exact language ➤

My first experience living with a roommate turned out to be a
First, Kate   *expenses*
disaster. ~~Kate~~ rarely paid her share of the ~~bills~~. She never
                 and she
paid the phone bill. ~~She~~ often borrowed money from me to pay

the rent. ~~She never bought supplies like toilet paper or detergent.~~
Moreover, she   *filthy*
~~She~~ was an incredibly messy person, she left her ~~dirty~~ laundry and
                          Also, to my chagrin, her
dirty dishes all over the apartament. ~~Her~~ annoying boyfriend was at

our place way to much. He ate my food without asking. When we
                                                          smelly
watch TV, he hogged the remote. Sometimes both of them left

cigarette butts in beer bottles. I was so happy when my landlord

finally aloud me to break my lease.

Edit for Errors

When you **edit,** you reread your writing and make sure that it is free of errors. Look for mistakes in grammar, punctuation, mechanics, and spelling. The editing guide on the inside front cover of this book contains some common editing codes that your teacher may use.

 **Spelling and Grammar Logs**

It is a good idea to put your text aside for a day or two before you edit it. You could also keep a spelling and grammar log.

- **Keep a spelling log.** In a notebook or binder, keep a list of all of your spelling mistakes. Then, you can refer to your list of spelling errors when you edit your writing.

- **Keep a grammar log.** After you receive each corrected assignment, choose an error. Write down the error and a rule about it in your grammar log.

See Appendix 5 for more information about the spelling and grammar logs.

MADHURI'S EDITING

Madhuri edited her paragraph. She corrected spelling and grammar errors.

My first experience living with a roommate turned out to be

a disaster. First, Kate rarely paid her share of the expenses. She

never paid the phone ~~bill and~~ *bill, and* she often borrowed money from me to

pay the rent. Moreover, she was an incredibly messy ~~person, she~~ *person. She*

left her filthy laundry and dirty dishes all over the ~~aparatment~~ *apartment*. Also,

to my chagrin, her annoying boyfriend was at our place way ~~to~~ *too*

much. He ate my food without asking. When we ~~watch~~ *watched* TV, he hogged

the remote. Sometimes both of them left smelly cigarette butts in

beer bottles. I was so happy when my landlord finally ~~aloud~~ *allowed* me to

break my lease.

The Writer's Desk Revise and Edit Your Paragraph

Choose a paragraph that you wrote for Chapter 2, or choose one
that you have written for another assignment. Carefully revise and
edit your paragraph.

TECHNOLOGY LINK

Word processors have spelling and
grammar checkers. If the program
suggests ways to correct errors,
carefully verify that the computer's
suggestions are valid before you
accept them.

Peer Feedback

After you write a paragraph or an essay, it is useful to get peer feedback. Ask
another person such as a friend, family member, or fellow student to read your
work and give you comments and suggestions on its strengths and weaknesses.

 **Offer Constructive Criticism**

When you peer-edit someone else's writing, try to make constructive suggestions
rather than destructive comments. Phrase your comments in a positive way. Look at
the following examples.

Instead of saying . . .	**You could say . . .**
Your examples are dull.	Perhaps you could add more details to your examples.
Your paragraph is confusing.	Your topic sentence needs a controlling idea.

When you are editing someone else's work, try using a peer feedback form
as a guideline. A sample form is on the next page.

Peer Feedback Form

Written by: _____   Feedback by: _____

Date: _____

1. Your main idea is _____

   _____

   _____

2. Your best supporting ideas are _____

   _____

   _____

   _____

3. I like _____

   _____

   _____

4. Perhaps you could change _____

   _____

   _____

   _____

5. My other comments are _____

   _____

   _____

   _____

   _____

The Final Draft

When you have finished making revisions on the first draft of your paragraph, write the final draft. Include all of the changes that you have made during the revising and editing phases. Before you hand in your final draft, proofread it one last time to ensure that you have caught any errors.

The Writer's Desk **Writing Your Final Draft**

You have developed, revised, and edited your paragraph. Now write the final draft. Before you hand it to your instructor, proofread it one last time to ensure that you have found all of your errors.

The Writer's Room **Paragraph Topics**

Writing Activity 1

Choose a paragraph that you have written for this course. Revise and edit that paragraph, and then write a final draft.

Writing Activity 2

Choose one of the following topics, or choose your own topic and write a paragraph. You could try exploring strategies to generate ideas. The first sentence of your paragraph should make a point about your topic. Remember to revise and edit your paragraph before you write the final draft.

General Topics

1. an interesting dream
2. a family story
3. travel
4. television
5. divorce

College or Work-Related Topics

6. an unusual experience at college
7. cheating
8. reasons to stay in college
9. a personality conflict at work
10. working with your spouse

REVISING AND EDITING CHECKLIST

When you revise and edit a paragraph, ask yourself the following questions.

Does my paragraph have **unity?** Ensure that every sentence relates to the main idea.

Does my paragraph have **adequate support?** Verify that there are enough details and examples to support your main point.

Is my paragraph **coherent?** Try to use transitional expressions to link ideas.

Does my paragraph have good **style?** Check for varied sentence patterns and exact language.

Does my paragraph have any errors? **Edit** for errors in grammar, punctuation, spelling, and mechanics.

Is my **final draft** error-free?

See Chapter 3 on the Visualizing Writing CD-ROM for additional audio and animated mini-lectures on **Revising and Editing Your Own Paragraph, Revising the Paragraph for Development, Revising the Paragraph for Organization,** and **Revising the Paragraph for Coherence.**

Paragraph Patterns

CHAPTER 4

> *Art is the imposing of a pattern on experience.*
> —ALFRED NORTH WHITEHEAD (1861–1947)
> *Mathematician and philosopher*

A furniture designer uses diverse patterns to create chairs with different functions. In this chapter, you will learn about various writing patterns.

CONTENTS

- What Are Paragraph Patterns?
- A) The Illustration Paragraph
- B) The Narrative Paragraph
- C) The Descriptive Paragraph
- D) The Process Paragraph
- E) The Definition Paragraph
- F) The Comparison and Contrast Paragraph
- G) The Cause and Effect Paragraph
- H) The Argument Paragraph

What Are Paragraph Patterns?

Paragraph patterns, or **modes**, are methods writers can use to develop a piece of writing. Each pattern has a specific purpose. For example, if you want to entertain your audience by telling a story about your recent adventure, you might write a narrative paragraph. If your purpose is to explain the steps needed to complete an activity, you might write a process paragraph. Sometimes, more than one pattern can fulfill your purpose. Take a moment to review eight different writing patterns.

Pattern	Definition
Illustration	To illustrate or prove a point using specific examples
Narration	To narrate or tell a story about a sequence of events that happened
Description	To describe using vivid details and images that appeal to the reader's senses
Process	To inform the reader about how to do something, how something works, or how something happened

(continued)

Pattern	Definition
Definition	To define or explain what a term or concept means by providing relevant examples
Comparison and Contrast	To present information about similarities (compare) or differences (contrast)
Cause and Effect	To explain why an event happened (the cause) or what the consequences of the event were (the effects)
Argument	To argue or to take a position on an issue and offer reasons for your position

A) The Illustration Paragraph

An **illustration paragraph** uses specific examples to **illustrate** or clarify the main point. For example, if you are writing a paragraph about your most valuable possessions, you might list your grandmother's ring, your photo album, your family videos, and so on.

Illustration writing is a pattern that you frequently use in college writing because you must support your main idea with examples.

PRACTICE I

Read the next paragraph and answer the questions that follow.

Ontario: a province in Canada

Quito: the capital of Ecuador

Riobamba: a city in Ecuador

San José: a city in Costa Rica

Ensenada: a city in Mexico

Mountie: a Canadian federal police officer; the name derives from the word *Mounted* in Royal Canadian Mounted Police.

In recent visits to Canada, Mexico, Costa Rica, and Ecuador, I saw adolescents routinely behaving in ways American experts condemn as horrifying. **Ontario** 19-year-olds queued in liquor stores and drank in pubs alongside elders. Teens in **Quito**, **Riobamba**, and **San José** thronged to late-night discos. Unchaperoned **Ensenada** middle-schoolers strolled hand-in-hand along late-night downtown streets after emerging from unrated movies. Latin American cybercafés (often managed by teens or children) overflowed with unsupervised youths clicking unfiltered computers. Laughed a **Mountie** when I asked if Toronto had a youth curfew, "Maybe for six-year-olds." By American expert thinking, European, Canadian, and Latin American adolescents should be developmentally damaged alcoholic felons.

—Mike Males, "Freedom: For Adults Only"

1. What is the subject? _____

2. Underline the topic sentence of this paragraph.

3. List five supporting examples.

_____

_____

_____

_____

4. What is the author's point of view about the treatment of teens in the United States?

The Writer's Desk **Exploring**

Think about the following questions, and write down the first ideas that come to mind. Try to write two or three ideas for each topic.

EXAMPLE: What clutter do you have in your home?

kitchen cupboard filled with junk, letters on hall table, shoes piled in closet, basement filled with boxes

1. What are some examples of traditions?

2. What are some qualities of a successful parent?

3. What are some traits of an effective leader?

The Topic Sentence

The topic sentence in an illustration paragraph controls the direction of the paragraph. It includes the topic and a controlling idea about the topic.

controlling idea   topic

<u>It is very difficult to</u> **patrol America's borders.**

The Writer's Desk **Write Topic Sentences**

Write a topic sentence for each of the following topics. Your sentence should have a controlling idea that expresses the direction of the paragraph. Remember that the goal of the paragraph is to give examples.

EXAMPLE:

Topic: Clutter in the home

Topic sentence: *Several places in my home are magnets for clutter.*

1. Topic: Traditions

Topic sentence: _____

_____

2. Topic: A successful parent

Topic sentence: _____

_____

3. Topic: An effective leader

Topic sentence: _____

_____

The Supporting Ideas

In an illustration paragraph, the examples support the topic sentence. A paragraph plan helps you organize your topic sentence and supporting details.

An Illustration Paragraph Plan

When you write an illustration paragraph plan, ensure that your examples are valid and that they relate to the topic sentence. In the following plan, the topic sentence is supported by several examples. Then, each example is supported with details.

TOPIC SENTENCE:	**Several places in my home are magnets for clutter.**
Support 1:	The front closet is a mess.
Details:	— shoes piled on top of each other
	— scarves, umbrellas, hats, gloves heaped at top of closet
Support 2:	The hallway table is never clear.
Details:	— covered with letters, newspapers, opened bills

Support 3: A kitchen cupboard attracts junk.
  Details: — coupons, pens, screwdriver, twist ties, and other odds and ends piled in it
Support 4: The bathroom vanity is in disarray.
  Details: — comb, hair clips, razor, toothbrushes, hair products, face cleanser all over the counter

The Writer's Desk **Develop Supporting Ideas**

Choose one of the topic sentences that you wrote for the Writer's Desk on page 46, and write a detailed paragraph plan. List at least three examples that could support the topic sentence.

Topic sentence: _____

_____

Support 1: _____

  Details: _____

Support 2: _____

  Details: _____

Support 3: _____

  Details: _____

Support 4: _____

  Details: _____

The Writer's Desk **Write an Illustration Paragraph**

You have made a list of supporting ideas for a topic. Now write an illustration paragraph. After you finish writing, remember to revise and edit your paragraph.

The Writer's Room   **More Topics for Illustration Paragraphs**

WRITING LINK

See the Writer's Rooms in the following grammar chapters for more illustration writing topics.

Chapter 8, Writer's Room topic 1 (page 158)

Chapter 12, Writer's Room topic 1 (page 222)

Chapter 20, Writer's Room topic 1 (page 314)

Chapter 22, Writer's Room topic 1 (page 342)

Chapter 25, Writer's Room topic 1 (page 381)

Writing Activity 1

Write an illustration paragraph about one of the following topics.

General Topics

1. mistakes
2. favorite clothing
3. dangerous habits
4. extreme sports
5. creative hobbies

College and Work-Related Topics

6. inappropriate workplace clothing
7. qualities of a roommate
8. undesirable or difficult jobs
9. excuses for missing work
10. excuses for not finishing something

Writing Activity 2

Examine the photo. As you look at it, think about things that frustrate you or drive you crazy. Then write an illustration paragraph.

READING LINK

The following readings use examples to support the main idea.

"The Appalling Truth" by Dorothy Nixon (page 438)

"The Rewards of Dirty Work" by Linda L. Lindsey and Stephen Beach (page 459)

ILLUSTRATION PARAGRAPH CHECKLIST

As you write your illustration paragraph, review the paragraph checklist on the inside rear cover. Also, ask yourself the next set of questions.

Does my topic sentence include a controlling idea that can be supported with examples?

Do my supporting ideas contain sufficient examples that clearly support the topic sentence?

Are the examples smoothly and logically connected?

B) The Narrative Paragraph

A **narrative** paragraph tells a story about what happened and generally explains events in the order in which they occurred.

There are two main types of narrative writing. When you use **first-person narration,** you describe a personal experience using *I* or *we* (first-person pronouns)—for example, "When I was a child, I played a terrible prank on my brother." When you use **third-person narration,** you describe what happened to somebody else, and you use *he, she,* or *they* (third-person pronouns). Most news reports use third-person narration. For example, a news article might state, "The billionaire inventor Dean Kamen has created a new type of engine. His invention, which is the size of a shoebox, works with any power source."

PRACTICE 2

Read the next paragraph and answer the questions that follow.

When I was in seventh grade, one of the big ninth-grade girls began bullying me. She didn't shake me down for lunch money or even touch me. But she stalked me in the halls, on the playground, and in the girls' lavatory. The way that **buffarilla** rolled her eyes and worked her neck in my direction, I could feel her fingers yanking out every hair on my head—and I didn't have that much. In class, instead of paying attention, I began to envision the after-school crowd that would gather to watch me get stomped into the ground. Every day, my adversary seemed to grow bigger, meaner, and stronger. In my mind she evolved from a menacing older girl into a monster. By the time I realized that she wasn't really interested in fighting me—just intimidating me with dirty looks—I was already bruised from kicking my own butt.

—Bebe Moore Campbell, "Dancing with Fear"

buffarilla: an invented word that is a combination of buffalo and gorilla

1. What type of narration is this selection?
   a. First person   b. Third person

2. Underline the topic sentence.

3. What organizational method does the author use?
   a. Time order   b. Space order   c. Emphatic order

4. List what happens in the paragraph. (List only the main events.)

   _____

   _____

   _____

   _____

5. What did the author learn?

   _____

The Writer's Desk   Exploring

Think about the following questions, and write down the first ideas that come to mind. Try to write two or three ideas for each topic.

EXAMPLE: What important lessons have you learned since you came to college?

> Must be more organized
>
> Should have clear goals and work hard at them
>
> It's easier to make friends than I thought it would be.

1. What interesting place have you visited? What did you do in that place?

   _____

   _____

2. Think about an accident or injury that you, or someone whom you know, had. What happened?

   _____

   _____

3. Think of a moment when you felt very proud. What happened?

   _____

   _____

The Topic Sentence

The **topic sentence** controls the direction of the paragraph and includes the topic and a controlling idea. To create a meaningful topic sentence for a narrative paragraph, you could ask yourself these questions: What did I learn? How did I change? How is the event important?

topic   controlling idea

When I visited Romania, <u>I learned about my heritage</u>.

The Writer's Desk   Write Topic Sentences

Write a topic sentence for each of the following topics. Your sentence should make a point about the topic. Remember that the goal of the paragraph is to tell a story.

EXAMPLE:

Topic: A lesson in college

Topic sentence: *In my first year of college, I gained a lot of self-confidence.*

1. Topic: A place I have visited

   Topic sentence: _____

   _____

2. Topic: An accident or injury

   Topic sentence: _____

   _____

3. Topic: A proud moment

   Topic sentence: _____

   _____

The Supporting Ideas

A narrative paragraph should contain details that explain what happened. To be as complete as possible, a good narrative paragraph should provide answers to most of the following questions.

- *Who* is the paragraph about?
- *What* happened?
- *When* did it happen?
- *Where* did it happen?
- *Why* did it happen?
- *How* did it happen?

WRITING LINK

For more information about organizing ideas using time, space, and emphatic order, see pages 23 to 26 of Chapter 2, "Developing."

A Narrative Paragraph Plan

When you write a narrative paragraph plan, ensure that your details are valid and that they relate to the topic sentence. Also, think about how you can organize your ideas. In the following plan, each detail explains what happened by using time order.

TOPIC SENTENCE: <u>In my first year of college, I gained a lot of self-confidence.</u>

Support 1: In high school, I felt shy and was nervous around people.
Details: — a lot of cliques in my school
— wasn't popular

Support 2: In college, I met new people right away.
Details: — met students who share my interests
— joined the chess club
— met my first girlfriend

Support 3: Now I feel more confident around others.
Details: — can initiate conversations
— make it a point to talk with new people

The Writer's Desk Develop Supporting Ideas

Choose one of the topic sentences that you wrote for the Writer's Desk on page 51, and write a detailed paragraph plan. List the events in the order in which they occurred.

Topic sentence: _____

_____

Support 1: _____

Details: _____

_____

_____

Support 2: _____

Details: _____

_____

_____

Support 3: _____

Details: _____

_____

The Writer's Desk **Write a Narrative Paragraph**

You have made a list of supporting ideas for a topic. Now write a narrative paragraph. After you finish writing, remember to revise and edit your paragraph.

The Writer's Room More Topics for Narrative Paragraphs

Writing Activity 1

Write a narrative paragraph about one of the following topics.

General Topics

1. a scandal
2. a frightening book or movie
3. an anxious moment
4. a good or bad financial decision
5. something you learned from a parent or relative

College and Work-Related Topics

6. a successful person
7. a smart career decision
8. a positive college experience
9. when you were first hired
10. when you lost or quit a job

WRITING LINK

See the Writer's Rooms in the following grammar chapters for more narrative writing topics.
Chapter 6, Writer's Room topic 1 (page 125)
Chapter 9, Writer's Room topics 1 and 2 (page 176)
Chapter 11, Writer's Room topic 2 (page 206)
Chapter 14, Writer's Room topic 1 (page 246)
Chapter 17, Writer's Room topic 1 (page 286)
Chapter 21, Writer's Room topic 2 (page 331)

Writing Activity 2

Examine the photo. As you look at it, think about a journey you have taken. Write a narrative paragraph about a spiritual or physical journey.

READING LINK

Narrative Essays
The following readings use examples to support the main idea.
"Sports and Life: Lessons to Be Learned" by Jeff Kemp (page 430)
"Birth" by Maya Angelou (page 432)

C) The Descriptive Paragraph

When writing a **descriptive** paragraph, use words to create a vivid impression of a subject. Descriptive writing often contains details that appeal to the five senses: seeing, smelling, hearing, tasting, and touching. You want readers to be able to imagine that they are experiencing what you are describing. For example, you might describe a frightening experience or a stunning landscape.

PRACTICE 3

Read the next paragraph and answer the questions that follow.

> On the train ride down to Asilah, I sat with my head and folded arms halfway out of the window so I could take in the country again. The train moved through the land slowly, just as I like it. We passed surprisingly green hills scattered with shepherds herding their sheep. We also saw children who waved at us and fetched water from wells and veiled women in colored robes who strolled along village roads. Ancient red-clay houses with tiny windows concealed mysteries of family life. Camels in contempt of the world knelt on the beach, and donkeys looked small and burdened in the fields. It was replenishing to be back in Morocco.
>
> —Laurie Gough, *Kite Strings of the Southern Cross: A Woman's Travel Odyssey*

1. Underline the topic sentence.

2. How does the writer describe Morocco? Write some descriptive words and phrases.

_____

_____

_____

The Writer's Desk **Exploring**

Think about the following questions, and write down the first ideas that come to mind. Try to write two or three ideas for each topic.

EXAMPLE: What do you remember about a difficult moment?

blackout, stuck in elevator, time I broke up with my
girlfriend, when my mom caught me smoking, when I was
accused of cheating

1. Where do you go when you want to relax? Think of two or three places.

   _____

   _____

   _____

2. What did you look like in the past? What fashions did you wear? What hairstyles did you have? (You might look at old photographs for inspiration.)

   _____

   _____

   _____

3. Have you ever experienced the fury of nature? What happened?

   _____

   _____

   _____

The Topic Sentence

In the **topic sentence** of a descriptive paragraph, you should convey a dominant impression about the subject. The dominant impression is the overall mood that you wish to convey. For example, the paragraph could convey an impression of tension, joy, nervousness, or anger.

          topic   controlling idea

When I saw my smashed windshield, <u>I hollered with rage</u>.

 **Expressing a Dominant Impression**

Sometimes, you can convey the dominant impression directly. However, you can also express it indirectly. For example, in the topic sentence "Our neighbor's yard was filled with junk," the dominant impression is *distaste*. In the body of the paragraph, you could further develop the dominant impression by including descriptions that help develop the sense of distaste. For example, you could describe the stench from a rotting pile of trash.

The Writer's Desk Write Topic Sentences

Write a topic sentence for each of the following topics. Your sentence should state what you are describing and express a dominant impression.

EXAMPLE:

Topic: A difficult moment

Topic sentence: *When the power went out in the elevator, I panicked.*

1. Topic: A relaxing place

   Topic sentence: _____

   _____

2. Topic: Yourself in the past

   Topic sentence: _____

   _____

3. Topic: Nature's fury

   Topic sentence: _____

   _____

The Supporting Ideas

To create a dominant impression, think about your topic and make a list of your feelings and impressions. These details can include things that you saw, heard, smelled, tasted, or touched.

 **Use Interesting and Detailed Vocabulary**

In your paragraph, try to use interesting descriptive vocabulary. Avoid overused words such as *nice, bad, mean,* and *hot.* For example, instead of writing "He was mean," you might write "He was as nasty as a raging pit bull." For more information about specific and vivid language, refer to Chapter 17, Sentence Variety and Exact Language.

The Writer's Desk List Images and Impressions

Think about images, impressions, and feelings that the following topics inspire in you. Make a list under each topic.

EXAMPLE:

A difficult moment: *Stuck in*
elevator

pitch black

no sound

perspiration trickling down
my back

scared and alone

stuffy air

my heart pounded

1. A relaxing place: _____

_____

_____

_____

_____

_____

_____

_____

2. Yourself in the past: _____

_____

_____

_____

_____

_____

_____

_____

_____

3. Nature's fury: _____

_____

_____

_____

_____

_____

_____

_____

_____

WRITING LINK

For more information about organizing ideas using time, space, and emphatic order, see pages 23 to 26 of Chapter 2, "Developing."

A Descriptive Paragraph Plan

When you write a descriptive paragraph plan, ensure that your details are valid and that they relate to the topic sentence. You could place your details in space order, time order, or emphatic order. The order that you use depends on the topic of your paragraph. In the following plan, the details, which are in time order, appeal to the senses and develop the dominant impression.

TOPIC SENTENCE:	**When the elevator jolted to a stop, I panicked.**
Support 1:	The light in the elevator went out.
Details:	— was pitch black
Support 2:	I was alone.
Details:	— scared
	— complete silence
Support 3:	My panic began.
Details:	— heart raced
	— pounding sounds in my ears
	— began pacing and touching the walls
Support 4:	I heard a loud banging noise.
Details:	— elevator lights came on
	— elevator began to move

The Writer's Desk Develop Supporting Ideas

Choose one of the topic sentences that you wrote for the Writer's Desk on page 56, and write a detailed paragraph plan. Remember to develop a dominant impression.

Topic sentence: _____

_____

Support 1: _____

Details: _____

Support 2: _____

Details: _____

Support 3: _____

Details: _____

Support 4: _____

Details: _____

The Writer's Desk **Write a Descriptive Paragraph**

You have made a list of supporting ideas for a topic. Now write a descriptive paragraph. After you finish writing, remember to revise and edit your paragraph.

The Writer's Room **Topics for Descriptive Paragraphs**

Writing Activity I

Write a descriptive paragraph about one of the following topics.

General Topics

1. an uncomfortable room
2. a fad or fashion trend
3. a shocking experience
4. a family member
5. a messy place

College and Work-Related Topics

6. a good meeting place on campus
7. a panicky moment
8. the place where you study
9. a bad day at work
10. the style of clothing you wear to work

WRITING LINK

See the Writer's Rooms in the following grammar chapters for more descriptive writing topics.

Chapter 11, Writer's Room topic 1 (page 206)
Chapter 19, Writer's Room topic 1 (page 303)
Chapter 21, Writer's Room topic 2 (page 331)
Chapter 23, Writer's Room topic 1 (page 357)
Chapter 25, Writer's Room topic 2 (page 381)
Chapter 26, Writer's Room topics 1 and 2 (page 392)

Writing Activity 2

Describe a time of the day that you love or hate. How do you feel at that time of the day? Write a descriptive paragraph about the best or worst time of day.

READING LINK

The following readings use descriptive writing.
"Fish Cheeks" by Amy Tan (page 421)
"What It Feels Like to Walk on the Moon" by Buzz Aldrin (page 449)

✓ **DESCRIPTIVE PARAGRAPH CHECKLIST**

As you write your descriptive paragraph, review the paragraph checklist on the inside rear cover. Also, ask yourself the next set of questions.

☐ Does my topic sentence clearly show what I will describe?

☐ Does my topic sentence make a point about the topic?

☐ Does my paragraph have a dominant impression?

☐ Does each body paragraph contain supporting details that may appeal to the reader's senses?

D) The Process Paragraph

A **process** is a series of steps done in chronological or emphatic order. In a **process paragraph,** you explain how to do something. For example, you might explain how to change the oil in your car, how to plan a party, or how to write a résumé. The reader should be able to follow the directions and do the process.

PRACTICE 4

Read the next paragraph and answer the questions that follow.

Sharks do not specifically hunt for humans, but swimmers can take some precautions to avoid becoming easy bait. First, sharks are active at dawn and dusk, so avoid swimming at those times. Also, because sharks are more likely to attack an individual swimmer, always swim in groups. Sharks look for color contrasts and light reflections to spot their prey under the water. To avoid being mistaken for a fish, do not swim if you have dark tan lines, brightly patterned swim gear, glittery jewelry, or flashy body art. Moreover, do not splash around or make erratic movements. Most important, do not take the plunge if you are bleeding or if you have lesions. Sharks have a keen sense of smell and are skilled at finding a source of blood.

—Sharmila Anand, student

1. Underline the topic sentence.

2. In process paragraphs, the support is generally a series of steps. List the steps you can take to reduce your chances of getting attacked by a shark.

_____

_____

_____

_____

_____

3. This paragraph does not have a concluding sentence. Write a concluding sentence.

_____

_____

The Writer's Desk **Exploring**

Think about the following questions, and write down the first ideas that come to mind. Try to write two or three ideas for each topic.

EXAMPLE: What are some ways to find a mate?

join a club, ask your friends, be open and receptive, don't
act desperate, be yourself, use an Internet dating service

1. What are some things you should do when you plan to move? _____

_____

_____

2. What should you do if you want to find a job? _____

_____

_____

3. What steps can you take to impress a date? _____

_____

_____

The Topic Sentence

The topic sentence in a process paragraph includes the process you are describing and a controlling idea.

topic (process)   controlling idea
Finding a job <u>requires persistence and organization</u>.

It is also possible to make a topic sentence that contains a map, or guide, to the details that you will present in your paragraph. To guide your readers, you could mention the main steps in your topic sentence.

topic   controlling idea

If you want to be a good boss, <u>treat your employees with respect, fairness, and honesty</u>.

The Writer's Desk Write Topic Sentences

Write a topic sentence for each of the following topics. Your sentence should have a controlling idea that expresses the direction of the paragraph. Remember that the goal of the paragraph is to explain how to do something.

EXAMPLE:

Topic: How to find a mate

Topic sentence: *With careful preparation and screening, you can find a mate on the Internet.*

1. Topic: How to plan a move

   Topic sentence: _____

   _____

2. Topic: How to find a job

   Topic sentence: _____

   _____

3. Topic: How to impress a date

   Topic sentence: _____

   _____

The Supporting Ideas

When you write the supporting ideas, decide which steps your reader needs to take to complete the process. Explain each step in detail. Organize your steps chronologically. Remember to mention any necessary tools or supplies.

 **Give Steps, Not Examples**

When you explain how to do a process, describe each step. Do not simply list examples of the process.

How to Relax

List of Examples	Steps in the Process
Read a book.	Change into comfortable clothing.
Take a bath.	Do some deep breathing.
Go for a long walk.	Choose a good book.
Listen to soothing music.	Find a relaxing place to read.

A Process Paragraph Plan

When you write a process paragraph plan, decide how you will organize your plan, and ensure that you explain each step clearly. The following plan shows how the writer used emphatic order to describe the process.

TOPIC SENTENCE: **With careful preparation and screening, you can find a mate on the Internet.**

Step 1: Prepare by finding a viable dating site.
Details: — Ask friends about possible sites.
— Make sure the site targets people in your area.

Step 2: Write an interesting profile.
Details: — Use positive terms to describe yourself, such as *dynamic* and *energetic.*
— Get a friend or a professional to look over your profile.

Step 3: Screen replies carefully.
Details: — Choose your favorite responses.
— Invite friends to help you sort potential dates.

Step 4: Meet only in public places.
Details: — Consider meeting in the daytime, maybe in a coffee shop.
— Avoid alcohol (will cloud judgment).

The Writer's Desk Develop Supporting Ideas

Choose one of the topic sentences that you wrote for the Writer's Desk on page 62, and write a detailed paragraph plan.

Topic sentence: _____

_____

Support 1: _____
Details: _____

Support 2: _____
Details: _____

Support 3: _____
Details: _____

Support 4: _____
Details: _____

The Writer's Desk Write a Process Paragraph

You have made a list of supporting ideas for a topic. Now write a process paragraph. After you finish writing, remember to revise and edit your paragraph.

The Writer's Room **More Topics for Process Paragraphs**

WRITING LINK

See the Writer's Rooms in the following grammar chapters for more process writing topics.
Chapter 10, Writer's Room topic 1 (page 195)
Chapter 22, Writer's Room topic 2 (page 342)
Chapter 23, Writer's Room topic 2 (page 357)
Chapter 27, Writer's Room topic 2 (page 405)

Writing Activity 1

Write a process paragraph about one of the following topics.

General Topics

1. how to vote
2. how to discipline a small child
3. how to find an apartment
4. how to organize your closet
5. how to listen

College and Work-Related Topics

6. how to use a particular machine
7. how to give a speech
8. how to dress for success
9. how to do an activity in your job
10. how to get fired from a job

READING LINK

The following readings contain examples of process writing.
"Political Activism" by Craig Stern (page 454)
"How to Handle Conflict" by P. Gregory Smith (page 457)

Writing Activity 2

Examine the photo. Write a process paragraph explaining how to get along with co-workers or how to do team work.

> ✔ **PROCESS PARAGRAPH CHECKLIST**
>
> As you write your process paragraph, review the paragraph checklist on the inside rear cover. Also, ask yourself the next set of questions.
>
> Does my topic sentence make a point about the process?
>
> Does my paragraph explain how to do something?
>
> Do I clearly explain each step in the process?
>
> Do I mention any supplies that my reader needs to complete the process?
>
> Do I use transitions to connect the steps in the process?

E) The Definition Paragraph

A **definition** tells you what something means. When you write a **definition paragraph,** you give your personal definition of a term or concept. Although you can define most terms in a few sentences, you may need to offer extended definitions for words that are particularly complex. For example, you could write a paragraph or even an entire book about the term *happiness.* The way that you interpret the term is unique, and you would bring your own opinions, experiences, and impressions to your definition paragraph.

PRACTICE 5

Read the next paragraph and answer the questions that follow.

> The Internet has provided writers with a new method of sharing information. A blogger is a writer who expresses his or her opinions in an Internet journal. To create the word "blogger," someone likely joined the words *Web* and *logger.* Some bloggers are professional writers or journalists who want an outlet for their private opinions and feelings. Rather than striving to be objective, a blogger can rant about issues and be highly controversial or personal. Although some bloggers are well-known and have large readerships, most are just average people from all walks of life who have something to say. Thus, the blog may be aimed at a large audience or simply at family members or co-workers. Also, the content of blogs varies. Some look like personal diaries, whereas others contain insightful commentary about politics, science, and social issues. Occasionally, bloggers become famous. For example, Salam Pax is the blog name of an Iraqi interpreter. He created a vivid Web log describing his experiences before, during, and after the 2003 invasion of Iraq. He came to the attention of editors at the prestigious British newspaper, *The Guardian,* and was invited to write a bi-weekly column. The word blogger, therefore, encompasses a variety of writers who express diverse messages.
>
> —Pedram Sabooni, student

1. What term does the author define? _____

2. Underline the topic sentence. Be careful; it may not be the first sentence in the paragraph.

3. List some supporting examples. _____

_____

_____

The Writer's Desk Exploring

Think about the following questions, and write down the first ideas that come to mind. Try to write two or three ideas for each topic.

EXAMPLE: What is *spam*?

Canned ham; too many emails; porn site links; advertising

1. What is a *bad hair day*? _____

_____

2. What is a *slob*? _____

_____

3. What is a *genius*? _____

_____

The Topic Sentence

In your **topic sentence,** indicate what you are defining, and include a definition of the term. Look at the three ways to define a term.

- **Definition by synonym.** You could give a word that means the same thing as the term.

  term   +   synonyms
  Gratuitous means "unnecessary" or "uncalled-for."

- **Definition by negation.** Explain what the term is not, and then explain what it is.

  term   +   what it is not   +   what it is
  Sexual harassment is not harmless banter; it is intimidating and unwanted sexual attention.

- **Definition by category.** Decide what larger group the term belongs to, and then determine the unique characteristics that set the term apart from others in that category.

  term   +   category   +   detail
  A blogger is a writer who expresses his or her opinions in an Internet journal.

The Writer's Desk **Write Topic Sentences**

Write a topic sentence for each of the following topics. Your sentence should have a controlling idea that expresses the direction of the paragraph. Remember that the goal of the paragraph is to define something.

EXAMPLE:

Topic: Spam

Topic sentence: *Spam is not just canned ham; it is annoying and unwanted emails.*

1. Topic: A bad hair day

   Topic sentence: _____

   _____

2. Topic: A slob

   Topic sentence: _____

   _____

3. Topic: A genius

   Topic sentence: _____

   _____

The Supporting Ideas

A definition paragraph should include a complete definition of a term, and it should have adequate examples that support the definition. Remember to provide various types of support. Do not simply repeat the definition.

A Definition Paragraph Plan

When you write a definition paragraph plan, ensure that your details are valid and that they relate to the topic sentence.

TOPIC SENTENCE:	**Spam is not just canned ham; it is annoying and unwanted emails.**
Support 1:	It increases in quantity.
Details:	— may begin with one or two unwanted emails
	— becomes an avalanche of spam
Support 2:	It offers unwanted advertising.
Details:	— products of questionable value
	— promotions often pornographic

Support 3: It is time-consuming to deal with.
Details: — sometimes open to see if email is from a friend
— must sort through and permanently trash each spam
— waste valuable time

The Writer's Desk Develop Supporting Ideas

Choose one of the topic sentences that you wrote for the Writer's Desk on page 67, and write a detailed paragraph plan.

Topic sentence: _____

_____

Support 1: _____

   Details: _____

_____

Support 2: _____

   Details: _____

_____

Support 3: _____

   Details: _____

The Writer's Desk Write a Definition Paragraph

You have made a list of supporting ideas for a topic. Now write a definition paragraph. After you finish writing, remember to revise and edit your paragraph.

The Writer's Room **Topics for Definition Paragraphs**

Writing Activity 1

Write a definition paragraph about one of the following topics.

General Topics

1. a mosh pit
2. mall rats
3. road rage
4. meticulous
5. collateral damage

College and Work-Related Topics

6. a golden handshake
7. a blue-collar worker
8. burnout
9. materialistic
10. an effective boss

WRITING LINK

See the Writer's Rooms in the following grammar chapters for more definition writing topics.

Chapter 10, Writer's Room topic 2 (page 196)

Chapter 16, Writer's Room topic 1 (page 273)

Chapter 19, Writer's Room topic 2 (page 303)

Chapter 23, Writer's Room topic 3 (page 357)

Writing Activity 2

What is a *nest egg?* Write a paragraph explaining the term.

READING LINK

Definition Essays

The following readings contain examples of definition writing.

"The Hijab" by Naheed Mustafa (page 423)

"The Point Is?" by John G. Tufts (page 428)

✓ DEFINITION PARAGRAPH CHECKLIST

As you write your definition paragraph, review the paragraph checklist on the inside rear cover. Also, ask yourself the next set of questions.

☐ Does my topic sentence contain a definition by synonym, negation, or category?

☐ Do all of my supporting sentences relate to the topic sentence?

☐ Do I use concise language in my definition?

☐ Do I include enough examples to help define the term?

F) The Comparison and Contrast Paragraph

You **compare** when you want to find similarities, and you **contrast** when you want to find differences. When writing a comparison and contrast paragraph, you prove a specific point by explaining how people, places, things, or ideas are the same or different. For example, you might compare two jobs that you have had, two different ways of disciplining, or two ideas about how to stimulate the national economy.

Before you write, you must make a decision about whether you will focus on similarities, differences, or both. As you explore your topic, it is a good idea to make a list of both similarities and differences. Later, you could use some of the ideas in your paragraph plan.

PRACTICE 6

Read the next paragraph and answer the questions that follow.

cacophony: an unpleasant combination of sounds

innocuous: dull; inoffensive

There are some major differences between the supermarket and a traditional marketplace. The **cacophony** of a traditional market has given way to programmed **innocuous** music, punctuated by enthusiastically intoned commercials. A stroll through a traditional market offers an array of sensuous aromas; if you are conscious of smelling something in a supermarket, there is a problem. The life and death matter of eating, expressed in traditional markets by the sale of vegetables with stems and roots and by hanging animal carcasses, is purged from the supermarket, where food is processed somewhere else, or at least trimmed out of sight. But the most fundamental difference between a traditional market and the places through which you push your cart is that in a modern retail setting nearly all the selling is done without people. The product is totally dissociated from the personality of any particular person selling it—with the possible exception of those who appear in its advertising. The supermarket **purges** sociability, because sociability slows down sales.

purge: to remove or get rid of

—Thomas Hine, "What's in a Package?"

1. Underline the topic sentence.

2. List the key features of a supermarket and a traditional market.

Supermarket	Traditional Market
_____	_____
_____	_____
_____	_____
_____	_____
_____	_____

The Writer's Desk **Exploring**

Think about the following questions, and write down the first ideas that come to mind. Try to write two or three ideas for each topic.

EXAMPLE: What are some key differences between a small town and a city?

Small Town	**City**
People know each other.	Larger, more impersonal
Mall or main street is main hangout.	Downtown is full of small shops.
Not many libraries or bookstores	Many libraries and bookstores

1. Compare one season with another season.

Season: _____   Season: _____

_____   _____

_____   _____

_____   _____

2. Compare two different jobs that you have had.

Job: _____   Job: _____

_____   _____

_____   _____

_____   _____

3. Compare what you do on two different holidays. For example, you could compare Thanksgiving and Halloween.

Holiday: _____   Holiday: _____

_____   _____

_____   _____

_____   _____

The Topic Sentence

The topic sentence in a comparison and contrast paragraph indicates whether you are making comparisons, contrasts, or both. When you write a topic sentence, indicate what you are comparing or contrasting, and express a controlling idea. The following are examples of topic sentences for comparison and contrast paragraphs.

My brother and father argue a lot, but they have very similar personalities.

Topic (what is being compared): father and brother

Controlling idea: similar personalities

Although women generally earn less than men, they must pay more than men do for everyday products.

Topic (what is being contrasted): men's and women's products

Controlling idea: women's products cost more

The Writer's Desk Write Topic Sentences

Write a topic sentence for each of the following topics. Your sentence should have a controlling idea that expresses the direction of the paragraph.

EXAMPLE:

Topic: Town and city

Topic sentence: <u>Although large cities are fascinating, I prefer my small hometown.</u>

1. Topic: Two seasons

   Topic sentence: _____

   _____

2. Topic: Two jobs

   Topic sentence: _____

   _____

3. Topic: Two holidays

   Topic sentence: _____

   _____

The Supporting Ideas

In a comparison and contrast paragraph, you can develop your supporting ideas in two different ways.

Point-by-Point Development

To develop a topic point by point, you look at similarities or differences by going back and forth from one side to the other.

Point A   Point B   Point A   Point B   Point A   Point B

Topic-by-Topic Development

To develop your ideas topic by topic, you discuss one topic in detail, and then you discuss the other topic in detail.

All of Topic A   All of Topic B

A Comparison and Contrast Paragraph Plan

When you write a comparison and contrast paragraph plan, decide which pattern you will follow: point by point or topic by topic. Then add some details.

TOPIC SENTENCE:	**Although large cities are fascinating, I prefer my small hometown.**
Support 1:	Large cities have a lot of attractions.
Details:	— many theaters, restaurants, music clubs
Support 2:	Large cities have diverse groups of people.
Details:	— people from all over the United States
	— immigrants and tourists from different nations
Support 3:	My hometown is small but friendly.
Details:	— not many clubs or restaurants
	— only one movie theater
Support 4:	But my hometown makes me feel secure.
Details:	— people I've known my whole life, including bus driver, post office clerk
	— old school friends and family live there

The Writer's Desk Develop Supporting Ideas

Choose one of the topic sentences that you wrote for the Writer's Desk, on page 72, and write a detailed paragraph plan.

Topic sentence: _____

_____

Support 1: _____

   Details: _____

_____

Support 2: _____

Details: _____

_____

Support 3: _____

Details: _____

_____

Support 4: _____

Details: _____

_____

The Writer's Desk **Write a Comparison and Contrast Paragraph**

You have made a list of supporting ideas for a topic. Now write a comparison and contrast paragraph. After you finish writing, remember to revise and edit your paragraph.

The Writer's Room **Topics for Comparison and Contrast Paragraphs**

WRITING LINK

See the Writer's Rooms in the following grammar chapters for more comparison and contrast writing topics.

Chapter 8, Writer's Room topic 2 (page 158)

Chapter 12, Writer's Room topic 2 (page 222)

Chapter 14, Writer's Room topic 2 (page 246)

Chapter 18, Writer's Room topic 1 (page 295)

Chapter 20, Writer's Room topic 2 (page 314)

Chapter 27, Writer's Room topic 1 (page 404)

Writing Activity 1

Write a comparison and contrast paragraph about one of the following topics.

General Topics

1. a new driver versus an experienced driver
2. two sports
3. your mother and your father
4. two close friends
5. two youth subcultures

College and Work-Related Topics

6. expectations about college and the reality of college
7. a small school or college and a large school or college
8. two different co-workers
9. working alone and working in a team
10. two different bosses

Writing Activity 2

Examine the photo, and think about things that you could compare and contrast. Some ideas might be spanking versus time out, two parenting styles, or two behavior problems. Then write a comparison and contrast paragraph.

READING LINK

The following readings use comparison and contrast writing.
"The New Addiction" by Josh Freed (page 442)
"The Zoo Life" by Yann Martel (page 452)

COMPARISON AND CONTRAST PARAGRAPH CHECKLIST

As you write your comparison and contrast paragraph, review the paragraph checklist on the inside rear cover. Also, ask yourself the next set of questions.

Does my topic sentence explain what I am comparing or contrasting?

Does my paragraph focus on either similarities or differences?

Does my paragraph include a point-by-point or topic-by-topic pattern?

Do all of my supporting examples clearly relate to the topics that are being compared or contrasted?

G) The Cause and Effect Paragraph

Cause and effect writing explains why an event happened or what the consequences of such an event were. You often analyze the causes or effects of something. You may worry about what causes your mate to behave in a certain manner, or you may wonder about the effects of fast food on your health.

Because a paragraph is not very long, it is best to focus on either causes or effects. If you do decide to focus on both causes and effects, make sure that your topic sentence expresses your purpose to the reader.

PRACTICE 7

Read the next paragraph and answer the questions that follow.

Although reality shows are widely criticized, they hook viewers for several reasons. First, reality-show contestants are ordinary people, and their reactions appear to be unscripted. Therefore, the viewer has the sensation of watching something that is authentic. Viewers also like to be voyeurs, smugly observing contestants who expose weaknesses. On *Survivor*, for example, contestants scheme and negotiate to advance in the game. Moreover, reality television makes real-life situations seem more exciting. For example, on dating shows, participants live in mansions, have romantic candlelight dinners, and have a chance to meet the perfect mate, all within a few weeks. Most important, reality programming allows viewers to live out their fantasies. They watch ordinary folks transform their bodies, become fashion models, get top-level jobs in finance, and live on exotic islands. And of course, the contestants become television stars, and viewers can imagine becoming stars, too. Therefore, in spite of strong criticisms, reality shows will likely continue to exist in one form or another for many years to come.

—Gaspare Bedrosian, student

1. Underline the topic sentence.

2. What does this paragraph focus on?
   a. Causes   b. Effects

3. Who is the audience? _____

4. List the supporting details.

   _____

   _____

   _____

   _____

   _____

The Writer's Desk Exploring

Write some possible causes and effects for the following topics. Think of two or three ideas for each topic. Then choose whether you would rather write about causes or effects.

EXAMPLE: Why do some parents spoil their children, and how does being spoiled affect the children?

Causes	Effects
want child to like them	children don't appreciate
don't have parenting skills	material goods
can't say no	hurts parent–child
	relationship
	children have no patience

Focus on: Causes

1. Why do people marry, and how does marriage affect people's lives?

Causes	Effects

Focus on: _____

2. What are some of the causes and effects of credit card debt?

Causes	Effects

Focus on: _____

3. What can cause a person to drive badly, and how can bad driving affect others?

Causes	Effects

Focus on: _____

The Topic Sentence

The topic sentence in a cause and effect paragraph must clearly demonstrate whether the focus is on causes, effects, or both.

topic   controlling idea (causes)
I buy fast food <u>for many reasons</u>.

topic   controlling idea (effects)
Fast food <u>has had negative effects on my health</u>.

topic   controlling idea (causes and effects)
Fast food, <u>which I eat for many reasons,</u> <u>has had some negative</u>

<u>effects on my health</u>.

 **Do Not Confuse** *Affect* **and** *Effect*

Affect is a verb, and *effect* is a noun. *Affect* (verb) means "to influence or change," and *effect* (noun) means "the result."

verb
Secondhand smoke can <u>affect</u> children's health.

noun
Secondhand smoke has many negative <u>effects</u> on children's health.

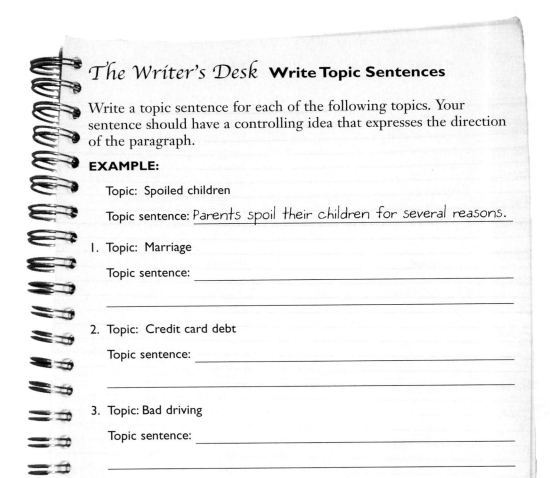

The Writer's Desk **Write Topic Sentences**

Write a topic sentence for each of the following topics. Your sentence should have a controlling idea that expresses the direction of the paragraph.

EXAMPLE:

Topic: Spoiled children

Topic sentence: Parents spoil their children for several reasons.

1. Topic: Marriage

   Topic sentence: _____

   _____

2. Topic: Credit card debt

   Topic sentence: _____

   _____

3. Topic: Bad driving

   Topic sentence: _____

   _____

The Supporting Ideas

After you have developed an effective topic sentence, generate supporting ideas. For a cause and effect paragraph, think of examples that clearly show the causes or effects. Then arrange your examples in emphatic order. Emphatic order means that you can place your examples from the most to the least important or from the least to the most important.

A Cause and Effect Paragraph Plan

When you write a cause and effect paragraph plan, think about the order of your ideas. List details under each supporting idea.

TOPIC SENTENCE: **Parents spoil their children for many reasons.**

Support 1: People are not educated about good parenting skills.
  Details: — Schools do not teach how to be a good parent.
  — Some people may follow the habits of their own parents.

Support 2: They want to be the child's friend instead of an authority figure.
  Details: — Parents won't say no.
  — Parents want to be liked.

Support 3: They believe that children should receive whatever they want.
  Details: — Parents think they are doing their children favors by buying toys, video games, and so on.
  — They feel that there is nothing wrong with instant gratification.

Support 4: Some parents are motivated by guilt to overspend on their children.
  Details: — They spend very little time with their children.
  — Parents buy gifts, unnecessary clothing, and so on.

The Writer's Desk Develop Supporting Ideas

Choose one of the topic sentences that you wrote for the Writer's Desk on page 78, and write a detailed paragraph plan.

Topic sentence: _____

_____

Support 1: _____
  Details: _____

_____

Support 2: _____
  Details: _____

_____

Support 3: _____

Details: _____

_____

Support 4: _____

Details: _____

The Writer's Desk **Write a Cause and Effect Paragraph**

You have made a list of supporting ideas for a topic. Now write a cause and effect paragraph. After you finish writing, remember to revise and edit your paragraph.

The Writer's Room   **Topics for Cause and Effect Paragraphs**

WRITING LINK

See the Writer's Rooms in the following grammar chapters for more cause and effect writing topics.

Chapter 6, Writer's Room topic 2 (page 125)

Chapter 13, Writer's Room topic 1 (page 238)

Chapter 15, Writer's Room topic 1 (page 259)

Chapter 22, Writer's Room topic 3 (page 342)

Chapter 24, Writer's Room topic 1 (page 368)

Writing Activity 1

Write a cause and effect paragraph about one of the following topics. As you consider each topic, think about both causes and effects.

General Topics

1. losing a good friend
2. buying a car
3. seeing a therapist
4. becoming famous
5. losing your temper

College and Work-Related Topics

6. going to college
7. workplace stress
8. achieving good grades
9. working with a friend, mate, or spouse
10. working nights

Writing Activity 2

Examine the photo. Why do people work out? What are the effects of exercise? Write a paragraph about the causes or effects of regular exercise.

READING LINK

The following readings use cause and effect writing.

"The Culture War" by Linda Chavez (page 444)

"Going Thin in Fiji" by Ellen Goodman (page 447)

CAUSE AND EFFECT PARAGRAPH CHECKLIST

As you write your cause and effect paragraph, review the paragraph checklist on the inside rear cover. Also, ask yourself the next set of questions.

- Does my topic sentence indicate clearly that my paragraph focuses on causes, effects, or both?

- Do I have adequate supporting examples for causes and/or effects?

- Do I make logical and valid points?

- Do I use the terms *effect* or *affect* correctly?

H) The Argument Paragraph

In an **argument paragraph**, you take a position on an issue, and you try to defend your position. For example, you might argue that taxes are too high, that a restaurant is excellent, or that a certain breed of dog should be banned.

Although some people may disagree with you, try to be direct in argument writing. State your point of view clearly and unapologetically.

PRACTICE 8

Read the next paragraph and answer the questions that follow.

According to the Children's Defense Fund Action Council, about 3,300 children and teens are killed by gunfire in the United States every year, and close to 15,000 children are injured by firearms. To stem the tide of gun-related deaths and injuries, public schools should teach gun-safety courses. First, guns are prevalent in our society, and we cannot stop children from being fascinated with them. Even if parents have no guns in their homes, their children could come across a gun in a friend's home or on the street. Second, children who understand the danger of guns will not be so attracted to weapons. If a child is permitted to hold a gun, feel its kick, hear its deafening blast, and witness its destructiveness, he or she will realize how hazardous a gun is. Furthermore, if children know how to use guns responsibly, there will be fewer gun accidents. An uninformed child may not realize that a gun is loaded or that the safety catch is off. After taking a gun safety course, that same child would immediately recognize that a gun is ready to fire and extremely dangerous. If children are not properly educated about gun use, the numbers of accidental deaths and injuries will rise.

—Dean Cochrane, student

1. Underline the topic sentence.

2. How does the author prove that there is a problem? _____

   _____

   _____

   _____

   _____

3. What are the three main arguments? _____

   _____

   _____

   _____

   _____

4. What are some transitional expressions that the writer uses? _____

   _____

5. How does the writer conclude his paragraph?
   a. A prediction   b. A quotation   c. A suggestion

The Writer's Desk Exploring

Think about the following questions, and write down the first ideas that come to mind. Try to write two or three ideas for each topic.

EXAMPLE: Should any dog breeds be banned?

I don't really know, maybe pit bulls. They have a bad reputation.

What else? Dobermans? Maybe the problem is with the owners.

1. Is college beneficial? Does it really change people's lives? Explain your answer.

   _____

   _____

   _____

2. What do you think about the legal drinking age? Is it useful? Should it be

   raised or lowered? _____

   _____

   _____

   _____

3. Is it a good idea to have a workplace romance? Why or why not? _____

   _____

   _____

   _____

The Topic Sentence

The **topic sentence** in an argument paragraph mentions the subject and a debatable point of view about the subject. You can use *should, must,* or *ought to* in your topic sentence.

controlling idea   topic (issue)

<u>Our police forces should not use</u> **racial profiling**.

Your topic sentence can further guide your readers by listing the specific arguments you will make in the paragraph.

controlling idea   topic (issue)   argument 1

<u>Parents should not</u> **spank their children** because it is a violent act,

argument 2   argument 3

it scares children, and it teaches children to become violent.

 **Write a Debatable Topic Sentence**

Your topic sentence should be a debatable statement. It should not be a fact or a statement of opinion.

Fact: Some breeds of dogs can be aggressive.

(Who can argue with that point?)

Opinion: I think that pit bulls should be banned.

(This is a statement of opinion. Nobody can deny that you want pit bulls to be banned. Do not use phrases such as *In my opinion*, *I think*, or *I believe* in your topic sentence.)

Argument: Pit bulls should be banned.

(This statement is debatable.)

The Writer's Desk Write Topic Sentences

Write a topic sentence for each of the following topics. Your sentence should have a controlling idea that expresses the direction of the paragraph. Remember that the goal of the paragraph is to express your viewpoint.

EXAMPLE:

Topic: Banning a dog breed

Topic sentence: Pit bulls should be banned for several reasons.

1. Topic: Benefits of college

   Topic sentence: _____

   _____

2. Topic: Changing the legal drinking age

   Topic sentence: _____

   _____

3. Topic: Workplace romance

   Topic sentence: _____

   _____

The Supporting Ideas

In the body of your paragraph, give convincing supporting arguments. Try to use several types of supporting evidence such as anecdotes, facts and statistics, and answers to the opposition.

- **Anecdotes** are specific experiences or stories that support your point of view.
- **Facts** are statements that can be verified in some way. **Statistics** are a type of fact. When you use a fact, ensure that your source is reliable.
- Think about your opponents' arguments, and provide **answers to the opposition** in response to their arguments.

 **Avoid Circular Reasoning**

Circular reasoning means that a paragraph restates its main point in various ways but does not provide supporting details. Avoid it by offering separate supporting ideas and precise examples.

Circular

Film actors, who lead decadent lives, should not earn huge salaries because so many average people struggle. Many ordinary folks work long hours and have trouble making ends meet. Some actors work only a few months, earn millions, and then buy ridiculous luxury items. They lose touch with reality. Film studios should avoid paying so much and encouraging self-indulgence.

Improved

Film actors, who often lead decadent lives, should not earn huge salaries while so many average people struggle. Many ordinary folks, **such as teachers and nurses,** work long hours and have trouble making ends meet. **Yet, actor Tom Cruise's $20-million-per-movie salary is more than the combined wages of a small city's police department.** Also, some actors lose touch with reality. **Consider the difference between John Travolta, who flies a private jet, and caregiver Luisa Moreno, who spends $18.40 a day commuting on public buses. And, in a nation with so much homelessness, actress Demi Moore owns a house that holds her doll collection.** Film studios should cut film actors' high salaries and then disburse the remaining amount to people who really need the money.

An Argument Paragraph Plan

When you write an argument paragraph plan, think about how you will organize your arguments. If possible, include different types of supporting evidence: facts, statistics, anecdotes, and answers to the opposition.

Topic sentence: <u>**Pit bulls should be banned for several reasons.**</u>

Support 1: Pit bulls often attack people.
Details:
— Three children in my state have been maimed or killed by pit bulls.
— The dogs have attacked owners.

Support 2: Pit bulls sometimes seem to "snap."
Details:
— The dogs sometimes attack without provocation.
— Some experts believe improper breeding has caused chemical "misfiring" in their brains.

Support 3: They are difficult to control when they become aggressive.
Details:
— Their jaws clench tightly on the victim in a vise-like grip.
— They have immensely powerful bodies.

The Writer's Desk **Develop Supporting Ideas**

Choose one of the topic sentences that you wrote for the Writer's Desk on page 84, and write a paragraph plan. Include supporting arguments, and list a detail for each argument.

Topic sentence: _____

_____

Support 1: _____

   Details: _____

_____

Support 2: _____

   Details: _____

_____

Support 3: _____

   Details: _____

Support 4: _____

   Details: _____

The Writer's Desk **Write an Argument Paragraph**

You have made a list of supporting ideas for a topic. Now write an argument paragraph. After you finish writing, remember to revise and edit your paragraph.

The Writer's Room

Topics for Argument Paragraphs

Writing Activity 1

Write an argument paragraph about one of the following topics. Remember to narrow your topic and to follow the writing process.

General Topics

1. length of compulsory schooling
2. watching too much television
3. wearing fur
4. right to privacy for politicians or celebrities
5. divorce

College and Work-Related Topics

6. an unfair college rule
7. living on campus
8. compulsory art courses in college
9. reasons for students' interest (or lack of interest) in politics
10. raising the minimum wage

WRITING LINK

See the Writer's Rooms in the following grammar chapters for more argument writing topics.
Chapter 6, Writer's Room topic 3 (page 125)
Chapter 7, Writer's Room topics 1 and 2 (page 145)
Chapter 13, Writer's Room topic 2 (page 238)
Chapter 15, Writer's Room topics 2 and 3 (page 259)
Chapter 16, Writer's Room topic 2 (page 274)
Chapter 17, Writer's Room topic 2 (page 286)
Chapter 18, Writer's Room topic 2 (page 295)
Chapter 24, Writer's Room topic 2 (page 368)

Writing Activity 2

Write an argument paragraph explaining the benefits or disadvantages of day care centers.

READING LINK

The following readings use argument writing.
"For Marriage" by Kirsteen Macleod (page 435)
"Against Marriage" by Winston Murray (page 436)

ARGUMENT PARAGRAPH CHECKLIST

As you write your argument paragraph, review the paragraph checklist on the inside rear cover. Also, ask yourself the next set of questions.

☐ Does my topic sentence clearly state my position on the issue?

☐ Do I support my position with facts, examples, or answers to the opposition?

☐ Do my supporting arguments provide evidence that directly supports the topic sentence?

See Chapter 4 on the Visualizing Writing CD-ROM for additional audio and animated mini-lectures on **Illustration**, **Narration**, **Description**, **Process**, **Definition**, **Classification**, **Comparison and Contrast**, **Cause and Effect**, and **Argument**.

Writing the Essay

CHAPTER 5

> *Words are tools that automatically carve concepts out of experience.*
>
> —JULIAN SORRELL HUXLEY (1887–1975)
> *British biologist*

CONTENTS

Exploring
* Exploring the Essay
* Explore Topics

Developing
* The Thesis Statement
* The Supporting Ideas
* The Essay Plan
* The Introduction
* The Conclusion
* The First Draft

Revising and Editing
* Revising and Editing the Essay
* The Final Draft

A suspension bridge is supported by columns and steel cables. In the same way, an essay is a sturdy structure that is supported by a strong thesis statement and solid body paragraphs.

EXPLORING

Exploring the Essay

An **essay** is a series of paragraphs that support one central idea. It is divided into three parts: an **introduction,** a **body,** and a **conclusion.** There is no perfect length for an essay. Some instructors prefer five-paragraph essays, and others may ask for two- or three-page essays. The important thing to remember is that all essays, regardless of length, have certain features: the introductory paragraph introduces the essay's thesis, the body paragraphs provide support for the thesis, and the concluding paragraph brings the essay to a satisfactory close.

Review the examples on pages 90 and 91 to see how different types of sentences and paragraphs can form an essay.

The Sentence

A **sentence** always has a subject and a verb and expresses a complete thought.

> Winning a lottery can lead to feelings of boredom, paranoia, and guilt.

The Paragraph

A **topic sentence** introduces the subject of a paragraph and shows the writer's attitude toward its subject.

The **body** of a paragraph contains details that support its topic sentence.

A paragraph ends with a **concluding sentence.**

> Winning a lottery can lead to feelings of boredom, paranoia, and guilt. With no financial incentive to work, people often quit their jobs. Lottery winners also complain that they lose their workplace friendships. Without work, winners may feel that their days are wasted. Ultimately people should not expect a lottery win to improve their lives.

The Essay

An **introduction** engages the reader's interest and contains a **thesis statement.**

Body paragraphs support the main idea of an essay.

A **conclusion** reemphasizes the main idea (thesis) and restates the main points of an essay. It brings an essay to a satisfactory close.

A concluding paragraph in the essay ends with a **concluding statement.**

> Winning a lottery can lead to feelings of boredom, paranoia, and guilt.
>
> Many lottery winners quit their jobs, but then they feel bored.
>
> Friendships and family relationships often disintegrate after a lottery win.
>
> Feelings of guilt are common in the newly rich.
>
> Ultimately, people should not expect a lottery win to improve their lives.

The Essay's Structure

Each body paragraph begins with a topic sentence.

The introductory paragraph introduces the essay's topic and contains its thesis statement.

The title gives a hint about the essay's topic.

The thesis statement contains the essay's topic and its controlling idea.

Winning the Lottery

Every week my father buys a Powerball lottery ticket hoping to win the grand prize. Even when money is tight, he puts aside a few dollars so that he can play his numbers. Like most Americans, he dreams of winning a fortune. However, winning a lottery may not bring the rewards that people dream of. In fact, a lottery win can cause many unexpected problems.

Many lottery winners quit their jobs, but then they feel bored. The workplace is part of the social network for the majority of people. They share professional and personal interests. Also, performing a job each day gives people a sense of personal accomplishment. Those who win lotteries may have a lot of money, but they also have a lot of empty time to fill.

Furthermore, friendships and family relationships can disintegrate after a lottery win. During a television interview on a local news program, a woman named Linda discussed her $7 million lottery win. Her mother sued her for a share of the winnings, arguing that they usually bought lottery tickets together. Family members took sides and fought over the issue. Meanwhile, some of the lottery winner's friends, jealous that she was so wealthy, either asked her for handouts or deserted her. Linda told the interviewer that the lottery win had made her very lonely.

Feelings of guilt are common in the newly rich. They often feel conflicted about having so much money when they know what it is like to have very little. The guilt can lead them into doing rash acts. They may give the money away, spend it wildly, or allow others to take advantage of them. For example, in the interview with Linda, she said that many strangers phoned her with dubious requests for aid, and she agonized over some of their stories. She gave away large sums of money to people who conned her.

Although it seems exciting to win a lottery, there can be many problems with such a windfall. People may feel paranoid, used, and guilty if they win the lottery. If you buy lottery tickets, prepare to have your life turned upside down.

—*Nick Zoubris, student*

The concluding paragraph brings the essay to a satisfactory close.

Each body paragraph contains details that support the thesis statement.

Explore Topics

When you are planning your essay, consider your topic, audience, and purpose. Your **topic** is who or what you are writing about. Your **audience** is your intended reader, and your **purpose** is your reason for writing. Do you hope to entertain, inform, or persuade the reader?

Narrowing the Topic

You may need to narrow your topic (make it more specific) to ensure that it suits your purpose for writing and fits the size of the assignment. To narrow your topic, you can use some exploring methods, such as questioning (asking and answering questions) or brainstorming (jotting a rough list of ideas that come to mind). These strategies are explained in more detail in Chapter 1.

SAM'S LIST TO NARROW THE TOPIC

Student writer Sam Kwan used brainstorming to narrow his broad topic, "divorce."

- Reasons people get divorced
- How to make divorce easier for the children
- People who commit adultery
- Dealing with blended families
- The role of stepparents
- How I reacted when my father left home
- Should fathers get custody of the children?
- The importance of having marriage classes
- How property should be divided after a breakup

The Writer's Desk Narrow the Topic

Each of the following topics is very broad. Practice narrowing each topic.

EXAMPLE:

Fame: Fans who are obsessed with celebrities

Problems associated with fame

How to become famous

1. Music: _____

_____

_____

2. War: _____

_____

_____

3. Housing: _____

_____

_____

DEVELOPING

The Thesis Statement

Once you have narrowed the topic of your essay, it is important to state clearly in one sentence what it is. Like the topic sentence in a paragraph, the **thesis statement** introduces what the essay is about and arouses the interest of the reader by making a point about the topic.

Characteristics of a Good Thesis Statement

A thesis statement has the following characteristics.

- It expresses the main topic of the essay.
- It contains a controlling idea.
- It is a complete sentence that usually appears in an essay's introductory paragraph.

> topic   controlling idea
> **Credit card fraud** <u>is a serious problem</u>.
>
> controlling idea   topic
> <u>The public has the right to know about</u> **the scandalous private lives of politicians.**

Writing an Effective Thesis Statement

When you develop your thesis statement, ask yourself the following questions.

1. **Is my thesis statement a complete statement that has a controlling idea?**
   Your thesis statement should always reveal a complete thought and make a point about the topic. It should not announce the topic.

Incomplete:	Campus drinking.
	(This is not a complete statement. A complete sentence has both a subject and a verb.)
Announcement:	I will write about campus drinking.
	(This announces the topic but says nothing relevant about the topic. Do not use expressions such as *I will write about* or *My topic is*.)
Thesis statement:	Binge drinking is a serious problem on college campuses.

2. **Does my thesis statement make a valid and supportable point?**
Your thesis statement should express a valid point that you can support with
details. It should not be a vaguely worded statement, and it should not be a
highly questionable generalization.

Vague:	Politicians spend too much money.
	(Which politicians? What do they spend it on?)
Invalid point:	Politicians are liars.
	(Is this really true for all politicians? This generalization might be difficult to prove.)
Thesis statement:	Our mayor has spent too much money on renovations to his office.

 **Give Specific Details**

Make sure that your thesis statement is very clear. You should give enough details to
make it interesting. Your instructor may want you to guide the reader through your
main points. You can do this by including specific points that you will later argue in the
body of your essay.

My years in high school taught me <u>to stand up for myself</u>, <u>to focus on my
goals</u>, and <u>to be a more open-minded person</u>.

PRACTICE I

Identify why each of the following thesis statements is not effective. There may
be more than one reason. Then revise each statement.

Announces   Incomplete   Invalid   Vague

EXAMPLE:

In this essay, I will discuss hazing in colleges.

Problem: _Announces_

Revised sentence: _Colleges should severely punish students who_
                    organize or participate in hazing events.

1. Bilingual education is good.

   Problem: _____

   Revised statement: _____

2. Censorship of the Internet.

   Problem: _____

   Revised statement: _____

3. I am going to write about why I left my job.

   Problem: _____

   Revised statement: _____

   _____

4. All criminals have had terrible childhoods.

   Problem: _____

   Revised statement: _____

   _____

5. In this paper, I will discuss sex education in schools.

   Problem: _____

   Revised statement: _____

   _____

The Writer's Desk Write Thesis Statements

For each item, choose a narrowed topic from the Writer's Desk on pages 92 and 93. Then write an interesting thesis statement. Remember that each thesis statement should contain a controlling idea

EXAMPLE:

Topic: **Fame**

Narrowed topic: Problems with fame

Thesis statement: Although fame seems exciting, there are many problems associated with fame.

1. Topic: **Music**

   Narrowed topic: _____

   Thesis statement: _____

   _____

2. Topic: **War**

   Narrowed topic: _____

   Thesis statement: _____

   _____

3. Topic: **Housing**

   Narrowed topic: _____

   Thesis statement: _____

   _____

The Supporting Ideas

The thesis statement expresses the main idea of the entire essay. In the illustration below, you can see how topic sentences relate to the thesis statement and how details support the topic sentences. Every idea in the essay is unified and supports the thesis.

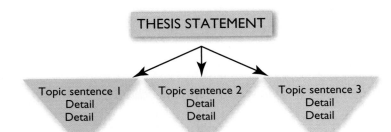

Generating Supporting Ideas

To generate ideas for the body paragraphs, you could use exploring strategies such as brainstorming, clustering, or freewriting. Come up with any ideas that can support your thesis statement.

OLIVIA'S SUPPORTING IDEAS

Student writer Olivia Riffo created a list to support her thesis statement. Then she reread her supporting points and removed ideas that she did not want to develop in her essay.

THESIS STATEMENT: **Although many people want to be famous, there are problems associated with fame.**

Supporting points:

—Lack of privacy
—Paparazzi follow celebrities
—Get swelled heads and believe they are special
—Have too much money
—~~Some people get famous on reality shows~~
—May develop addictions to drugs or alcohol
—~~Some celebs are so good-looking~~

The Writer's Desk List Supporting Ideas

Choose one of your thesis statements from the Writer's Desk on page 95, and create a list of possible supporting ideas.

Thesis statement: _____

Supporting ideas: _____

_____

_____

_____

_____

_____

_____

_____

_____

_____

The Essay Plan

When you write an **essay plan** or **outline,** organize your ideas logically by using time, space, or emphatic order. To create an essay plan, do the following:

- Look at your list of ideas and identify the best supporting ideas.
- Write topic sentences that express the main supporting ideas.
- Add details under each topic sentence.

WRITING LINK

For more information about organizing ideas using time, space, and emphatic order, see pages 23 to 26 of Chapter 2, "Developing."

OLIVIA'S ESSAY PLAN

Olivia wrote topic sentences and supporting examples and organized her ideas into a plan. Notice that her plan begins with a thesis statement, and she indents her supporting ideas.

THESIS STATEMENT: **Although many people want to be famous, there are problems associated with fame.**

    I. Celebrities have little to no privacy.
       –Paparazzi hound them (J. Lo, Princess Diana's death, the Olsen twins).
       –They can never relax in public because fans want to meet them.
   II. Many famous people start believing that they are special.
       –They are surrounded by people who praise them.
       –They become egotistical and demanding.
  III. Money and pressure lead some celebrities to abuse substances.
       –Some become alcoholics (Colin Farrell, Nick Nolte).
       –Some develop serious addictions to drugs (Kurt Cobain; Whitney Houston; Robert Downey, Jr.).

The Writer's Desk   Write an Essay Plan

Write an essay plan using your thesis statement and the supporting details you came up with in the previous Writer's Desk. Organize those ideas, and then write them in the essay plan below.

Thesis statement: _____

_____

I. _____

Details: _____

_____

II. _____

Details: _____

_____

III. _____

Details: _____

_____

Concluding idea: _____

_____

The Introduction

After you have made an essay plan, develop the sections of your essay by creating an effective introduction, linking body paragraphs, and forming a conclusion.

The **introductory paragraph** introduces the subject of your essay and contains the thesis statement. A strong introduction will capture the reader's attention and make him or her want to read on.

Introduction Styles

You can develop the sentences in the introduction in several different ways. To attract the reader's attention, your introduction can include various types of material.

- General background information
- Historical background information
- An interesting anecdote or a vivid description
- A contrasting position (an idea that is the opposite of the one you will develop)

 **Placement of the Thesis Statement**

Most introductions begin with sentences that introduce the topic and lead the reader to the main point of the essay. Generally, the thesis statement is the last sentence in the introduction.

PRACTICE 2

In the following introductions, the thesis statements are in bold print. Read each introduction, and circle the letter of the introduction style that each writer has used.

OLIVIA'S INTRODUCTION

All around the world, a lot of people dream of becoming big stars. They watch television and envy successful actors and actresses. Some people think that being famous is always a good thing. They associate celebrity with money, fun, and freedom. **Although many people want to be famous, there are problems associated with fame.**

Style: a. Anecdote   b. General   c. Historical   d. Contrasting position

1.   Dorothy Duke, the tobacco heiress, was rich, but she was renowned as an unhappy woman. She was alone during the last years of her life. She had no friends or family at her bedside during her final hours; indeed, some speculate that her own staff helped bring about her death. In Dorothy Duke's case, money did not buy her happiness or peace of mind. **Although many people feel that money will solve their problems, having too much money may cause more problems than it solves.**

Style: a. Anecdote   b. General   c. Historical   d. Contrasting position

2.   Life would be great if you won the lottery. There would be no work-related stress. You could stay home, sit by the pool, or play a game of golf. With a lot of money, you would not worry about your retirement; you could retire now! That nice house by the beach could be yours. It sounds great, right? But living a life of ease may not be so fantastic after all. **Money does not necessarily lead to happiness.**

Style: a. Anecdote   b. General   c. Historical   d. Contrasting position

3.   In the past, civilizations bartered with items. A cow could be traded for a small plot of land. Later, silver and gold were formed into coins. Because the coins translated into more goods or more land, they were coveted. Today, we are a money-obsessed nation. Everybody wants the dream house, the nice car, and the vacation by

a beach. **However, if you want to be truly happy, the pursuit of money should not guide your life.**

Style: a. Anecdote   b. General   c. Historical   d. Opposite position

4.   This is a materialistic nation. Advertisements instill a longing for consumer goods. At a young age, people learn that money equals success. Consequently, many average folks spend their lives pursuing wealth. Some may work long hours or have two jobs. Others buy lottery tickets or invest in stocks, dreaming of the wealth they will have one day. **However, when money becomes the primary focus, people may neglect other, much more important aspects of their lives.**

Style: a. Anecdote   b. General   c. Historical   d. Opposite position

The Writer's Desk **Write an Introduction**

In the Writer's Desk on page 98, you made an essay plan. Now, write an introduction for your essay on a separate piece of paper.

The Conclusion

Every essay ends with a **conclusion.** The concluding paragraph rephrases the thesis statement and summarizes the main points in the essay.

OLIVIA'S CONCLUSION

Olivia concluded her essay by restating her main points.

> Many celebrities lack privacy. They can also develop huge egos because they get praised constantly. Some celebrities have a hard time handling fame and become addicted to various substances.

To make her conclusion more interesting and original, Olivia could incorporate a prediction, a suggestion, or a quotation.

Prediction:	Those who become famous might end up with very difficult lives.
Suggestion:	People should not chase fame; instead, they should try to appreciate the life that they have.
Quotation:	A Chinese proverb states, "As great trees attract the winds, so great fame attracts envy."

 **Avoiding Problems in the Conclusion**

In your conclusion, do not contradict your main point, and do not introduce new or irrelevant information.

PRACTICE 3

The following essay is missing an introduction and a conclusion. Read the essay's body paragraphs, and underline the topic sentence in each. Then, on a separate sheet of paper, write an interesting introduction and an effective conclusion to make this a complete essay.

Body Paragraph 1

First, let the dog know that you are the boss. Animals in social units invariably have a hierarchy or rank, and dogs, like many other mammals, often want to be leaders. If you are not clearly positioned as the master, and if you feel a little insecure in the role, a puppy can become a dog that bites, attacks others, and destroys property simply because it thinks that it is the boss.

Body Paragraph 2

If you are not familiar with training methods, consider taking your pet to obedience school. The trainer will show you how to be assertive and consistent with your animal. If you are insecure, or if you act inconsistently, you could end up with major problems. Kylie Owens, a dog trainer from Miami, has dealt with very strong-willed pups: "I recently trained a dog that would tear the stuffing out of upholstered furniture, open cupboards, chew up carpets, and shred newspapers every time the owners left the house. After ten weeks of training, the dog has learned to behave."

Body Paragraph 3

Most importantly, plan to give your dog some time and attention. Dogs don't bathe themselves; someone has to do it. Dogs need to be taken on walks daily, in good weather and bad. And remember, it is cruel and inhumane to keep a large dog locked up in a city apartment all day. Dogs are not ornaments. They need attention, fresh air, and adequate exercise.

The Writer's Desk **Write a Conclusion**

In previous Writer's Desks in this chapter, you wrote an introduction and an essay plan. Now write a conclusion for your essay on a separate sheet of paper.

The First Draft

After creating an introduction and conclusion, and after arranging the supporting ideas in a logical order, you are ready to write your first draft. The first draft includes your introduction, several body paragraphs, and your concluding paragraph. Also, think of a title for your first draft.

The Writer's Desk **Write the First Draft**

Using the introduction, conclusion, and essay plan that you created in the previous Writer's Desk exercises, write the first draft of your essay.

REVISING AND EDITING

Revising and Editing the Essay

Revising and editing is an extremely important step in the writing process. When you revise your essay, you modify it to make it stronger and more convincing. You do this by reading the essay critically, looking for faulty logic, poor organization, or poor sentence style. Then you reorganize and rewrite it, making any necessary changes.

- **Revise for unity.** Verify that all of your body paragraphs support the essay's thesis statement. Also look carefully at each body paragraph and ensure that the sentences support the topic sentence.

- **Revise for adequate support.** Ensure that there are enough details and examples to make your essay strong and convincing.

- **Revise for coherence.** Make sure that your paragraphs flow smoothly and logically. To guide the reader from one idea to the next, or from one paragraph to the next, try using transitional words or expressions. Here are some examples.

finally	first	furthermore
in conclusion	moreover	second

- **Edit for errors.** Proofread your essay and check for errors in punctuation, spelling, grammar, and mechanics. There is an editing guide on the inside front cover of this book. It contains some common editing codes that your instructor may use.

WRITING LINK

For more information about revising, you may wish to review Chapter 3.

GRAMMAR LINK

To practice your editing skills, try the exercises in Chapter 28, "Editing Practice."

The Writer's Desk Revising and Editing Your Essay

In previous Writer's Desks, you developed an essay and wrote the first draft. Now revise and edit your essay.

The Final Draft

When you have finished revising the first draft of your essay, write the final version. This draft should include all the changes that you have made during the revision phase of your work. You should proofread the final copy of your work to check for mistakes in grammar, spelling, mechanics, and punctuation.

The Writer's Desk Writing Your Final Draft

You have developed, revised, and edited your essay. Now write the final draft. Before you give it to your instructor, proofread it one last time to ensure that you have found as many errors as possible.

The Writer's Room **Essay Topics**

Writing Activity

Choose any of the following topics, or choose your own topic. Then, write an essay. Remember to follow the writing process.

General Topics

1. moving out of the family home
2. a great or terrible movie
3. women on professional men's sports teams
4. financial mistakes
5. choosing a pet

College and Work-Related Topics

6. shift work
7. the value of work
8. feeling pressure
9. overwork
10. positive thinking

 ESSAY CHECKLIST

Exploring

☐ Think about your topic, audience, and purpose.

☐ Try exploring strategies such as brainstorming or clustering to find and narrow your topic.

Developing

☐ Write a thesis statement that introduces the topic and states the controlling idea.

☐ Support the thesis statement with facts and examples.

☐ Organize your ideas using time, space, or emphatic order.

☐ Write an essay plan to help you visualize the main and supporting ideas.

☐ Write the first draft.

Revising and Editing

- Revise for unity.

- Revise for adequate support.

- Revise for coherence. Use transitional expressions to link ideas.

- Edit for errors in spelling, punctuation, grammar, and mechanics.

- Write the final draft.

 See Chapter 5 on the Visualizing Writing CD-ROM for additional audio and animated mini-lectures on **Recognizing the Essay**, **Thesis Statements**, **Specific Details**, **Introductions**, **Conclusions**, and **Revising and Editing Your Own Essay**.

The Editing Handbook

Why Grammar Is Important

Clear writing begins with a well-developed sentence. At the very least, a sentence needs a noun, or pronoun, and a verb. However, a sentence can become richer when it also includes adjectives, adverbs, conjunctions, interjections, or prepositions.

Clear writing also requires grammatically correct sentences. If your writing contains errors in grammar, you may distract readers from your message, and they may focus, instead, on your inability to communicate clearly. To improve your writing skills, it is useful to understand how the English language works. When your knowledge of grammar conventions increases, you will be better able to identify and correct errors in your writing.

In the Editing Handbook, you will learn to spot errors and you will also learn about the underlying rule that applies to each error. Before you begin working through the chapters, review the images on the adjacent pages, which may help you think about grammar concepts in different ways.

◄ SECTION 1: Some Parts of Speech
THEME: SOCIAL SCIENCES

Train signals must work properly so that trains can avoid accidents. In sentences, certain parts of speech act as signals. If the wrong part of speech is used, the sentence may not transmit a clear message.

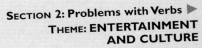

SECTION 2: Problems with Verbs ►
THEME: ENTERTAINMENT AND CULTURE

A movie requires a main character and action to drive the story forward. In the same way, a sentence needs both a subject and a verb to convey a message.

◄ SECTION 3: Verb Agreement and Consistency

THEME: BELIEFS

Each stone in a pyramid must be an accurate size and shape for the structure to be stable. For a sentence to function properly, the subject and verb must fit together.

SECTION 4: Effective Sentences ►
THEME: POLITICS

The political cartoonist combines a vivid image with a clever message to get the attention of the readers. In the next chapters, you will learn to combine sentences to make your writing more appealing.

◀ SECTION 5: Common Sentence Errors
THEME: SCIENCE

Skilled chefs are knowledgeable about food chemistry. They know that adding too much of one ingredient or too little of another can ruin a meal. In the same way, a sentence must have certain ingredients to make it complete and balanced.

SECTION 6: Modifiers ▶
THEME: RELATIONSHIPS

When Shah Jahan created the Taj Mahal as a symbol of his love, he used specific elements of design, color, and texture to make the architectural wonder more visually appealing. In the same way, adjectives and adverbs add color and definition to the nouns and verbs that they describe.

◀ SECTION 7: Word Use and Spelling
THEME: ZOOLOGY

To preserve a species, conservationists must make accurate analyses of things such as population sizes, animal habitats, and food sources. In the same way, when you write you should carefully examine your text to ensure that your spelling and choice of words is accurate.

SECTION 8: Punctuation and Mechanics ▶
THEME: THE BUSINESS WORLD

A button joins two pieces of fabric together. In the same way, a sentence has punctuation that links parts together.

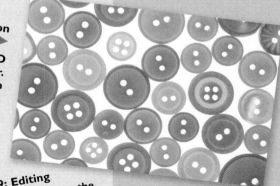

◀ SECTION 9: Editing

An interior decorator takes the time to ensure that the details in a room are complete. When you edit, you ensure that your writing is refined.

CHAPTER 6

Nouns, Determiners, and Prepositions

Section Theme: **SOCIAL SCIENCES**

CONTENTS

- Nouns
- Count Nouns and Noncount Nouns
- Determiners
- Prepositions

In this chapter, you will read about topics in anthropology and sociology, including ecotourism, education, and aging.

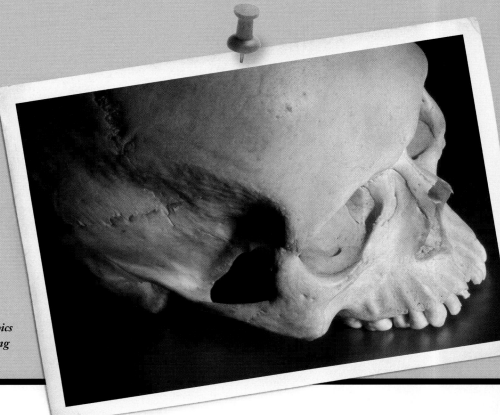

Grammar Snapshot

Looking at Nouns, Determiners, and Prepositions

In her essay "My Body Is My Own Business," Naheed Mustafa recounts her reasons for wearing the hijab. In the following excerpt, the nouns, determiners, and prepositions are highlighted.

> Young Muslim **women** are reclaiming the **hijab**, reinterpreting it in **light** of its original **purpose**—to give back to **women** ultimate **control** of their own **bodies**. The **Qur'an** teaches us that **men** and **women** are equal, that **individuals** should not be judged according to **gender**, **beauty**, **wealth**, or **privilege**.

In this chapter, you will identify and write nouns, determiners, and prepositions.

Nouns

Nouns are words that refer to people, places, or things. Nouns are divided into common nouns and proper nouns.

- **Common nouns** refer to general people, places, or things. Each begins with a lowercase letter. For example, *books, computer,* and *village* are common nouns.
- **Proper nouns** refer to particular people, places, or things. Each begins with a capital letter. For example, *Margaret Mead, the Amazon,* and *Thanksgiving* are proper nouns.

Section 1
SOME PARTS OF SPEECH

Singular and Plural Nouns

Nouns are either singular or plural. A **singular noun** refers to one of something, while a **plural noun** refers to more than one of something. Regular plural nouns end in *-s* or *-es.*

	Singular	**Plural**
People:	father	fathers
	sister	sisters
Places:	town	towns
	room	rooms
Things:	dish	dishes
	chair	chairs

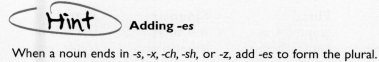

> ### Hint — Adding -es
>
> When a noun ends in -s, -x, -ch, -sh, or -z, add -es to form the plural.
>
> wish, wish**es**   box, box**es**   batch, batch**es**

Irregular Plural Nouns

Irregular plural nouns do not end in *-s* or *-es.* Here are some common irregular nouns.

Singular	**Plural**
child	children
foot	feet
goose	geese
man	men
mouse	mice
person	people
tooth	teeth
woman	women

Other Plural Noun Forms

Some nouns use other rules to form the plural. It is a good idea to memorize both the rules and the exceptions.

1. For nouns ending in *f,* or *fe,* change the *f* to *v* and add *-es.*

Singular	**Plural**	**Singular**	**Plural**
life	li**ves**	self	sel**ves**
thief	thie**ves**	shelf	shel**ves**

Some exceptions: belief, beliefs; roof, roofs.

2. For nouns ending in a consonant + *y*, change the *y* to *i* and add *-es*.

Singular	Plural	Singular	Plural
baby	bab**ies**	cherry	cherr**ies**
berry	berr**ies**	lady	lad**ies**

If a vowel comes before the final *y*, simply add *-s*.

Singular	Plural	Singular	Plural
boy	boy**s**	key	key**s**

3. Some nouns remain the same in both singular and plural forms.

Singular	Plural	Singular	Plural
deer	deer	moose	moose
fish	fish	sheep	sheep

4. Some nouns are thought of as being only plural and therefore have no singular form.

Only Plural			
clothes	goods	proceeds	scissors
eyeglasses	pants	savings	tweezers

5. Some nouns are **compound nouns,** or nouns with two or more words. To form the plural of compound nouns, add *-s* or *-es* to the last word of the compound noun.

Singular	Plural	Singular	Plural
graphic art	graphic art**s**	test tube	test tube**s**
human being	human being**s**	water pump	water pump**s**

If the first word in a hyphenated compound noun is a noun, add *-s* to the noun.

Singular	Plural	Singular	Plural
attorney-at-law	attorney**s**-at-law	passer-by	passer**s**-by
brother-in-law	brother**s**-in-law	runner-up	runner**s**-up

6. Some nouns that are borrowed from Latin keep the plural form of the original language.

Singular	Plural	Singular	Plural
alumnus	alumn**i**	medium	medi**a**
datum	dat**a**	phenomenon	phenomen**a**

 *Persons* **versus** *People*

There are two plural forms of *person*. *People* is the common plural form.

> Some **people** love to visit museums. Many **people** like to see the dinosaur exhibit.

Persons is used only in a legal or official context.

> The dinosaur skeleton was stolen by **persons** unknown.

PRACTICE I

Fill in each blank with either the singular or plural form of the noun. If both the singular and the plural forms are the same, put an *X* in the space.

Singular	**Plural**
EXAMPLES:	
lottery	*lotteries*
X	pants
1. child	
2. shelf	
3. _____	phenomena
4. sister-in-law	
5. community	
6. _____	media
7. _____	shorts
8. deer	
9. calf	
10. _____	goggles
11. tooth	
12. _____	scarves
13. _____	sunglasses
14. high school	
15. credit card	
16. _____	strawberries
17. factory	
18. _____	human rights
19. _____	data
20. person	

Section I
SOME PARTS OF SPEECH

PRACTICE 2

Each sentence contains an incorrect plural noun form. Correct the errors.

EXAMPLE:

Anthropologists study human beings and their ~~societys~~. *societies*

Section 1
SOME PARTS OF SPEECH

1. Traditionally, mens have dominated the field of anthropology.

2. However, one famous anthropologist, Margaret Mead, was a women.

3. She wanted to study the everyday lifes of people in other cultures.

4. After she completed her university studys, she went to American Samoa to study adolescent girls.

5. Then she traveled to New Guinea where she studied young childs at play.

6. She also used binocular to observe landscapes.

7. In Mead's notebook, she wrote notes and drew sketch of the people that she observed.

8. She published many books and articles that allowed American persons to understand different cultures.

9. After her death in 1978, the Library of Congress received Mead's enormous research collection and her personal diarys.

⟨ **Hint** ⟩ **Key Words for Singular and Plural Nouns**

• Use a singular noun after words such as *a, an, one, each, every,* and *another.*
   As **a** <u>young girl</u>, Margaret Mead lived in Philadelphia.
   Every <u>paleontologist</u> must examine **each** <u>fossil</u> very carefully.
• Use a plural noun after words such as *two, all, both, many, few, several,* and *some.*
   Many <u>anthropologists</u> have benefited from Mead's research.
   Some <u>journalists</u> interviewed her.

PRACTICE 3

Underline the key words that help to determine whether the noun in each sentence is singular or plural. Then, correct the errors in singular and plural nouns.

EXAMPLE:

Anthropologists have examined <u>several</u> case ~~study~~ of ancient humans.

1. Human history contains many story of famous hoaxes.

2. But historians generally agree that one hoaxes was very interesting.

3. In 1911, in Piltdown, England, some workers digging a hole found several fossil.

4. Many researcher believed that the fossils belonged to one individual and were the missing link between humans and their early ancestors.

5. One famous paleontologist spent five year researching this individual, whom researchers referred to as Piltdown man.

6. In 1925, a paleontologist, Raymond Dart, found a fossils in South Africa.

7. He called it the Taung child and believed that his discovery was another links in human evolution.

8. Few scientist believed him because his discovery did not match the information obtained from Piltdown man.

9. Technology progressed, and each new chemical testing methods proved that the Piltdown fossil was younger than paleontologists had thought.

10. By 1952, two mans named Oakley and Weiner proved that Piltdown man was a fake and was only between 520 and 720 years old.

Section 1
SOME PARTS OF SPEECH

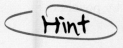 **Plural Nouns Follow "*of the*" Expressions**

Use a plural noun after expressions such as *one of the, all of the, each of the,* and so on.
<u>One of the</u> most famous **anthropologists** in the twentieth century was Louis Leakey.

PRACTICE 4

Correct ten errors with singular and plural nouns.

EXAMPLE:

                                                                    subjects
Anthropology is one of the most interesting ~~subject~~ to study.

1. Anthropology has several subfields. One of the branch is the study of primate behavior. Primates such as chimpanzees and apes exhibit behavior that has many similarity to human behavior. Two of the most famous primatologist are Jane Goodall and Dian Fossey. Both womans did their fieldwork in Africa under the supervision of Louis Leakey. They have made important contributions to the field of primatology.

2. Several scientists regarded Jane Goodall's research methods as unconventional. For example, she gave names to all of the chimpanzee that she studied. Dr. Goodall was also the first primatologist to observe that chimpanzees used some tool.

3. Dian Fossey studied the mountain gorillas in East Africa. She observed several groups of gorilla family. Each groups was led by a dominant male called a silverback. The silverback protects the group from predators and leads the group to food sources.

4. Because of Fossey's research, international interest in the lifes of mountain gorillas has grown. Unfortunately, mountain gorillas are an endangered species because of poaching. Fossey attempted to defeat poachers, but she was viciously murdered in 1985 at her camp. Most person believe that she was murdered by poachers.

Count Nouns and Noncount Nouns

In English, nouns are grouped into two types: count nouns and noncount nouns.

- **Count nouns** refer to people or things that can be counted, such as *car*, *book*, or *boy*. Count nouns have both a singular and a plural form.

    Louisa read **one** <u>book</u> about the life of Margaret Mead.

    Her anthropology professor wrote **five** <u>books</u> about language development.

- **Noncount nouns** refer to things that cannot be counted because they cannot be divided, such as *education* or *paint*. Noncount nouns generally have only the singular form.

Traditional Samoan <u>clothing</u> is different from traditional Western <u>dress</u>.

Archeologists have gathered a lot of <u>information</u> on Samoan culture.

To express a noncount noun as a count noun, you would have to refer to it in terms of *types, varieties,* or *amounts.*

Anthropologists do many different <u>types of research</u>.

The next table shows some common noncount nouns.

Section 1
SOME PARTS OF SPEECH

Common Noncount Nouns

Categories of Objects		Food	Nature	Substances
clothing	machinery	bread	earth	chalk
equipment	mail	fish	electricity	charcoal
furniture	money	honey	fire	hair
homework	music	meat	water	ink
luggage	software	milk	wind	paint

Abstract Nouns

advice	effort	information	progress	violence
attention	evidence	knowledge	proof	
behavior	health	luck	research	

PRACTICE 5

Change each word in italics to the plural form, if necessary. If you cannot use the plural form, write an *X* in the space. Hint: If the word ends in *y*, you may have to change the *y* to *i* when you make the plural form.

EXAMPLE:

There are many *theory* ___ies___ about the origins of human beings.

1. Africa is the home of many archeological *discovery* _____.

2. In 1974, Dr. Donald Johanson and his student, Tom Gray, were searching a *gully* _____ in Ethiopia when they noticed some *bone* _____.

3. They paid careful *attention* _____ to the area when they did their *research* _____.

4. Within two *week* _____, they had found several bone *fossil* _____ belonging to one *individual* _____.

5. They used special *equipment* _____ to date the skeleton.

6. The skeleton, which archaeologists named Lucy, was over 3 million *year* _____ old.

7. Named after the Beatles song "Lucy in the Sky with Diamonds," Lucy provided a lot of *information* _____ about hominids.

8. *Hominid* refers to all human *species* _____ that developed after humans branched out from the apes.

9. The skeleton provided *evidence* _____ that Lucy was an adult female weighing around sixty-five *pound* _____.

10. Currently, researchers use *mold* _____ of her bones for scientific study, while the real Lucy is kept at the National Museum in Addis Ababa, Ethiopia.

Determiners

Determiners are words that identify or determine whether a noun is specific or general.

> **The** chimpanzee named Moe used **a** twig as his tool.

You can use many words from different parts of speech as determiners.

Articles:	a, an, the
Indefinite pronouns:	any, all, both, each, either, every, few, little, many, several
Demonstrative pronouns:	this, that, these, those, such
Numbers:	one, two, three

A, An, The

Some determiners can be confusing because you can use them only in specific circumstances. *A* and *an* are general determiners, and *the* is a specific determiner.

> general   specific
> I want to watch a new film. The films in that collection are fascinating.

■ Use *a* and *an* before singular count nouns but not before plural or noncount nouns.

> singular count noun   noncount noun
> Dr. Johanson drove a **jeep**. He made quick **progress** in his work.

 *A or An*

- Use *a* before words that begin with a consonant (*a* man, *a* house).

  Exception: When *u* sounds like *you*, put *a* before it (*a* uniform, *a* university).

- Use *an* before words that begin with a vowel (*an* exhibit, *an* umbrella.)

  Exception: When *h* is silent, put *an* before it (*an* hour, *an* honest man).

■ Use *the* before nouns that refer to a specific person, place, or thing.

<u>The</u> anthropologist, Dr. Johanson, found <u>the</u> skeleton of Lucy.

> **Avoid Overusing *The***
>
> Do not use *the* before nouns that refer to certain types of things or places.
>
> | | |
> |---|---|
> | **Languages:** | He studies ~~the~~ Swahili. |
> | **Sports:** | We played ~~the~~ football. |
> | **Most cities and countries:** | Lucy was found in ~~the~~ Ethiopia. |
> | Exceptions: | *the* United States, *the* Netherlands |

Section 1
SOME PARTS OF SPEECH

PRACTICE 6

Write either *a*, *an*, or *the* in the space before each noun. If no determiner is necessary, write *X* in the space.

EXAMPLE:

Most people enjoy looking at ___X___ beautiful artwork.

1.   The earliest examples of _____ art are found in _____ caves and on _____ rocks. In 1940, teenagers in Lascaux, France, accidentally discovered _____ important example of cave art. They discovered the entrance to _____ cave and explored it. They saw murals on _____ walls of _____ cave. Since then, many other caves with _____ art have been found in _____ France.

2.   Early humans known as Cro-Magnons lived around 40,000 years ago. They painted scenes of _____ animals and _____ hunters on _____ walls of the caves in Lascaux. The cave painters used _____ minerals to make colors. They were very familiar with _____ anatomy of _____ animals. Therefore, on the cave walls, _____ drawing of _____ antelope is usually detailed, but _____ drawing of _____ human looks like _____ stick figure.

3.   _____ drawing of _____ hand appears on one of _____ cave walls. Perhaps one of _____ artists wanted to leave his or her signature near the paintings.

4.   Nobody knows why _____ caves in Lascaux contain paintings. The paintings may have been used in _____ religious ceremonies. It is _____ mystery.

Many, Few, Much, Little

Use *many* and *few* with count nouns.

> <u>Many</u> **archeologists** have tried to find the origins of human beings, but <u>few</u> **experts** have found complete skeletons.

Use *much* and *little* with noncount nouns.

> Dr. Meghana Kale spent <u>much</u> **time** and very <u>little</u> **money** doing important research.

This, That, These, Those

Both *this* and *these* refer to things that are physically close to the speaker in time or place. Use *this* before singular nouns and *these* before plural nouns.

> <u>These</u> **days,** many articles are written about fossils. <u>This</u> **article** in my bag is about some new discoveries in Siberia.

Use *that* and *those* to refer to things that are physically distant from the speaker in time or place. Use *that* before singular nouns and *those* before plural nouns.

> In the 1970s, anthropologists traveled to Africa. In <u>those</u> **years,** many anthropologists did groundbreaking fieldwork. In <u>that</u> **building,** there is some very old equipment for dating fossils.

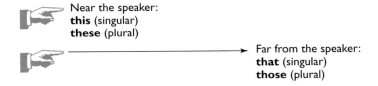

Near the speaker:
this (singular)
these (plural)

Far from the speaker:
that (singular)
those (plural)

PRACTICE 7

Underline the best determiner in each set of parentheses. If no determiner is needed, underline the *X*.

EXAMPLE:
There are not (<u>many</u>, much) gorillas in the wild.

1.   (A, The, X) hundred years ago, there were thousands of mountain gorillas in (the, X) Africa. At (this, that) time, gorilla habitats were isolated. Later, war, environmental destruction, and hunting contributed to (X, the) decline in gorilla populations.

2.   In (a, X, the) 1970s, poachers killed (much, many) gorillas and used gorilla hands as ashtrays. In (these, those) days,

primatologist Dian Fossey worked hard to prevent the slaughter of the gorillas.

3.   Recently, there has been (a, the) resurgence in gorilla poaching. (Much, Many) attention has been focused on the problem. (These, Those) days, there are only about 660 mountain gorillas left in Africa. In (X, the) Rwanda, for example, very (few, little) gorillas remain.

4.   Currently, (much, many) poachers kill adult female gorillas and then sell (a, the) baby gorillas to wealthy collectors. Since (the, X) 1972, no gorillas have been taken from (a, the) wild and brought to zoos in (the, X) North America. However, there are (many, much) disreputable collectors who covet (a, the) rare animals. Recently, (a, the) Nigerian dealer asked for $1.6 million for four baby gorillas. To date, authorities have had (few, little) success in combating (a, the, X) gorilla-poaching problem.

Section I
SOME PARTS OF SPEECH

PRACTICE 8

Correct ten errors with singular nouns, plural nouns, and determiners.

EXAMPLE:

One of the most exciting ~~find~~ *finds* of Stone Age Europeans is Oetzi.

1.   In 1991, hikers discovered an body in the Alps. At first, the hikers thought that it was the body of someone who had had a accident in the mountains. Using special equipments, scientists examined the body and realized that it was a 5,300-year-old mummy. The man, whom archeologists named Oetzi, was found in a valley between the Austria and Italy. The hikers who found Oetzi think that they received too few money as a reward.

2.   Although many ancient mummy are found in Egypt and Peru, Oetzi is the oldest mummy in the world. He is now displayed in a museum in Bolzano, Italy. Oetzi is surrounded by blocks of ices to preserve his body. The scientists have made

several discovery about him. They know that he died from a wound by a arrow. Oetzi was also carrying much tools, including a copper axe, a bow, and several arrows.

Section 1
**SOME PARTS
OF SPEECH**

Prepositions

Prepositions are words that show concepts such as time, place, direction, and manner. They show connections or relationships between ideas. Some common prepositions are *about, around, at, before, behind, beside, between, for, in, of, on, to, toward,* and *with.*

Anthropologists go **to** many different areas **for** their work.

In the spring, my brother will travel **to** Papua, New Guinea.

He will go **with** a group **of** other anthropologists.

Prepositions of Time and Place

Generally, as a description of a place or time becomes more precise, you move from *in* to *on* to *at.*

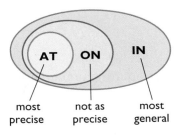

Preposition	Prepositions of Time	Prepositions of Place
in	in a year (in 2006) in a month (in February) in the morning, afternoon, evening in the spring, summer, fall, winter	in a city, country, etc. (in Houston, in Japan, in Africa)
on	on a day of the week (on Tuesday) on a specific date (on January 25) on a specific holiday (on Memorial Day) (on my birthday) on time ("punctual")	on a specific street (on Main Street) on a planet (on Mars) on certain technological devices (on TV, on the radio, on the phone, on the computer) on top
at	at a specific time of day (at 1:30) at night at breakfast, lunch, dinner	at a specific address (at 32 Cardinal Crescent) at a specific building (at the hotel)
from ... to	from one time to another (from 10 AM to 6 PM)	from one place to another (from New York to Boston)
for	for a period of time (for two hours)	for a distance (for five miles)

To versus At

- Use *to* after verbs that indicate movement from one place to another.

  go to   walk to   run to   move to   return to

  Exception: Do not put *to* directly before *home*.

  I'll go ~~to~~ home with you. I won't go to his home.

- Use *at* after verbs that indicate being in one place (and not moving from one place to another).

  wait at   stay at   sit at   look at   work at

Section 1
**SOME PARTS
OF SPEECH**

PRACTICE 9

Underline the correct prepositions in parentheses. If no preposition is needed, underline the *X*.

EXAMPLE:

(In, On, At) Kenya, Louis Leakey learned to speak Kikuyu.

1. The famous anthropologist Louis Leakey was born (at, in) British East Africa, which is now called Kenya, (in, on) 1903.

2. He traveled (at, to) England, where he studied anthropology (at, on) Cambridge University, but he longed to go (X, at) home.

3. He returned (in, to) Africa because he believed that it was the birthplace of early humans.

4. He searched for fossils (in, on) the Olduvai Gorge (in, on) Kenya (in, for) twenty years without finding anything.

5. Eventually Leakey and his wife Mary discovered fossils (at, in) the site.

6. One day (in, on) 1959, Mary went for a walk (in, at) 6:00 (in, on) the morning and found a skull that was 1.8 million years old.

7. The couple became famous and gave interviews that were broadcast (for, in, on) the radio.

8. (From, In) approximately 1949 (in, to) 1952, Leakey also spied for the British government.

9. Leakey died of a heart attack and was buried (in, on) October 4, 1972, (at, in) Kenya.

Section 1
SOME PARTS OF SPEECH

Hint **For versus During**

Sometimes people confuse the prepositions *for* and *during* because both indicate that an activity happened over a period of time. However, these words are not interchangeable. Use *during* to explain when something happened. Use *for* to explain how long it took to happen.

The tourist shop closed **for** <u>two hours</u> **during** <u>the blackout</u>.

The environmentalists protested **for** <u>six hours</u> **during** <u>the economic summit</u>.

PRACTICE 10

Correct six errors with prepositions.

EXAMPLE:

My sister and I went scuba diving ~~during~~ ^{for} three hours.

Many people travel at exotic destinations for their holidays. Last year, my family and I flew on a small island in the Caribbean during a week. We were there on November. Each morning we went to the beach. We did some snorkeling during two hours. We tried not to disturb the fish. After snorkeling, we returned at our hotel.

Common Prepositional Expressions

Many common expressions contain prepositions. A preposition can follow an adjective or a verb. These types of expressions usually express a particular meaning.

Example: This morning, I <u>listened **to**</u> the radio.

The next list contains some of the most common prepositional expressions.

accuse (somebody) of	ask for	confronted with
acquainted with	associate with	consist of
add to	aware of	count on
afraid of	believe in	deal with
agree with	belong to	decide on
angry about	capable of	decide to
angry with	care about	depend on
apologize for	care for	disappointed about
apply for	commit to	disappointed with
approve of	comply with	dream of
argue with	concerned about	escape from

excited about
familiar with
feel like
fond of
forget about
forgive (someone) for
friendly with
good for
grateful for
happy about
hear about
hope for
hopeful about
innocent of
insist on
insulted by
interested in
introduce to
jealous of
keep from

located in
long for
look forward to
opposed to
participate in
patient with
pay attention to
pay for
pray for
prepared for
prevent (someone) from
protect (someone) from
proud of
provide (someone) with
qualify for
realistic about
refer to
related to
rely on
  rescue from

responsible for
sad about
satisfied with
scared of
search for
similar to
specialize in
stop (something) from
succeed in
take advantage of
take care of
thank (someone) for
think about
think of
tired of
upset about
upset with
willing to
wish for
worry about

Section 1
**SOME PARTS
OF SPEECH**

PRACTICE 11

Write the correct prepositions in the following sentences. Use the preceding list
of common prepositional expressions to help you.

EXAMPLE:

Paolo belonged _____to_____ a travel club.

1.   More and more people are interested _____ adventure

   travel. They want to participate _____ kayaking, mountain

   climbing, and other dangerous activities. For example, shark

   diving is popular in Australia, in the Bahamas, and off the coast

   of California. The divers are not afraid _____ sharks. They

   look forward _____ viewing marine life.

2.   Why do people like adventure tourism? Some people long

   _____ an adrenaline rush. Others want to associate

   _____ wildlife. Often, tourists are bored, and they dream

   _____ an escape _____ their routine lives. They

   get excited _____ swimming with dolphins or scaling a

   mountain peak because they want to challenge themselves.

3.   In Rwanda and Uganda, some agencies specialize _____

   gorilla trekking. The trek consists _____ a six-hour hike

to heights in excess of 7,500 feet. Tourists are not prevented

_____ getting close to the wild beasts. They must be willing

_____ spend over $3,000 for a one-week adventure. Cash-

strapped countries in Central Africa depend _____ the

foreign dollars that gorilla trekking provides.

4.   Some adventure tourists are concerned _____ the

impact of their actions on the environment. However, others are

not aware _____ the fragile ecosystems that they may

disrupt. For example, tourists are not supposed to disturb coral

reefs, but sometimes they do not pay attention _____ the

rules of conservation. Perhaps adventure tourists should consider

the impact of tourism on local cultures.

FINAL REVIEW

A. Correct thirteen errors in singular and plural nouns and determiners.

                                                 evidence

Example: Paleontologists have discovered a lot of ~~evidences~~ regarding the
origin of early humans.

1.   Many scientists believe that early humans lived in the Africa

in a period of times that is known as the Stone Age. According

to evidences, early humans learned how to make stone tool and

weapons such as axes and knifes, and they used this tools to hunt

for food. However, as agricultural method improved, hunting

also developed as a sports.

2.   Some persons think that hunting is barbaric. They believe

that it is cruel and endangers animals such as the elephants and

tigers. They argue that, in fact, there are so little tigers

remaining in the world that we must protect them. Much hunters,

on the other hand, state that responsible hunting is necessary and

humane. Some animals such as wolfs are hunted if their numbers

increase. People on both sides of the hunting debate have strong

opinions.

B. Correct six preposition errors.

Example: $\overset{In}{\cancel{At}}$ 2003, adventure tourism became popular.

Section 1
**SOME PARTS
OF SPEECH**

1.　　Many people travel at exotic destinations. Tourism can be both beneficial and harmful. By creating jobs, tourism helps the local economy. However, it may also have a negative impact at the culture. Often local families must migrate in order to work on a tourist resort, so they must leave their homes during many months. Furthermore, it is necessary to speak the language of the tourist in order to take advantage at the tourism industry. Therefore, indigenous people who depend of tourism may lose their languages, and they may reject traditional food, clothing, and values.

The Writer's Room

Write a paragraph about one of the following topics. After you finish writing, circle any plural nouns and underline any determiners.

1. Describe an interesting vacation you have taken. Where did you go? What did you do?

2. What are some reasons people take vacations? What are the effects of taking a vacation? Write about the causes or effects of taking time off work and school.

3. Should people hunt for sport? What is your opinion?

CHECKLIST: NOUNS, DETERMINERS, AND PREPOSITIONS

When you edit your writing, ask yourself the next set of questions.

　Do I use the correct singular or plural form of nouns? Check for errors with the following:

　–spelling of regular plurals

　–count and noncount nouns

　–spelling of irregular plurals

According to $\overset{research}{\cancel{researches}}$, most $\overset{families}{\cancel{familys}}$ have two $\overset{children}{\cancel{childrens}}$.

(continued)

☐ Do I use the correct determiners? Check for errors with the following:

—*a, an, the*

—*much, many, few, little*

—*this, that, these, those*

<u>These</u> much the
~~This~~ days, there is not ~~many~~ information about ~~a~~ impact of tourism on cultures.

☐ Do I use the correct prepositions? Check for errors with the following:

—*in, on, at, to*

—*for, during*

—prepositional expressions

For on
~~During~~ two months each summer, the town depends ~~of~~ tourists
at
who stay ~~to~~ the hotel.

 See Chapter 6 on the Visualizing Writing CD-ROM for an additional audio and animated mini-lecture on **Parts of Speech** and **Phrases and Clauses**.

Section Theme: **SOCIAL SCIENCES**

CONTENTS

- Pronoun-Antecedent Agreement
- Indefinite Pronouns
- Vague Pronouns
- Pronoun Shifts
- Pronoun Case
- Problems with Possessive Pronouns
- Relative Pronouns
- Reflexive Pronouns

In this chapter, you will read about social issues related to families, education, and aging.

Grammar Snapshot

Looking at Pronouns

Dorothy Nixon is a freelance writer who writes about families. In this excerpt, Nixon writes about families in the past. The pronouns are underlined.

> <u>I</u> know <u>I</u> have no right to complain. Medieval moms (<u>I</u> read somewhere) had seven kids on average. The mothers and children worked <u>their</u> farms while hubby was away fighting important battles. Mothers worried about wild beasts carrying off <u>their</u> young ones; <u>they</u> fretted over <u>their</u> babies falling into the hearth. And for all this angst and back-breaking labor, <u>they</u> lost <u>their</u> teeth.

In this chapter, you will identify and write pronouns.

127

Pronoun-Antecedent Agreement

Pronouns are words that replace nouns (people, places, or things), other pronouns, and phrases.

Max Weber was a famous sociologist. ~~Max Weber~~ wrote many books.

A pronoun must agree with its **antecedent,** which is the word to which the pronoun refers. Pronouns must agree in person and number with their antecedents.

> The <u>sociologist</u> was frustrated because **she** did not receive enough recognition for **her** work.
>
> (*Sociologist* is the antecedent of *she* and *her.*)
>
> My <u>son</u> went to work at a college in Taiwan. **He** took **his** family with **him.**
>
> (*Son* is the antecedent of *he, his,* and *him.*)
>
> In Chinese culture, the <u>elderly</u> receive great respect. **They** often live with their sons.
>
> (*Elderly* is the antecedent of *they.*)

Hint   **Compound Antecedents**

Compound antecedents consist of two or more nouns joined by *and* or *or.* When the nouns are joined by *and,* you must use a plural pronoun to refer to them.

> <u>Susan Brown and Alan Booth</u> published **their** book in 1997.

When the nouns are joined by *or,* you may need a singular or plural pronoun. If both nouns are singular, then use a singular pronoun. If both nouns are plural, use a plural pronoun.

> Does <u>California or Florida</u> have **its** own child welfare agency?
>
> Have more <u>men or women</u> completed **their** degrees in sociology?

PRACTICE 1

The pronouns in the following sentences are in bold print. Underline each antecedent.

EXAMPLE:

The first sociology <u>course</u> in the United States started in 1890, and **it** was given at the University of Kansas.

1. Sociology is a science, and **it** is studied in colleges across the nation.

2. Sociologists struggle to understand why people do the things that **they** do.

3. Auguste Comte studied societies, and **he** coined the term *sociology* in 1838.

4. In the United States, the first sociology department was founded at the University of Chicago in 1892, and **it** became a very prestigious department.

5. At that time, many immigrants came to Chicago, and **it** grew rapidly.

6. Chicago sociologists spent **their** time studying social issues such as poverty, crime, and immigration.

7. The professional association for sociologists was originally called the American Sociology Society, but **its** name was changed because the abbreviation was embarrassing.

8. The name changed to the American Sociological Association, and today, the members are proud of **their** professional organization.

Section 1
SOME PARTS OF SPEECH

PRACTICE 2

Underline the antecedents, and write the appropriate pronoun in each blank.

EXAMPLE:

<u>Robert Moses</u>, a teacher at the Horace Mann School, wanted ____*his*____ students to go to college.

1. In 1982, Robert Moses realized that some students were not being offered many advanced courses because _____ were from poor school districts.

2. If the students could study courses such as algebra, then _____ would have the opportunity to qualify for college.

3. Moses realized that there was a problem, and he decided to do something about _____.

4. Moses started the Algebra Project, and _____ began to teach algebra to groups of middle-school children.

5. The children studied in after-school classes, and _____ seemed eager to learn.

6. If the children could learn algebra, then _____ could go to college.

7. Moses decided that _____ needed help, so he recruited African American college graduates to help teach the students.

8. Before long, parents were pleased because _____ could see their children's progress.

9. Educators, parents, and students praise the Algebra Project because _____ realize that it has changed the lives of many children.

10. Today, the Algebra Project is a great success, and _____ has grown to include more than one hundred schools.

Indefinite Pronouns

Most pronouns refer to a specific person, place, or thing. You can use **indefinite pronouns** when you talk about people or things whose identity is not known or is unimportant. The following table shows some common singular and plural indefinite pronouns.

Indefinite Pronouns				
Singular:	another	each	nobody	other
	anybody	everybody	no one	somebody
	anyone	everyone	nothing	someone
	anything	everything	one	something
Plural:	both, few, many, others, several			
Either singular or plural:	all, any, some, half (and other fractions), more, most, none			

Singular Pronouns

When you use a singular indefinite antecedent, also use a singular pronoun to refer to it.

> Everybody wonders what will happen when **he or she** becomes elderly.

> No one, in **his or her** lifetime, wants to be a burden on others.

Plural Pronouns

When you use a plural indefinite antecedent, also use a plural pronoun to refer to it.

> Our town has many social problems, and several of **them** are difficult to conquer.

> Although most elderly people would like to live independently, many must leave **their** homes.

Pronouns That Can Be Singular or Plural

Some indefinite pronouns can be either singular or plural, depending on the noun to which they refer.

Many sociologists came to the conference. <u>All</u> were experts in **their** fields.

(*All* refers to sociologists; therefore, the pronoun is plural.)

We read <u>all</u> of the report and agreed with **its** recommendations.

(*All* refers to the report; therefore, the pronoun is singular.)

Section 1
SOME PARTS OF SPEECH

Hint   Using *"of the"* Expressions

The subject of a sentence appears before the words *of the*. For example, in sentences containing the expression *one of the* or *each of the,* the subject is the indefinite pronoun *one* or *each.* You must use a singular pronoun to refer to the subject.

<u>One</u> of the books is missing **its** cover.

If the subject could be either male or female, then use *his or her* to refer to it.

<u>Each</u> of the students has **his or her** own copy of the book.

PRACTICE 3

Underline the correct pronouns.

EXAMPLE:

Some say (his or her, <u>their</u>) pensions will not be adequate for retirement.

1.   Some cultures have high regard for (its, their) elderly members. In India and China, for instance, the elderly have a lot of status. Every family member has (his or her, their) role regarding elderly parents. For example, each son must take care of (his, their) aging mother or father. Everyone in the family must show respect for (his or her, their) elderly relatives. In India, younger members of the family show (his or her, their) respect by touching the feet of older people. Every child is expected to speak politely to (his or her, their) grandparents.

2.   In some countries, such as England, the United States, and Germany, a modern problem called *ageism* is growing. Ageism is discrimination and prejudice on the basis of age. Each country has (its, their) own way of dealing with an aging population. In some places, there is a mandatory retirement age, so every person over sixty-five must leave (his or her, their) job. Furthermore, many countries have aging populations that make

demands on the social network. Some who contribute to social security may see (his or her, their) pension funds shrink. Every nation must deal with the problem in (its, their) own way.

Vague Pronouns

Avoid using pronouns that could refer to more than one antecedent.

Vague:	Manolo introduced me to his friend and <u>his</u> sister.
	(Whose sister is it: Manolo's or his friend's?)
Clearer:	**Manolo** introduced me to **his** friend and his friend's sister.

Avoid using confusing pronouns like *it* and *they* that have no clear antecedent.

Vague:	<u>They</u> say that seniors should receive more tax breaks.
	(Who are *they*?)
Clearer:	**Critics of government policy** say that seniors should receive more tax breaks.
Vague:	<u>It</u> stated in the newspaper that many seniors live in poverty.
	(Who or what is *it*?)
Clearer:	**The newspaper article** stated that many seniors live in poverty.

Use *this, that,* and *which* only to refer to a specific antecedent.

Vague:	The nursing home's fees were raised. <u>This</u> caused many residents to panic.
	(What is *this*?)
Clearer:	The nursing home's fees were raised. **This information** caused many residents to panic.

 **Avoid Repeating the Subject**

When you clearly mention a subject, do not repeat the subject in pronoun form.

Dr. MacKenzie, ~~he~~ is more than eighty years old.

His course on contemporary culture, ~~it~~ is really interesting.

PRACTICE 4

Correct any vague pronoun or repeated subject errors.

EXAMPLE:

Many senior citizens, ~~they~~ are productive members of society.

1. They say that senior citizens should retire because young people need jobs.

2. I do not agree with this.

3. It stated in my book that many older people have accomplished great things.

4. For example, Ronald Reagan he was elected president of the United States when he was almost seventy years old.

5. It also says that Eleanor Roosevelt became a member of the U.S. delegation to the United Nations when she was sixty-one.

6. Roosevelt she helped draft the Universal Declaration of Human Rights.

7. This was an achievement.

8. Many older people they continue working into their seventies and eighties.

Pronoun Shifts
Making Pronouns Consistent in Person

Person is the writer's perspective. In some writing assignments, you may use the first person (*I, we*). For other assignments, you may use the second person (*you*) or the third person (*he, she, it, they*). Make sure that your pronouns are consistent in person. Therefore, if you begin writing from one point of view, do not shift unnecessarily to another point of view.

              we
If we had studied, ~~one~~ would have passed the exam.

                    we
We visited every library, but ~~you~~ could not find the book.

Making Pronouns Consistent in Number

Pronouns and antecedents must agree in **number.** If the antecedent is singular, then the pronoun must be singular. If the antecedent is plural, then the pronoun must be plural.

                   his or her
Each social worker encouraged ~~their~~ clients to talk openly.

                 he or she
When a parent needs advice, ~~they~~ should talk to a professional.

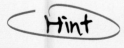 **Avoiding Pronoun Shifts in Paragraphs**

Sometimes it is easier to use pronouns consistently in individual sentences than in larger paragraphs or essays. When you write paragraphs and essays, always check that the pronouns agree with the antecedents in person.

    In the next example, the pronouns are consistent in the first two sentences. However, they shift in person in the third sentence.

    I visited two sociology departments. **I** talked to many sociology students about

                                                  I

    different courses. But there were so many courses that **you** could not decide

    which ones to take.

PRACTICE 5

Correct the sentences that have pronoun shift errors. Write *C* beside any sentences that are already correct.

EXAMPLE:

We
~~One~~ learned many interesting things about the late actor and comedian George Burns when we studied him in class.

Section 1
SOME PARTS OF SPEECH

1. _____ After we read a biography about George Burns, you were amazed at all the things he had accomplished in his later years.

2. _____ As I read his biography, you could see that Burns's career blossomed as he got older.

3. _____ He was rediscovered by his fans when he was in his eighties.

4. _____ In fact, he received an Academy Award for best supporting actor when he was eighty years old.

5. _____ My friends and I went to see his movie *The Sunshine Boys* but decided to go another time because you had to wait in a long line to get tickets.

6. _____ Burns wrote several books when he was in his nineties.

7. _____ I managed to watch his one hundredth birthday special on television, and one could see that he was very happy and healthy.

8. _____ When you get older, one always thinks that you will not be able to work, but as George Burns demonstrated, that is not always true.

Pronoun Case

Pronouns are formed according to the role they play in a sentence. A pronoun can be the subject or object of the sentence, or it can show possession. This chart shows the three main pronoun cases: subjective, objective, and possessive.

Pronoun Case

Singular	Subjective	Objective	Possessive Possessive Adjective	Possessive Pronoun
First person:	I	me	my	mine
Second person:	you	you	your	yours
Third person:	he, she, it, who, whoever	him, her, it whom, whomever	his, her, its, whose	his, hers
Plural				
First person:	we	us	our	ours
Second person:	you	you	your	yours
Third person:	they	them	their	theirs

Section 1
SOME PARTS OF SPEECH

Subjective Case

A **subject** performs an action in a sentence. When a pronoun is the subject of the sentence, use the subjective form of the pronoun. In the following sentences, *she* and *we* are the subjects.

> **She** was a social worker for about twenty-five years.

> **We** listened to a lecture on television addiction yesterday.

Objective Case

An **object** receives an action in a sentence. When a pronoun is the object in the sentence, use the objective form of the pronoun. In the following sentences, *him* and *us* are objects.

> My sociology class sent **him** an invitation to speak at the ceremony.

> My sister told **us** about her sociology exam.

Possessive Case

A possessive pronoun shows ownership.

- **Possessive adjectives** are always placed before the noun that they modify. In the next sentences, *his* and *her* are possessive adjectives.

  > He finished **his** <u>book report</u> about the life of Max Weber, but she did not finish **her** <u>book report</u>.

- **Possessive pronouns** replace the possessive adjective and noun. In the next sentence, *her* is a possessive adjective and *theirs* is a possessive pronoun.

  > She finished **her** <u>essay</u> about sociologist Max Weber, but they did not finish **theirs.**

Section I
SOME PARTS OF SPEECH

PRACTICE 6

Underline the pronouns in each sentence. Then identify the case of each pronoun. Write *S* for subjective case, *O* for objective case, and *P* for possessive case.

EXAMPLE:

<u>S</u>   P
<u>I</u> read the writings of Max Weber. <u>His</u> theories were ingenious.

1. Max Weber was born in Germany in 1864, and he is considered one of the founders of modern sociology.

2. His parents had seven children, and he was their eldest son.

3. He studied law, and then he did graduate work in Italy and Spain.

4. He held many academic positions, and his students respected him.

5. His important works showed how capitalism functioned.

6. We get the term *Protestant work ethic*, or the desire for hard work in order to acquire wealth, from him.

7. Initially, many of his colleagues thought that his ideas were too controversial and laughed at them.

8. However, his scholarly works remain influential today, and many people admire him.

Problems with Possessive Pronouns

When using the possessive pronouns *hers* and *theirs*, be careful that you do not add an apostrophe before the *-s*.

                                  hers   theirs
The sociology book is ~~her's~~. The magazine is ~~their's~~.

GRAMMAR LINK

See Chapter 26 for more detailed information about apostrophes.

Some possessive adjectives sound like certain contractions. Review these examples of commonly confused words.

Possessive adjective:	<u>Their</u> field trip was canceled.
Contraction:	<u>They're</u> going to go next week. (*They're = they are.*)
Possessive adjective:	<u>Your</u> guidance counselor will help you choose the right courses.
Contraction:	<u>You're</u> going to enjoy the course on the history of education. (*You're = you are.*)

Possessive adjective: <u>Its</u> theme is about the influence of technology on everyday life.

Contraction: <u>It's</u> a book that you should read. (*It's = it is.*)

 *His or Her?*

To choose the correct possessive adjective, think about the possessor, *not* the object that is possessed.

• If something belongs to or is a relative of a female, use *her* + noun.

Allison and **her** father both worked at a college.

• If something belongs to or is a relative of a male, use *his* + noun.

Max Weber wanted **his** colleagues to be supportive.

PRACTICE 7

Underline the correct pronoun or possessive adjective in each set of parentheses.

EXAMPLE:

The family and (it's, <u>its</u>) definition is changing.

1.   Many sociologists and (they're, their, theirs) students are doing research on the role of the family in society. In America, the traditional family is usually referred to as a nuclear family. (It's, Its) members include the parents and (their, theirs) children. In Western culture, the family usually has a blood or legal tie for (it's, its) members. Other societies value the extended family, which includes several generations such as grandparents, parents, and children. (They, Them) all live together.

2.   In a traditional Indian family, the parents and (they're, their, theirs) sons' families live in the same house. After a daughter is married, she lives with (her, his, their) in-laws.

3.   I come from an extended Indian family. My brother and I grew up in the same house as (my, mine) cousins. They shared their problems with (us, ours), and we shared (our, ours) with (theirs, them). What kind of family do (you, your) have? Is (your, you're) family large or small?

Pronouns in Comparisons with *Than* or *As*

Avoid making errors in pronoun case when the pronoun follows *than* or *as*. If the pronoun is a subject, use the subjective case. If the pronoun is an object, use the objective case.

If you use the incorrect case, your sentence may have a meaning that you do not intend it to have. Look at the differences in the meanings of the next sentences.

Objective case:	I like sociology as much as **him.**
	(I like sociology *as much as I like him.*)
Subjective case:	I like sociology as much as **he.**
	(I like sociology *as much as he likes sociology.*)

> ### Hint   Complete the Thought
>
> If you are unsure which pronoun case to use, test by completing the thought.
>
> He likes to work with the elderly more than **I** [like to work with the elderly].
>
> He likes to work with the elderly more than [he likes to work with] **me.**

Pronouns in Prepositional Phrases

A **prepositional phrase** is made up of a preposition and its object. Therefore, always use the objective case of the pronoun after a preposition.

<u>To</u> **him,** Max Weber was a man with great ideas.

<u>Between</u> **you** and **me,** our sociology professor is very eccentric.

Pronouns with *And* or *Or*

Use the correct case when nouns and pronouns are joined by *and* or *or.* If the pronouns are the subject, use the subjective case. If the pronouns are the object, use the objective case.

~~Him and me~~ had to do a presentation on modern American culture.

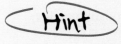
The instructor asked ~~he and I~~ to present first.

> ### Hint   Finding the Correct Case
>
> An easy way to determine that your case is correct is to say the sentence with just one pronoun.
>
> The teacher asked her and (**I, me**) to do the presentation.
>
> **Possible choices:** The teacher asked **I** . . . *or* The teacher asked **me** . . .
>
> **Correct answer:** The teacher asked her and **me** to do the presentation.

PRACTICE 8

Correct any errors with pronoun case. Write *C* in the space if the sentence is already correct.

EXAMPLE:

Donor anonymity is an ethical issue that interests my friend and ~~I~~.   _____me_____

1. Angela and me attend the same college.   _____

2. She is more outgoing than me; she knows everyone.   _____

3. Last week, she introduced her friend, Paul, to me.   _____

4. While chatting, Paul told Angela and I that he was looking for his biological father.   _____

5. He explained that his mother conceived him through artificial insemination.   _____

6. Angela and me were surprised by this information.   _____

7. Between you and I, Paul might have problems obtaining the identity of his father.   _____

8. Some countries allow donor-born children to access information about theirs biological fathers.   _____

9. Perhaps sperm donors will no longer donate if their anonymity is taken away.   _____

10. Tomorrow, him and his friend Rohan are going to the fertility clinic to get more information.   _____

PRACTICE 9

Correct eight pronoun errors in the next paragraphs.

EXAMPLE:

My friend and ~~me~~ $\overset{\text{I}}{}$ discussed an ethical issue related to families.

1.   Currently, many governments are considering the rights of a

certain group of people. Should children born of sperm or egg

donation have the right to know who they're biological parents

are? In the past, it was illegal to give them any information.

However, an adopted child has a right to know who his or hers

biological parents are, so shouldn't a child conceived through donation have the right to know who his or her's are?

2. The CBS program *60 Minutes* did a segment about sperm donors. Dr. Joseph Feldschuh, owner of a sperm donation clinic, said that secrecy benefits sperm donors. However, others feel that all children should have access to there birth records.

3. Documentary filmmaker Barry Stevens and his sister are the children of a sperm donor. His parents did not tell he or his sister that they were donor children. Stevens says that the lies hurt the relationship between he and his parents. Today, him and his sister want information about their biological father. However, his sister does not feel as strongly about the issue as him. Stevens has made a documentary about his search.

Relative Pronouns

Relative pronouns can join two short sentences. Here is a list of relative pronouns.

who	whom	which	that	whose
whoever	whomever			

- *Who* (or *whoever*) and *whom* (or *whomever*) always refer to people. *Who* is the subject of the clause, and *whom* is the object of the clause.

    The <u>sociologist</u> **who** specializes in adoption is speaking today.
    The <u>sociologist</u> **whom** you met is my sister.
- *Which* always refers to things. *Which* clauses are set off with commas.

    Modern <u>sociology</u>, **which** has many subfields, was founded in the nineteenth century.
- *That* refers to things.

    Sociologist Robert Merton wrote the <u>book</u> **that** first included the term "self-fulfilling prophecy."
- *Whose* always shows that something belongs to or is connected with someone or something. It usually replaces the possessive pronoun *his*, *her*, or *their*. Do not confuse *whose* with *who's*, which means "who is."

GRAMMAR LINK

Clauses with *which* are set off with commas. For more information, see Chapter 25, "Commas."

The social worker was waiting for his clients when his car got towed.

The social worker, **whose** car got towed, was waiting for his clients.

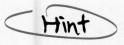

Hint ▷ *Who or Whom?*

If you are unsure whether to use *who* or *whom*, test yourself in the following way. Replace *who* or *whom* with another pronoun. If the replacement is a subject such as *he* or *she*, use *who*. If the replacement is an object such as *her* or *him*, use *whom*.

I know a math teacher **who** tutors after school.
(He tutors after school.)

The man to **whom** you gave your assignment is a teaching assistant.
(You gave your assignment to him.)

Section 1
SOME PARTS OF SPEECH

PRACTICE 10

Underline the correct relative pronoun in each set of parentheses.

EXAMPLE:

Many children (<u>who</u>, which) are of school age do not go to a regular school.

1. Home schooling is an idea (who, that) has always been around.

2. In fact, the home schooling movement, (who, which) has grown in recent years, has generated a lot of controversy.

3. Some parents (who, whom) believe that public schools are flawed have chosen to homeschool their children.

4. For example, Mike and Donna Wakefield, (who, which) live in Oregon, have homeschooled their children for several years.

5. The Wakefields, for (who, whom) moral education is important, want their children to learn certain values.

6. In addition, school violence, (who, which) has escalated in recent years, has caused many parents to withdraw their children from public schools.

7. The National Education Association, (who, which) is America's largest schoolteachers' union, is against home schooling.

8. Some teachers (who, which) have studied the issue believe that home schooling does not provide a complete educational experience.

9. According to the association, children (who, whose) parents homeschool them are not exposed to everyday social interactions.

10. Americans, (who, whose) ideas on mass schooling developed around the time of the Civil War, will continue to debate the issue of home schooling.

Section 1
**SOME PARTS
OF SPEECH**

PRACTICE 11

In each sentence, write the correct relative pronoun from the list below. Remember that you cannot use *which* unless the clause is set off with commas.

who   whom   whose   which   that

EXAMPLE:

Americans _____*who*_____ strongly support public education must deal with the problem of school segregation.

1. Several social scientists _____ research shows important findings advocate desegregating schools. For example, some studies have shown that children _____ are from a lower-income bracket perform better in economically and racially integrated schools. In the 1970s and 1980s, lawmakers for _____ these findings were important ruled to desegregate schools through busing.

2. Busing of poor students to schools in wealthy districts, _____ created great controversy in the past, continues to be hotly debated. Some people _____ views support busing state that minority students have shown improvement in their schoolwork. Opponents of busing think that it overlooks other problems _____ contribute to poor school performance, such as poverty and racism. Parents for _____ busing is a problem have other options, such as school choice programs. Segregation is a problem _____ still needs a creative solution.

Reflexive Pronouns (*-self, -selves*)

Use **reflexive pronouns** when you want to emphasize that the subject does an action to himself or herself.

<u>We</u> ask **ourselves** many questions.

The <u>book</u> sells **itself** because it is so good.

Do not use reflexive pronouns for activities that people do to themselves, such as washing or shaving. However, you can use reflexive pronouns to draw attention to a surprising or an unusual action.

My three-year-old **sister** dressed **herself.**

(The girl probably could not dress herself at a previous time.)

The next chart shows subjective pronouns and the reflexive pronouns that relate to them.

Section 1
SOME PARTS OF SPEECH

Pronouns that end with *-self* or *-selves*

Singular	Antecedent	Reflexive Pronouns
First person:	I	myself
Second person:	you	yourself
Third person:	he, she, it	himself, herself, itself
Plural		
First person:	we	ourselves
Second person:	you	yourselves
Third person:	they	themselves

 **Common Errors with Reflexive Pronouns**

Do not use *hisself* or *theirselves*. These are incorrect ways to say *himself* or *themselves*.

themselves
The students went by ~~theirselves~~ to the lecture.

himself
Max Weber worked by ~~hisself~~.

PRACTICE 12

Fill in the blanks with the correct reflexive pronouns.

EXAMPLE:

He wanted to read by ___himself___ .

1. My classmates and I were talking among _____ about our first

   teaching assignment.

2. I had to teach by _____ for the first time.

Section 1
**SOME PARTS
OF SPEECH**

3. My teaching partner could not be present because she had hurt

   _____.

4. Most of the students began studying by _____.

5. However, one student, Alex, was excited about having a new teacher and
   would not work by _____.

6. Eventually, I was able to get Alex to settle down, and he did some math
   problems by _____.

7. At the end of the school day, I said to the students, "You should
   congratulate _____ on a job well done."

8. Tired after a long day, I treated _____ to a relaxing massage.

FINAL REVIEW

Read the following paragraphs and correct any pronoun inconsistencies. There
are fifteen errors.

EXAMPLE:

                                       her
Grandma Moses was known for ~~hers~~ paintings of rural scenes.

1.   An art lover would gasp in delight when they heard that

      Grandma Moses started to paint at the age of seventy. She was

      born on a farm in 1860, and in 1887, she married Thomas Moses.

      They lived in upstate New York for the rest of theirs lives.

2.   They say that Grandma Moses used to enjoy embroidering

      and started to paint because she got arthritis. Each of her friends

      had their own way of encouraging Moses to paint. One of them

      suggested that Grandma Moses display his work at the local

      pharmacy. Because of this, Grandma Moses received recognition.

      Her friends congratulated theirselves when an art dealer noticed

      her work.

3.   In 1939, Otto Kallir he exhibited her paintings in New York

      City. Grandma Moses went to the art gallery, and her and her

      friends enjoyed the exhibit. Moses, which was almost eighty

years old, received a lot of public attention. Until her death at
101 years of age, Grandma Moses continued to paint and to
receive recognition for her work.

4.   My friend and me went to see an exhibit of Grandma Moses's
work. We had to wait to see each painting, and you could not
believe how crowded it was. My friend liked the paintings better
than me. I liked some of them. We both bought posters of
paintings by Grandma Moses. My friend really liked his poster,
but I liked my better. Probably, each member of the public has
their own preferences.

The Writer's Room

Write a paragraph about one of the following topics. After you finish writing,
circle the pronouns and underline their antecedents.

1. How are the elderly treated in society? Explain your views.
2. What is your opinion of home schooling? Can children receive a
   complete education at home?

✓ CHECKLIST: PRONOUNS

When you edit your writing, ask yourself the next set of
questions.

Do I use the correct pronoun case? Check for errors with the
following:

–subjective, objective, and possessive case

–comparisons with *than* or *as*

–prepositional phrases

–pronouns after *and* or *or*

Between you and ~~I~~ me, my parents were stricter with my brother
than ~~I~~ me.

Do I use the correct relative pronouns? Check for errors with *who,*
whom, or *whose.*

My husband, ~~who~~ whom you have met, is a sociologist.

(continued)

Section 1
**SOME PARTS
OF SPEECH**

Do my pronouns and antecedents agree in number and person? Check for errors with indefinite pronouns and collective nouns.

                                   its
The government announced ~~their~~ new policy: everyone will have
his or her
~~their~~ own identity card.

Are my pronoun references clear? Check for vague pronouns and inconsistent points of view.

Policy makers
~~They~~ say that family sizes are shrinking. I read the report, and ~~you~~ *I*
could not believe what it said.

 The Writers' Circle

Work with a group of three to five students. Your team will compete with other teams in a short contest.

Look at the two words below. Using letter combinations from those words, brainstorm and form as many new words as possible. For example, you could create the word *car*. You can only use the letters given; you cannot add or double any letters. The team that forms the most words wins the contest.

anthropological discovery

READING LINK

Social Sciences

To read more about issues related to social sciences, see the next essays.

"Fish Cheeks" by Amy Tan
    (page 421)
"The Hijab" by Naheed Mustafa
    (page 423)
"A Conversation with John E.
    Smelcer" by Dale E. Seeds
    (page 425)

 See Chapter 7 on the Visualizing Writing CD-ROM for additional audio and animated mini-lectures on **Pronoun-Antecedent Agreement**, **Vague Pronouns**, and **Pronoun Shift**.

Subjects and Verbs

CHAPTER 8

Section Theme: **ENTERTAINMENT AND CULTURE**

CONTENTS

• Identifying Subjects
• Identifying Prepositional Phrases
• Identifying Verbs

In this chapter, you will read about music and musicians.

Grammar Snapshot

Looking at Subjects and Verbs

Sonia Margossian teaches singing. In the next excerpt from a speech, she discusses proper breathing techniques. Notice that subjects are in bold type and the verbs are underlined. Also observe that some sentences have no visible subjects.

> <u>Stand</u> straight, and <u>place</u> your hands on your stomach, just below the ribs. Then <u>take</u> a long, deep breath and <u>carry</u> the air to the bottom of your lungs. Your **shoulders** <u>should</u> not <u>move</u> as you breathe. As **you** <u>continue</u> to inhale, your **chest** <u>will inflate</u>.

In this chapter, you will identify subjects and verbs.

Identifying Subjects

A **sentence** has a subject and verb, and it expresses a complete thought. The **subject** tells you who or what the sentence is about. The **verb** expresses an action or state. If a sentence is missing a subject or a verb, it is incomplete.

subject   verb

Prehistoric **humans** <u>banged</u> on hollow logs to make music.

Singular or Plural Subjects

Subjects may be singular or plural. To determine the subject of a sentence, ask yourself who or what the sentence is about.

A **singular subject** is one person, place, or thing.

> **Mozart** learned to play piano at an early age.

> The **violin** is difficult to master.

A **plural subject** is more than one person, place, or thing.

> **People** still listen to Mozart's music.

> Some **instruments** are easy to learn.

Pronouns as Subjects

A **subject pronoun** (*he, she, it, you, we, they*) can act as the subject of a sentence.

> Greg wants that guitar, but **it** is very expensive.

> Louisa has a great voice. **She** should sing more often.

Gerunds (*-ing* Words) as Subjects

Sometimes a **gerund** (the *-ing* form of a verb, acting as a noun) is the subject of a sentence.

> **Listening** is an important skill.

> **Dancing** can improve your cardiovascular health.

Section 2
PROBLEMS WITH VERBS

 **Simple versus Complete Subject**

In a sentence, the **simple subject** is the noun or pronoun. The complete name of a person, place, or organization is a simple subject.

    he   guitar   Tupac Shakur   Sony Music Corporation

The **complete subject** is the noun, plus the words that describe the noun. In the examples, the descriptive words are underlined.

    <u>new accoustic</u> guitar   <u>Michael's silver</u> flute   <u>the tiny</u> microphone

simple subject

<u>The expensive old **violin**</u> is very fragile.

complete subject

PRACTICE 1

Underline the complete subject in each sentence. (Remember to underline the subject and the words that describe the subject.) Then circle the simple subject.

EXAMPLE:

Mexico's most famous recording (artist) is Juan Gabriel.

1. His birth name was Alberto Aguilera Valadez.

2. Gabriel's family was extremely poor.

3. His hardworking mother was a housekeeper for a rich family in Juarez.

4. Twelve-year-old Gabriel started writing songs.

5. The talented young man sang in local nightclubs such as El Noa Noa.

6. El Noa Noa's name appeared in a Juan Gabriel song.

7. The young singer eventually moved to Mexico City.

8. His songs became extremely popular.

9. Gabriel's family bought a mansion in Juarez a few years ago.

10. His mother had been a housekeeper in that mansion.

Section 2
PROBLEMS WITH VERBS

Compound Subjects

Many sentences have more than one subject. These are called compound subjects. Notice that *and* is not part of the compound subject.

> **Boys** and **girls** can learn music.

> **Reporters** and **photographers** took pictures of the singer.

PRACTICE 2

Complete each sentence by adding one or more logical subjects.

EXAMPLE:

__Beyoncé Knowles__ sings and dances.

1. In my opinion, _____ is the most interesting type of music.

2. _____ and _____ are great singers.

3. My feathered yellow _____ sings every morning.

4. _____ stopped making music a long time ago.

5. _____ and _____ recorded many number one hits.

6. Last year, _____ released a new CD.

7. The _____ is my least favorite instrument.

8. _____ is important in our lives.

Special Subject Problems
Unstated Subjects (Commands)

In a sentence that expresses a command, the subject is unstated, but it is still understood. The unstated subject is *you*.

> Practice every day.

> Do not judge the musician harshly.

Here, There

Here and *there* are not subjects. In sentences that begin with *here* or *there*, the subject follows the verb.

> verb   subject
> There <u>are</u> five **ways** to improve your voice.

> verb subject
> Here <u>is</u> my **CD**.

Section 2
PROBLEMS WITH VERBS

 **Ask Who or What**

When you are trying to determine the subject, read the sentence carefully and ask yourself who or what the sentence is about. Do not presume that all nouns are the subjects in a sentence. For example, in the next sentence, *music, dance,* and *occasions* are nouns, but they are not the subject.

Most **cultures** use music and dance to celebrate special occasions.

PRACTICE 3

Underline one or more simple subjects in these sentences. If the subject is unstated, write *you*.

EXAMPLE:
You listen
~~Listen~~ to music as often as possible.

1. Every known human group has a form of music.

2. Music stimulates many parts of the brain.

3. Do not listen to extremely loud music on earphones.

4. There are various musical styles in North America.

5. Some cultures do not distinguish between musicians and ordinary people.

6. For example, music is as natural as breathing in Indonesia.

7. Some animal species use musical sounds to communicate.

8. There are many exotic birds that are unable to sing.

9. Douglas Nelson taught songs to some sparrows.

10. If possible, try to learn a musical instrument.

Identifying Prepositional Phrases

A **preposition** is a word that links nouns, pronouns, and phrases to other words in a sentence. It expresses a relationship based on movement, motion, or position.

Common Prepositions

about	before	during	of	toward
above	behind	except	off	under
across	below	for	on	until
after	beside	from	onto	up
against	between	in	out	with
along	beyond	inside	outside	within
among	by	into	over	
around	despite	like	through	
at	down	near	to	

A **phrase** is a group of words that is missing a subject, a verb, or both, and it is not a complete sentence. A **prepositional phrase** is made up of a preposition and its object (a noun or a pronoun).

Preposition	**+**	**Object**
in		the morning
among		the shadows
over		the rainbow
with		some friends

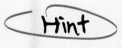 **Nouns Are Not Always Subjects**

Because the object of a preposition is a noun, it may look like a subject. However, the object in a prepositional phrase is never the subject of the sentence.

To help you identify the subject of a sentence, it is a good idea to put parentheses around prepositional phrases, cross them out, or identify them in some other way. In each of the following sentences, the subject is in bold type and the prepositional phrase is in parentheses.

(In most countries,) particular **musical styles** exist.

The **studio** (on Slater Street) is closed.

The **information** (in that magazine) is true.

Section 2
**PROBLEMS
WITH VERBS**

PRACTICE 4

In each sentence, place parentheses around one or more prepositional phrases. Then circle the simple subject.

EXAMPLE:

(According to Kristin Leutwyler of *Scientific American,*) prehistoric (humans) listened to music.

1. In a cave in France, archeologists have found sophisticated wind instruments.

2. In the past, Neanderthals made flutes out of animal bones.

3. The sweet-sounding flutes from the cave are more than 50,000 years old.

4. In spite of the evidence, scientists do not agree about the origins of music.

5. Some scientists with the National Research Institute study the musical ability of animals.

6. At the California Academy of Sciences, curator Luis Baptista studies bird sounds.

7. In a symposium, Baptista made an interesting demonstration.

8. The curator, in front of the audience, played the white-breasted wood wren's call.

9. With a smile, he then played the opening notes of Beethoven's Fifth Symphony.

10. The sounds from the two recorded pieces were similar.

PRACTICE 5

If the underlined word is the subject, write *C* (for "correct") in the space. If the underlined word is not the subject, then circle the correct subject(s).

EXAMPLES:

In the 1930s, (Elvis Aaron Presley) was born.   _____

The musical legend was born on Jan. 8, 1935.   *C*

1. His twin brother was named Jesse.   _____

2. <u>Jesse</u> died at birth. _____

3. In the <u>summer</u> of 1953, the young Southerner made his first
   demo record. _____

4. Elvis, Scotty Moore, and <u>Bill Black</u> recorded "That's All Right." _____

5. Sun Records, in <u>Memphis</u>, was a very small recording studio. _____

6. <u>Elvis's</u> first number one song was called "Mystery Train." _____

7. Elvis's manager was <u>Colonel Tom Parker</u>. _____

8. <u>Elvis's</u> only non-U.S. concert was in Vancouver, Canada. _____

9. In March, 1956, <u>"Heartbreak Hotel"</u> became the most popular
   song in the United States. _____

10. In his last <u>year</u>, Elvis performed at 150 concerts. _____

Section 2
**PROBLEMS
WITH VERBS**

Identifying Verbs

Every sentence must contain a verb. The **verb** either expresses what the subject
does or links the subject to other descriptive words.

Action Verbs

Action verbs describe the actions that the subject performs.

> The violinist <u>performed</u> in Carnegie Hall.

> She <u>has</u> a son.

Compound Verbs

When a subject performs more than one action, the verbs are called **compound
verbs.**

> Mr. Gibson <u>makes</u>, <u>polishes</u>, and <u>sells</u> good-quality guitars.

PRACTICE 6

Fill in each space with an appropriate and interesting action verb.

EXAMPLE:

The Petersons ___paid___ for their tickets and ___entered___ the theater.

1. Marcella, the violinist, _____ the audience.

2. She then _____ beautifully.

3. At the end of the performance, the audience _____
   and _____.

4. The performer _____ to her dressing room.

5. She _____ on her sofa, exhausted.

6. Somebody _____ on the door and

   _____.

Linking Verbs

Linking verbs (or state verbs) do not describe an action; instead, they describe a state of being or give information about the subject. The most common linking verb is *be* (*am, are, is, was, were*).

Section 2
PROBLEMS WITH VERBS

> The harp <u>is</u> a lovely instrument.
>
> Those sound systems <u>are</u> unreliable.

Other linking verbs link the subject with descriptive words.

subject   linking verb   descriptive word
That **music**   <u>sounds</u>   *good.*

subject   linking verb   descriptive words
Mr. Wayland   <u>seems</u>   *quite eccentric.*

Here are some common linking verbs:

act	feel	seem
appear	get	smell
be (am, is, are, was, were)	look	sound
become	remain	taste

PRACTICE 7

Underline the linking verb in each sentence.

EXAMPLE:

In some cultures, musicians <u>are</u> important people in the community.

1. Among the Mandiki of Senegal, the jali is a highly specialized musician.

2. The jali acts as the official singer of the tribe.

3. His songs sound haunting and powerful.

4. The tribe's history becomes part of the jali's repertoire.

5. The music seems simple.

6. However, it is actually quite complex.

7. The jali appears confident during his performance.

8. The tribe members are ready for the jali to commemorate important events.

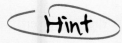 **Infinitives Are Not the Main Verb**

Infinitives are verbs preceded by *to,* such as *to sing, to play,* and *to run.* An infinitive is never the main verb in a sentence.

verb infinitive   verb   infinitive

Chuck Berry <u>wanted</u> <u>to be</u> famous. He <u>hoped</u> <u>to become</u> a music legend.

Section 2
**PROBLEMS
WITH VERBS**

PRACTICE 8

Circle the subjects and underline the verbs in the following sentences. Some sentences have more than one verb. Write *L* beside any sentence that contains a linking verb.

EXAMPLE:

(Andrew Young) <u>changed</u> his name to Dr. Dre.

1. Andrew Young's mother raised him in a Los Angeles housing project.

2. The gangs in his environment influenced him and later affected his music.

3. Young admired basketball superstar Dr. J.

4. Later, the future music producer took the name Dr. Dre.

5. Violence was widespread in his environment.

6. Dre's brother died during a fight in the neighborhood.

7. The young musician began as a disc jockey at parties.

8. Dre, Ice Cube, and Easy Z became the founders of West Coast hip-hop in the late 1980s.

9. Then Dre and Suge Knight founded Death Row Records in the early 1990s.

10. Their "gansta rap" became the target of censorship groups.

11. *Rolling Stone* calls Dre "the most influential rapper/producer of his time."

12. Eminem and other wealthy music stars owe their careers to Dre.

Helping Verbs

Many verbs contain two or more words: a main verb and a helping verb. The **main verb** expresses what the subject does or links the subject to descriptive words. The **helping verb** combines with the main verb to indicate tense, negative structure, or question structure.

Be, Have, Do

The common helping verbs *be*, *have*, and *do* combine with the main verb to indicate a tense, negative structure, or question structure.

HV   HV   V
Some songs <u>have been</u> <u>banned</u> from radio station play lists.

Modals

A modal is another type of helping verb. It indicates ability (*can*), obligation (*must*), possibility (*may, might, could*), advice (*should*), and so on.

HV   V
Violent lyrics <u>can</u> <u>influence</u> children.

Questions

In question forms, the first helping verb usually appears before the subject.

HV   subject   V
<u>Should</u> radio **stations** <u>censor</u> song lyrics?

HV   subject   V
<u>Do</u> violent, sexist, or racist **songs** <u>influence</u> young listeners?

 **Interrupting Words and Phrases**

Interrupting words may appear between verbs, but they are *not* part of the verb. Some interrupting words are *always, easily, ever, never, not, often, sometimes,* and *usually.*

HV interrupter V
Blues music <u>can</u> **sometimes** <u>be</u> sorrowful.

PRACTICE 9

Underline each complete verb once. Then underline each main verb twice.

EXAMPLE:

Musicians with perfect pitch <u>are</u> <u>envied</u>.

1. According to an article in *Scientific American*, very few people have achieved perfect pitch.

2. Human beings with absolute pitch will easily sing an F sharp.

3. Most people do not have this ability.

4. Only one person in 10,000 can identify a note perfectly.

5. Musical ability may be an inherited trait.

6. In languages such as Vietnamese and Mandarin, one word can have several different meanings.

7. The meaning of each word may depend on the tone of the word.

8. Diana Deutch of the University of California has discussed the topic in her lectures.

9. According to Deutch, native speakers of tonal languages, even those with no musical training, could recognize and repeat notes perfectly.

10. The best way to teach children perfect pitch could be to train them with tonal words.

Section 2
**PROBLEMS
WITH VERBS**

FINAL REVIEW

Circle each simple subject and underline each complete verb. Underline each main verb twice. If prepositional phrases confuse you, you can cross them out.

EXAMPLE:

(Aaron Wherry) wrote an article about music and consumerism. (It) is called "Say Yes to Logos."

1.   Most young music consumers do not associate their favorite sounds with advertising. However, according to journalist Aaron Wherry, a lot of contemporary musicians consciously promote merchandise.

2.   Lucian James is a marketing consultant in San Francisco. He has compiled a list of products. Mercedes, Lexus, and Gucci are frequently mentioned brands in the *Billboard* Top 20 list. For example, the hip-hop artist 50 Cent often mentions his Mercedes-Benz automobile in his music.

3.   Hip-hop artists, according to Wherry, do not apologize for combining music and commerce. Back in 1986, Run-DMC recorded a track called "My Adidas." Then, rap mogul Russell Simmons invited Adidas executives to a Run-DMC concert. Audience members lifted up their running shoes on cue. Naturally, the running shoe company offered the rappers an endorsement deal.

4.   Some musicians have refused to promote products in their music. They do not want to become "sellouts." Other musicians have chosen to actively publicize products in their songs. They do not see any problems with the practice. In the end, most music fans do not care about the debate. They will continue to support musicians on both sides of the issue.

Section 2
PROBLEMS WITH VERBS

 The Writer's Room

Write a paragraph about one of the following topics. After you finish writing, circle your subjects and underline your verbs. Underline main verbs twice.

1. What qualities does a professional singer need? List at least five qualities.

2. Compare two different singers. How are they similar or different?

 CHECKLIST: SUBJECTS AND VERBS

To identify **subjects,** look for words that tell you who or what the sentence is about.

To identify **verbs,** look for words that express what the subject does or link the subject to descriptive words.

To identify **action verbs,** look for words that describe the action that the subject performs.

To identify **linking verbs,** look for words that describe a state of being or link the subject with descriptive words.

To identify **helping verbs,** look for words that combine with the main verb to indicate tense, negative structure, or question structure.

To identify a **prepositional phrase,** look for words that consist of a preposition and its object. The object of a prepositional phrase cannot be the subject.

prepositional phrase   subject   helping verb   verb
In spite of criticism, Madonna's fame   has   endured.

 See Chapter 8 on the Visualizing Writing CD-ROM for an additional audio and animated mini-lecture on **Subjects and Verbs**.

Present and Past Tenses

CHAPTER 9

Section Theme: **ENTERTAINMENT AND CULTURE**

CONTENTS

- Understanding Verb Tense
- The Simple Present Tense
- The Simple Past Tense
- Avoiding Double Negatives

In this chapter, you will read about literature and the media.

Grammar Snapshot

Looking at Present and Past Tenses

Kate Chopin, the mother of six children, began writing shortly after her husband died. In this abridged excerpt from her short story "The Storm," written in 1898, the past tense verbs are underlined.

> She <u>went</u> and <u>stood</u> at the window with a greatly disturbed look on her face. She <u>wiped</u> the moist frame. It <u>was</u> stiflingly hot. Alcée <u>got</u> up and <u>joined</u> her at the window, looking over her shoulder. The playing of the lightning <u>was</u> incessant. A bolt <u>struck</u> a tall chinaberry tree at the edge of the field. It <u>filled</u> all visible space with a blinding glare.

In this chapter, you will identify and write present and past tense verbs.

Understanding Verb Tense

A verb shows an action or a state of being. A **verb tense** indicates when an action occurred. For example, review the various tenses of the verb *write*.

Past time:	J. K. Rowling <u>wrote</u> parts of her first book in a coffee shop.
Present time:	She <u>writes</u> every morning.
Future:	Perhaps she <u>will write</u> a new book next year.

Section 2
PROBLEMS WITH VERBS

 **Use Standard Verb Forms**

Nonstandard English is used in everyday conversation and may differ according to the region in which you live. **Standard American English** is the common language generally used and expected in schools, businesses, and government institutions in the United States. Most of your instructors will want you to write using standard American English.

Nonstandard:	She be busy. She don't have no time to talk.
Standard:	She is busy. She doesn't have any time to talk.

The Simple Present Tense

The **simple present tense** shows that an action is a general fact or habitual activity.

Fact:	Harry Potter books <u>sell</u> in countries throughout the world.
Habitual activity:	J. K. Rowling <u>writes</u> every morning.

Simple present tense verbs (except *be*) have two forms.

- **Base form.** When the subject is *I, you, we,* or *they,* do not add an ending to the verb.

  They <u>read</u> magazines. We often <u>borrow</u> their magazines.
- **Third-person singular form.** When the subject is *he, she, it,* or the equivalent (*Joe, Anne, New York*), add an *-s* or *-es* ending to the verb.

  The story <u>ends</u> badly. The main character <u>leaves</u> his family.

Look at the two forms of the verb *eat*. Notice the *-s* in bold print in the third-person singular form.

Present Tense of *Eat*

	Singular	Plural
First person:	I eat	We eat
Second person:	You eat	You eat
Third person:	He eat**s** She eat**s** It eat**s**	They eat

Subject-Verb Agreement

In the present tense, the subject and verb must **agree** in number. If the subject is third-person singular (*he, she, it*), the corresponding verb must have the singular form, too.

Although plural nouns usually end in *–s*, plural verbs do not. Instead, singular verbs have the *–s* or *–es* ending. Read the following sentences and notice the errors in subject-verb agreement.

writes

Jan Freeman ~~write~~ for the *Boston Globe*. Her columns ~~appears~~ *appear* every Sunday.

GRAMMAR LINK

See Chapter 13, "Subject-Verb Agreement," for more detailed information.

Section 2
PROBLEMS WITH VERBS

PRACTICE 1

George Orwell, the author of *Animal Farm* and *1984*, wrote an essay called "Why I Write." The following sentences summarize his ideas. Underline the correct present tense form of each verb in parentheses.

EXAMPLE:

Authors (<u>write</u>, writes) for several reasons.

1. Every writer (want, wants) to seem clever and to be talked about, according to George Orwell.

2. Most human beings (like, likes) to be remembered.

3. Also, a beautiful or moving moment (become, becomes) immortal with writing.

4. A good writer (attempt, attempts) to show others the beauty of certain places.

5. People also (write, writes) to create a historical record of events.

6. Some writers (hope, hopes) to persuade others with their words.

7. Literary works (need, needs) to document political events.

8. George Orwell's book *Animal Farm* (show, shows) certain injustices, and it (criticize, criticizes) Soviet-style communism.

9. Some lies (need, needs) to be exposed.

10. Art (have, has) a relationship with politics.

Irregular Present Tense Verbs: *Be, Have*

Two common present tense verbs are irregular and do not follow the usual pattern for endings. Review the forms of the verbs *be* and *have*.

Present Tense of *Be* and *Have*

Singular	Be	Have
First person:	I am	I have
Second person:	You are	You have
Third person:	He is	He has
	She is	She has
	It is	It has
Plural		
First person:	We are	We have
Second person:	You are	You have
Third person:	They are	They have

Section 2
**PROBLEMS
WITH VERBS**

 **Using the Irregular Verb Be**

Use the verb *be* to identify age, hunger, thirst, and temperature. Remember that the form of the verb must also agree with the subject of the sentence.

> **Age:** He ~~has~~ *is* forty years old.
>
> **Hunger and thirst:** He ~~has~~ *is* thirsty, and I ~~have~~ *am* hungry.
>
> **Temperature:** It ~~be~~ *is* cold outside.

Do not use *be* to express agreement.

> I ~~am~~ agree.

PRACTICE 2

Write present tense verbs in the spaces provided. Use the correct forms of *be* and *have*.

EXAMPLE:

J. K. Rowling __*is*__ the world's most successful children's author.

1. Her full name _____ Joanne Katherine Rowling. She _____ from Bristol, England, and she _____ the child of middle-class parents. Currently, she _____ about forty years old.

2. Rowling's books _____ about a child named Harry Potter. The child _____ no parents. His cruel aunt and uncle _____ his guardians. They _____ their own

child, whom they spoil, but they treat Harry horribly. Harry
_____ a tiny bedroom under the stairs, and he _____
extremely unhappy.

3.   As the story progresses, Harry goes to a special private
school. He _____ two close friends in the new school, and
he _____ able to use his special powers to fight evil.

4.   The *Harry Potter* novels follow a literary tradition. Many
fairy tales _____ about an orphan who overcomes obstacles.
Often, cruel relatives or stepparents _____ in charge of the
orphan. The child _____ no option but to grow up quickly
and escape from the evil surrogate family.

Section 2
**PROBLEMS
WITH VERBS**

Question Forms: *Do or Does*

To create present tense questions, begin each question with *do* or *does*.

Statement	**Question**
He complains a lot.	**Does** he complain a lot?
They read each night.	**Do** they read each night?

In the following chart, notice when to use the third-person singular form *does*.

Question Forms Using *Do or Does*

	Singular	**Plural**
First person:	Do I work?	Do we work?
Second person:	Do you work?	Do you work?
Third person:	Does he work? Does she work? Does it work?	Do they work?

Exception: When the main verb is *be* (*is, am, are*), just move *be* before the subject
to form a question.

   Is the story suspenseful? **Are** they safe?

PRACTICE 3

Fill in each blank with the correct present tense form of the verb *do* or *be*. Then
underline the complete subject in each question.

EXAMPLES:

____Does____ it have a happy ending?   ____Is____ it interesting?

1. _____ we have time to discuss the novel?

2. _____ you a fan of murder mysteries?

3. _____ you want to read something else?

4. _____ the main character about forty years old?

5. _____ you like the author's writing style?

6. _____ he a good storyteller?

7. _____ the characters interesting?

8. _____ you know what the critics think?

9. _____ the newspaper critic fair?

Negative Forms: *Do Not, Does Not*

To form the negative of present tense verbs, place *do* or *does* and the word *not* between the subject and the verb.

> We **do not** read her novels. (Contraction: **don't** read)

> Simon **does not** write every day. (Contraction: **doesn't** write)

Negative Forms of *Do* and *Does*

	Singular Forms	**Contraction**
First person:	I do not work.	don't
Second person:	You do not work.	don't
Third person:	He does not work. She does not work. It does not work.	doesn't
	Plural Forms	
First person:	You do not work.	don't
Second person:	We do not work.	don't
Third person:	They do not work.	don't

Exception: When the main verb is *be* (*is, am, are*), just add *not*.

> The story **is not** suspenseful. (Contraction: **isn't**)

> They **are not** happy with the ending. (Contraction: **aren't**)

PRACTICE 4

A. Add *-s* or *-es* to each italicized verb if necessary. Then, write the negative form and contraction in the spaces provided.

EXAMPLE:

	Negative Form	**Contraction**
Frodo *do* __es__ many strange things.	does not do	doesn't do
1. In *The Lord of the Rings*, a little hobbit *make* _____ friends with a wizard.	_____	_____

2. He *live* _____ in a small house.

   _____ _____

3. His best friend, Sam, *eat* _____
   a lot of greasy food.

   _____ _____

4. They *leave* _____ their village
   to go on a journey.

   _____ _____

5. Frodo *own* _____ a special ring.

   _____ _____

6. They *stay* _____ up late every
   night.

   _____ _____

7. The hobbits *meet* _____ some
   elves.

   _____ _____

B. Write the correct form of the verb *be* in each blank. Then, write the negative form and contraction.

EXAMPLE:

	Negative Form	**Contraction**
Frodo's feet __are__ very large.	are not	aren't

8. Their journey _____
   dangerous.

   _____ _____

9. The hobbits _____
   brave.

   _____ _____

10. J. R. R. Tolkien's books _____
    expensive.

    _____ _____

Hint **Correcting Question and Negative Forms**

In question and negative forms, always use the base form of the main verb even when the subject is third-person singular. Put the -*s* or -*es* ending only on the helping verb (*does*).

>   *have*
> Why does the magazine ~~has~~ so many subscribers?

>   *contain*
> The magazine does not ~~contains~~ many advertisements.

PRACTICE 5

Correct errors in present tense verb forms.

EXAMPLE:

   does
What ~~do~~ your brother like to read?

1. According to the tabloid headline, aliens visits the earth every day.

2. Why tabloids are so popular?

3. That newspaper do not have a small circulation.

4. Do that newspaper be over fifty years old?

5. Do that tabloid sometimes breaks a story before the mainstream newspapers?

6. The magazine editor do not want to print false stories.

7. Today, some regular newspapers doesn't look very different from tabloids.

8. Often a celebrity do something crazy, and the story becomes front-page news.

9. During difficult times, perhaps readers doesn't want to read about wars or famines.

10. Stories about the lives of celebrities provides readers with an escape from reality.

Section 2
**PROBLEMS
WITH VERBS**

The Simple Past Tense

The **simple past tense** shows that an action occurred at a specific past time. In the past tense, there are regular and irregular verbs.

Regular Past Tense Verbs

Regular past tense verbs have a standard *-d* or *-ed* ending (*talked, ended, watched*). Use the same form for both singular and plural past tense verbs.

Singular subject:	F. Scott Fitzerald **published** his stories in several languages.
Plural subject:	The journalists **asked** for an interview.

GRAMMAR LINK

See Chapter 23, "Spelling," for more spelling tips.

 **Spelling of Regular Verbs**

Most regular past tense verbs are formed by adding *-ed* to the base form of the verb.

    talk–talk**ed**   mention–mention**ed**

Exceptions

• When the regular verb ends in *-e*, add just *-d*.
    hope–hope**d**   bake–bake**d**

• When the regular verb ends in a consonant + *y*, change the *y* to *i* and add *-ed*.
    fry–fr**ied**   apply–appl**ied**

Note: if the regular verb ends in a vowel + *y*, add just *-ed*.

    play–play**ed**   destroy–destroy**ed**

• When the regular verb ends in a consonant-vowel-consonant combination, double the last consonant and add *-ed*.
    stop–stop**ped**   jog–jog**ged**

PRACTICE 6

Write the past tense forms of the following verbs.

EXAMPLE:

watch   _watched_

1. hope   _____   6. plan   _____
2. try   _____   7. rain   _____
3. stay   _____   8. rest   _____
4. employ _____   9. deny   _____
5. study   _____   10. ban   _____

Section 2
**PROBLEMS
WITH VERBS**

 **Hint**   *Past versus Passed*

Some people confuse *past* and *passed*. *Past* is a noun that means "in a previous time; before now."

> She has many secrets in her <u>past</u>. Her mistakes are in the <u>past</u>.

Passed is the past tense of the verb *pass,* which has many meanings. In the first example, it means "went by"; in the second example, it means "to successfully complete."

> Many days <u>passed</u>, and the nights got shorter.
> She <u>passed</u> her exams.

PRACTICE 7

Write the simple past form of each verb in parentheses. Make sure that you have spelled your past tense verbs correctly.

EXAMPLE:

Writer F. Scott Fitzgerald's wife, Zelda, (inspire) ____inspired____ many of his stories.

1. During the jazz era, Fitzgerald (chronicle) _____ life among upper-middle-class youths.

2. Initially, Zelda Fitzgerald (act) _____ like a typical flapper.

3. She (dress) _____ in loose-fitting clothing, and her hair was short.

4. The Fitzgeralds (live) _____ a Bohemian existence, meeting regularly with other writers and artists.

5. Eventually, Zelda (want) _____ her own career.

6. She (dislike) _____ living in Scott's shadow, and she (hope) _____ to be a writer or a dancer.

7. Zelda (try) _____ writing her own novels in the 1930s.

8. According to some biographers, Scott (use) _____ some of Zelda's words in his stories.

9. However, during their lifetimes, critics never (discover) _____ proof of any artistic theft by F. Scott Fitzgerald.

10. The Fitzgerald's marriage (end) _____ tragically.

11. Zelda (pass) _____ her last years in an asylum, and Scott (abuse) _____ alcohol.

12. Their dreams of wealth and fame (disappear) _____.

Section 2
PROBLEMS WITH VERBS

Irregular Past Tense Verbs

Irregular verbs do not end in any specific letter. Because their spellings change from the present to the past forms, these verbs can be challenging to remember.

Irregular Verbs

Base Form	Simple Past	Base Form	Simple Past	Base Form	Simple Past
be	was, were	catch	caught	fight	fought
beat	beat	choose	chose	find	found
become	became	cling	clung	flee	fled
begin	began	come	came	fly	flew
bend	bent	cost	cost	forget	forgot
bet	bet	cut	cut	forgive	forgave
bind	bound	deal	dealt	freeze	froze
bite	bit	dig	dug	get	got
bleed	bled	do	did	give	gave
blow	blew	draw	drew	go	went
breed	bred	drink	drank	grind	ground
break	broke	drive	drove	grow	grew
bring	brought	eat	ate	hang	hung
build	built	fall	fell	have	had
burst	burst	feed	fed	hear	heard
buy	bought	feel	felt	hide	hid

Base Form	Simple Past	Base Form	Simple Past	Base Form	Simple Past
hit	hit	rise	rose	steal	stole
hold	held	run	ran	stick	stuck
hurt	hurt	say	said	sting	stung
keep	kept	see	saw	stink	stank
kneel	knelt	sell	sold	strike	struck
know	knew	send	sent	swear	swore
lay	laid	set	set	sweep	swept
lead	led	shake	shook	swim	swam
leave	left	shoot	shot	swing	swung
lend	lent	shrink	shrank	take	took
let	let	shut	shut	teach	taught
lie*	lay	sing	sang	tear	tore
light	lit	sink	sank	tell	told
lose	lost	sit	sat	think	thought
make	made	sleep	slept	throw	threw
mean	meant	slide	slid	thrust	thrust
meet	met	slit	slit	understand	understood
mistake	mistook	speak	spoke	upset	upset
pay	paid	speed	sped	wake	woke
put	put	spend	spent	wear	wore
quit	quit	spin	spun	weep	wept
read	read	split	split	win	won
rid	rid	spread	spread	wind	wound
ride	rode	spring	sprang	withdraw	withdrew
ring	rang	stand	stood	write	wrote

Section 2
PROBLEMS WITH VERBS

*When *lie* means "tell a false statement," it is a regular verb: *lie, lied, lied.*

PRACTICE 8

Write the correct past form of each verb in parentheses. Some verbs are regular, and some are irregular.

EXAMPLE:

In the 1950s, journalists at *The Confidential* (write) ___wrote___ about show-business scandals.

1.　　　In 1833, the first American tabloid, the *New York Sun*,

(hit) _____ the streets. It (sell) _____ on

the street for one penny. Journalists (give) _____

readers stories about political scandals, murders, and other crimes.

2.   In the 1952, a new tabloid (rise) _____ to prominence. An Italian publisher, Generoso Pope, Jr., (buy) _____ a newspaper called the *Enquirer*. It (be) _____ full of horse-racing tips.

3.   Pope (pay) _____ about $70,000 for the *Enquirer*. The paper's focus (change) _____ from horse racing to bizarre and gory stories about cannibalism and other crimes. The *Enquirer*'s staff (make) _____ up incredible stories. Readers usually (think) _____ that the stories were true.

Section 2
PROBLEMS WITH VERBS

The Past Form of *Be* (*Was* or *Were*)

The verb *be* has two past forms: *was* and *were*.

Past Tense of *Be*

	Singular	Plural
First person:	I was	We were
Second person:	You were	You were
Third person:	He was	They were
	She was	
	It was	

PRACTICE 9

Fill in each blank with *was* or *were*.

EXAMPLE:
During the early years of Hollywood, people ___*were*___ curious about celebrities.

1.   In the early 1950s, there _____ many hoax stories in the *National Enquirer*. However, in the late 1950s, that situation changed. Each journalist _____ careful to include true stories about celebrities. The friends and employees of the famous _____ often greedy, and they _____ ready to sell information to the tabloids.

2.   Some popular celebrities _____ on the front covers of the tabloids each week. For example, during the 1960s, the love

life of Elizabeth Taylor _____ front-page news. Her many

marriages _____ the fodder for gossip columnists. Often,

reporters _____ disguised as bellhops or police officers.

By wearing disguises, they _____ able to get close to

movie stars. For example, a photographer _____ able

to take photographs of Taylor by posing as a waiter.

Negative Forms of Past Tense Verbs

To form the negative of past tense verbs, place *did* and the word *not* between the subject and the verb.

Section 2
**PROBLEMS
WITH VERBS**

> The actress **did not** want to appear in tabloids. (Contraction: **didn't**)

> We **did not** buy that newspaper. (Contraction: **didn't**)

Exception: When the main verb is *be* (*was, were*), just add *not*.

> The story **was not** suspenseful. (Contraction: **wasn't**)

> They **were not** happy with the ending. (Contraction: **weren't**)

PRACTICE 10

Write the contracted negative forms of the underlined verbs.

EXAMPLE:

He <u>worked</u>.   *didn't work*   They <u>were</u> hungry.   *weren't*

1. She <u>was</u> busy. _____
2. Joe <u>ate</u> a lot. _____
3. You <u>made</u> it. _____
4. We <u>spoke</u>. _____
5. I <u>lied</u>. _____

6. I <u>did</u> it. _____
7. We <u>washed</u> up. _____
8. They <u>were</u> late. _____
9. Kay <u>went</u> out. _____
10. He <u>opened</u> it. _____

Question Forms of Past Tense Verbs

To create past tense questions, add *did* before the subject.

She wrote a lot.   **Did** she write a lot?
They liked the story.   **Did** they like the story?

Exception: When the main verb is *be* (*was, were*), just move *be* before the subject to form a question.

> **Was** the story exciting?

> **Were** you ready?

 **Use the Base Form After** *Did*

In question and negative forms, remember to use the base form—not the past form—of the main verb.

use
Did he ~~used~~ a computer to write his book?

Section 2
**PROBLEMS
WITH VERBS**

PRACTICE 11

Correct the errors with question or negative forms.

EXAMPLE:

did he seem
Why ~~he seem~~ so surprised by his success?

1. J. R. R. Tolkien don't be born in England.

2. He did not remained in South Africa.

3. When he moved to Birmingham, England?

4. Why did Tolkien wrote about hobbits?

5. His friends not believed in the value of myths.

6. Tolkien wasn't agree with his friends.

7. *The Lord of the Rings* didn't be popular at first.

8. Why the book became popular ten years after its release?

9. Why did the book sold more than 100 million copies?

10. When Amazon.com customers voted for *The Lord of the Rings* as the book

    of the millennium?

Common Errors with *Be* and *Have*

Some writers find it particularly difficult to remember how to use the irregular verbs *be* and *have*.

- Use *were*, not *was*, when the subject is plural.

    were
    The photographers ~~was~~ extremely persistent.

- Use the standard form of the verb (*is* or *was*), not *be*.

    was
    The camera ~~be~~ small enough to fit in a button hole.

■ Use the past form of the verb (*had*), not the present form (*have* or *has*), when speaking about a past event.

                had

Mike Wallace ~~has~~ to work in dangerous war zones during his early days as a reporter.

PRACTICE 12

If the underlined past tense verb is incorrectly formed or in the wrong tense, write the correct form above it. There are fifteen errors.

EXAMPLE:

              was

Hoax journalism <u>be</u> common in past eras.

Section 2
PROBLEMS WITH VERBS

1.   In the nineteenth century, many famous writers <u>maked</u> up stories for newspapers. The hoax stories <u>was</u> completely untrue. Even respected newspapers sometimes <u>printed</u> hoaxes.

2.   Some of literature's greatest writers <u>loved</u> to make up hoax stories. Mark Twain, for example, <u>created</u> a false story about a headless killer. Edgar Allen Poe <u>wroted</u> a story about a giant balloon that could cross oceans. The first blimps only <u>become</u> a reality many years later.

3.   One of the most widespread hoaxes <u>involved</u> "moon men." In 1835, the *New York Sun* <u>print</u> articles about the moon's furry, winged creatures. According to the newspaper, Sir John Hershel, a respected astronomer, <u>builded</u> a giant, powerful telescope. Each article <u>be</u> full of details about Hershel's observations.

4.   People <u>was</u> ready to believe the moon men stories. The articles <u>haved</u> enough facts to seem plausible. An astronomer named Hershel actually <u>existed</u>. Also, many citizens <u>be</u> worried about Halley's comet, so they often <u>looked</u> at the skies. They soon <u>realize</u> that they should not believe everything in newspapers.

5.   More recently, in 1999, newspapers and magazines <u>reported</u>
dubious "facts" about the millennium bug. People <u>buyed</u> supplies
and <u>digged</u> bomb shelters. They <u>was</u> scared of widespread power
failures. The media <u>contributed</u> to the mass hysteria. Many
people <u>was</u> amazed when nothing major happened on January 1,
2000.

Section 2
**PROBLEMS
WITH VERBS**

Avoiding Double Negatives

A **double negative** occurs when a writer combines a negative word such as *no*,
nothing, *nobody*, or *nowhere* with a negative adverb such as *not*, *never*, *rarely*, or
seldom. The result is a sentence that has a double negative. Such sentences can be
confusing because the negative words cancel each other.

> **Double negative:**   She <u>doesn't</u> give <u>no</u> interviews.
>
> He <u>never</u> received <u>no</u> royalties.

How to Correct Double Negatives

There are two ways to correct double negatives.

- Completely remove *one* of the negative forms.

Incorrect	**Correct**
She **doesn't** give **no** interviews.	She **doesn't** give interviews.
	She gives **no** interviews.
He **never** received **no** royalties.	He **never** received royalties.
	He received **no** royalties.

- Change *no* to *any* (*anybody, anything, anywhere*).

Incorrect	**Correct**
She **doesn't** give **no** interviews.	She doesn't give **any** interviews.
He **never** received **no** royalties.	He never received **any** royalties.

PRACTICE 13

Correct six errors with double negatives. You can correct each error in more than
one way.

EXAMPLE:

Amy Tan's novel didn't have ~~no~~ ^{any} negative reviews.

Amy Tan's novel ~~didn't have~~ ^{had} no negative reviews.

1.   Amy Tan's mother, Daisy, left an abusive husband in China

and went to the United States. She had three daughters, but her husband did not let her take none of her daughters with her. Daisy married John Tan, and they had a daughter named Amy. Her parents did not have no other daughters, but they had two sons.

2.   Amy's mother did not want her daughter to make no mistakes. She pushed Amy to enter medical school, but Amy didn't have no ambition to be a doctor. Amy rebelled and decided to study English instead. Amy also rebelled by moving to San Francisco so that she could be near her boyfriend. There wasn't no reason for her to stay in Oakland.

3.   Amy's relationship with her mother improved in later years. In 1987, they traveled to China together to meet Mrs. Tan's long-lost daughters. Amy's first novel, *The Joy Luck Club*, was inspired by her mother's life, and it became an international best-seller. Most reviewers didn't say nothing bad about the novel.

Section 2
PROBLEMS WITH VERBS

FINAL REVIEW

Correct fifteen errors. There are present tense, past tense, and double negative errors.

EXAMPLE:

The books ~~was~~ *were* offensive.

1.   The Federal Anti-Obscenity Act past in 1873. After that, citizens was not able to buy certain novels. For example, in 1915, the U.S. government did not permitted Americans to import James Joyce's classic novel *Ulysses*. Officials called the book obscene. Some activists fighted the government, and in 1930, they winned the right to publish the book in the United States. In 2000, the Modern Library choosed *Ulysses* as the best book of the twentieth century.

Section 2
**PROBLEMS
WITH VERBS**

2.   Between 1873 and 2000, school districts and libraries in the United States banned hundreds of novels for a variety of reasons. For example, in 1939, administrators at the St. Louis Public Library stoped lending John Steinbeck's classic *The Grapes of Wrath* because they thought that the novel's language was vulgar. In the 1960s, some people goed to other countries to buy the American classic *The Catcher in the Rye* because many states banned the novel. In the 1990s, some officials didn't want to stock no copies of Mark Twain's *Huckleberry Finn* because they believed that the book portrayed African Americans in a negative way. Some people also disliked the portrayal of Shylock, a Jewish merchant, in Shakespeare's play *The Merchant of Venice.* They sayed that Shakespeare stereotyped certain members of society in his play.

3.   Generally, book banners wants to safeguard the values of their communities. They don't see no problem with book banning. Others believes that people should have the freedom to choose their own reading material. They feels that books give insight into the social attitudes of different eras. Book banning is an emotional issue, and people will continue to debate the subject.

 The Writer's Room

Write a paragraph about one of the following topics. After you finish writing, underline your verbs. Verify that you have formed your present and past tense verbs correctly.

1. Describe your major source of entertainment during your childhood. Did you read? If not, why not? What other types of things did you do?

2. Describe what happens in a story, poem, play, or article that you have read.

CHECKLIST: PRESENT AND PAST TENSES

When you edit your writing, ask yourself the following questions.

Do I use the correct present tense forms? Check for errors in these cases:

–verbs following third-person singular nouns

–irregular present tense verbs

–question and negative forms

Zoey Cervantes, a young author, ~~need~~ *needs* to find a literary agent. ~~Does~~ *Do* you know of anyone she could contact?

Do I use the correct past tense forms? Check for spelling errors and other mistakes with the following words:

–regular past tense verbs

–irregular past tense verbs

–negative and question forms

In 1969, Maya Angelou ~~wroted~~ *wrote* her first novel. Why ~~decided~~ she *did decide* to write a novel?

Do my sentences have standard English? Check for errors in the following cases:

–use of *ain't* instead of *is not*, *am not*, or *are not*

–use of double negatives instead of correct negative forms

J. D. Salinger, the author of *Catcher in the Rye*, never gives ~~no~~ *any* interviews.

Section 2
PROBLEMS WITH VERBS

See Chapter 9 on the Visualizing Writing CD-ROM for an additional audio and animated mini-lecture on **Verb Tense**.

CHAPTER 10

Past Participles

Section Theme: **ENTERTAINMENT AND CULTURE**

CONTENTS

- Past Participles
- The Present Perfect Tense
- The Past Perfect Tense
- The Past Participle as an Adjective
- The Passive Voice

In this chapter, you will read about topics related to television and film.

Grammar Snapshot

Looking at Past Participles

Silent film actor George Arliss wrote several autobiographies, including *Up the Years from Bloomsbury*. In this excerpt, Arliss discusses film acting. The past participles of verbs are underlined.

> I had always <u>believed</u> that, for the movies, acting must be <u>exaggerated</u>, but I saw in this one flash that restraint was the chief thing that the actor had to learn in transferring art from the stage to the screen. The art of restraint and suggestion on the screen may any time be <u>studied</u> by watching the acting of the inimitable Charlie Chaplin.

In this chapter, you will identify and write past participles.

Past Participles

A **past participle** is a verb form, not a verb tense. You cannot use a past participle as the only verb in a sentence. Instead, you must use it with a helping verb. The most common helping verbs are forms of *have* or *be* (*have, has, had,* or *is, was, were*).

helping   past
verb   participle

My sister and I **were** <u>raised</u> in New York City.

Many movies **have been** <u>filmed</u> there.

Regular Verbs

Regular verbs end in *-d* or *-ed*. The past tense and the past participle of regular verbs are the same. Here are some examples.

Base Form	Past Tense	Past Participle
talk	talked	talked
cry	cried	cried
hope	hoped	hoped

Section 2
**PROBLEMS
WITH VERBS**

PRACTICE I

Underline each helping verb that appears before the word in parentheses. Then write the past participle of the verb in parentheses.

EXAMPLE:

Some consumers <u>have</u> (complain) ___*complained*___ about reality programs.

1. In the past few years, reality television has (dominate) _____ the airwaves.

2. Many viewers have (develop) _____ a taste for reality shows.

3. Reality programming is not new, though. It has (appear) _____ on network television since the 1940s.

4. *Wanted*, a show that was (produce) _____ in 1955 by CBS television, contained interviews with fugitives and their families.

5. *Candid Camera*, which was (create) _____ by its host Alan Funt in 1948, showed regular people reacting to surprising events.

6. Many other producers have (copy) _____ Funt's ideas.

7. Ashton Kutcher's *Punk'd* was (base) _____ on Funt's show.

8. Reality shows are (watch) _____ by viewers of all ages.

9. In 2003, many viewers were (attract) _____ to shows about finding the perfect mate.

10. For example, *The Bachelor* was (view) _____ by millions of people.

11. However, dating reality shows have (decline) _____ in the ratings.

12. Some reality shows have (remain) _____ popular.

Section 2
PROBLEMS WITH VERBS

Irregular Verbs

Certain verbs have irregular past forms and can be challenging to remember. Review the next list of common irregular verbs. Put an *X* next to verbs that you commonly misspell.

Irregular Verbs

Base Form	Simple Past	Past Participle	Base Form	Simple Past	Past Participle
arise	arose	arisen	deal	dealt	dealt
be	was, were	been	dig	dug	dug
beat	beat	beat, beaten	do	did	done
become	became	become	draw	drew	drawn
begin	began	begun	drink	drank	drunk
bend	bent	bent	drive	drove	driven
bet	bet	bet	eat	ate	eaten
bind	bound	bound	fall	fell	fallen
bite	bit	bitten	feed	fed	fed
bleed	bled	bled	feel	felt	felt
blow	blew	blown	fight	fought	fought
breed	bred	bred	find	found	found
break	broke	broken	flee	fled	fled
bring	brought	brought	fly	flew	flown
build	built	built	forbid	forbade	forbidden
burst	burst	burst	forget	forgot	forgotten
buy	bought	bought	forgive	forgave	forgiven
catch	caught	caught	freeze	froze	frozen
choose	chose	chosen	get	got	got, gotten
cling	clung	clung	give	gave	given
come	came	come	go	went	gone
cost	cost	cost	grind	ground	ground
cut	cut	cut	grow	grew	grown

Base Form	Simple Past	Past Participle	Base Form	Simple Past	Past Participle
hang	hung	hung	sing	sang	sung
have	had	had	sink	sank	sunk
hear	heard	heard	sit	sat	sat
hide	hid	hidden	sleep	slept	slept
hit	hit	hit	slide	slid	slid
hold	held	held	slit	slit	slit
hurt	hurt	hurt	speak	spoke	spoken
keep	kept	kept	speed	sped	sped
kneel	knelt	knelt	spend	spent	spent
know	knew	known	spin	spun	spun
lay	laid	laid	split	split	split
lead	led	led	spread	spread	spread
leave	left	left	spring	sprang	sprung
lend	lent	lent	stand	stood	stood
let	let	let	steal	stole	stolen
lie	lay	lain	stick	stuck	stuck
light	lit	lit	sting	stung	stung
lose	lost	lost	stink	stank	stunk
make	made	made	strike	struck	struck
mean	meant	meant	swear	swore	sworn
meet	met	met	sweep	swept	swept
mistake	mistook	mistaken	swim	swam	swum
pay	paid	paid	swing	swung	swung
put	put	put	take	took	taken
quit	quit	quit	teach	taught	taught
read	read	read	tear	tore	torn
rid	rid	rid	tell	told	told
ride	rode	ridden	think	thought	thought
ring	rang	rung	throw	threw	thrown
rise	rose	risen	thrust	thrust	thrust
run	ran	run	understand	understood	understood
say	said	said	upset	upset	upset
see	saw	seen	wake	woke	woken
sell	sold	sold	wear	wore	worn
send	sent	sent	weep	wept	wept
set	set	set	win	won	won
shake	shook	shaken	wind	wound	wound
shoot	shot	shot	withdraw	withdrew	withdrawn
show	showed	shown	write	wrote	written
shut	shut	shut			

Section 2
PROBLEMS WITH VERBS

PRACTICE 2

Write the simple past and the past participle of the following verbs.

	Base Form	**Past Tense**	**Past Participle**
EXAMPLE:	lose	lost	lost
1.	cost		
2.	choose		
3.	drive		
4.	break		
5.	ring		
6.	bring		
7.	drink		
8.	think		
9.	build		
10.	become		
11.	grow		
12.	hit		
13.	sit		
14.	go		
15.	do		

Section 2
**PROBLEMS
WITH VERBS**

PRACTICE 3

The irregular past participles are underlined. Correct the twelve past participle errors, and write *C* above correct verbs.

EXAMPLE:

learned
Many acting students have <u>learn</u> the Stanislavsky method.

1.   Most people have <u>thinked</u> about becoming famous actors.

Acting seems like an easy thing to do; however, most successful

actors have <u>spend</u> years developing their craft.

2.   If you want to be an actor, take some acting classes. Acting is

<u>teached</u> in many colleges and private institutes. In acting classes,

students are <u>given</u> the basic techniques. Acting students are often

<u>telled</u> to read novels and plays as well as reference books and biographies. Most actors have <u>readed</u> many classic works.

3.   According to talent agent Myra Daly, after you have <u>took</u> your classes, you should develop your "persona." An actor is like a product; his or her persona is <u>selled</u>. Perhaps you have <u>became</u> the femme fatale, the bitter comic, the nice guy, the menacing criminal, or the girl next door. If you have <u>finded</u> a persona, it is easy for your agent to promote you. Although good actors can play many types of roles, even many well-known actors have <u>falled</u> into a "type." For example, some people say Renée Zellweger has not <u>shaken</u> her "girl next door" persona even though she has <u>been</u> in a variety of different roles. Some actors have <u>feeled</u> upset and frustrated when they have <u>been</u> typecast.

4.   The last step is to prepare your résumé and get references from teachers and other influential people who have <u>saw</u> your work. Traditionally, good acting jobs have <u>been</u> hard to find. If you persevere, and if you believe in your abilities, you have a chance at succeeding.

Section 2
**PROBLEMS
WITH VERBS**

The Present Perfect Tense: *Have/Has* + Past Participle

A past participle combines with *have* or *has* to form the **present perfect tense.** You can use this tense in two different circumstances.

- Use the present perfect to show that an action began in the past and continues to the present time. Some key words and expressions to look for are *since, for, ever, not, yet, so, far,* and *up to now.*

PAST   PRESENT PERFECT   NOW

Makeup artist Ella Chu **has lived** in Los Angeles since 1982.

■ Use the present perfect to show that one or more completed actions occurred at unimportant and unspecified past times. Some key words and expressions to look for are *already*, *once*, *twice*, *several times*, and *many times*.

PAST (unspecified past times)   NOW

Ella Chu **has returned** to her hometown in Canada many times.

Look at the difference between the past and the present perfect tenses in the following examples.

Simple past: In 2004, Jude Law <u>appeared</u> in *Alfie*.
(This event occurred at a known past time.)

Present perfect: Jude Law <u>has been</u> a popular actor for more than ten years.
(The action began in the past and continues to the present moment.)

He <u>has appeared</u> in more than twenty movies.
(The repeated past actions have occurred at unspecified past times.)

Section 2
PROBLEMS WITH VERBS

PRACTICE 4

Write the present perfect form of each verb in parentheses.

EXAMPLE:
Horror movies (be)___*have*___ ___*been*___ around for almost a century.

1. Some of America's most respected actors (appear) _____
_____ in horror movies. Since 1958, Jack Nicholson (act)
_____ _____ in many low-budget scary
movies with titles such as *The Cry Baby Killer*. Of course, he (have)
_____ _____ the chance to act in quality
horror movies, too, including Stanley Kubrick's film *The Shining*. Jack
Nicholson (be) _____ not _____ in a horror
movie since 1980.

2. For years, Johnny Depp (play) _____ _____
diverse roles, including that of a pirate, a detective, and an eccentric
journalist. However, did you know that he (be) _____ also
_____ in horror movies? Horror movie buffs who (see)
_____ _____ *Nightmare on Elm Street* may
recall that he appeared in the original 1984 film. Although Johnny Depp

is an American actor, he (live) _____ _____

in France since 2001.

3.   Brad Pitt (act) _____ _____ in horror

movies, too. He appeared in 1989's *Cutting Class*, which was about a maniac

who went on a killing spree. Jennifer Aniston (do) _____

also _____ roles in several low-budget features, including

the 1993 horror movie *The Leprechaun*. Leonardo DiCaprio (work)

_____ _____ professionally since he was

eleven years old, and he (be) _____ _____

in horror movies such as *Critters*, a 1991 flick about hairy little monsters.

Clearly, horror movies (provide) _____

_____ some of the most popular actors with essential

film experience.

Section 2
**PROBLEMS
WITH VERBS**

> ## Hint   Time Markers
>
> **Time markers** are words that indicate when an action occurred.
>
> **Simple Past Tense**
> To refer to an incident that occurred at a specific past time, use the following time markers.
>
> | | | | |
> |---|---|---|---|
> | yesterday | ago | when I was . . . | last (week, month, year . . .) |
> | in the past | in 1925 | during the 1990s | in the early days of . . . |
>
> <u>In 1989</u>, Spike Lee **directed** the film *Do the Right Thing*.
>
> **Present Perfect Tense**
> To refer to an action that began in the past and is still continuing, use the following time markers.
>
> | | | | |
> |---|---|---|---|
> | since | ever, never | so far | up to now |
> | not yet | for (a period of time up to now) | lately, recently | |
>
> I **have been** a Spike Lee fan <u>since 1990</u>.
>
> To refer to an action that occurred at an unspecified past time or past times, use the following time markers.
>
> | | | |
> |---|---|---|
> | many | several times | repeatedly | once, twice, three times |
>
> I **have watched** *Jungle Fever* <u>once</u> and *Malcolm X* <u>twice</u>.

PRACTICE 5

Underline the correct past or present perfect tense of each verb in parentheses.

EXAMPLE:

In recent years, visual effects (became, <u>have become</u>, has become) quite
sophisticated.

1. In the 1930s, special effects in movies (was, were, have been) ingenious.

2. In 1934, the movie *King Kong* (contained, has contained, have contained) sets with miniature skyscrapers and model airplanes.

3. To make the ape movie back then, *King Kong* artists (created, have created, has created) a model of the giant ape and then (moved, have moved, has moved) the model slightly every few frames of film.

4. Since 1934, audiences (appreciated, have appreciated, has appreciated) special effects.

5. Since the 1980s, computerized animation (became, have become, has become) more sophisticated.

6. In recent years, film studios (developed, have developed, has developed) eleven new animation techniques.

7. In 1995, *Toy Story* (was, has been, have been) the first completely computer-animated film.

8. Since then, many other computer-animated films (hit, have hit, has hit) movie screens.

9. Additionally, makeup (improved, have improved, has improved) since the 1980s.

10. Recently, the use of latex (allowed, have allowed, has allowed) makeup artists to create interesting effects.

11. In the 2001 film *The Lord of the Rings*, the hobbits (wore, have worn, has worn) large latex feet.

12. Since then, many actors (wore, have worn, has worn) latex masks and suits.

Section 2
PROBLEMS WITH VERBS

PRACTICE 6

Fill in the blanks with either the simple past or the present perfect verb tense.

EXAMPLE:

I (watch) ___have watched___ *General Hospital* since I was seven years old.

1.   Daytime soap operas (change) _____
a lot since they began. In the 1930s, soap companies (sponsor)
_____ daytime radio dramas. For example, the

program *The Guiding Light* (begin) _____ in
the 1930s as a radio show. Then, in the 1940s, the television network
CBS (film) _____ *The Guiding Light.* It (be)
_____ a popular daytime drama since then.

2.   Over the years, some well-known actors (appear) _____
_____ in soap operas. For example, Josh Duhamel
(act) _____ in *All My Children* when he
was younger.

3.   Soap operas are popular in many nations. Since 1980, Mexican
producers (sell) _____ soap operas to
nations around the world. Actress Salma Hayek (have) _____
_____ the lead role in the Mexican soap opera *Teresa*
in 1989. Her career (take) _____ off since
then. Since the late 1990s, Mexican soap operas (be)
_____ very popular in Russia.

4.   For many years, critics (complain) _____
that the actors in soap operas are too beautiful. However, since the
1960s, British studios (bring) _____ regular-
looking people to television screens. Since its debut, the long-running
soap opera *Coronation Street* (star) _____ a
variety of ordinary-looking actors. For more than fifty years, daytime
soap operas (be) _____ an essential part of
afternoon television schedules.

Section 2
**PROBLEMS
WITH VERBS**

The Past Perfect Tense: *Had* + Past Participle

The **past perfect tense** indicates that one or more past actions happened before
another past action. To form the past perfect, use *had* plus the past participle.

PAST PERFECT	PAST	NOW
▼	▼	▼

The movie **had started** when Vladimir arrived.

Notice the differences between the simple past, the present perfect, and the past perfect tenses.

Simple past:	Last night I <u>rented</u> the video *Lost in Translation.*
	(The action occurred at a known past time: *last night.*)
Present perfect:	I <u>have seen</u> most of Sophia Coppola's movies.
	(The actions have occurred at unspecified past times.)
Past perfect:	When Bill Murray appeared in *Lost in Translation,* he <u>had</u> already <u>acted</u> in several successful films.
	(All of the actions happened in the past, but Murray had acted in good movies before he appeared in *Lost in Translation.*)

Section 2
**PROBLEMS
WITH VERBS**

PRACTICE 7

Underline the correct verb tense. Choose either the simple past or the past perfect verb.

EXAMPLE:
When Charlie Chaplin left England, he (already acted, <u>had already acted</u>) in many productions.

1. Charles Spencer Chaplin was born into a London slum on April 16, 1889, and then, in 1910, he (arrived, had arrived) in America.

2. Because Chaplin (accumulated, had accumulated) a lot of acting experience in England, Mack Sennett hired him to work in Sennett comedies.

3. In 1920, Chaplin earned $10,000 per week, which was more than he (ever earned, had ever earned) in his life!

4. He (developed, had developed) his Tramp character, which was inspired by the poverty that he (experienced, had experienced).

5. When he turned twenty-six years old, he fulfilled a dream that he (had, had had) for several years.

6. Chaplin (acted, had acted) and (directed, had directed) in his own movies, and, in his films, he expressed sympathy for the poor.

7. FBI agents investigated Chaplin because they thought that he (joined, had joined) the Communist party.

8. At that time, Chaplin didn't have American citizenship even though he (spent, had spent) most of his professional life in the United States.

9. In 1952, the U.S. immigration authorities revoked Chaplin's re-entry permit after he (sailed, had sailed) for England.

10. Although Chaplin (made, had made) many successful American comedies, he (spent, had spent) most of the next years living in exile.

11. In 1972, Chaplin (returned, had returned) to America to accept an Academy Award for Lifetime Achievement.

12. When Chaplin passed away in 1977, his children knew that he (lived, had lived) an extremely full and rewarding life.

PRACTICE 8

Underline the correct tense of each verb in parentheses. You may choose the simple past, the present perfect, or the past perfect tense.

EXAMPLE:

For decades, parents (<u>have worried</u>, had worried) about the effects of television on children.

1.　In 1999, journalist Ellen Goodman (wrote, had written) the article "Going Thin in Fiji" about the influence of television on Fijian society. In 1994, people on the island of Fiji (appreciated, had appreciated) large women. In fact, big women (received, had received) many compliments.

2.　Then, in 1995, something (changed, has changed) on the island. That year, television (appeared, had appeared) for the first time in Fiji. Most islanders (never saw, had never seen) a TV show when the first televisions arrived.

3.　Since 1995, television (changed, has changed, had changed) the lives of people in Fiji. In recent years, young girls in Fiji (have watched, had watched) American television shows filled with thin actresses. The images (have affected, had affected) the self-esteem of Fijian women.

4.　In 1998, 75 percent of Fijian girls said that they (felt, have felt) too fat, yet most of those same girls (have never worried, had never worried) about their weight when they were younger. In that same interview, 62 percent of Fijian girls (said, had said) that they (dieted, had dieted) in the previous month. Clearly, media images influence the way people see themselves.

The Past Participle as an Adjective

A past participle can function as an adjective by modifying or describing the noun that follows it.

> He sat near the **broken** window.
> (*Broken* modifies *window*.)

Section 2
PROBLEMS WITH VERBS

PRACTICE 9

Write a logical past participle in each blank. Use the past participle form of the following verbs. Do not use the same verb more than once.

~~break~~	chip	fry	know	respect
bruise	dress	hide	qualify	tear

EXAMPLE:
She was shocked when she saw the ___broken___ lock.

1. Brad Pitt wore _____ clothing for his boxing scenes in the 1999 film *Fight Club*.

2. Some actors had _____ faces after the fight scenes.

3. Ed Norton, who narrated the movie, is a loved and _____ actor.

4. For some scenes, Brad Pitt removed the dental cap from his _____ front tooth.

5. Sometimes, tiny _____ microphones recorded the actors' dialogue.

6. Helena Bonham Carter played a poorly _____ woman named Marla Singer.

7. A _____ doctor was always on the set.

8. The caterers sometimes served _____ food.

9. The well-_____ movie won many awards.

The Passive Voice: *Be* + Past Participle

In sentences with the **passive voice**, the subject receives the action and does not perform the action. To form the passive voice, use the appropriate tense of the verb *be* + the past participle.

> passive
> Acting is the art of lying well. I <u>am **paid**</u> to tell elaborate lies.
> —Mel Gibson, actor

Look carefully at the following two sentences. Notice the differences between the active and the passive voice.

Active: Alejandro González Iñárritu **released** *21 Grams* in 2003.

(This sentence is active because the subject, Iñárritu, performed the action.)

Passive: The movie **was filmed** in 2002.

(This sentence is passive because the subject, the movie, did not perform the action.)

Active and Passive Voice

Verb Tenses	Active	Passive: *Be* + Past Participle
	The subject performs the action.	The subject receives the action.
Simple present:	They produce movies.	Movies <u>are</u> produced by them.
Present progressive:	are producing	<u>are being</u> produced
Simple past:	produced	<u>were</u> produced
Present perfect:	have produced	<u>have been</u> produced
Future:	will produce	<u>will be</u> produced
Modals:	can produce	<u>can be</u> produced
	could produce	<u>could be</u> produced
	should produce	<u>should be</u> produced

 **Avoid Overusing the Passive Voice**

Generally, try to use the active voice instead of the passive voice. The active voice is more direct and friendly than the passive voice. For example, read the next two versions of the same message.

Passive voice: Your questions about our cable service have been received by us. You will be contacted.

Active voice: We have received your questions about our cable service. Our sales representative will contact you.

PRACTICE 10

Decide whether each underlined verb is active or passive, and write *A* (for "active") or *P* (for "passive") above each verb.

EXAMPLE:

      P

The story <u>is based</u> on a fictional event.

1.   In the early 1940s, a radio <u>was owned</u> by almost every

American family. Then, in 1941, the first television show <u>was</u>

<u>broadcast</u>. In 1942, some veteran radio performers <u>predicted</u> that

television would never catch on. However, television <u>has been</u> a permanent fixture in American homes since then.

2. It is hard for us to imagine the excitement that <u>was felt</u> in the 1940s. In those years, one television <u>was watched</u> by many people, including friends and relatives of the owners. In fact, TV watching <u>was</u> a social event. For example, in 1946, the first TV sports extravaganza <u>was staged</u> by NBC. The program <u>featured</u> boxing great Joe Louis. The match <u>was seen</u> by about 150,000 people, or about 30 viewers per television. Today, the average television <u>is watched</u> by only 3 people.

Section 2
**PROBLEMS
WITH VERBS**

> ### Hint — The *by . . .* Phrase
>
> In many passive sentences, it is not necessary to write the *by . . .* phrase.
>
> The film was released in 2005 ~~by United Artists~~.
> The costumes were made in France ~~by costume designers~~.

PRACTICE 11

A. Complete the following sentences by changing each italicized verb to the passive form. Do not alter the verb tense. For some, you do not have to include the *by . . .* phrase in your sentences.

EXAMPLE:

Producers *make* movies all over the world.

Movies are made all over the world (by producers).

1. Fame *attracts* many ordinary people.

    Many ordinary people _____

2. People *view* movie stars as happy, exciting people.

    Movie stars _____

3. In 2005, a producer *offered* Maria Figuera a job in a movie.

    In 2005, Maria Figuera _____

4. The director *filmed* the movie in Boston.

    The movie _____

5. Perhaps people *will recognize* Maria in the future.

   Perhaps Maria _____

B. The following sentences are in the passive voice. Change the verbs in italics to the active voice, but do not alter the verb tense.

EXAMPLE:

Some actors *are paid* too much money by the studios.

Studios *pay some actors too much money.* _____

6. Famous actors *have been stalked* by overzealous fans.

   Overzealous fans _____

7. A few years ago, Orlando Bloom's privacy *was invaded* by journalists.

   A few years ago, journalists _____

8. Many complaints *are made* by actors about their lack of privacy.

   Many actors _____

9. Perhaps actors *should not be chased* by paparazzi.

   Perhaps paparazzi _____

10. Tabloids *are enjoyed* by some ordinary people.

    Some ordinary people _____

Section 2
**PROBLEMS
WITH VERBS**

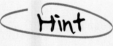 **Using the Passive Form**

In the passive voice, sometimes a form of the verb *be* is suggested but not written. The following sentence contains the passive voice.

Be is suggested:	Many movies **made** in the 1970s have become classics.
Be is written:	Many movies **that were** made in the 1970s have become classics.

PRACTICE 12

Correct twelve errors with past participles.

EXAMPLE:

    seen
I have <u>saw</u> *Bridget Jones's Diary* twice.

1.   Many successful novels have been turn into movies. *Bridget Jones's*

   Diary, publish in 1996, became a successful film with Renée

   Zellweger. Also, many screenwriters have been influence by the work of British novelist Jane Austin. Her book *Emma* was update in the film *Clueless*. In the story, the main character, portray by Alicia Silverstone, is a rich Beverly Hills teenager who likes matchmaking. The story was modernize by director Amy Heckerling.

2.   William Shakespeare has been the most influential writer of all time. Many movies have been based on his plays. *Othello*, for example, was transform into the urban drama *O*. The movie, produce in 2001, starred Mekhi Phifer as Odin, a talented black athlete who is envy by his peers. Odin falls in love with the headmaster's daughter. Hugo, the coach's son, is consume with jealousy, and he eventually causes Odin's downfall.

3.   Many studios hold the rights to contemporary best-sellers. In fact, as soon as a new book is embrace by the public, producers try to determine whether the book should become a movie. Definitely, future filmmakers will be influence by great novels.

Section 2
**PROBLEMS
WITH VERBS**

FINAL REVIEW

Correct fifteen errors with past participles or verb tense.

EXAMPLE:

               born
Jackie Chan was ~~borned~~ in 1954.

1.   Action star Jackie Chan has haved a difficult life. Chan was raised in Hong Kong. When he was a baby, he was nearly sold by his parents to pay his mother's hospital bill. In various interviews, Chan has said that the asking price was $26.

2.   In 1960, when Chan's parents worked in Australia, they left their son behind. Chan was enroll in the Peking Opera School.

The school had a reputation for developing talented singers, dancers, and acrobats. Chan was teached to do things such as leap over tables in a single bound and do headstands for hours at a time. The teachers were extremely strict, and Chan was hitted on a regular basis. He has stayed in the school until he was seventeen years old.

3.   Since his days with the Opera School, Chan enjoys a lot of success. In the early 1980s, Chan said that Bruce Lee had influence him. However, Chan knew that he did not have Lee's style. To separate himself from his idol, Chan incorporated comedy into his kung fu movies. A new movie genre was create in 1981: kung fu comedies.

4.   Since his debut in movies, Chan has broke almost every bone in his body. He has hurted himself many times over the years. In the 1980s, Hong Kong stunt actors did not wear protective equipment. When Chan was first hire in Hollywood, he was surprised that stunt actors wore shoulder pads and elbow pads.

5.   Jackie Chan's movies have not always maked a lot of money. Since the beginning of Chan's career, journalists have criticize his movies. However, Chan has undoubtedly create some of cinema's most surprising action sequences.

 The Writer's Room

Write a paragraph about one of the following topics. Identify all verbs, and verify that you have used and formed each verb correctly.

1. Some people spend more than four hours a day in front of the television. What steps can a television addict take to reduce his or her dependence on television?

2. Examine this photo. What are some terms that come to mind? Some ideas might be *reality television*, *talk show*, *couch potato*, or *sitcom*. Define a term or expression that relates to the photo.

Section 2
PROBLEMS WITH VERBS

CHECKLIST: PAST PARTICIPLES

When you edit your writing, ask yourself the next questions.

Do I use the correct form of past participles? Check for spelling errors in the following:

–regular past participles
–irregular past participles

Novels are often ~~turn~~ *turned* into films and the screenplays are ~~wrote~~ *written* by the author.

Do I use the present perfect tense correctly?

Since 2004, I ~~refused~~ *have refused* to watch television.

Do I use the past perfect tense correctly?

Ursula did not watch the movie because she ~~already saw~~ *had already seen* it.

Do I use the active and passive voice correctly? Check for overuse of the passive voice and errors with verb form and usage.

Last month, ~~the documentary was watched by many people.~~ *many people watched the documentary.*

Progressive Tenses

CHAPTER 11

Section Theme: **ENTERTAINMENT AND CULTURE**

CONTENTS

- Understanding Progressive Tenses
- Present Progressive
- Past Progressive
- Using Complete Verbs
- Other Progressive Forms

In this chapter, you will read about well-known artists and issues in the art world.

Grammar Snapshot

Looking at Progressive Tenses

In this excerpt from one of his letters, impressionist artist Vincent Van Gogh explains his progress in drawing. Notice the underlined progressive verbs.

> Recently I <u>have been drawing</u> from the model a good deal. And I have all kinds of studies of diggers and sowers, both male and female. At present I <u>am working</u> with charcoal and black crayon, and I have also tried sepia and watercolor. Well, I cannot say that you will see progress in my drawings, but most certainly you will see a change.

In this chapter, you will identify and write progressive verb tenses.

Understanding Progressive Tenses

A **progressive tense** indicates that an action was, is, or will be in progress. Progressive verb tenses always include a form of the verb *be* and the present participle (or *-ing* form of the verb).

Past progressive:	She <u>was trying</u> to finish her painting when the phone rang.
Present progressive:	Right now, Marg <u>is visiting</u> the Louvre.
Present perfect progressive:	She <u>has been working</u> as a painter for twelve years.
Future progressive:	Tomorrow morning, at 11 a.m., she <u>will be working</u>.

Section 2
PROBLEMS WITH VERBS

Present Progressive

The **present progressive** shows that an action is happening now or for a temporary period of time. Use this tense with key words such as *now*, *currently*, *at this moment*, *this week*, and *this month*.

This month, Tamayo <u>is exhibiting</u> several paintings in an art gallery.

Right now, Tamayo <u>is painting</u> a portrait.

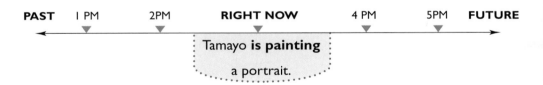

| PAST | 1 PM | 2PM | **RIGHT NOW** | 4 PM | 5PM | **FUTURE** |

Tamayo **is painting** a portrait.

Affirmative, Question, and Negative Forms

Review the present progressive forms of the verb *work*.

Affirmative	Question Form Move *be* before the subject.	Negative Form Add *not*.
I am She is He is It is } working. We are You are They are	Am I Is she Is he Is it } working? Are we Are you Are they	I am She is He is It is } not working. We are You are They are

> **Spelling of Present Participles (-ing Verbs)**

To form most regular present participles, add -ing to the base form of the verb.

    try–try**ing**   question–question**ing**

Exceptions

• When the regular verb ends in e, remove the e and add -ing.
    realize–realiz**ing**   appreciate–appreciat**ing**

• When the regular verb ends in a consonant + ie, change the ie to y and add -ing.
    lie–l**ying**   die–d**ying**

• When the regular verb ends in a consonant-vowel-consonant combination, double the last consonant and add -ing.
    stop–stop**ping**   jog–jog**ging**

• When a verb of two or more syllables ends in a stressed consonant-vowel-consonant combination, double the last consonant and add -ing.
    refer–refer**ring**   begin–begin**ning**

Note: If the two-syllable verb ends in an unstressed syllable, add just -ing.

    offer–offer**ing**   open–open**ing**

Section 2
**PROBLEMS
WITH VERBS**

PRACTICE I

Change each verb to the present progressive form.

EXAMPLE:

He runs. ___is running___

1. I paint. _____
2. We fly. _____
3. She studies. _____
4. You carry. _____
5. He writes. _____
6. I sculpt. _____
7. They fix. _____

8. I hope. _____
9. She plans. _____
10. We open. _____
11. It rains. _____
12. He shops. _____
13. It happens. _____
14. It begins. _____

Compare the Simple Present and the Present Progressive

Use the present progressive when an action is happening right now or for a temporary period of time. Use the simple present tense when the action happens habitually or when the action is a fact.

    Ellen is cleaning her brushes. (Action is in progress.)

    Ellen cleans her brushes. (Action is habitual or factual.)

 **A Common Tense Error**

Sometimes people overuse the progressive tense. If an action happens on a regular basis, do not use the progressive tense.

                                                      complain
Every week Tamayo's students ~~are complaining~~ about the number of assignments.

Section 2
**PROBLEMS
WITH VERBS**

PRACTICE 2

In each sentence, underline the correct verb tense. Then identify the action by writing *G* if it is a general fact or habit or *N* if it is happening now.

EXAMPLE:

This month, the Museum of Modern Art (exhibits, <u>is exhibiting</u>)
the work of Jackson Pollock.   N

1. The Barth Gallery usually (changes, is changing) exhibits each
   month.   _____

2. Right now, the gallery owner (negotiates, is negotiating)
   with a hot young artist.   _____

3. Usually, Fandra Chang (combines, is combining) photography,
   silkscreening, and painting.   _____

4. These days, she (works, is working) on a large cityscape
   photograph.   _____

5. Currently, she (tries, is trying) to sell her photos at the gallery.   _____

6. She (develops, is developing) new art techniques each year.   _____

7. Another artist, Barri Kumar, (experiments, is experimenting)
   with European and Asian images these days.   _____

8. He (doesn't want, isn't wanting) to give up his art career.   _____

9. Today he (works, is working) on a new piece.   _____

10. Both artists (are, are being) successful.   _____

Past Progressive

The **past progressive** indicates that an action was in progress at a specific past time. It can also indicate that an action in progress was interrupted.

Yesterday at 1 p.m., Tamayo <u>was cleaning</u> his studio.

Tamayo <u>was cleaning</u> his studio when the fire started.

The fire started.

He **was cleaning** his studio.

NOW

Affirmative, Question, and Negative Forms

Review the past progressive forms of the verb *work*.

Affirmative	**Question Form** Move *be* before the subject.	**Negative Form** Add *not*.
I was She was He was It was } working. We were You were They were	Was I Was she Was he Was it } working? Were we Were you Were they	I was She was He was It was } not working. We were You were They were

Section 2
PROBLEMS WITH VERBS

PRACTICE 3

Fill in the blanks with the past progressive forms of the verbs in parentheses.

EXAMPLE:

Diego Rivera (work) __was working__ on a mural when he met his future wife, artist Frida Kahlo.

1. Diego Rivera, Mexico's most famous muralist, (draw) _____ _____ on a wall when he discovered his passion for art.

2. At age 21, while he (visit) _____ friends in France, he discovered the artwork of Cézanne, Gauguin, and Matisse.

3. Later, Rivera and some friends (tour) _____ Italy when he developed a passion for fresco paintings.

4. In 1932, Americans (live) _____ through the Great Depression when Rivera visited.

5. Rivera (relax) _____ at home when Henry Ford called and asked Rivera to do a mural on the wall of the Detroit Institute of Fine Arts.

6. In Detroit, Rivera (work) _____ on his mural about American workers when critics first saw the image.

7. The artist and his assistants (paint) _____ the mural when some journalists arrived.

8. The next morning, the painter (read) _____ a Detroit newspaper when he saw a headline calling him a communist.

9. Later, while Rivera (return) _____ home to Mexico on a train, Henry Ford's son, Edsel, defended the mural.

10. Rivera said that he (try) _____ to depict the struggles of the working class when he created the mural.

Section 2
PROBLEMS
WITH VERBS

Using Complete Verbs

In progressive forms, always include the complete form of the helping verb *be*. Also make sure that the main verb ends in *-ing*.

                                is
Right now, the photographer examining the scene.

             taking
Adam was ~~take~~ a picture when I entered the room.

 **A Past Progressive Pitfall**

Do *not* use the past progressive to talk about past habits or about a series of past actions.

                   drew
Renoir ~~was drawing~~ pictures of his friends when he was younger.

PRACTICE 4

Correct eight past progressive errors.

EXAMPLE:

                                                 worked
When Vincent Van Gogh was a young man, he ~~was working~~ in many different jobs.

1.   When Van Gogh was twenty-five years old, he became a minister and worked in a poor coal-mining district in southwestern Belgium. One day, while he listening to a poor woman, he had an idea. He was deciding to stop eating. He

wanted to give his food money to the poor miners. On another

day, he noticed that a poor child wearing no shoes, so Van Gogh

gave away his own clothing and other possessions. Eventually, he

was fired. His superiors worried about Van Gogh's "excessive

enthusiasm."

Section 2
**PROBLEMS
WITH VERBS**

2.   Penniless and in despair, he isolated himself and began

to draw. His brother Theo was agreeing to support Vincent

financially. Soon, Van Gogh developed a passion for painting.

3.   Van Gogh settled in southern France where he wanted to

start an artists' colony. He invited a fellow artist, Paul Gauguin,

to come live with him. While the two men living together, they

engaged in some violent arguments. After one terrible fight, Van

Gogh was cutting off the lower portion of his own ear with a razor.

4.   Van Gogh voluntarily entered an asylum in Saint Remy.

While he was stay in the asylum, he created beautiful, vivid

pictures of wildflowers, fields, and houses. He spent twelve

months in the asylum. In December 1889, in a letter to his friend

Emile Bernard, Van Gogh said that his health improving a great

deal. Unfortunately, six months later, Van Gogh committed

suicide, and the world lost a great artist.

Other Progressive Forms

Many other tenses also have progressive forms. Review the information about
the future progressive and the present perfect progressive.

Future Progressive

The future progressive indicates that an action will be in progress at a future
time.

Tomorrow morning, do not disturb Tamayo because he <u>will be
working</u> in his studio.

Present Perfect Progressive

The present perfect progressive indicates that an action has been in progress, without interruption, from a past time up to the present.

Tamayo <u>has been painting</u> for eight hours, so he is very tired.

Nonprogressive Verbs

Some verbs do not take the progressive form because they indicate an ongoing state or a perception rather than a temporary action.

Section 2
**PROBLEMS
WITH VERBS**

Examples of Nonprogressive Verbs

Perception Verbs	Preference Verbs	State Verbs	Possession
hear	care*	believe	have*
feel*	desire	know	own
look*	hate	mean	
smell*	like	realize	
see	love	suppose	
seem	prefer	think*	
taste*	want	understand	

*Some verbs have more than one meaning and can be used in the progressive tense.

Compare the following pairs of sentences to see how these verbs are used.

Nonprogressive: He **has** two Picassos. (Expresses ownership)

I **think** it is expensive. (Expresses an opinion)

The photo **looks** good. (Expresses an observation)

Progressive: He **is having** a bad day.

I **am thinking** about it.

He **is looking** at the photo.

PRACTICE 5

Examine each underlined verb. Write *C* above correct verbs, and fix any verb errors. Some verbs may be incomplete or nonprogressive.

EXAMPLE:

     has

Miguel <u>been living</u> in Austin, Texas, for several years.

1. Currently, Miguel <u>working</u> in a contemporary art gallery.

2. Generally, he <u>is loving</u> his job, but this morning something strange

    happened.

3. Sharon, an installation artist, entered and dropped paper and envelopes on the floor while Miguel <u>was cleaning</u> the gallery.

4. Sharon <u>been working</u> as an artist for twelve years.

5. This week, she <u>is exhibit</u> an art project called *Lost Mail.*

6. Miguel <u>is wanting</u> to understand what a work of art is.

7. He <u>is liking</u> abstract paintings, and he <u>sees</u> the value in a lot of contemporary art.

8. However, he <u>is not understanding</u> what Sharon <u>is trying</u> to do.

9. According to Miguel, some contemporary artists <u>are preferring</u> to create art for each other rather than for the general public.

10. Sharon, however, <u>is believing</u> in the value of her art, and she <u>treats</u> each exhibit seriously.

Section 2
**PROBLEMS
WITH VERBS**

FINAL REVIEW

Correct fifteen errors with progressive verbs.

EXAMPLE:

was
Cindy Sherman living in New York in 1981 when she had her first photography show.

1.   One of America's most original photographers is Cindy Sherman. In 1980, Sherman was watch an old movie when she had an idea. She decided to take photographs of herself. In each photo, Sherman was dressing like a 1950s movie star. In 1981, her first one-woman exhibit, *Untitled Film Stills*, was a huge success. Later that year, while she preparing for her second show, she received a call from a museum curator in the Netherlands. So, in 1982, she had her first European show at the Stedelijk Museum in Amsterdam. Sherman's original photos now appear

in many museums. Presently, Sherman producing a new series of photos.

Section 2
**PROBLEMS
WITH VERBS**

2.   It is difficult for modern artists to find an original style. Alison Stone, a California-based art student, says, "While I working on a piece, I am always aware of influences. I am try to find my own style, but it is difficult." Stone adds, "We been studying art for two years. Each one of us is attempt to do original work."

3.   Stone is also interested in photography. These days, many contemporary photographers are move out of darkrooms and renting offices. Basically, digital technology is change the way that photographers work. Recently, Stone been spending more time in her office than in her studio. When asked what she is doing these days, Stone said, "Right now, I manipulating digital images. I creating surreal images. This new technology is exciting, and I am loving it." Stone has lofty career goals: "I am wanting to be as famous as Cindy Sherman."

 The Writer's Room

Write a paragraph about one of the following topics. Ensure that you have used and formed your verbs correctly.

1. Describe your favorite work of art. It could be a painting, a sculpture, a piece of architecture, or an illustration.

2. Choose a place on campus. You could go to the cafeteria, the lawn outside, a student center, the library, the hallway, or anywhere else on campus. Then, sit and observe what is going on around you. Use your five senses. Write a paragraph describing the things that are happening.

3. Irish author Oscar Wilde once said, "All art is useless." What is your opinion about art?

CHECKLIST: PROGRESSIVE VERBS

When you edit your writing, ask yourself the next questions.

Do I use the correct verb tenses? Check for the overuse or misuse of progressive forms.

> created
> Every year, Picasso ~~was creating~~ new types of paintings.

Are my progressive verbs complete? Check for errors in the following:

–the verb *be*

–incomplete *-ing* forms

> am posing   taking
> Right now, I ~~posing~~ beside a fountain and Christa is ~~take~~ a picture of me.

Section 2
**PROBLEMS
WITH VERBS**

CHAPTER 12

Other Verb Forms

Section Theme: **ENTERTAINMENT AND CULTURE**

CONTENTS

- Modals
- Nonstandard Forms: *Gonna, Gotta, Wanna*
- Conditional Forms
- Gerunds and Infinitives

In this chapter, you will read about cultural differences.

Grammar Snapshot

Looking at Other Verb Forms

In this excerpt from their book *Cultural Anthropology*, Carol R. Ember and Melvin Ember discuss body types. Notice the modals in bold print.

> There is a tendency in our society to view "taller" and "more muscled" as better, which **may reflect** the bias toward males in our culture. Natural selection **may have favored** these traits in males, but different ones in females. For example, because females bear children, selection **may have favored** earlier cessation of growth, and therefore less ultimate height, in females so that the nutritional needs of a fetus **would** not **compete** with the growing mother's needs.

In this chapter, you will identify and write modals, conditionals, gerunds, and infinitives.

Modals

Modals are helping verbs that express possibility, advice, and so on. Review the list of some common modals and their meanings.

Common Modal Forms

Modal	Meaning	Present Form	Past Form
can	Ability	Amir **can draw** very well.	**could draw**
could	Possibility	He **could sell** his work.	**could have sold**
may **might**	Possibility	Amir **may become** famous. Amir **might become** famous.	**may have become** **might have become**
must	Obligation Probability	We **must work** late. The buyers **must be** impatient.	**had to work**[*] **must have been**
should **ought to**	Advice	He **should see** a lawyer. He **ought to see** a lawyer.	**should have seen** **ought to have seen**
will	Future action or willingness	They **will buy** his products.	**would buy**
would	Desire	I **would like** to see his designs.	**would have liked**

[*]Exception: To show the past tense of *must* (meaning "obligation"), use the past tense of the regular verb *have to.*

Section 2
PROBLEMS WITH VERBS

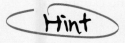 **Modal Forms Are Consistent**

Each modal has a fixed form. When the subject changes, the verb remains the same. In the example, *can* is the modal.

I **can** go.   You **can** go.   She **can** go.
We **can** go.   They **can** go.

PRACTICE 1

Read the following sentences. In the space, indicate the function of each underlined modal.

Ability   Possibility   Advice   Obligation   Desire

EXAMPLE:

People <u>ought to learn</u> about cultural differences.   *Advice*

1. You <u>could say</u> that culture is learned behavior that involves shared language, gestures, arts, attitudes, beliefs, and values.   _____

2. In the United States, people <u>may call</u> you by your first name.   _____

3. Many Americans <u>can speak</u> both English and Spanish.   _____

4. You <u>ought to remove</u> your shoes when you enter a home in India.   _____

5. In Japan, you <u>should bow</u> when you greet someone. _____

6. In Australia, instead of saying "Good day," you <u>could say</u> "G'day." _____

7. Many people <u>would like</u> to visit Australia. _____

8. In Great Britain, you <u>must drive</u> on the left side of the road. _____

9. In England, some people <u>might say</u> "I shall not" to mean "I will not." _____

10. In Japan, you <u>should not make</u> direct eye contact with people. _____

Section 2
PROBLEMS WITH VERBS

Present and Past Forms

For some modals, you must use a completely different word in the past tense. Review the differences between *can* and *could, will* and *would*.

Can and Could

Use *can* to indicate a present ability.

> Amir **can speak** Arabic.

Use *could* to indicate a past ability.

> When he was younger, he **could write** in Arabic, but he cannot do so now.

Also use *could* to show that something is possible.

> With globalization, some cultures **could disappear.**

Will and Would

Use *will* to discuss a future action from the present perspective.

> Myriam **will visit** Haiti next summer.

Use *would* to discuss a future action from a past perspective.

> Last month, I told her that I **would go** with her.

Also use *would* to indicate a desire.

> Myriam **would like** to visit her ancestral home.

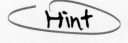   **Negative Forms of Modals**

Negative Forms

When you add *not* to modals, the full form consists of two words—for example, *could not* and *should not*. However, when you add *not* to the modal *can,* it becomes one word.

| **cannot** | should not | could not | would not | will not |

Contracted Forms

You can contract the negative forms of modals. Note that *will* + *not* becomes *won't.*

| can't | shouldn't | couldn't | wouldn't | won't |

PRACTICE 2

Underline the correct modal forms.

EXAMPLE:

Today, people (<u>can</u>, could) pass messages around the world instantly. For example, on December 26, 2003, when there was an earthquake in Iran, people in China (can, <u>could</u>) read about it the same day.

Section 2
**PROBLEMS
WITH VERBS**

1.   Right now, there are almost 7,000 languages in the world, but only about 10 percent of them are widely used. Some languages (will, would) definitely disappear in the next century. In Australia, for example, an aboriginal language called Lardil (will, would) likely disappear soon. Today, only a few people (can, could) speak that language.

2.   Norvil Richards, a linguistics professor at MIT, (will, would) like to preserve Lardil. In 2002, he visited Mornington Island in Australia, and he said that he (will, would) try to find as many Lardil speakers as possible. That year, he (can, could) find only a few elderly people who knew the language, and only one ninety-year-old man (can, could) speak the language fluently.

3.   Today, some island children (can, could) say a few insults in Lardil, but they (cannot, could not) conduct a conversation in their native language. Norvil Richards (cannot, could not) speak the language, but he (will, would) learn it in the future. In coming months, he (will, would) record the voices of people on Mornington Island.

4.   When you were a child, (can, could) you speak a language other than English? When my father was young, he (can, could) speak Russian, but he stopped using that language when he went to school. Today, my father (can, could) speak only English.

5.   Language is an important factor in defining culture. In the future, more languages (will, would) disappear unless new generations actively learn their native languages.

Past of *Should, Could,* and *Would*

To form the past tense of *should, could,* and *would,* add *have* + the past participle. Review the examples on the next page.

Before Anik and Richard went to Mexico, they **should have learned** a few words in Spanish. They **could have communicated** with the locals, and they **would have had** a better time.

 **Use Standard Past Forms**

Some people say *should of* or *shoulda*. These are nonstandard forms, and you should avoid using them, especially in written communication. When you write the past forms of *should, would,* and *could,* always include *have* + the past participle.

          should have
Before he did business in Japan, he ~~shoulda~~ learned about Japanese business etiquette.

Section 2
PROBLEMS WITH VERBS

PRACTICE 3

Correct eight errors with modal forms.

EXAMPLE:

      should have read
In high school, I ~~shoulda read~~ Chang's novel.

1. Jung Chang's historical novel, *Wild Swans: Three Daughters of China*, shoulda been made into a movie. Her fascinating novel describes the lives of her ancestors.

2. Chang's grandmother, Yu-fang, was born in 1909. Yu's father would of preferred a son. When Yu-fang was a child, her toes were broken and her feet were bound tightly in cloth. She would have liked to escape such a fate, but at that time, a woman with unbound feet wouldn't of found a husband. Yu-fang's younger sister was luckier. She could have suffer the same fate, but by 1917, the practice of foot-binding had been abandoned.

3. When she was fifteen, Yu-fang became a concubine for a much older man, General Xue. She would of liked to be a first wife instead of a concubine, but she had no choice. General Xue built a large house for Yu-fang, and he stayed with her for one week. Then he left her alone for the next six years. Yu-fang

would have like to spend time with her friends in the village, but she was confined to her house day and night.

4.   In one generation, life in China changed drastically. Yu-fang's daughter had more freedom than women of her mother's generation. She studied medicine, but she coulda studied something else. She married a soldier, but she coulda chosen another man for a husband.

Section 2
PROBLEMS WITH VERBS

Nonstandard Forms: *gonna, gotta, wanna*

Some people commonly say *I'm gonna, I gotta,* or *I wanna.* These are nonstandard forms, and you should not use them in written communication.

Write *going to* instead of *gonna.*

> My uncle is ~~gonna~~ going to help me learn Hungarian.

Write *have to* instead of *gotta.*

> I ~~gotta~~ have to learn to speak with my grandparents.

Write *want to* instead of *wanna.*

> Next year, I ~~wanna~~ want to go to Hungary.

Hint   **Forming the Main Verb**

When you use modals, make sure to form your main verb correctly. Use the base form of the verb that directly follows a modal.

> We **should** ~~visited~~ visit France. We **can** ~~going~~ go in March.

PRACTICE 4

Correct ten errors with nonstandard verbs and modal forms.

EXAMPLE:

You ~~are gonna learn~~ are going to learn about gestures.

1.   If you take a trip to a foreign country, you should studied nonverbal communication. According to experts, humans can expressing up to eighty percent of their thoughts nonverbally.

2.   One gesture can had different meanings in different countries. For example, in the United States, if you wanna indicate that you like something, you can join your thumb and forefinger into an "okay" gesture. However, you are gonna insult a waiter in France if you give the okay sign because the gesture means "zero" or "worthless." In Russia, use the okay sign only if you wanna insult someone.

3.   If you gotta go on a business trip to Brazil, do not use the thumbs up gesture because it is highly offensive. If you raise your forefinger and your pinky in Italy, you are gonna make someone very angry because the sign means that a man's wife is cheating on him. In Australia, if you wanna lose friends, make the V for "victory" sign with your palm facing towards you. It is Australia's most obscene gesture.

4.   Clearly, if you wanna get along with people from other cultures, it is a good idea to learn about their gestures.

Section 2
**PROBLEMS
WITH VERBS**

Conditional Forms

In a **conditional sentence,** there is a condition and a result. This type of sentence usually contains the word *if* and has two parts, or clauses. The main clause depends on the condition set in the *if* clause. There are three conditional forms.

First Conditional Form: Present or Possible Future
Use the "possible future" form when the condition is true or very possible.

If + present tense   ⟶   present or future tense

Condition (*if* clause)	**Result**
If he needs help,	he can call me.
If you visit Mexico,	you will see some amazing murals.

Second Conditional Form: Unlikely Present
Use the "unlikely present" form when the condition is not likely and probably will not happen.

If + past tense ⟶ *would* (expresses a condition)

could (expresses a possibility)

Condition (*if* clause)
If I knew how to speak Spanish,
If she were taller,

Result
I would live in Mexico for a year.
she could be a runway model.

> ⟨**Hint**⟩ **If I Were ...**
>
> In informal English, you occasionally hear *was* in the *if* clause. However, in academic writing, when the condition is unlikely, always use *were* in the *if* clause.
>
> If I **were** rich, I <u>would buy</u> a new car.
>
> If my sister **were** rich, she <u>would save</u> the money.

Section 2
**PROBLEMS
WITH VERBS**

Third Conditional Form: Impossible Past

Use the "impossible past" form when the condition cannot happen because the event is over.

If + past perfect tense ⟶ *would have* (+ past participle)

Condition (*if* clause)
If Bruno had invited me,
If I had spoken up sooner,

Result
I would have visited him.
I could have gone with him.

PRACTICE 5

In each case, identify the type of conditional sentence, and write *A*, *B*, or *C* in the blank.

A (possible future): If you ask me, I will help.
B (unlikely present): If you asked me, I would help.
C (impossible past): If you had asked me, I would have helped.

EXAMPLE:

If I could, I would travel to Spain.   <u>   B   </u>

1. If Carmen Morales were younger, she would return to school.   <u>   </u>

2. If she had known how difficult it is to make a career in dance,
   she would have found a different profession.   <u>   </u>

3. If you want to learn the tango, she will teach it to you.   <u>   </u>

4. According to Carmen, the tango is not difficult to master if you
   practice a lot.   <u>   </u>

5. If she had taken better care of herself, she would not have required
   knee surgery.   <u>   </u>

6. Today, if she takes it easy, she can teach three dance classes a week. _____

7. She would teach more classes if her doctor permitted it. _____

8. Perhaps if she had not danced with passion, she would have felt unfulfilled. _____

 **Avoid Mixing Conditional Forms**

Avoid mixing conditional forms. If you are discussing a past event, use the third conditional form. Do not mix the second and third forms.

             had been
If I ~~were~~ you, I would have done the assignment.

Section 2
PROBLEMS WITH VERBS

PRACTICE 6

Fill in the blanks with the correct forms of the verbs in parentheses.

EXAMPLE:

If you (plan) __plan__ to do business abroad, you will benefit from diversity training courses.

1.   Eric Zorn went on a business trip to Japan, and, unfortunately, he made some cultural etiquette errors. While there, he made eye contact with his hosts, and he got down to business immediately. If he (take) _____ more time for small talk, his hosts would have felt more comfortable. Also, if he had avoided direct eye contact, he (appear) _____ less aggressive. Basically, if he (understand) _____ the cultural differences, he would not have insulted his hosts.

2.   Roger Axtell is an international business traveler. He has written a book called *Do's and Taboos of Humor Around the World.* If Axtell (travel, not) _____ extensively, he would have been unable to write about cultural differences.

3.   Axtell has had some interesting experiences. A few years ago, when he visited Saudi Arabia, he met with an important customer. One day, the customer grabbed his hand while they were walking. In Saudi Arabia, hand-holding is a sign of friendship

and respect. If Axtell (pull) _____ away,

he would have offended his host. If he (know) _____

_____ in advance about the hand-holding, he

(feel, not) _____ so uncomfortable.

4.　　Many readers have appreciated learning from this author's

experiences. Axtell says that if he (be, not) _____

_____ so busy, he would write more books about

cultural diversity.

) **Problems with the Past Conditional**

In "impossible past" sentences, the writer expresses regret about a past event or expresses the wish that a past event had worked out differently. Avoid the following errors.

- Do not use *would have . . .* in the *if* clause. Instead, use the past perfect tense.
　　　　　had asked
　If you ~~would have asked~~ me, I would have traveled with you.

- Do not write *woulda* or *would of*. These are nonstandard forms. When you use the past forms of *should, would,* and *could,* always include *have* + the past participle.
　　　　　had done　　　　　　　　　*have*
　If you ~~would have done~~ the work, you would ~~of~~ passed the course.

PRACTICE 7

Correct ten errors with conditional forms.

EXAMPLE:

　　　　　　　　　　　　　　would have
If Mawlid had stayed in Somalia, his life ~~woulda~~ been different.

1.　　In 1994, Mawlid and Myriam Abdul moved to San Diego

from Somalia. If he would have had a choice, Mawlid would

have stayed in his native country. He misses his mother and his

extended family.

2.　　Mawlid is impressed by the respectful treatment of the

elderly in Somalia: "My grandparents were treated with love

and attention until their deaths. If my grandparents had moved to the United States, they would of been surprised by the treatment of old people. If they would have visited a typical nursing home, they woulda been shocked."

3. Mawlid's wife, Myriam, would not like to live in Somalia again, even if she was able to. She says, "In the United States, if I want to study or work, I can do it easily. However, if I would have stayed in Somalia, my brothers and aunts would have expected me to take care of them. When I was a child, my mother had to take care of my uncle's children because he wanted them to be educated in the city. He didn't ask my mother for permission. If she had refused to care for her nephews, family members woulda been angry with her. If she would have had a choice, she would have preferred a quieter life."

4. Mawlid says that he will return to his native country if he amassed enough money because he misses his close-knit family. If Mawlid and Myriam wanted to resolve their differences, they will have to compromise.

Gerunds and Infinitives

Sometimes a main verb is followed by another verb. The second verb can be a gerund or an infinitive. A **gerund** is a verb with an *-ing* ending. An **infinitive** consists of *to* and the base form of the verb.

Verb + gerund:	We <u>finished</u> **reading** *Wild Swans*.
Verb + infinitive:	I <u>want</u> **to write** about it.

Using Gerunds

Some verbs in English are always followed by a gerund. Do not confuse gerunds with progressive verb forms. Compare a progressive verb and a gerund.

Verb:	Julie is studying now.	(*Studying* is in the present progressive form. Julie is in the process of doing something.)
Gerund:	Julie <u>finished</u> **studying**.	(*Studying* is a gerund that follows *finish*. After *finish*, you must use a gerund.)

Some Common Verbs and Expressions Followed by Gerunds

acknowledge	discuss	practice
adore	dislike	quit
appreciate	enjoy	recall
avoid	finish	recollect
can't help	involve	recommend
can't stand	keep	regret
complete	loathe	resent
consider	mention	resist
delay	mind	risk
deny	miss	(be) worth
detest	postpone	

Using Prepositions Plus Gerunds

Many verbs have the structure **verb + preposition + object.** If the object is another verb, the second verb is a gerund.

> I am excited <u>about</u> **traveling** to Greece.

Some Common Verbs Followed by Prepositions Plus Gerunds

accuse of	excited about	forgive <u>me</u> for	prohibit from
apologize for	enthusiastic about	insist on	succeed in
be good at	feel like	(be) interested in	think about
discourage <u>him</u>* from	fond of	look forward to	(be) tired of
dream of	forbid <u>them</u> from	prevent <u>him</u> from	warn <u>her</u> about

*Certain verbs must have a noun or pronoun before the preposition. Here, the pronouns are underlined.

Using Infinitives

Some verbs are followed by the infinitive (*to* + base form of verb).

> Helen wants **to travel** with me.

> (*To travel* is an infinitive that follows the verb *wants*.)

Some Common Verbs Followed by Infinitives

afford	decide	manage	seem
agree	demand	mean	swear
allow	deserve	need	threaten
appear	expect	plan	volunteer
arrange	fail	prepare	want
ask	have	pretend	wish
(be) best	hesitate	promise	would like
claim	hope	refuse	
consent	learn		

Using Gerunds or Infinitives

Some common verbs can be followed by gerunds or infinitives. Both forms have the same meaning.

begin	continue	hate	like
love	prefer	start	try

Elaine <u>tried</u> **to eat** snails.

Elaine <u>tried</u> **eating** snails.

(Both sentences have exactly the same meaning.)

Section 2
PROBLEMS WITH VERBS

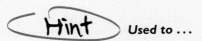

> **Hint**   *Used to . . .*
>
> You can follow *used to* with a gerund or an infinitive, but there is a difference in meaning.
>
> • *Used to* + infinitive expresses a past habit.
>
>   Rowan does not smoke now, but she <u>used to</u> **smoke**.
>
> • *Be used to* + gerund expresses something you are accustomed to.
>
>   Rowan has been on her own for years, so she <u>is used to</u> **living** alone.

PRACTICE 8

Correct any errors in the underlined gerund and infinitive forms. If the verb is correct, write *C* above it. (Be careful. You may have to change the preposition before the gerund.)

EXAMPLES:

                                    to have
Gustavo and Beth expect ~~having~~ a long mariage.

1. Gustavo is from Mexico City and Beth is from California. They got married in 2003, and they <u>hope having</u> a small family.

2. The couple rents an apartment near San Diego, but they <u>dream to own</u> a house one day.

3. Every weekend, Beth <u>enjoys to hike</u> in the woods, but Gustavo <u>is not interested in doing</u> outdoor activities.

4. Beth <u>is enthusiastic about creating</u> a large garden in their yard.

5. Gustavo does not like gardens. He <u>is used to have</u> a small cement courtyard, and he <u>does not want to spend</u> any time pulling weeds.

6. They have other differences as well. Gustavo <u>likes cooking</u> spicy food, but Beth <u>refuses eating</u> hot and spicy dishes.

7. Beth <u>avoids to be</u> in the house while Gustavo <u>practices playing</u> Mexican folk songs.

8. In spite of the differences, they <u>are learning respecting</u> each other.

9. For example, they do not share musical tastes, but it <u>does not prevent them to enjoy</u> a night out at local music clubs.

10. Although they have different backgrounds, Beth and Gustavo <u>are looking forward to have</u> a long life together.

Section 2
**PROBLEMS
WITH VERBS**

FINAL REVIEW

Identify and correct fifteen verb errors in the next letter.

EXAMPLE:

going to
You are ~~gonna~~ enjoy reading this letter.

Dear Anne,

1   I gotta tell you about my adventures. As you know, I recently returned from a trip to England. While there, I made some mistakes. If I had understood British English, I coulda avoided some problems. I shoulda found out about British expressions and customs.

2   For example, soon after I arrived, I met a man on the airport bus. When I mentioned where I was staying, he chuckled and called my hotel a "tip." I had no idea what he meant, and although I shoulda asked him to explain himself, I didn't bother. Unfortunately, when I arrived at the hotel, I learned that the term means "a big mess." If I had understood the word beforehand, I certainly would of avoided that hotel.

3   When I arrived at my hotel, I was given the keys to a tiny room on the fourth floor. It was hard to climb the stairs everyday, but I could doing it.

When I looked at the room, I noticed that the wallpaper was peeling and the bathroom was dirty. Clearly, I shoulda done more research before making the reservations. If you wanna visit England one day, definitely ask someone to recommend a hotel.

Section 2
PROBLEMS WITH VERBS

4   The next day, when I went into a restaurant, I noticed an item on the menu called "Bubble and Squeak." I shoulda tried the item, but I did not wanna eat something unfamiliar. After I ordered, I learned that it was only cabbage and potatoes. After my meal, I asked the waiter to direct me to the ladies' room. The waiter looked suspicious. If I would have asked for the "loo," I would have been directed to the appropriate place.

5   In spite of my language blunders, I thoroughly enjoyed my stay. If I had the chance to visit England again, I will take it. In fact, I look forward going there again. I know that you are gonna visit England soon, so call me before you leave, and I promise giving you some more information.
Best regards,

Julia

The Writer's Room

Write a paragraph about one of the following topics. Ensure that you have formed any modals or conditionals correctly.

1. What can people learn when they interact with other cultures? List some things.
2. Think about someone you know who is from another culture. How are you and that person similar or different?

CHECKLIST: OTHER VERB FORMS

When you edit your writing, ask yourself these questions.

Do I use the correct modal forms? Check for errors in the following:

–*will* vs. *would* and *can* vs. *could*

–past forms

       have
I should ~~of~~ packed an umbrella when I visited Ireland.

Do I use the correct conditional forms? Check for errors in the following:

–possible future forms ("If I meet . . . , I will go . . .")

–unlikely present forms ("If I met . . . , I would go . . .")

–impossible past forms ("If I had met . . . , I would have gone . . .")

    had
If I ~~would have~~ more money, I would stay in good hotels.

Do I use the correct gerund or infinitive form?

    traveling
I enjoy ~~to travel~~ during my spring break.

Section 2
**PROBLEMS
WITH VERBS**

 The Writers' Circle

Work with a group of about three students. You need one sheet of paper for this activity.

STEP 1   Write down as much as you know about the life of a famous entertainer (such as a musician, an artist, an athlete, or an actor). Do not mention the name of the entertainer. Write at least six sentences about the person.

> **Example:**   She was born in Hawaii, but she grew up in Australia. She sang in a group when she was a teenager. She married a famous actor. Their divorce was covered extensively. She won an Academy Award. She is very tall and thin.

STEP 2   Read your sentences aloud to another group of students. They must guess who your mystery person is. If they cannot guess, continue to give them more clues.

READING LINK

Entertainment and Culture
To read more about entertainment and culture, see the following essays:

"Sports and Life: Lessons to Be Learned" by Jeff Kemp (page 430)

"The Appalling Truth" by Dorothy Nixon (page 438)

"The New Addiction" by Josh Freed (page 442)

"The Culture War" by Linda Chavez (page 444)

 See Chapter 12 on the Visualizing Writing CD-ROM for an additional audio and animated mini-lecture on **Regular and Irregular Verbs**.

CHAPTER 13

Subject-Verb Agreement

Section Theme: **BELIEFS**

CONTENTS

- Basic Subject-Verb Agreement Rules
- Verb Before the Subject
- More Than One Subject
- Special Subject Forms
- Interrupting Words and Phrases

In this chapter, you will read about mysteries and urban legends.

Grammar Snapshot

Looking at Subject-Verb Agreement

David A. Locher is the author of *Collective Behavior*. In the following excerpt from his book, he describes an urban legend. The subjects are in bold print, and the verbs are underlined.

> An **urban legend** <u>gives</u> specific details about an **event** that <u>has</u> supposedly <u>occurred</u>. For example, there <u>is</u> a **legend** about a **man** who <u>wakes</u> up in a bathtub full of ice. **He** <u>finds</u> a note left by the attractive woman **he** <u>met</u> at a party or bar the night before. **She** <u>has</u> purportedly <u>stolen</u> his kidney. This **urban legend** <u>gives</u> specific **details** that <u>may change</u> every time the **story** <u>is told</u>.

In this chapter, you will practice making subjects and verbs agree.

Basic Subject-Verb Agreement Rules

Subject-verb agreement simply means that a subject and verb agree in number. A singular subject needs a singular verb, and a plural subject needs a plural verb.

Singular subject: Jay believes in urban legends.

Plural subject: The **stories** have strange endings.

Simple Present Tense

Writers use **simple present tense** to indicate that an action is habitual or factual. Review the rules for simple present tense agreement.

- Add -*s* or -*es* to the verb when the subject is *he, she, it,* or the equivalent (*Mike, Ella, Texas*). This is also called the **third-person singular form.**

    Mr. Roy believes in ghosts. (one person)

    The **museum** displays many exhibits. (one place)

    Perhaps a **giant ape** roams the forests (one thing)
    of the northwestern United States.

- When the subject is *I, you, we, they,* or the equivalent (*the Smiths, the books, Jay and I*), do not add an ending to the verb.

    The moment **we** want to believe something, **we** suddenly see all the arguments for it, and become blind to the arguments against it.

    —George Bernard Shaw

To see how these rules work, review the forms of the verb *run.*

Section 3
VERB AGREEMENT AND CONSISTENCY

Present Tense of *Run*

	Singular Forms	Plural Forms
First person:	I run	We run
Second person:	You run	You run
Third person:	He runs	They run
	She runs	
	It runs	

PRACTICE 1

In each sentence, underline the subject and circle the correct verb. Make sure that the verb agrees with the subject.

EXAMPLE:

Some stories (seem, seems) fantastic.

1. Generally, an urban legend (appear, appears) mysteriously.

2. The stories (spread, spreads) rapidly.

3. A particular legend (deal, deals) with a common fear.

4. For example, in one story a hitchhiker (vanish, vanishes).

5. Usually, the speaker (say, says), "This happened to a friend of a friend."

6. Many urban legends (focus, focuses) on insects or other creatures.

7. For example, a woman (buy, buys) a cactus, and she (take, takes) it home.

8. Suddenly, the woman (hear, hears) a humming sound, and she (call, calls) the plant store.

9. The store owner (tell, tells) the woman to put her plant outside.

10. She (put, puts) the cactus in her backyard.

11. Suddenly, the cactus (split, splits) in two and tarantulas pour out of it.

12. Many people (believe, believes) such urban legends.

Troublesome Present-Tense Verbs: *Be, Have, Do*

Some present-tense verbs are formed in special ways. Review the verbs *be, have,* and *do.* Be particularly careful when writing these verbs.

Section 3
**VERB AGREEMENT
AND CONSISTENCY**

	Be	**Have**	**Do**
Singular Forms			
First person:	I am	I have	I do
Second person:	You are	You have	You do
Third person:	He **is**	He **has**	He **does**
	She **is**	She **has**	She **does**
	It **is**	It **has**	It **does**
Plural Forms			
First person:	We are	We have	We do
Second person:	You are	You have	You do
Third person:	They are	They have	They do

PRACTICE 2

Fill in each blank with the correct form of *be, have,* or *do.*

EXAMPLE:

I _____*have*_____ a book about urban legends. The stories_____*are*_____ not true.

1.   Many urban legends _____ scary. I _____ not a superstitious person, but I _____ a good friend who _____ very gullible. My friend, Anthony, _____ tax preparation for a pet store in New York City. The store _____ baby alligators for sale.

2.   Anthony _____ sure that some customers buy

alligators as pets. The alligators _____ from Florida.

Usually, after a few months, the alligators _____ too

big to fit into their aquariums. Customers _____ an

odd thing: they throw the alligators into the sewers. According

to Anthony, alligators _____ alive in New York City's

sewer system. I _____ not believe this urban legend.

I _____ to see things before I believe them.

PRACTICE 3

In the following paragraphs, the verbs are underlined. Identify and correct ten
subject-verb agreement errors. Write *C* above the correct verbs.

EXAMPLE:

      has
Mario <u>have</u> strange opinions about urban legends.

1.   Urban legends <u>is</u> not new. The "earwig" legend <u>is</u> over 1,000

years old. In the story, an earwig <u>have</u> an unusual idea. It <u>climb</u>

into the ear of a woman to lay eggs. The eggs <u>hatch</u>, and tiny

earwigs <u>eats</u> the brain of the woman. Perhaps people <u>repeat</u> this

story because they <u>is</u> afraid of insects. Personally, I <u>is</u> not afraid

of the creatures.

2.   Urban legends <u>serve</u> a purpose. They <u>is</u> about ordinary people

in frightening situations, and each legend <u>warn</u> us about a possible

danger. Sometimes, a story <u>have</u> a moral. Additionally, when

people <u>speaks</u> about a scary or traumatic event, they <u>release</u> their

collective anxiety.

Agreement in Other Tenses
Simple Past Tense

Writers use the **simple past tense** to indicate that an action was completed at a
past time. In the past tense, all verbs except *be* have one form.

Regular: I worked.   He worked.   We worked.   You worked.   They worked.
Irregular: I ate.   He ate.   We ate.   You ate.   They ate.

Exception: In the past tense, the only verb requiring subject-verb agreement is the verb *be*. It has two past forms: *was* and *were*.

Past Tense of Be

Was	Were
I was	You were
He was	We were
She was	They were
It was	

GRAMMAR LINK

For more information about using the present perfect, see Chapter 10.

Section 3
VERB AGREEMENT AND CONSISTENCY

Present Perfect Tense

The present perfect tense is formed with *have* or *has* before the past participle. If the subject is third-person singular, always use *has*.

She <u>has</u> <u>finished</u> a book about Native American legends. **I** <u>have</u> <u>read</u> it.

Other Tenses

When writing in most other verb tenses and in modal forms (*can, could, would, may, might . . .*), use the same form of the verb with every subject.

Future	Past Perfect	Modals
I <u>will</u> read.	I <u>had</u> finished.	I <u>can</u> go.
She <u>will</u> read.	She <u>had</u> finished.	She <u>should</u> go.
He <u>will</u> read.	He <u>had</u> finished.	He <u>might</u> go.
They <u>will</u> read.	They <u>had</u> finished.	They <u>could</u> go.

PRACTICE 4

In each sentence, underline the subject and circle the correct verb. Make sure that the subject and verb agree.

EXAMPLE:
Some <u>mysteries</u> (have, has) been solved.

1. Benjamin Radford (have, has) written many books, including *Hoaxes, Myths, and Manias: Why We Need Critical Thinking*.

2. Most mysteries (is, are) not mysterious at all, according to Radford.

3. For example, perhaps giant apelike creatures (live, lives) in the mountainous region between British Columbia and California.

4. Radford (have, has) visited the sites where Bigfoot sightings were reported, but he (is, are) not convinced that the evidence is legitimate.

5. He (give, gives) interesting reasons for his opinion.

6. First, when a giant ape (die, dies), there should be a dead body, yet no bodies (have, has) been found.

7. Second, many people (claim, claims) that they have seen Bigfoot, but these eyewitness testimonies (is, are) likely unreliable.

8. Sometimes a large mammal may (look, looks) like a giant ape.

9. Finally, believers (refer, refers) to sightings of giant footprints, but in 2000, a man named Ray Wallace admitted that he and his son made fake footprints.

10. They (was, were) just making a joke, and they (was, were) surprised when many people believed them.

11. Many people (continue, continues) to believe in Bigfoot.

12. Radford (admit, admits) that the legend will probably continue for centuries.

Section 3
**VERB AGREEMENT
AND CONSISTENCY**

Verb Before the Subject

Usually the verb comes after the subject, but in some sentences, the verb comes *before* the subject. In such cases, you must still ensure that the subject and verb agree.

Sentences Beginning with *There* or *Here*

When a sentence begins with *there* or *here*, the subject always follows the verb. *There* and *here* are not subjects.

> V   S   V   S
> Here is a new **book** about Atlantis. There are many new **theories** about it.

Questions

In most questions, the helping verb, or the verb *be*, appears before the subject. In the next examples, the main verb is *be*.

> V   S   V   S
> Where is the mysterious **island?** Was Plato's **story** about Atlantis fictional or factual?

In questions in which the main verb is not *be*, the subject usually agrees with the helping verb.

> H   S   V   H   S   V
> Where does the sunken **city** rest? Do **scientists** have any answers?

PRACTICE 5

In each sentence, underline the subject and circle the correct verb.

EXAMPLE:

(Have, Has) you ever read *Lost Horizon*, by James Hilton?

1. (Do, Does) the book *Lost Horizon* appear on Web sites?

2. (Have, Has) many authors written about utopias?

3. (Is, Are) there real places that are idyllic?

4. (Is, Are) Shangri-la a real place?

5. Why (do, does) an American woman visit Shangri-la?

6. (Do, Does) she understand the valley's residents?

7. Why (do, does) she want to know about their religious beliefs?

8. (Is, Are) her tour guide helpful?

9. When (does, do) he explain his philosophy?

10. Why (do, does) the lamas devote themselves to contemplation and the pursuit of wisdom?

Section 3
**VERB AGREEMENT
AND CONSISTENCY**

PRACTICE 6

Correct any subject-verb agreement errors. If a sentence is correct, write *C* in the blank.

EXAMPLE:

                is
There ~~are~~ a fascinating woman in my neighborhood.   _____

1. There is many stories about Anna Madeo.   _____

2. Do she see the future?   _____

3. There are five customers waiting for Anna to read their palms.   _____

4. Is her predictions often correct?   _____

5. There is some strange coincidences.   _____

6. Do that woman have a special gift?   _____

7. Do you know Anna Madeo?   _____

8. There is many possible reasons for her popularity.   _____

More Than One Subject

There are special agreement rules when there is more than one subject in a sentence.

- When two or more subjects are joined by *and*, use the plural form of the verb.
    And: **Florida, Bermuda,** and **Puerto Rico** <u>form</u> the Bermuda Triangle.
- When two or more subjects are joined by *or* or *nor*, the verb agrees with the subject that is the closest to it.

    Nor: Neither Clara Jackson nor her **children** <u>like</u> to fly in airplanes.

    Or: Either the children or **Clara** <u>is</u> claustrophobic.

PRACTICE 7

In each sentence, underline the subject and circle the correct verb. Make sure the verb agrees with the subject.

EXAMPLE:

There (is, are) an interesting <u>legend</u> about a ship that disappeared.

1. In 1872, the *Mary Celeste* (was, were) launched from New York.

2. There (was, were) ten people on the ship when it left port.

3. Later, the ship (was, were) found floating in the sea, but no survivors (was, were) on board.

4. Neither the captain nor the crew members (was, were) ever found.

5. Today, there (is, are) many versions of the story.

6. Many theories (have, has) been put forward.

7. Maybe strong winds or a giant storm (was, were) responsible for the missing crew members.

8. Perhaps either one or several crew members (was, were) violent and murderous.

9. Maybe man-eating monsters (live, lives) in the sea.

10. (Do, Does) you (know, knows) the true story?

Special Subject Forms

Some subjects are not easy to identify as singular or plural. Two common types are indefinite pronouns and collective nouns.

Indefinite Pronouns

Indefinite pronouns refer to a general person, place, or thing. Carefully review the following list of indefinite pronouns.

Indefinite Pronouns

Singular:	another	each	nobody	other
	anybody	everybody	no one	somebody
	anyone	everyone	nothing	someone
	anything	everything	one	something
Plural:	both	many	others	
	few	several		

Section 3
**VERB AGREEMENT
AND CONSISTENCY**

Singular Indefinite Pronouns

In the following sentences, the subjects are singular, so they require third-person singular verb forms.

> Almost **everyone** <u>has</u> theories about the Bermuda Triangle.

> According to Norm Tyler, **nothing** <u>proves</u> that the Bermuda Triangle is dangerous.

Plural Indefinite Pronouns

Both, *few*, *many*, *others*, and *several* are all plural subjects. The verb is always plural.

> The two survivors talked about their journey. **Both** <u>have</u> frequent nightmares.

> **Many** <u>were</u> still on the boat when it mysteriously disappeared.

PRACTICE 8

Underline the subject and circle the correct verb in each sentence.

EXAMPLE:

<u>Everybody</u> (has, have) an opinion on the role of religion in schools.

1.   In 1859, Charles Darwin wrote *On the Origin of Species.* In Victorian England, Darwin's ideas (was, were) regarded as a threat to Christianity. Years later, the theory of evolution (was, were) still controversial.

2.   In 1925, John Scopes (was, were) accused of breaking the "Butler Act" by teaching Tennessee biology students about evolution. According to the Butler Act, if anybody (teach, teaches) a theory that denies the story of divine creation,

it is unlawful. The Scopes Monkey Trial lasted for fifteen days, but nobody (was, were) prepared for defense lawyer Clarence Darrow's decision. He asked the jury to find his client guilty because he wanted to take the case to the Tennessee supreme court.

3.   Today, there (is, are) debates about the teaching of religion and science in schools. In this country, one controversial issue (is, are) school prayer. Some (think, thinks) that students should pray every day under the direction of a teacher. Others (disagree, disagrees) and (argue, argues) that parents, not schools, should teach religion and morality.

4.   If someone (say, says) that the United States is a multicultural society with a variety of religious beliefs, then someone else (reply, replies) that it was founded on a Christian theistic base and that school prayer is necessary. Certainly, everyone (has, have) an opinion about this issue.

Section 3
VERB AGREEMENT
AND CONSISTENCY

Collective Nouns as Subjects

Collective nouns refer to a group of people or things. The group acts as a unit. Here are some common collective nouns.

army	class	crowd	group	population
association	club	family	jury	public
audience	committee	gang	mob	society
band	company	government	organization	team

Generally, each group acts as a unit, so you must use the singular form of the verb.

The **public** <u>loves</u> to hear about urban myths.

PRACTICE 9

Underline the subject of each sentence. Then, circle the correct form of the verb.

EXAMPLE:

In many communities throughout the world, <u>people</u> ((believe), believes) in ghosts.

1.   Scientists and other rational thinkers (is, are) likely to question the existence of a spirit world. However, even skeptics (admit, admits) that they may not know the whole truth.

2.   In *The Power of Myth*, Joseph Campbell (state, states), "A fairy tale is the child's myth. There (is, are) proper myths for proper times of life. As you (grow, grows) older, you (need, needs) a sturdier mythology." Every society (invent, invents) stories to try to explain basic truths.

3.   In the Chinese lunar tradition, the seventh month (is, are) "ghost month." During ghost month, a gate (separate, separates) the spirit world from the normal world. It (open, opens), and the spirits (enter, enters) the human world. Buddhist priests (pray, prays) to subdue the spirits. A band (play, plays) music to welcome the spirits, and the crowd (listen, listens) with reverence. In China, a typical family (welcome, welcomes) the ghosts during ghost month.

4.   Each nation (have, has) its own version of ghost stories. As long as everyone (have, has) questions about death and the afterlife, religious scholars will continue to examine the spirit world.

Section 3
**VERB AGREEMENT
AND CONSISTENCY**

Interrupting Words and Phrases

Words that come between the subject and the verb may confuse you. In these cases, look for the subject and make sure that the verb agrees with the subject. To help you see the interrupting words in the following two examples, we have put parentheses around the words that come between the subject and verb.

Some old **legends** (about vampires and spirits) <u>continue</u> to scare people.

A **student** (in my creative writing class) <u>writes</u> updated vampire stories.

 **Identify Interrupting Phrases**

To make it easier to find subject-verb agreement errors as you edit for subject-verb agreement, place parentheses around any words that separate the subject and the verb in the sentence. Then you can see whether the subjects and verbs agree.

Many **directors**, (including the late Stanley Kubrick), <u>have made</u> horror films.

When interrupting phrases contain *of the,* the subject appears before the phrase.

One (of the neighbors) <u>knows</u> everybody's secrets.

PRACTICE 10

Place parentheses around any words that come between each subject and verb. Then, circle the correct form of the verb.

EXAMPLE:

Anne Rice, (a popular author,) write / (writes) about vampires.

1. One of this era's most enduring legends <u>is / are</u> the Dracula legend.

2. Tales about vampires <u>was / were</u> common in Eastern Europe and India.

3. The story about the blood-drinking human <u>was / were</u> especially popular after Bram Stoker wrote the novel *Dracula* in 1897.

4. Current myths about vampires <u>emphasize / emphasizes</u> the creature's aversion to sunlight, garlic, and the symbol of the cross.

5. Some believers in Eastern Europe <u>surround / surrounds</u> their homes with garlic.

6. Many Internet sites, such as Vampires.com, <u>cater / caters</u> to people's interest in vampires.

7. Several movies, such as one with Boris Karloff, <u>is / are</u> about vampires.

8. Some legends, especially the Dracula legend, <u>last /lasts</u> a long time.

Section 3
**VERB AGREEMENT
AND CONSISTENCY**

PRACTICE 11

Correct any subject-verb agreement errors. If the sentence is correct, write *C* in the blank.

EXAMPLE:

Many of us, in the opinion of Dr. Raoul Figuera, ~~enjoys~~ *enjoy* horror stories. _____

1. Villains and heroes in most gothic novels is very distinct. _____

2. Evil characters, including Dracula, does not have a good side. _____

3. One novel, *Dr. Jekyll and Mr. Hyde*, show us two sides of human nature. _____

4. The hero of the story has a dark side. _____

5. Sometimes Dr. Jekyll, away from the prying eyes of others, drink a powerful potion. _____

6. His personality, usually very sweet and friendly, changes completely.   _____

7. The doctor, with a lack of control, become the evil Mr. Hyde.   _____

8. Both characters, however, resides within the same man.   _____

9. In the novel, Robert Louis Stevenson shows us a shocking truth.   _____

10. Both good and evil exist within us.   _____

11. A play about Dr. Jekyll and Mr. Hyde are at the regional theater.   _____

12. Tickets to Saturday's show is sold out.   _____

Section 3
**VERB AGREEMENT
AND CONSISTENCY**

Interrupting Words: *Who, Which,* and *That*

If a sentence contains a clause beginning with *who, which,* or *that,* then the verb agrees with the subject preceding *who, which,* or *that.*

> There is a **man** in southern Mexico **who** <u>writes</u> about Aztec beliefs.
>
> Here are some old **books that** <u>discuss</u> unsolved mysteries.
>
> One **book, which** <u>contains</u> stories about crop circles, is very interesting.

PRACTICE 12

The following excerpt originally appeared in Chapter 13 of Bram Stoker's 1897 novel, *Dracula*. In the novel, the news story was supposed to have appeared in *The Westminster Gazette,* the town's local newspaper. Read the excerpt, and circle the correct verb forms.

EXAMPLE:

A mysterious man who (wear, wears) a dark cloak is in our town.

1.   During the past two or three days, several cases of young children straying from home (have, has) occurred. In all these cases, the children (was, were) too young to give properly **intelligible** accounts of events. Most of the children who (have, has) gone missing (say, says) that they (have, has) been with a "bloofer lady." It (have, has) always been late in the evening when they (have, has) been missed, and on two occasions the children (have, has) not been found until early the following morning.

intelligible: understandable

2.   Some of the children, indeed all who (have, has) been missed at night, (have, has) been slightly torn or wounded in the throat. The wounds (seem, seems) such as might be made by a rat or a small dog. The animal that (inflict, inflicts) the wounds (have, has) a system or method of its own. The police officers of the division (have, has) been instructed to keep a sharp lookout for straying children, especially those who (is, are) very young.

FINAL REVIEW

Identify and correct fifteen errors in subject-verb agreement.

EXAMPLE:

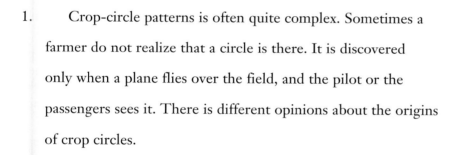

Crop circles is patterns that appear in farmers' fields.

1.   Crop-circle patterns is often quite complex. Sometimes a farmer do not realize that a circle is there. It is discovered only when a plane flies over the field, and the pilot or the passengers sees it. There is different opinions about the origins of crop circles.

2.   Explanations for these circles varies greatly. There is those people who believe that aliens made them and others who think that the circles occurs naturally. For example, Colin Andrews and Pat Delgado, authors of a book about crop circles, attempts to persuade readers that crop circles transmits spiritual messages. Other researchers, such as Dr. Terrence Meaden, suggests that spiral patterns are caused by a whirlwind vortex. Neither Meaden nor his colleagues believes that the circles are caused by supernatural forces.

3.   Skeptics think that somebody create each crop circle by dragging a heavy wooden plank in a circular pattern. However,

Section 3
VERB AGREEMENT AND CONSISTENCY

crop-circle enthusiasts such as Colin Andrews insists that humans always break the wheat instead of bending it. Others points out that moist green wheat bends easily during the summer.

4.   Nobody know why the patterns appear in farmers' fields or why the crop-circle sightings have increased tremendously since the 1970s.

Section 3
**VERB AGREEMENT
AND CONSISTENCY**

 The Writer's Room

Write a paragraph about one of the following topics. When you finish writing, underline each subject, and ensure that all of your subjects and verbs agree.

1. What are the causes of urban legends? Why do people pass along such stories?

2. Many adults tell children stories about magical or mythical people, creatures, or events. For example, they might tell a tale about the tooth fairy, elves, or a stork that brings babies. Children often believe the stories. Should parents tell such yarns to children? Why or why not?

CHECKLIST: SUBJECT-VERB AGREEMENT

When you edit your writing, ask yourself these questions.

Do my subjects and verbs agree? Check for errors with the following:

–present tense verbs

–*was* and *were*

                                    were   *are*
Dr. Figuera and his associates ~~was~~ surprised; men ~~is~~ more superstitious than women.

Do I use the correct verb form with indefinite pronouns? Check for errors with singular indefinite pronouns such as *everybody*, *nobody*, and *somebody*.

                     knows
Everybody ~~know~~ about urban legends.

Do my subjects and verbs agree when there are interrupting phrases? Check for errors in these cases:

–when prepositional phrases separate the subject and verb

–when relative pronouns such as *who* or *that* separate the subject and verb

                          rents
One of our cousins often ~~rent~~ horror movies. She is a girl who
      gets
never ~~get~~ scared.

Do my subjects and verbs agree when the subject comes after the verb? Check for errors with the following:

–sentences containing *here* and *there*

–question forms

        are
There ~~is~~ two horror movies on television tonight.

Section 3
VERB AGREEMENT AND CONSISTENCY

See Chapter 13 on the Visualizing Writing CD-ROM for an additional mini-lecture on **Subject-Verb Agreement**.

Tense Consistency

Section Theme: **BELIEFS**

CONTENTS

• Consistent Verb Tense

In this chapter, you will read about folk tales, myths, and astrology.

Grammar Snapshot

Looking at Tense Consistency

In this excerpt from David A. Locher's *Collective Behavior*, the author describes what happened during the Y2K millennium panic. The verbs are underlined.

Intense, credible media coverage <u>plays</u> a role in spreading false beliefs in many collective delusions. This <u>was</u> certainly true for the Y2K hysteria. Mainstream media sources <u>circulated</u> false rumors of "Y2K failures" that <u>had</u> supposedly already <u>occurred</u>. It <u>was</u> constantly <u>reported</u> that sewage systems, electrical systems, financial and school records, and a variety of other systems <u>had shut</u> down completely or wildly <u>malfunctioned</u> when <u>tested</u> for Y2K compliance.

In this chapter, you will identify and correct tense inconsistencies.

Consistent Verb Tense

When you write, the verb tense you use tells the reader when the event occurred. A **tense shift** occurs when you shift from one tense to another for no logical reason. If you shift verb tenses unnecessarily, you risk confusing your audience. The next sentence begins in the past tense but then shifts to the present tense.

Tense shift:	Nostradamus had a great memory and <u>becomes</u> a well-known doctor.
Consistent tense:	Nostradamus had a great memory and <u>became</u> a well-known doctor.

Sometimes the time frame in a narrative really does change. In those circumstances, you would change the verb tense. The following example accurately shows two different time periods. Notice that certain key words (*In 1550, today*) indicate what tense the writer should use.

In 1550, Nostradamus <u>wrote</u> a book of prophesies. Today, some

researchers <u>debate</u> his ideas.

Section 3
**VERB AGREEMENT
AND CONSISTENCY**

PRACTICE I

Correct each tense shift. If a sentence is correct, write *C* in the blank.

EXAMPLES:

"The Village of Idiots" is a simple folktale showing that beliefs shape a
person's reality.   ___C___

My father read the story, and then he ~~explains~~ *explained* what it meant.   _____

1. A long time ago, a man named Schmendrik was feeling particularly

   bored and unhappy, so he decided to run away.   _____

2. He no longer wanted to be near his screaming wife and children,

   so he packed a bag and walks down the road, leaving the town

   of Chelm behind him.   _____

3. During his journey, he gets tired and decided to stop for a nap. _____

4. When he woke up, he continued on his journey.   _____

5. He thinks that he was on the road toward Warsaw, but he was

   actually on the road back to Chelm.   _____

6. When Schmendrik arrived in Chelm, he was sure that it was
Warsaw and was surprised because everything looks familiar. _____

7. He came to a house that appears exactly like his house, and he
met a woman and children who were exactly like his family. _____

8. He moved in with the new family and felt happy and content. _____

9. At first, Schmendrik was bored and unhappy with his wife and
children, yet when he met them again, in what he believes is a
new city, he appreciates them. _____

10. The story illustrates that a person's attitude has a profound effect
on his or her appreciation of life. _____

Section 3
VERB AGREEMENT
AND CONSISTENCY

> ⟨ **Hint** ⟩ **Would and Could**
>
> When you tell a story about a past event, use *would* instead of *will*, and use *could*
> instead of *can*.
>
>   *would*
> Nostradamus predicted that in the year 1999, a great terror ~~will~~ descend
>   *could*
> from the skies and nobody ~~can~~ stop the event.

PRACTICE 2

Correct the six tense inconsistencies in the following paragraphs.

EXAMPLE:
Fortune-tellers and psychics try to predict the future, and some psychics
               believe
genuinely ~~believed~~ that they have a special gift.

1. A fifteenth-century British woman, Ursula Shipton, made
many accurate predictions about the future. For example, she
predicted that iron boats will float on water, and she also said
that thoughts will fly around the world. She spoke of human
flight, modern ships, submarines, and wireless communications.

However, one of her most famous predictions does not come true. She predicted that the world will end in 1881.

2.   In 1990, Gordon Stein wrote an article expressing his doubts about Shipton. He said that her predictions were often vague and can be interpreted in many different ways. In addition, Charles Hindley, who edited an 1862 version of Shipton's verses, admits that he added his own verses to make her prophecies seem more accurate. Perhaps readers should be skeptical when they read about ancient prophecies.

Telling a Story

When you narrate, or tell a story, you can describe events using the present, past, or future tense. The important thing is to be consistent. The next two paragraphs tell the same story using different tenses.

Past Tense

Mark Twain **went** to see a magic show. At the show, a hypnotist **made** the audience members do ridiculous things. Twain **asked** to go onstage, and he **did** not fall under the hypnotist's spell. However, he **decided** to act out everything that the hypnotist **asked**. He **realized** that the hypnotist **was** a fraud.

Present Tense

Mark Twain **goes** to see a magic show. At the show, a hypnotist **makes** the audience members do ridiculous things. Twain **asks** to go onstage, and he **does** not fall under the hypnotist's spell. However, he **decides** to act out everything that the hypnotist **asks**. He **realizes** that the hypnotist **is** a fraud.

PRACTICE 3

The following paragraph shifts between the present and the past tenses. Edit the paragraph to make the tenses consistent. You might choose to tell the story using the present or past tense.

According to Chinese astrology, one day Buddha invites all of the animals in the kingdom to the Chinese New Year's celebration. An invitation was sent to the rat, and the rat was asked to invite the cat.

However, the rat was jealous of the cat, and he did not pass along the information. On the day of the celebration, only twelve animals can attend; the first to arrive is the rat and the last to arrive is the pig. Buddha assigned each animal a year of its own, and people born in that year were then said to have the characteristics of the animal. The next day, the cat heard about the celebration, and she sent word that she will soon arrive. Later, when the cat met Buddha, she asked to have a year named after her, but she is told that it is too late. Buddha decides that there will be no year of the cat.

Section 3
**VERB AGREEMENT
AND CONSISTENCY**

FINAL REVIEW

Correct fifteen tense inconsistencies in the following paragraphs.

EXAMPLE:

Some people read horoscopes because they ~~wanted~~ *want* to know about the future.

1. The word *astrology* is an ancient Greek word that means "science of the stars." Early humans used the stars to guide them and to help them choose when to hunt, fish, and migrate. Then, as soon as people can write, they looked to the stars and write of relationships between the sky and humans.

2. In the past, ancient Greeks, Aztecs, Babylonians, and Chinese all develop sophisticated astrological charts. For centuries, astrology's appeal has endured. There is a brief setback when, in 1594, Galileo proved that the earth was not the center of the universe. However, Sir Isaac Newton pointed out that astrology was about the relationships between the planets;

therefore, it did not matter what the center of the universe was. Today, in this age of reason, people around the globe still consulted horoscopes.

3.   It is common to find horoscopes on Internet sites and in daily newspapers and magazines. College students have mixed reactions to horoscopes. Jessie Irwin is a first-year college student, and she swears that her horoscope has been eerily accurate. In 1998, she read that she will have an accident, and that evening she broke her arm in a car crash. Then, last year, her horoscope said that she will find love, and she soon fell head over heels for someone. However, most of Jessie's peers are dismissive of horoscopes, and they did not believe in astrology. Her friend Brian Bowman says, "They are worthless. Anybody who believed in horoscopes is a little crazy."

Section 3
VERB AGREEMENT AND CONSISTENCY

4.   In the past, many astrologers focused on predictions. One of the most famous fortune-tellers was Jeanne Dixon, who died in 1997. In 1960, Dixon predicted that the next president will be a Democrat and will be assassinated. When President John F. Kennedy was elected and subsequently killed, Dixon's fame skyrocketed. However, many of Dixon's predictions were inaccurate. For example, she predicted that World War III will begin in 1958, and she said that the Russians can and will beat the Americans to the moon. Today, most astrologers avoided making predictions about future events. Instead, they concentrate on making links between astrological signs and personality traits.

The Writer's Room

Write a paragraph about one of the following topics. When you finish writing, ensure that your verb tenses are consistent.

1. Think of a typical fairy tale, myth, or legend, such as "The Three Little Pigs" or "Little Red Riding Hood." You could also think of a tale that is special in your culture. Retell the story using more modern names and places.

2. Were you superstitious when you were a child? For example, did you consult your horoscope, or did you have a lucky charm? Are your beliefs different today? Compare your past and current beliefs.

 CHECKLIST: TENSE CONSISTENCY

When you edit your writing, ask yourself the following question.

Are my verb tenses consistent? Check for errors with the following:
–shifts from past to present or from present to past
–*can, could* and *will, would*

If a black cat crossed your path, ~~will~~ *would* you have bad luck?

Section 3
VERB AGREEMENT AND CONSISTENCY

 The Writers' Circle

Survey an equal number of males and females. Try to survey at least three people of each sex. Ask them if they believe, or do not believe, in the following. Write *M* (for "male") and *F* (for "female") in the spaces.

	Don't Believe	Believe
1. Dead people visit the earth as ghosts.		
2. It is possible to create a society in which everyone has equal wealth.		
3. Some people can contact the dead or predict future events.		
4. Horoscopes provide useful information about future events.		
5. Capital punishment helps lower the crime rate.		
6. Aliens have visited the earth and kidnapped some people.		
7. Human beings have walked on the moon.		
8. There is life on other planets.		
9. The universe is expanding.		

Next, ask people why they believe a certain thing. Did they read about it? Did someone tell them about it? Keep notes about their answers. Then work with your team members, and write a paragraph about one of the following topics. Ensure that your verb tenses are consistent.

READING LINK

To learn more about beliefs, read the following essays:
"The Point Is?" by John G. Tufts (page 428)
"Going Thin in Fiji" by Ellen Goodman (page 447)

1. Choose one person you asked about his or her beliefs, and write a paragraph about that person. What does he or she believe in? Why does he or she have those beliefs? (Because you are writing about one person, take extra care to ensure that your subjects and verbs agree.)

2. Write a paragraph about the results of the survey. You could discuss any differences between males and females regarding superstitions and beliefs.

See Chapter 14 on the Visualizing Writing CD-ROM for an additional audio and animated mini-lecture on **Consistent Verb Tense** and **Active Voice**.

Section 3
**VERB AGREEMENT
AND CONSISTENCY**

CHAPTER 15

Sentence Combining 1

Section Theme: **POLITICS**

CONTENTS

• Comparing Simple and Compound Sentences

• Combining Sentences Using Coordinating Conjunctions

• Combining Sentences Using Semicolons

• Combining Sentences Using Transitional Expressions

In this chapter, you will read about political history and great leaders.

Grammar Snapshot

Looking at Compound Sentences

Seneca Chief Red Jacket spoke to the Iroquois nation in 1805. In this excerpt, compound sentences are underlined.

> The white people had now found our country. <u>Tidings were carried back, and more came amongst us.</u> Yet we did not fear them. We took them to be friends. They called us brothers. <u>We believed them, and we gave them a large seat.</u> At length their numbers had greatly increased. <u>They wanted more land; they wanted our country.</u> <u>Our eyes were opened, and our minds became uneasy.</u>

In this chapter, you will practice identifying and writing compound sentences.

Comparing Simple and Compound Sentences

When you write, you can use sentences of varying lengths to make your writing more appealing. One of the easiest ways to create variety is to combine simple sentences to form compound sentences.

A **simple sentence** expresses a complete idea. It has one or more subjects and verbs.

One subject, one verb:	**Josh** <u>writes</u> for the campus newspaper.
Two subjects:	**Housing** and **transportation** <u>are</u> hotly discussed issues on campus.
Two verbs:	The **student president** <u>speaks</u> and <u>writes</u> about serious issues.

A **compound sentence** contains two or more simple sentences, and the two complete ideas can be joined in several ways.

Josh is ambitious. + He hopes to win.

Add a coordinator:	Josh is ambitious, **and** he hopes to win.
Add a semicolon:	Josh is ambitious; he hopes to win.
Add a semicolon and conjunctive adverb	Josh is ambitious; **therefore,** he hopes to win.

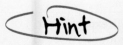

Section 4
EFFECTIVE SENTENCES

Combining Sentences Using Coordinating Conjunctions

A **coordinating conjunction** joins two complete ideas and indicates the connection between them. When you combine two sentences with a coordinating conjunction, put a comma before the conjunction.

Complete idea	**, for** **, and** **, nor** **, but** **, or** **, yet** **, so**	complete idea.

Martin Luther King experienced injustice, **but** he was not a bitter person.

Hint Recognizing Compound Sentences

To be sure that a sentence is compound, place your finger over the coordinator, and then ask yourself whether the two clauses are complete sentences.

Simple:	Mr. Webb contacts businesspeople and asks them for support.
Compound:	Mr. Webb contacts businesspeople, and he asks for their support.

PRACTICE I

Indicate whether the following sentences are simple (*S*) or compound (*C*). Underline the coordinating conjunction in each compound sentence.

EXAMPLE:

Today women can vote, <u>but</u> they did not always have that right.   _C_

1. Often, charismatic individuals gain power and keep it.   _____

2. Sometimes a particular social class controls a government.   _____

3. Democratic governments first flourished in ancient Greece, and they eventually spread around the world.   _____

4. In Athens, ordinary men could influence decision making.   _____

5. However, women, slaves, and poor people were not allowed to vote.   _____

6. In 1881, the Isle of Man became the first place in the world to give property-owning women the vote in national elections.   _____

7. Unmarried women and wealthy widows could participate in decision making, but they could not run in elections.   _____

8. For over two hundred years, American women could not vote, and they could not go to college.   _____

9. Some women made speeches and campaigned for the right to vote, and many men joined them in their fight.   _____

10. In 1920, American women won the right to vote in national elections.   _____

Section 4
EFFECTIVE SENTENCES

Meanings of Coordinating Conjunctions

Each coordinating conjunction has a specific meaning. Review the next table to see how each coordinator can be used.

Coordinating Conjunction	Usage	Example
and	To join two ideas	Royal families receive public money, **and** each member gets an allowance.
but	To contrast two ideas	Spain has a monarchy, **but** the United States does not have a king or queen.
for	To indicate a reason	A monarchy is expensive to maintain, **for** it costs a lot to upkeep royal institutions.
nor	To indicate a negative idea	Americans do not have a monarchy, **nor** do they want one.
or	To offer an alternative	A king can rule, **or** he can abdicate the throne.

Coordinating Conjunction	Usage	Example
so	To indicate a cause and effect relationship	Some monarchies have abolished their "males only" rule, **so** some women now assume the throne.
yet	To introduce a surprising idea	Britain's Prince William is very popular, **yet** he is also quite shy.

PRACTICE 2

Underline the best coordinating conjunction in each sentence.

EXAMPLE:

We should learn about the suffragist movement, (but, <u>for</u>, yet) it is an important part of our history.

1.   I read a book about the famous women's rights crusader Elizabeth Cady Stanton, (and, but, or) I learned a lot about her. Stanton was born in 1815, (yet, and, so) her father was a lawyer, judge, and congressman.

2.   In her childhood, Elizabeth read about an unfair law, (so, but, or) she decided to do something about it. The law restricted a woman's right to own property, (so, and, but) it appeared on a page in her father's law book. She was only seven years old, (nor, or, but) she understood the difference between right and wrong. To Elizabeth, the law was unjust, (so, but, or) she cut the page out of the law book. She thought that if it were removed from the book, the law would be canceled.

3.   Her father was not happy, (yet, or, so) he did not react harshly. He did not become angry, (but, or, nor) did he punish Elizabeth. Instead, he put down his pen, (and, but, or) he gave his daughter some advice. He explained that she had two choices. She could either do nothing, (and, but, or) she could try to help women secure certain rights.

4.   She could not change things alone, (or, but, so) she would have to find like-minded people to help her. She could prepare a speech, (and, but, nor) she could present it to a group of legislators.

Section 4
EFFECTIVE SENTENCES

5. In 1848, Elizabeth Cady Stanton organized an important convention in Seneca Falls, New York, (but, or, and) she spent the next fifty years fighting for women's rights. She lived for many years, (yet, or, so) in 1902, at the time of her death, women still did not have the right to vote.

PRACTICE 3

Create compound sentences by adding a coordinating conjunction and another complete sentence to each simple sentence. Remember that the two ideas must be related. Try to use a variety of coordinating conjunctions.

EXAMPLE:

Many people vote, *but they do not always know about the issues.*

1. Kyle has unusual opinions _____

    _____

2. The drinking age is twenty-one in most states _____

    _____

3. Many teenagers drink alcohol illegally _____

    _____

4. Some laws are passed to protect people _____

    _____

5. Drinking and driving is dangerous _____

    _____

6. Barry continually drives too fast _____

    _____

Section 4
EFFECTIVE SENTENCES

PRACTICE 4

In the following paragraphs, join eight pairs of sentences using coordinating conjunctions. You can keep some of the short sentences so that your paragraph has variety.

EXAMPLE:

                                , and we
We read the report. ~~We~~ did not know what to do.

1. In 1870, for the first time, the U.S. government published statistics about child labor. Many people believed that work was

good for children. Others worried about the harsh conditions faced by child workers. At that time, millions of children had full-time jobs in the United States. They were all under the age of sixteen. In Pennsylvania, children between the ages of eight and ten worked in coal mines. Some of them worked as domestics. Many states permitted children to work twelve hours a day. They could also work night shifts.

2.   In the late nineteenth century, concerned people started a movement to protect child laborers in America. Leaders in this effort wanted children to get schooling. They tried to convince lawmakers to regulate child labor. For example, in Georgia, very young children worked in cotton mills. Some of them were only seven years old. The Georgia legislature refused to pass laws regulating child labor. Florence Kelley, a child advocate, worked to change the laws. She was not able to vote or be elected. She decided to organize boycotts of cotton mills. Kelley's strategies were somewhat successful. Many laws restricting child labor were passed. In 1916 and 1918, Congress passed federal child labor laws. The Supreme Court declared them unconstitutional. Finally, in 1939, the Fair Labor Standards Act was passed. It prohibited children under sixteen years of age from working in manufacturing or mining.

Section 4
EFFECTIVE SENTENCES

Combining Sentences Using Semicolons

A semicolon can join two complete sentences. The semicolon replaces a conjunction.

> Complete idea   ;   complete idea.

The election offices closed; many ballots were missing.

PRACTICE 5

Each sentence is missing a semicolon. Put a semicolon in the appropriate place.

EXAMPLE:

In 1945, George Orwell was discouraged ; he was very disillusioned with communism.

1. Orwell did not like state intervention in people's lives he also worried about unemployment and the exploitation of the poor.

2. According to Orwell, no book is genuinely free from political bias most of his novels had political undertones.

3. In 1945, George Orwell published a political allegory called *Animal Farm* the story traces the rise of communism in the former Soviet Union.

4. At the beginning of the story, old farmer Jones drinks too much whiskey he forgets to lock up the farm.

5. A pig called Old Major influences the animals he makes speeches about evil humans.

6. The animals feel upset with their master's incompetence they decide to revolt and take over the farm.

7. Mr. Jones and his wife flee the animals celebrate by eating a feast.

8. At first, two pigs lead the animals the animal farm runs smoothly.

9. Then the two leaders begin to fight one pig drives the other from the farm.

10. The leader becomes an evil dictator the other animals are treated badly.

Section 4
EFFECTIVE SENTENCES

   **Use a Semicolon to Join Related Ideas**

Do not use a semicolon to join two unrelated sentences.

Incorrect:	George Orwell wrote about political issues; he believed in voodoo.
	(The second idea has no clear relationship with the first idea.)
Correct:	George Orwell wrote about political issues; he criticized communism in his book *Animal Farm*.

PRACTICE 6

Create compound sentences by adding a semicolon and another complete sentence to each simple sentence. Remember that the two ideas must be related.

EXAMPLE:

Last year I returned to college; *I wanted to change careers.* _____

1. Some adults return to college _____

   _____

   _____

2. Many students drive cars to campus _____

   _____

   _____

3. Some students live in dorms _____

   _____

   _____

4. Students look forward to spring break _____

   _____

   _____

5. I am on the student council _____

   _____

   _____

Section 4
**EFFECTIVE
SENTENCES**

Combining Sentences Using Transitional Expressions

A **transitional expression** can join two complete ideas and show how they are related. The next table shows some common transitional expressions.
If the second sentence begins with a transitional expression, put a semicolon before it and a comma after it.

Transitional Expressions

Addition	Alternative	Contrast	Time	Example or Emphasis	Result or Consequence
additionally	in fact	however	eventually	for example	consequently
also	instead	nevertheless	finally	for instance	hence
besides	on the contrary	nonetheless	later	namely	therefore
furthermore	on the other hand	still	meanwhile	of course	thus
in addition	otherwise		subsequently	undoubtedly	
moreover					

> Complete idea **;** **transitional expression** **,** complete idea.

Sheila Chow lost the election**; nevertheless,** she resolved to remain active in politics.

> ; **still,**
> ; **however,**
> ; **nonetheless,**

PRACTICE 7

Punctuate the following sentences by adding any necessary semicolons and commas.

EXAMPLE:

Nelson Mandela was born into the royal family of the Thembu ; however , he was educated in a British missionary school.

Section 4
EFFECTIVE
SENTENCES

1. Mandela went to Fort Hare University eventually he was expelled because of his political actions.

2. He returned home meanwhile his family expected him to agree to an arranged marriage.

3. His potential bride was in love with another man therefore Mandela ran away from his village and went to Soweto.

4. Mandela became a lawyer later he turned his attention to the repressive race laws of South Africa.

5. He was politically active against the apartheid system consequently he was arrested.

6. Mandela defended himself during his 1964 trial however the jury was biased.

7. He was not freed instead he was sentenced to life imprisonment.

8. Some of the prison guards were cruel nevertheless many of the guards grew to respect Mandela.

9. Mandela left prison twenty-five years later without bitterness in fact he forgave his opponents.

PRACTICE 8

Create compound sentences using the following transitional expressions. Try to use a different expression in each sentence.

consequently	furthermore	however
in fact	nevertheless	therefore

EXAMPLE:

Each vote is important *; in fact, one vote can change the outcome of an election.*

1. Most students are not politically active _____

   _____

2. An American president can remain in office for only two terms _____

   _____

3. There are two main political parties in the United States _____

   _____

4. The mayor committed a crime _____

   _____

5. The last election was quite close _____

   _____

6. The new senator is outspoken _____

   _____

Section 4
**EFFECTIVE
SENTENCES**

PRACTICE 9

Add a transitional expression to join each pair of sentences. Choose an expression from the following list, and try to use a different expression in each sentence.

consequently	for example	for instance	however
in fact	therefore	thus	

EXAMPLE:

; thus, I

I vote in every election. ~~I~~ want to know about the issues.

1. Every four years, there is a presidential election in the United States.

   Voters are bombarded with campaign advertising.

2. Sometimes the campaign advertisements attack the opponent's platform. Some ads attack the opponent's personal life.

3. In 1988, attack ads appeared on television. They accused presidential candidate Michael Dukakis of being soft on crime.

4. Today, many attack ads appear on Web sites. In the 2004 presidential election, a Republican Web site criticized Democratic candidate John Kerry's antiwar activities.

5. At the same time, a Democrat-supported Web site attacked George Bush. It questioned his service in the National Guard.

6. Most voters do not like attack advertising. Political parties should try to focus on issues instead of making personal attacks.

Section 4
EFFECTIVE SENTENCES

Final Review

Read the following paragraphs. Create compound sentences by adding semicolons, conjunctive adverbs (*however, therefore,* etc.) or coordinating conjunctions (*for, and, nor, but, or, yet, so*). Try to create at least ten compound sentences.

EXAMPLE:

Political leaders have traditionally been male~~. Many~~ , but many countries have elected female leaders.

1. In the twentieth century, there were over forty female presidents or prime ministers. Sirimavo Bandaranaike was the world's first female prime minister. She was elected in Sri Lanka on July 20, 1960. She made Sri Lanka a republic. She nationalized private companies. Parliament expelled her in 1980. However, she was reelected in 1993.

2. Indira Gandhi was elected in 1966. She led India for nearly twenty years. Indira's last name was Gandhi. She was not related

to Mahatma Gandhi. Her husband's name was Feroze Gandhi. She took his name. Some of Indira Gandhi's policies were unpopular. She made many enemies.

3.   In Pakistan, citizens also voted for a female leader. Benazir Bhutto was elected prime minister in 1988. She was the first female head of state in the Muslim world. However, a military coup by army generals forced her out of office. She was accused of corruption. She spent nearly six years in prison.

4.   All three women had connections to powerful men. Bandaranaike's husband was the prime minister of Sri Lanka. He was assassinated. Then his wife became prime minister. Indira Gandhi and Benazir Bhutto were the daughters of prime ministers. They inherited the leadership of their fathers' political parties. However, some female leaders, such as England's former prime minister, Margaret Thatcher, and Iceland's former president, Vigdis Finnbogadottir, had no family connections.

Section 4
**EFFECTIVE
SENTENCES**

 The Writer's Room

Write a paragraph about one of the following topics. First, write at least ten simple sentences. Then, combine some of your sentences to create compound sentences. When you have finished, edit your writing and ensure that your sentences are combined correctly.

1. What are some common reasons that people give for not voting?
2. Do you think that the voting age should be raised or lowered? Explain your position.
3. Are you happy with the current administration in the White House? Why or why not?

CHECKLIST: COMPOUND SENTENCES

When you edit your writing, ask yourself these questions.

Are my compound sentences correctly punctuated? Remember to do the following:

–place a comma before a coordinating conjunction.

Students should get involved, and they should vote in elections.

–use a semicolon between two complete ideas.

A woman may run for president; she may not win.

–use a semicolon before a transitional expression and a comma after it.

The results will be close; **therefore,** it is important to cast your vote.

See Chapter 15 on the Visualizing Writing CD-ROM for an additional audio and animated mini-lecture on **Combining Sentences**.

Section 4
**EFFECTIVE
SENTENCES**

Sentence Combining 2

CHAPTER 16

Section Theme: **POLITICS**

CONTENTS

- Understanding Complex Sentences
- Using Subordinating Conjunctions
- Using Relative Pronouns
- Combining Questions

In this chapter, you will read about political activists.

Grammar Snapshot

Looking at Complex Sentences

In this excerpt from Nelson Mandela's *The Long Road Home*, he describes his prison cell. The complex sentences are underlined.

Many mornings, a small pool of water would have formed on the cold floor overnight. <u>When I raised this with the commanding officer, he told me our bodies would absorb the moisture.</u> <u>We were each issued three blankets so flimsy and worn that they were practically transparent.</u> Our bedding consisted of a single sisal, or straw, mat. Later we were given a felt mat, and we placed the felt mat on top of the sisal one to provide some softness. <u>At that time of year, the cells were so cold and the blankets provided so little warmth that we always slept fully dressed.</u>

In this chapter, you will identify and write complex sentences.

Understanding Complex Sentences

A **complex sentence** contains one independent clause (complete idea) and one or more dependent clauses (incomplete ideas).

■ An **independent clause** has a subject and a verb and can stand alone because it expresses one complete idea.

> Rosa Parks did not give up her seat.

■ A **dependent clause** has a subject and verb, but it cannot stand alone. It "depends" on another clause to be complete.

Incomplete:	Although she was asked to move.
Complete:	dependent clause independent clause Although she was asked to move, Rosa Parks did not give up her seat.

Section 4
EFFECTIVE SENTENCES

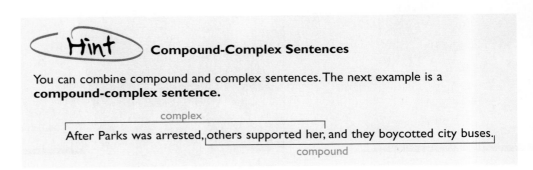

Hint **Compound-Complex Sentences**

You can combine compound and complex sentences. The next example is a **compound-complex sentence.**

complex
After Parks was arrested, others supported her, and they boycotted city buses.
compound

Using Subordinating Conjunctions

When you add a **subordinating conjunction** (a word such as *after, because,* or *although*) to a clause, you make the clause dependent. *Subordinate* means "secondary," so subordinating conjunctions are words that introduce secondary ideas.

Main idea   **subordinating conjunction**   secondary idea.

Crowds gathered **whenever** the candidate spoke.

Subordinating conjunction   secondary idea,   main idea.

Whenever the candidate spoke, crowds gathered.

Some Subordinating Conjunctions

after	because	since	until	whereas
although	before	so that	when	wherever
as	even if	that	whenever	whether
as if	even though	though	where	while
as though	if	unless		

Subordinating conjunctions create a relationship between the clauses in a sentence. Review the next table to see how you can use subordinating conjunctions.

Subordinating Conjunction	Usage	Example
as, because, since	To indicate a reason or a cause	John F. Kennedy ran for office <u>because</u> he thought he could change things.
as long as, even if, if, provided that, unless	To indicate a condition	A person cannot become president <u>unless</u> he or she was born in the United States.
although, even though, though	To contrast ideas	<u>Although</u> Kennedy had a bad back, he remained active.
where, wherever	To indicate a location	<u>Wherever</u> he traveled, large crowds gathered.
so that	To show a purpose	He often went to Hyannis Port <u>so that</u> he could relax with his family.
after, before, since, until, when, whenever	To show a point in time	Americans were stunned <u>when</u> President Kennedy was assassinated.

Section 4
EFFECTIVE SENTENCES

PRACTICE I

Practice identifying dependent and independent clauses. Circle the subordinating conjunction and then underline the dependent clause in each sentence.

EXAMPLE:

Gandhi was well-respected (because) he used nonviolent action to spark political change.

1. Although such restraint is extremely rare, some political leaders refuse to use violent methods.

2. When he was still a teenager, Mahatma Gandhi developed his beliefs about nonviolence.

3. Gandhi did not believe in the use of force because he believed that "an eye for an eye leads to a world of the blind."

4. Although his political career began in South Africa, Gandhi is most known for his passive resistance movement in India.

5. When he returned to Bombay in 1915, British rulers controlled all of India.

6. After assessing the situation, Gandhi led textile workers and planters in acts of civil disobedience.

7. When he toured India in 1919, he persuaded people across the country to stop working for one day.

8. Sometimes the country's rulers used force to stop people from going on strike even if the strikers were peaceful.

9. Gandhi complained because officials often used "a hammer to strike a fly."

10. Even though his supporters were violently attacked, Gandhi would not respond to violence with violence.

11. After twenty-eight years of peaceful noncooperation, Mahatma Gandhi's passive resistance movement was successful.

12. India became independent in 1947, although the country then split up along religious lines.

Section 4
**EFFECTIVE
SENTENCES**

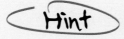 **Punctuating Complex Sentences**

If you use a subordinator at the beginning of a sentence, put a comma after the dependent clause. Generally, if you use a subordinator in the middle of the sentence, you do not need to use a comma.

Comma:	**Even though** she did not like the candidates, she voted in the election.
No comma:	She voted in the election **even though** she did not like the candidates.

PRACTICE 2

The following selection is adapted from Mahatma Gandhi's autobiography, *The Story of My Experiments with Truth*. In the excerpt, Gandhi describes his first trip to England. Underline each subordinating conjunction, and add five missing commas.

EXAMPLE:

<u>Although</u> I did not feel at all seasick ʼas the days passed ᐱ I became fidgety.

1.   I felt shy even when I spoke to the steward. I was not used to speaking English because I had had very little practice. The other passengers were English although my friend, Mazmudar, was not. Whenever they were friendly and tried to speak with me I could not understand them. Even if I understood an Englishman I could not reply.

2.   Mazmudar had no difficulty communicating whenever he mixed with the others. While I hid in the cabin he would move about freely on deck. Because Mazmudar was a lawyer he told me about his legal experience. He advised me to take every possible opportunity to speak in English even though I might make mistakes. Although I wanted to please him nothing could make me conquer my shyness.

Section 4
**EFFECTIVE
SENTENCES**

PRACTICE 3

Each of the sentences in this practice is missing a subordinating conjunction. Write one of the following conjunctions in each blank. Use a different conjunction each time.

~~after~~	before	until
although	even though	whenever
because	so that	when

EXAMPLE:

<u>After</u> Frederick Douglass's birth in 1818 ʼhe was separated from his mother.

1.   Douglass's grandmother took him to her master's plantation _____ he turned six years old.

_____ Douglass understood why his grandmother gave him to the master, he always felt the pain of abandonment.

2.   _____ he turned nine years old, he was sent to work as the houseboy for a Baltimore family. Sophia Auld, his mistress, taught Douglass the alphabet _____ it was illegal to instruct slaves in reading. _____

Douglass knew how to read, he could tap into the power of the written word.

3.   Douglass waited _____ he turned twenty. Then he escaped from slavery by disguising himself as a sailor. He worked with the Massachusetts antislavery society _____ he could influence public opinion. _____ he could, he spoke about the abolition of slavery and of women's rights.

 **Putting a Subject After the Subordinator**

When you combine sentences to form complex sentences, always remember to put a subject after the subordinator.

>   *it*
> The protest was unsuccessful because was not well organized.

Section 4
EFFECTIVE SENTENCES

PRACTICE 4

Add five missing subjects to this selection. Remember that a subject can be a noun or a pronoun.

EXAMPLE:

                                                            he

Arnold Schwarzenegger was born in Austria, although currently has a U.S. passport.

      Many well-known actors and actresses have gotten involved in politics. In 2003, Arnold Schwarzenegger became the governor of California. The former bodybuilder is a successful actor, although is not as popular as he was in the 1980s. He was mainly known as "the Terminator" when threw his hat into the political arena. He apparently ran for office because wanted to help Californians. His wife, Maria Shriver, is also in the media industry, although is not an actress. She is a reporter and newscaster. Another actor turned politician was former president

Ronald Reagan. He was no longer making movies when ran as a presidential candidate. President Reagan served two terms in the 1980s.

PRACTICE 5

Combine the sentences by adding a subordinating conjunction. Write each sentence twice: once with the dependent clause at the beginning of the sentence, and once with the dependent clause at the end of the sentence. From the following list, use each conjunction once.

after   although   ~~because~~   even though   when

EXAMPLE:

I vote. It is important.

I vote because it is important.

Because it is important, I vote.

1. I was very busy on election day. I still voted.

   _____

   _____

2. I got home. I watched the election results on television.

   _____

   _____

3. The ballots were counted. A winner was declared.

   _____

   _____

4. The losing candidate congratulated the winner. He was disappointed.

   _____

   _____

   _____

   _____

Section 4
**EFFECTIVE
SENTENCES**

Using Relative Pronouns

A **relative pronoun** describes a noun or pronoun. You can form complex sentences by using **relative pronouns** to introduce dependent clauses. Review the most common relative pronouns on the next page.

who	whomever	which
whom	whose	that

Use *who* (*whom, whomever, whose*) to add information about a person.

Martin Luther King, Jr., **who** <u>was a minister</u>, fought for civil rights.

Use *that* to add information about a thing.

He made speeches **that** <u>moved people</u>.

Use *which* to add information about a thing.

In his greatest speech, **which** <u>he wrote in 1963</u>, he speaks about his dream for a better America.

 **Punctuating Sentences with Relative Pronouns**

Which
Use commas to set off clauses that begin with *which*.

The movie, **which** <u>was very interesting</u>, was about the first presidential election.

That
Do not use commas to set off clauses beginning with *that*.

On the day **that** <u>we met</u> it was raining.

Who
When a clause begins with *who,* you may or may not need a comma. If the clause contains nonessential information, put commas. If the clause is essential to the meaning of the sentence, then it does not require commas.

Essential:	The two young men **who** <u>started the riot</u> were arrested.
Not essential:	Reporter Eli Marcos, **who** <u>once worked for the *Los Angeles Times*</u>, took photos of the event.

Section 4
**EFFECTIVE
SENTENCES**

GRAMMAR LINK

For more information about punctuating relative clauses, refer to Chapter 25, "Commas."

PRACTICE 6

In each of the following sentences, underline the relative clause.

EXAMPLE:
Winona LaDuke, <u>who is a Chippewa</u>, is director of the White Earth Land Recovery Project.

1. Winona LaDuke has done work that others have avoided. She has helped native people who live in Minnesota learn about their Ojibwe language. She has also helped women who have

been abused find security and peace. Furthermore, LaDuke, who is only in her forties, has worked tirelessly to retrieve Anishinabe land. In fact, nearly 1,000 acres that had been lost over the decades have been retrieved with the help of the White Earth Project.

2.   In 1994, *Time* magazine, which is found on most newsstands, honored LaDuke for her work. Today, LaDuke's group, which is located in Minnesota, continues to buy back native land.

PRACTICE 7

Combine each set of sentences by using the relative pronoun in parentheses. There may be more than one way to combine some sets of sentences.

Section 4
EFFECTIVE SENTENCES

EXAMPLE:

(who) In Tiananmen Square, students were arrested. They protested against the government.

In Tiananmen Square, students who protested against the government were arrested.

1. (who) In 1989, Chinese students wanted change. They sat in a square in Beijing.

2. (who) The protesters were asking for democracy. They sang and held signs.

3. (that) Army tanks entered the square. The tanks fired on the students.

4. (who) An unknown man stood in front of the tanks. He has become a symbol of resistance to tyranny.

_____

_____

_____

5. (which) The photo appeared in newspapers around the world. It had a strong emotional impact.

_____

_____

PRACTICE 8

Add dependent clauses to each sentence. Begin each clause with a relative pronoun (*who, which,* or *that*). Add any necessary commas.

EXAMPLE:

People ____*who get involved*____ can change things in our society.

Section 4
**EFFECTIVE
SENTENCES**

1. Washington, D. C., _____ has many attractions.

2. The students _____ rented a bus.

3. The president of the college student union _____ _____ has done a good job.

4. The posters _____ are eye-catching.

5. This college _____ has an excellent student newspaper.

6. I do not vote for candidates _____.

7. My friend _____ is not interested in politics.

8. According to my friend, political issues are things _____ _____.

Combining Questions

It is possible to combine a question with a statement or to combine two questions to form a complex sentence. An **embedded question** is a question that is part of a larger sentence.

Question: How can she raise funds?

Embedded question: The candidate wonders <u>how she can raise funds</u>.

In questions, there is generally a helping verb before the subject. However, when a question is embedded in a larger sentence, either place the helping verb after the subject or remove it. As you read the following examples, pay attention to the word order in the embedded questions.

Combine two questions.

Separate: Do you know the answer? Why **do** they like the candidate?

   (The second question includes the helping verb *do*.)

Combined: Do you know <u>why they like the candidate?</u>

   (The helping verb *do* is removed from the embedded question.)

Combine a question and a statement.

Separate: I wonder about it. How **can** we help?

   (In the question, the helping verb *can* appears before the subject.)

Combined: I wonder <u>how we can help</u>.

   (In the embedded question, *can* is placed after the subject.)

 **Use the Correct Word Order**

When editing your writing, ensure that you have formed embedded questions properly.

I wonder why ~~do~~ people use drugs? I asked the mayor what ~~did she think~~ *she thought* about the war on drugs.

PRACTICE 9

Edit the eight embedded question errors in this paragraph.

EXAMPLE:

The writer explains how ~~did Prohibition begin~~. *Prohibition began.*

1.   I wonder why did the United States ban alcohol in 1920. Does

anybody understand why would officials do that? According to

Dr. K. Austen Kerr, many Americans were worried about social

problems related to alcohol consumption. But then you have to

wonder how could a government legislate morality.

2.   The Volstead Act prohibited the sale and distribution of alcohol. Do you know why was it called the Volstead Act? The author of the act was a prominent Republican named Andrew Volstead. Many citizens wondered how could the act be enforced.

3.   At first, Prohibition appeared to work, and alcohol consumption dropped. But then, illegal distillers popped up, and a huge black market appeared. Do you know why were people illegally producing alcohol? They did it because it was an extremely lucrative business. Many well-known families, including the Bronfmans and the Kennedys, made fortunes during the Prohibition era. At the time, Prohibition supporters wondered why were prominent citizens breaking the law.

Section 4
EFFECTIVE
SENTENCES

4.   Ultimately, in 1933, Prohibition was repealed. Do you know why could Prohibition never succeed? Perhaps as long as people are willing to buy intoxicating drinks or drugs, there will be others who are ready to supply those items.

FINAL REVIEW

The following paragraphs contain simple sentences. To give the paragraphs more sentence variety, try to form ten complex sentences by combining pairs of sentences. You will have to add some words and delete others.

EXAMPLE:

<s>Some</s> When some people fight for our rights and <s>freedoms. They</s> freedoms, they risk getting jailed.

1.   Henry David Thoreau was an honest man. He did not pay poll taxes. He protested against the Mexican War. He was arrested. He subsequently wrote "On the Duty of Civil Disobedience." In his text, he stressed that some laws are immoral. It is okay to disobey such laws. There have been many other acts of civil disobedience. Such acts have changed American history. For example, there was

the Boston Tea Party. Citizens threw boxes of tea into the harbor. They did not want to pay taxes to Britain.

2. Back in 1958, Ralph Nader was studying law at Harvard University. At that time, about 5 million car accidents happened every year. Carmakers were concerned about the style, cost, and performance of automobiles. They were not concerned about safety. In 1965, Nader wrote a best-selling book. It was called *Unsafe at Any Speed.* General Motors attempted to discredit Nader. Then he sued GM for invasion of privacy. GM executives settled the case. They admitted to harassing Nader. In 1966, new safety laws were passed. Automakers had to redesign autos. They had to make them safer. Sometimes one person works hard. That person influences large corporations.

The Writer's Room

Write a paragraph about one of the following topics. After you finish writing, ensure that you have formed and punctuated the complex sentences correctly.

1. Examine this photo. What are some terms that come to mind? Some ideas might be *left wing, right wing, American,* or *slogan.* Define a term or expression that relates to the photo.

2. Do you care about politics? Are you politically active? Do you vote in elections? Give your opinion about politics.

CHECKLIST: COMPLEX SENTENCES

When you edit your writing, ask yourself these questions.

Are my complex sentences complete?

He resigned because
~~Because~~ of the scandal.

Are my complex sentences correctly punctuated?

He resigned from office╱ because of the scandal.
The ballot box, which was full, was taken to the election office.

Do I have any embedded questions? Check for errors in these cases:
  –word order
  –unnecessary helping verbs

I will
I don't know which candidate ~~will I~~ vote for. I wonder which one ~~do~~ you like.

Section 4
**EFFECTIVE
SENTENCES**

Sentence Variety and Exact Language

Section Theme: **POLITICS**

CONTENTS

- Achieving Sentence Variety
- Using Specific Vocabulary
- Avoiding Clichés
- Slang versus Standard English

In this chapter, you will read about political scandals.

Grammar Snapshot

Looking at Sentence Variety

On August 8, 1974, President Richard Nixon resigned because of a political scandal. Notice the variety of sentence lengths in this excerpt from his resignation speech.

> For more than a quarter of a century in public life, I have shared in the turbulent history of this evening. I have fought for what I believe in. I have tried, to the best of my ability, to discharge those duties and meet those responsibilities that were entrusted to me. Sometimes I have succeeded, and sometimes I have failed.

In this chapter, you will practice varying the length and structure of sentences. You will also identify and correct clichés and slang.

Achieving Sentence Variety

Sentence variety means that your sentences have assorted patterns and lengths. When you write, you can vary your sentences by consciously considering their lengths and by altering opening words.

Vary the Lengths of Sentences

If a passage contains only simple sentences, it can be quite boring. You can vary the lengths of sentences by combining some short simple sentences to make compound and complex sentences.

No Sentence Variety

In the 1970s, there was a huge political scandal. The Watergate break-in dominated the news. President Nixon's aides committed an illegal act. They broke into the Democratic party headquarters. They stole documents. President Nixon claimed innocence. He recorded himself. He made incriminating statements. Investigators heard the tapes. Nixon was forced to resign. He knew about the break-in. He was devastated.

With Sentence Variety

In the 1970s, the Watergate break-in dominated the news and became a prominent political scandal. President Nixon's aides committed an illegal act when they broke into Democratic party headquarters and stole documents. The president initially claimed innocence. However, he recorded himself making incriminating statements, and investigators heard the tapes. Because he knew about the break-in, Nixon was forced to resign. He was devastated.

Section 4
EFFECTIVE SENTENCES

PRACTICE I

Rewrite the following paragraph. You can combine the sentences in any way that you want. As you combine, pay attention to your sentence length. Remember to include both long and short sentences.

In 1998, there was a political scandal. It involved President Bill Clinton. Clinton had a relationship with an intern named Monica Lewinsky. However, he publicly denied having an affair. He was worried about his reputation. He eventually had to testify before a grand jury. He admitted to having had the affair. Clinton was impeached. His presidency survived.

_____

_____

_____

_____

_____

Vary the Opening Words

One way to make your sentences more effective is to vary the opening words. Instead of beginning each sentence with the subject, you could try these two strategies: begin with an adverb or begin with a prepositional phrase.

Begin with an Adverb

An **adverb** is a word that modifies a verb, and it often ends in *-ly*. *Slowly, carefully, clearly,* and *suddenly* are adverbs. Non *-ly* adverbs include words such as *sometimes, often, always,* and *never.*

> Gradually, the truth dawned on the governor.
>
> Clearly, she had made a big mistake.
>
> Sometimes, she felt very discouraged.

PRACTICE 2*

Read the following sentences. Identify and cross out each adverb, and then rewrite it in the blank at the beginning of the sentence.

EXAMPLE:

__Secretly__ , Vice President Thomas Jefferson ~~secretly~~ hired a newspaper editor named James Callender.

Section 4
EFFECTIVE SENTENCES

1. _____, the newspaper editor sometimes published scandalous material about President John Adams.

2. _____, he generally wrote negative things about Alexander Hamilton, who was Secretary of the Treasury.

3. _____, the married Hamilton was clearly having an affair.

4. _____, the scandals obviously helped Jefferson win the next election.

5. _____, President John Adams gracefully admitted defeat.

Begin with a Prepositional Phrase

A **prepositional phrase** consists of a preposition and its object. *After the election, beside the river,* and *in my lifetime* are prepositional phrases.

> In past decades, the press showed more restraint.
>
> During the election campaign, media coverage was intense.
>
> Without any warning, the candidate resigned.

*The information in Practices 2 through 4 was adapted from information in William Safire's book *Scandalmonger.*

PRACTICE 3

Read the following sentences. Identify and cross out each prepositional phrase, and rewrite it in the blank at the beginning of the sentence.

EXAMPLE:

_____In 1798_____, the Alien and Sedition Acts were passed ~~in 1798~~.

1. _____, James Callender was jailed without any
   warning.

2. _____, vocal critics of the government could be
   jailed under the Sedition Act.

3. _____, Jefferson basically abandoned his
   controversial friend after the election.

4. _____, Jefferson repealed the Sedition Act
   in 1802.

5. _____, Callender was released from prison
   in the spring.

Section 4
**EFFECTIVE
SENTENCES**

Hint   **Punctuation Tip**

Generally, when a sentence begins with an adverb or a prepositional phrase, put a comma after the opening word or phrase.

   Suddenly, he threw his papers onto the floor.

   Without any warning, he got up and left the room.

PRACTICE 4

Following are some adverbs and prepositional phrases. For a variety of sentence openings, place these words and phrases at the beginnings of appropriate sentences. Do not repeat your choices. There are many possible answers.

additionally	at the time	eventually	~~likely~~	probably
at first	~~clearly~~	in his newspaper	obviously	without a doubt

EXAMPLE:

Thomas Jefferson pardoned James Callender. Jefferson then distanced himself
from the infamous editor. ~~The~~ *Clearly, the* President wanted the public to forget about past

scandals.

1.   Callender, a newspaper editor, was extremely upset with his former ally. He vowed to get revenge on Thomas Jefferson. He wrote that Jefferson "kept as a concubine, one of his own slaves." He mentioned the slave, Sally, and he added that Jefferson had several children by her. There had already been stories about Jefferson and Sally Hemings. Callender's story spread the rumor across the country.

2.   Jefferson didn't respond to the reports about his illegitimate children. Most Americans refused to believe the shocking news about the president. Very few historians accepted Callender's assertions.

3.   Some of Hemings's descendents had DNA testing done. The test showed a link between descendants of Hemings and the Jefferson family. The media showed an interest in the private lives of presidents long before the Nixon or Clinton years.

Section 4
**EFFECTIVE
SENTENCES**

Using Specific Vocabulary

When you revise your writing, ensure that your words are exact. Replace any vague words with more specific ones. For example, the following words are vague.

good	nice	interesting
bad	mean	dull

Vague: Diane Sawyer is a <u>good</u> journalist.

More precise: Diane Sawyer is a <u>respected</u>, <u>award-winning investigative</u> journalist.

How to Create Vivid Language

When you choose the precise word, you convey your meaning exactly. To create more vivid and detailed vocabulary, try the next strategies.

Modify Your Nouns

If the noun is vague, make it more specific by adding one or more adjectives. You could also rename the noun with a more specific term.

Vague:	the woman	
Vivid:	the agreeable editor	the nervous voter

Modify Your Verbs

Use more vivid, precise verbs. You could also use adverbs.

Vague:	said
Vivid:	commanded, spoke sharply, suggested, whispered, yelled

Include More Details

Add information to make the sentence more complete.

Vague:	His decision was bad for the party.
Precise:	His immoral conduct destroyed the political party's chances for reelection.

Section 4
**EFFECTIVE
SENTENCES**

PRACTICE 5

Underline vivid, detailed words and phrases in this excerpt from British author George Orwell's *1984*.

EXAMPLE:

The hallway smelled of <u>boiled cabbage and old rag mats</u>.

At one end of the hallway, a coloured poster, too large for indoor display, depicted an enormous face more than a metre wide; it was the face of a man of about forty-five with a heavy black moustache and ruggedly handsome features.

Winston made for the stairs. The flat was seven flights up, and Winston, who was thirty-nine and had a varicose ulcer above his right ankle, went slowly, resting several times on the way. On each landing, opposite the lift-shaft, the poster with the enormous face gazed from the wall. It was one of those pictures which are so contrived that the eyes follow you about when you move. BIG BROTHER IS WATCHING YOU, the caption beneath it ran.

PRACTICE 6

In each of the following sentences, replace the underlined word or phrase with more precise words or add more vivid details.

EXAMPLE:

He is (bad) _fiery, opinionated, and overbearing._____

1. The housing crisis is (bad) _____.

2. Some students must live in (bad) _____ conditions.

3. They must wait for weeks or months to get (good) _____ _____ housing.

4. The student dorms are (in poor condition) _____ _____.

5. (Someone) _____ _____ should focus on the housing problem.

6. In our city, (many people) _____ _____ will help.

7. For example, Geo Construction has already (been helpful) _____ _____.

8. Perhaps visiting students can be housed in (different locations) _____ _____.

9. You could (do something) _____ _____.

Section 4
**EFFECTIVE
SENTENCES**

Avoiding Clichés

Clichés are overused expressions. Because they are overused, they lose their power and become boring. Avoid using clichés in your writing.

In each example, the underlined cliché has been replaced with a more direct word.

Clichés	Direct Words
The senator was as <u>cool as a cucumber</u>.	relaxed
She worked <u>like a dog</u>.	efficiently
She liked <u>the finer things in life</u>.	luxuries

Some Clichés and Their Substitutions

Cliché	Possible Substitution	Cliché	Possible Substitution
a dime a dozen	common	as luck would have it	fortunately
apple of my eye	my favorite	axe to grind	a problem with
as big as a house	very big	under the weather	ill
in the blink of an eye	quickly	rude awakening	shock
bear the burden	take responsibility	slowly but surely	eventually
break the ice	start the conversation	top dog	supervisor
busy as a bee	very busy	tried and true	experienced
finer things in life	luxuries	true blue	trustworthy

Section 4
**EFFECTIVE
SENTENCES**

PRACTICE 7

Underline each clichéd expression, and replace it with words that are more direct.

EXAMPLE:

a large and imposing man

The king was <u>as big as a house</u>.

1. Books about Henry VIII are a dime a dozen.

2. When Henry VIII married Catherine of Aragon, his young bride was like a deer caught in the headlights.

3. Henry VIII's second wife, Anne Boleyn, liked the finer things in life.

4. During their courtship, Henry was as busy as a bee when he tried to impress the young maiden.

5. Anne Boleyn refused to be the king's mistress; as his legitimate wife, she would be the top dog.

6. After their marriage, King Henry was kind to Anne once in a blue moon.

7. On August 26, 1533, Queen Anne gave birth to a little bundle of joy named Elizabeth.

8. Henry got bored with Anne, and, in the blink of an eye, Anne was arrested and taken to the Tower of London.

9. Finding no support, Anne was as cool as a cucumber when she accepted her fate.

10. In May 1536, Anne Boleyn, who was as pretty as a picture, was charged with treason and executed.

11. Anne's cousin, Catherine Howard, also married Henry and was also executed; in fact, very few of Henry's wives lived to ripe old ages.

12. Henry searched for another wife, but the royal women of Europe, unwilling to throw caution to the wind, were understandably reluctant to marry the British monarch.

Slang versus Standard English

Most of your instructors will want you to write using standard American English. The word *standard* does not imply "better." Standard American English is the common language generally used and expected in schools, businesses, and government institutions in the United States.

Slang is nonstandard language. It is used in informal situations to communicate common cultural knowledge. In any academic or professional context, do not use slang. Read the following examples. The first example contains slang, while the second example uses standard English.

**Section 4
EFFECTIVE
SENTENCES**

Slang

J. Roe, the candidate, <u>hung out</u> with a member of a criminal organization. He got <u>miffed</u> when a journalist published a story about him. He thought that the reporter was a <u>total jerk</u>.

Standard English

J. Roe, the candidate, <u>spent time</u> with a member of a criminal organization. He got <u>angry</u> when a journalist published a story about him. He thought that the reporter was <u>unprofessional</u>.

PRACTICE 8

In the sentences that follow, the slang expressions are underlined. Substitute the slang with the best possible choice of words in standard English. You may have to rewrite part of each sentence.

EXAMPLE:

During the McCarthy era, it was not <u>a cakewalk</u> to defend oneself.
easy

1. In 1947, Republican Senator Joseph McCarthy became <u>freaked out</u> about communists.

2. According to McCarthy, many government employees had <u>buddies</u> in the Communist party.

3. For the next eight years, <u>dudes</u> and <u>chicks</u> who worked for the government had to take loyalty oaths.

4. Also, actors, writers, directors, and other <u>bigwigs</u> had to testify before a committee headed by Senator McCarthy.

5. McCarthy even <u>took potshots at</u> esteemed comedian Lucille Ball.

6. Some Hollywood directors provided the committee with the names of people who might be <u>pinkos</u>.

7. Hollywood director Elia Kazan, for example, <u>ratted on</u> some people.

8. Playwright Arthur Miller refused to be <u>a stool pigeon</u>.

9. In 1954, the McCarthy trials were televised for the first time, and many Americans became <u>ticked off</u> with the senator.

10. Government officials then asked the unpopular senator to <u>chill out</u> and stop harassing innocent people.

Section 4
EFFECTIVE
SENTENCES

FINAL REVIEW

A. Read the following paragraph. Introduce sentence variety by moving some adverbs and prepositional phrases. Also, combine some short sentences so that the paragraph has more sentence variety.

EXAMPLE:
Often, politicians
~~Politicians~~ are ~~often~~ involved in political scandals.

1. Many politicians commit unusual or disagreeable acts in their private lives. One former Canadian prime minister regularly spoke to spirits. He visited fortune-tellers. His departed mother gave him advice. The advice helped him run the nation. François

Mitterand, France's former president, had a mistress. The public
knew about the story. Nobody really cared. Mitterand died in
1996. His wife, mistress, and illegitimate daughter were at the
funeral.

B. Edit the following paragraphs. Replace ten clichés and slang expressions with
direct English.

EXAMPLE:

Somebody ~~ratted on~~ Gary Hart.

> *told the media about*

2.   Many reporters like to dig up dirt on the private lives of
politicians. In the past, however, journalists were more prudent.
John F. Kennedy, for example, had a lot of extramarital affairs,
but journalists minded their own beeswax and did not publish
information about the affairs. Today, journalists look for scandals
regarding the head honchos. Rival politicians, who are often
green with envy, help the journalists.

Section 4
**EFFECTIVE
SENTENCES**

3.   In 1987, Gary Hart made a whopper of a mistake. In the
middle of a campaign, he dared journalists to follow him. During
a party on a boat, someone took a picture of the married
presidential candidate with a bimbo sitting on his lap. Then, a
few days later, a journalist took a picture of the same woman
leaving the dude's hotel room. Hart could not ditch the
reporters.

4.   After the scandal exploded, Hart insisted that he was a loyal
husband and would never dump his wife, but it was too late. His
career tanked. Hart took a big risk when he dared the media to
follow him.

The Writer's Room

Write a paragraph about one of the following topics. Make sure that your paragraph has sentences of varying lengths. Also ensure that the sentences have varied opening words.

1. Write about a political issue or scandal. You could write about an issue that affects your college campus, or you could write about an issue in your city, town, state, or country. What happened?

2. Should journalists report on the private lives of politicians? For example, do you think it is important to know whether an elected official has committed adultery or has had drug, alcohol, or other kinds of problems? Explain your views.

Section 4
EFFECTIVE SENTENCES

 CHECKLIST: SENTENCE VARIETY AND EXACT LANGUAGE

When you edit your writing, ask yourself the following questions.

Are my sentences varied? Check for problems in these areas:
–too many short sentences
–long sentences that are difficult to follow

Many journalists report on the extramarital affairs of politicians
                                                    act. Their
whom they catch in the ~~act and then their~~ spouses have bad reactions, and marriages have fallen apart.

Do I use clear and specific vocabulary? Check for problems with these elements:
–vague words
–clichés
–slang

A journalist exposed
~~Somebody ratted on~~ the married senator.

 *The Writers' Circle*

Think of ten slang terms that you commonly use. Beside each slang word, write down a standard English word that means basically the same thing. Avoid using obscene words. Then, with a team of students, write a paragraph using the standard terms. Make sure that your paragraph has a variety of sentence lengths.

EXAMPLE:

Slang	Standard English
homie	good friend from the neighborhood

 See Chapter 17 on the Visualizing Writing CD-ROM for additional audio and animated mini-lectures on **Varying Sentence Structure** and **Standard versus Nonstandard English**.

READING LINK

Politics
To read more about political issues, see the following essays:
"Political Activism" by Craig Stern (page 454)
"The Hijab" by Naheed Mustafa (page 423)

Section 4
EFFECTIVE SENTENCES

CHAPTER 18

Fragments

Section Theme: **SCIENCE**

CONTENTS

- Understanding Fragments
- Phrase Fragments
- Explanatory Fragments
- Dependent-Clause Fragments

In the next chapters, you will read about the world of chemistry and hazardous substances.

Grammar Snapshot

Looking at Fragments

Student writer Amin Baty Konde wrote a paragraph about working with chemicals. The underlined errors are called fragments.

<u>Working with hazardous chemicals.</u> It can have far-reaching consequences on a person's life. I have personal experience because for three years I worked for a pesticide company. I sprayed large expanses of lawn with commercial pesticides each day. I was not always careful about wearing a protective mask or gloves. After two years, I began to develop red rashes on my arms. <u>Then, asthma.</u> Although I cannot be certain that exposure to chemicals caused my problems, the timing of my illness has convinced me that it is possible.

In this chapter, you will identify and correct sentence fragments.

Understanding Fragments

A **sentence** must have a subject and verb, and it must express a complete thought. A **fragment** is an incomplete sentence. Either it lacks a subject or a verb, or it fails to express a complete idea. You may see fragments in newspaper headlines and advertisements ("Three-month trial offer"). However, in college writing, it is unacceptable to write fragments.

Sentence:	Exposure to radium is very serious.
Fragment:	Causes various illnesses.

The following sections explain common types of fragments.

Phrase Fragments

Phrase fragments are missing a subject or a verb. In the examples, the fragment is underlined.

No subject:	My father did a dangerous job. <u>Worked with hazardous chemicals.</u>
No verb:	<u>First, sulfuric acid.</u> It is very dangerous.

How to Correct Phrase Fragments

To correct phrase fragments, add the missing subject or verb, or join the fragment to another sentence. Here are ways to correct the two previous examples of phrase fragments.

Add a word(s):	My father did a dangerous job. **He** worked with hazardous chemicals.
Join sentences:	First, sulfuric acid is very dangerous.

Section 5
**COMMON
SENTENCE
ERRORS**

> **Hint** **Incomplete Verbs**
>
> If a sentence has an incomplete verb, it is a phrase fragment. The following example contains a subject and part of a verb. However, the helping verb is missing; therefore, the sentence is not complete.
>
> | | |
> |---|---|
> | **Fragment:** | Many of the experiments with radium done by Marie Curie. |
>
> To make this sentence complete, you must add the helping verb.
>
> | | |
> |---|---|
> | **Sentence:** | Many of the experiments with radium <u>were</u> done by Marie Curie. |

PRACTICE I

Underline and correct five phrase fragments.

EXAMPLE:

<u>First, Marie Curie.</u> ~~She~~ was a great scientist.

Marie Curie discovered radium. In 1898. After her discovery, there was a radium craze. Across the United States. Companies added radium to different products. In some factories, the workers used paint with radium in it. To paint the faces of clocks and wristwatches. Sometimes they licked their paintbrushes to make the ends pointed. Very dangerous, indeed. The factory owners knew the radium-laced paint was not safe. They were more concerned with protecting their business interests than with protecting the health of their workers. Unfortunately.

Section 5
**COMMON
SENTENCE
ERRORS**

Explanatory Fragments

An **explanatory fragment** provides an explanation about a previous sentence and is missing a subject, a complete verb, or both. These types of fragments begin with one of the following words.

as well as	especially	for example	including	particularly
also	except	for instance	like	such as

In these two examples, the fragment is underlined.

We did many new experiments. <u>For example, with mercury.</u>

Some new chemical compounds are useful. <u>Particularly in the production of fabrics.</u>

How to Correct Explanatory Fragments

To correct explanatory fragments, add the missing subject or verb, or join the explanation or example to the previous sentence. Here are ways to correct the two previous examples of explanatory fragments.

Add words: We did many new experiments. For example, **we learned** about mercury.

Join sentences: Some new chemical compounds are useful, particularly in the production of fabrics.

PRACTICE 2

Underline and correct five explanatory fragments.

EXAMPLE:

, such

Radium poisoning causes many terrible health problems. ~~Such~~ as bone decay.

1.   One day in 1920, while factory employee Grace Flyer was
   working, she felt pain. Especially in her head and back. Doctors
   discovered that she had advanced bone decay in her mouth and
   spine. In the next months, strange things happened. For
   example, her teeth. They fell out. Including her back molars.

2.   Some of her co-workers also had symptoms of radium
   poisoning. Such as the loss of teeth. Five years later, Grace and
   her co-workers decided to sue U.S. Radium. They hoped to
   receive compensation for their pain and suffering. As well as
   for their medical expenses. The workers became known as the
   Radium Girls.

Section 5
**COMMON
SENTENCE
ERRORS**

PRACTICE 3

Correct five phrase and explanatory fragments.

EXAMPLE:

across

The lawsuit made headlines. ~~Across~~ the nation.

1.   The Radium Girls wanted $250,000 each. As compensation.
   Unfortunately, their lawsuit took a long time to be heard by a
   judge. Finally, members of the media. They became involved.
   Journalists wanted interviews. Particularly with Grace Flyer, the
   first worker to show symptoms of radium poisoning. However,
   by that time, the Radium Girls were very ill. And were close
   to death. U.S. Radium tried to avoid paying out any money by

using many delaying tactics. The company eventually decided to settle out of court.

2.   Several years later, reporters uncovered a disturbing fact. The judge mediating the settlement was a stockholder in the radium company. The public only learned about the judge's conflict of interest. At a later date.

Dependent-Clause Fragments

A **dependent clause** has a subject and verb, but it cannot stand alone. It "depends" on another clause to be a complete sentence. Dependent clauses may begin with subordinating conjunctions or relative pronouns. This chart contains some of the most common words that introduce dependent clauses.

Common Subordinating Conjunctions				Relative Pronouns
after	before	though	whenever	that
although	even though	unless	where	which
as	so that	until	whereas	who(m)
because	that	what	whether	whose

Section 5
**COMMON
SENTENCE
ERRORS**

In each example, the fragment is underlined.

Marie Curie had a successful professional life. <u>Although her personal life was plagued with scandal</u>.

<u>Marie Curie, who won the Nobel Prize for chemistry</u>. She was born in Poland.

How to Correct Dependent-Clause Fragments

To correct dependent-clause fragments, join the fragment to a complete sentence, remove words, or add the necessary words to make it a complete idea. Here are ways to correct the two previous examples of dependent-clause fragments.

Join sentences:	Marie Curie had a successful professional life, although her personal life was plagued with scandal.
Join sentences and remove words:	Marie Curie, who won the Nobel Prize for chemistry, was born in Poland.

Another way to correct dependent-clause fragments is to delete the subordinating conjunction or relative pronoun that makes the sentence incomplete.

Delete *although*:	Her personal life was filled with scandal.
Delete comma and *who*:	Marie Curie won the Nobel Prize for chemistry.

PRACTICE 4

Underline and correct five dependent-clause fragments.

EXAMPLE:

Few have heard about the women. ~~Who~~ *who* worked for U.S. Radium.

1.   The Radium Girls did not receive very much money. U.S. Radium gave only $10,000 to each woman. Who had wanted $250,000. Although the Radium Girls eventually died. Their case made labor history in the United States. Safety in the workplace became an important topic. That the public passionately debated.

2.   The Radium Girls' case also inspired the public. Citizens learned something important. That workers can fight large corporations. People who had been harmed by workplace toxins. They could use the court system to get compensation.

Section 5
**COMMON
SENTENCE
ERRORS**

PRACTICE 5

Write *C* next to correct sentences and *F* next to fragments.

EXAMPLE:

There are many poisonous chemicals. __C__ In our environment. __F__

1.   Sometimes people do not know that they have been exposed to hazardous chemicals. _____ In their homes. _____ Many household-cleaning products contain toxic chemicals. _____ Some people may have adverse reactions to these products. _____ For example, hives. _____

2.   Furthermore, sometimes there are dangerous chemicals in the land around residential neighborhoods. _____ In the 1970s,

people who lived in the Love Canal region of Niagara Falls, New York, did not know a very important fact. _____ That their homes had been built on a toxic dump. _____ Parents in Love Canal became worried. _____ When their children got sick. _____ Eventually, the parents found out the cause of sickness. _____ The school. _____ It was built on a site where an old factory had dumped poisonous chemicals. _____

3.   Moreover, in our professions. _____ Many of us are exposed to hazardous materials. _____ For instance, scientists in laboratories. _____ They work with dangerous chemicals every day. _____ Also in nuclear power plants. _____ There are sometimes spills or leaks that can poison workers. _____ For example, Karen Silkwood worked at the Kerr-McGee plutonium plant laboratory. _____ Polishing plutonium pellets. _____ She discovered that she had radiation poisoning. _____ Because there were inadequate safety measures at the plant. _____

4.   On a positive note. _____ Today's labor laws require that employers tell employees about the possible effects of working with hazardous materials. _____ There are also strict safety regulations in workplaces. _____ That have hazardous products. _____ Therefore, governments and industries are doing something about the problem. _____

Section 5
COMMON
SENTENCE
ERRORS

PRACTICE 6

The next paragraphs contain various types of fragments. Correct ten fragment errors.

EXAMPLE:

Early chemists experimented. With many substances.

1.   The legend of Nicolas Flamel. It is very interesting. His life has been made into stories and legends. For example, he appeared as a character in *Harry Potter and the Sorcerer's Stone.* By J. K. Rowling.

2.   Nicolas Flamel lived in France. In the fourteenth century. One day he received an unusual book. That was called *The Book of Abraham.* It had seven drawings depicting what seemed to be a chemical process.

3.   The book described the process of how to turn any metal into gold. Flamel made a powder. From the instructions in the book. The powder was called the Philosopher's Stone. According to legend, Flamel successfully transformed metal. Into gold using the powder. He became a rich man. And gained notoriety.

4.   Many people at that time thought that the Philosopher's Stone was the elixir of life. After Flamel's death, many people came to his grave and carried off pieces of the tombstone. Because they thought the magic powder lay at the gravesite. Some people believe that Flamel is still alive. Because of the Philosopher's Stone. Nobody really knows what happened. To the book. It remains a mystery.

Section 5
**COMMON
SENTENCE
ERRORS**

FINAL REVIEW

Identify and correct fifteen fragment errors.

EXAMPLE:

Each year, the Nobel Prize is awarded to people. ~~Who~~ are exceptional.
who

1.   Most people have heard of the Nobel Prize. However, they may not know a lot about the founder. Of that prize. Alfred

Nobel is most famous for his invention of dynamite. He started the Nobel Prize. For the world's greatest scientific and literary advances.

2.   Nobel was born on October 21, 1833. In Stockholm, Sweden. He died in 1896. In Italy. He developed an interest in chemistry. At an early age. While he was visiting Paris in 1847, he met Ascanio Sobrero. Who had developed nitroglycerine. Nitroglycerine was a liquid. That was highly explosive. Nobel realized that if the substance could be controlled, then it would be valuable for industrial use. For example, in mining.

3.   Nobel experimented with many methods. To control and transport the nitroglycerine safely. At last, he was successful. He mixed nitroglycerine with silica and made a paste that could be safely transported. He also invented a detonator. And named his new discovery dynamite.

Section 5
**COMMON
SENTENCE
ERRORS**

4.   Nobel also invented other products. Such as synthetic rubber and artificial silk. In addition to his interest in science, he loved all types of literature. Including poetry. In his will, he bequeathed $9 million to a foundation. That would give prizes in physics, chemistry, medicine, literature, and peace. A prize in economics was added. In 1969.

5.   Curiously, Nobel did not create a prize for mathematics. For many years, there was a rumor stating that Nobel did not give a prize in mathematics because his wife had run off with a famous mathematician. However, there is no historical evidence. That can back up this rumor.

Understanding Run-Ons

Sometimes two or more complete sentences are joined together without correct connecting words or punctuation. In other words, a **run-on sentence** "runs on" without stopping. There are two types of run-on sentences.

- A **fused sentence** is a run-on sentence that has no punctuation to mark the break between ideas.

Fused sentence:	Geologists learn about the origins of the earth they study rocks.
Correct sentence:	Geologists learn about the origins of the earth through their study of rocks.

- A **comma splice** is a run-on sentence that uses a comma to connect two complete ideas. In other words, the comma "splices" or "splits" the sentence.

Comma splice:	Mount St. Helens is an active volcano, it violently erupted on May 18, 1980.
Correct sentence:	Mount St. Helens is an active volcano. It violently erupted on May 18, 1980.

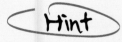 **Identifying Run-Ons**

To identify run-on sentences in your writing, look for sentences that are too long. Such sentences may either lack punctuation or have incorrect comma placement.

Section 5
COMMON SENTENCE ERRORS

PRACTICE I

Write *C* beside correct sentences and *RO* beside run-ons.

EXAMPLE:

A volcano is a fissure in the earth's crust, it allows lava to come out.   *RO*

1. The earth is composed of the core, the mantle, and the crust.   _____

2. Geologists developed a new theory in the 1960s it is called plate tectonics.   _____

3. The earth's crust is made of hard material, it is formed into several "plates."   _____

4. As the plates move over the mantle, they go toward or away from each other.   _____

5. The plates move slowly the movement causes molten rock to seep out.   _____

6. The molten rock oozes up through gaps in the earth's surface.   _____

7. The molten rock is called lava, it is extremely hot and dangerous.   _____

8. The lava can move quickly down the volcano's side, burning everything in its path. _____

How to Correct Run-Ons

You can correct run-on sentences in a variety of ways.

> **Run-On:** Some volcanoes erupt violently others erupt very slowly.

1. **Make two separate sentences by adding end punctuation, such as a period.**

   Some volcanoes erupt violently**.** **Others** erupt very slowly.

2. **Add a subordinator** (*after, although, as, because, before, since, when, while*).

   Some volcanoes erupt violently**,** **while** others erupt very slowly.

3. **Add a coordinator** (*for, and, nor, but, or, yet, so*).

   Some volcanoes erupt violently**,** **but** others erupt very slowly.

4. **Add a semicolon.**

   Some volcanoes erupt violently**;** others erupt very slowly.

PRACTICE 2

A. Correct each run-on by writing two complete sentences.

EXAMPLE:

. Some
There are about 500 active volcanoes ~~some~~ have caused massive destruction.

1. Mount St. Helens erupted for nine hours it covered 230 square miles of forest with ash.

2. Over fifty people died many animals and fish also died.

B. Correct the run-ons by joining the two sentences with a semicolon.

EXAMPLE:

; they
Geologists monitor volcanic activity**,** ~~they~~ share their information.

3. Mount Vesuvius is a famous volcano, it buried Pompeii in A.D. 79.

4. Vesuvius is located near Naples, Italy, over 2 million people live near it.

C. Correct the run-ons by joining the two sentences with a coordinator (*for, and, nor, but, or, yet, so*).

EXAMPLE:

, and he
In 1748, a farmer tried to dig in his vineyard ~~he~~ discovered some ruins.

Section 5
**COMMON
SENTENCE
ERRORS**

5. Pliny the Younger saw the volcano erupt he wrote an account of the event.

6. Pompeii was first discovered by laborers digging a well nobody thought the discovery was significant.

D. Correct the run-ons by joining the two sentences with a subordinator such as *after, although,* or *when.*

EXAMPLE:

In A.D. 63, many houses fell to the ground,͞ ͞when Vesuvius rumbled loudly.

7. Archeologists excavated the site they found loaves of bread from the time of the eruption.

8. The bread was almost 2,000 years old. It was still intact.

PRACTICE 3

Correct eight run-on errors, using a variety of correction methods.

EXAMPLE:

~~The~~ Because the Hope Diamond had a reputation of bad ~~luck many~~ luck, many people refused to buy it.

1. Throughout history, diamonds have intrigued kings, queens, and commoners. Diamonds were first discovered in India around 800 B.C. they were found in riverbeds. The Indians valued them for their beauty, they also thought that diamonds would protect them from evil. India was the world's main source of diamonds until the nineteenth century. Since then, discoveries of diamond deposits have been made in Brazil, South Africa, Siberia, and Canada.

2. The world's largest diamond is called the Star of Africa. In 1905, Frederick Wells, the superintendent of the Premier Mine in South Africa, discovered it. He saw something shining on the mine wall, it was a crystal. Tests showed that the crystal was a diamond, and it weighed about 1⅓ pounds. In 1907, the

Transvaal government of South Africa gave the stone to King Edward VII it was a gift to mark his sixty-sixth birthday. This diamond remains a part of the British crown jewels.

3. Another diamond, the Kohinoor, has an interesting history. Legend says that the Kohinoor is part of a larger diamond, the Great Mogul. This diamond has disappeared, nobody knows its whereabouts. The Kohinoor came into history around 1304, an Indian prince obtained it. The diamond was very beautiful many princes coveted it. In the early 1700s, Nadir Shah of Persia obtained it with his victory over the Delhi Sultanate. Legend says that Nadir Shah was overcome with emotion when he saw the beautiful gem. He cried the word *kohinoor*, in Urdu it means "mountain of light." Eventually, the British seized it from Ranjit Singh of Punjab and gave it to Queen Victoria in 1850. The Kohinoor is now a part of the British crown jewels.

Section 5
COMMON SENTENCE ERRORS

FINAL REVIEW

Correct ten run-on sentence errors. Use a variety of correction methods.

1. Diamonds have been a symbol of love and glamour they have also become a symbol of violence and exploitation. In many countries, diamonds are linked to severe human rights abuses. In those countries, diamonds are used to perpetuate wars, they are also used to finance the activities of terrorist groups.

2. Sierra Leone had a ten-year civil war, it ended in 2001. The cause of the conflict was greed. Sierra Leone has many diamond deposits, antigovernment groups waged military warfare to gain control of the diamonds. Rebel groups in Angola and Liberia have also financed wars, they used money obtained from the diamond trade to do so.

3.   Terrorist groups also benefit from the illegal diamond trade they use diamonds to buy arms and pay informants. *Washington Post* reporter Douglas Farah brought attention to this problem at a congressional hearing in 2003. FBI investigators also looking for the sources of funding for al-Qaeda and Hezbollah they are looking into West African diamonds. Diamonds are small, they are easy to move from one country to another. Therefore, officials find them harder to trace than other contraband items.

4.   Trade in diamonds has come under international scrutiny, to decrease the trade, many countries have agreed to abide by the Kimberley Process. This agreement requires that all international diamonds have a certificate of origin such regulations will curb violence created by the illegal diamond trade.

 The Writer's Room

Write a paragraph about one of the following topics. After you finish writing, ensure that you do not have any run-on sentences.

1. Describe your jewelry. What is your favorite type of jewelry? If you do not like to wear jewelry, explain why not.

2. Examine this photo and think of a term that you could define. Some ideas might be *bling bling, costume jewelry,* or *ostentatious*. Write a definition paragraph about any topic related to the photo.

CHECKLIST: Run-Ons

When you edit your writing, ask yourself the next questions.

Are my sentences joined together without punctuation or with incorrect punctuation? Check for fused sentences and comma splices.

volcano, and it

Mauna Loa is the world's largest ~~volcano it~~ is located in Hawaii.

volcano. It

Kilauea is the world's most active ~~volcano, it~~ has been erupting continuously since 1983.

See Chapter 19 on the Visualizing Writing CD-ROM for an additional audio and animated mini-lecture on **Run-Ons**.

Section 5
COMMON SENTENCE ERRORS

Faulty Parallel Structure

CHAPTER 20

Section Theme: **SCIENCE**

CONTENTS

- Identifying Parallel Structure
- Correcting Faulty Parallel Structure

In this chapter, you will read about astronomy and learn about discoveries, conspiracy theories, and space tourism.

Grammar Snapshot

Looking at Parallel Structure

President John F. Kennedy's 1962 speech at Rice University was about the U.S. space program. Review the underlined ideas to see how they are parallel.

> There is <u>no strife</u>, <u>no prejudice</u>, and <u>no national conflict</u> in outer space as yet. <u>Its hazards</u> are hostile to us all. <u>Its conquest</u> deserves the best of all mankind, and <u>its opportunity</u> for peaceful cooperation may never come again.

In this chapter, you will identify and correct faulty parallel structure.

Identifying Parallel Structure

Parallel structure occurs when pairs or groups of items in a sentence are balanced. By using parallel grammatical structure for words, phrases, or clauses, you will make your sentences clearer and your writing smoother.

In the following sentences, the underlined phrases contain repetitions of grammatical structure, but not repetitions of ideas. Each sentence has parallel structure.

The <u>United States</u>, <u>Russia</u>, and <u>Japan</u> have spent funds on the space station.
(The nouns are parallel.)

The astronomer went <u>through the doors</u>, <u>up the stairs</u>, and <u>into the observatory</u>.
(The prepositional phrases are parallel.)

She <u>observes</u>, <u>records</u>, and <u>predicts</u> planet cycles.
(The present tenses are parallel.)

I am <u>awed</u>, <u>excited</u>, and <u>terrified</u> at the prospect of space flight.
(The adjectives are parallel.)

Copernicus was a scientist <u>who took risks</u>, <u>who made acute observations</u>, and <u>who developed new theories</u>.
(The "who" clauses are parallel.)

Section 5
**COMMON
SENTENCE
ERRORS**

PRACTICE I

All of the following sentences contain parallel structures. Underline the parallel items.

EXAMPLE:
The space race was a <u>hazardous</u>, <u>exciting</u>, and <u>innovative</u> adventure.

1. In 1957, the space race began when Soviet scientists developed, built, and launched the space satellite *Sputnik*.

2. Soviet engineers, scientists, and politicians worked together.

3. American government officials felt shock, anxiety, and then determination.

4. The officials wanted to build their own satellite, to launch it quickly, and to surpass the Soviet achievements.

5. With an injection of funds, with some planning, and with the support of many scientists, the United States launched a satellite called *Explorer* in 1958.

6. The National Aeronautics and Space Administration (NASA) began operations on October 1, at noon, in Florida.

7. U.S. scientists who used available resources, who took risks, and who believed in their vision were able to create an automated moon probe.

8. President John F. Kennedy said that humans choose to go to the moon and do other difficult things "not because they are easy, but because they are hard."

Correcting Faulty Parallel Structure

Faulty parallel structure occurs when you present equivalent ideas with different grammatical structures. The result is a sentence with ideas that are not balanced. To avoid imbalances, use parallel structure.

A Series of Words or Phrases

Use parallel structure when words or phrases are joined in a series.

Not parallel: I like to read articles, watch documentaries, and listening to seminars.

Parallel: I like <u>to read</u> articles, <u>to watch</u> documentaries, and <u>to listen</u> to seminars.
(The infinitives are parallel.)

Not parallel: The expanding universe, black holes, and scientists studying matter are all problems relating to the study of cosmology.

Parallel: <u>The expanding universe</u>, <u>black holes</u>, and <u>matter</u> are all problems relating to the study of cosmology.
(The nouns are parallel.)

Section 5
**COMMON
SENTENCE
ERRORS**

Paired Clauses

Use parallel structure when independent clauses are joined by *and*, *but*, or *or*.

Not parallel: The space station is costing a lot of money, but it provides essential data.

Parallel: The space station <u>costs</u> a lot of money, but it <u>provides</u> essential data.
(The present tense verbs are parallel.)

Not parallel: Copernicus observed the stars carefully, and he recorded his findings with accuracy.

Parallel: Copernicus observed the stars <u>carefully</u>, and he recorded his findings <u>accurately</u>.
(The adverbs are parallel.)

Correcting Faulty Parallel Structure

When you identify faulty parallel structure, correct it by looking carefully at repeated grammatical units and then rewriting the unit that is not parallel.

sends
The satellite collects data, stores it, and ~~is sending~~ images.

PRACTICE 2

Correct the faulty parallel structure in each sentence.

EXAMPLE:

Today, amateur astronomers are looking for satellites, watching the
observing
constellations, and <u>to observe</u> shooting stars.

Section 5
COMMON SENTENCE ERRORS

1. Scientists are doing research on the expanding universe, on the Big Bang theory, and black and white holes.

2. To observe the universe, astrophysicists not only use powerful telescopes, but they are also relying on modern satellite images.

3. In ancient times, the Babylonians, the Greeks, and people from Egypt observed and predicted the position of planets and stars.

4. Copernicus worked quietly and at a slow pace on his observations.

5. With his announcement that the sun was the center of the universe, Copernicus surprised the public, was angering the clergy, and upset other scientists.

6. Galileo Galilei invented the telescope to look at the night sky and recording his observations.

7. Galileo's observations validated Copernicus' earlier observation, and Galileo was opening new doors for the study of astronomy.

8. Large telescopes and cameras that are powerful have helped scientists observe poorly lit celestial bodies.

9. Early photographers attempted to take pictures of the moon, the stars, and photograph solar eclipses.

10. The general public can learn about the universe by going to planetariums, to observatories, and science museums.

Comparisons

Use parallel structure in comparisons containing *than* or *as*.

Not parallel:	I wanted a better explanation rather than to remain confused.
Parallel:	I wanted <u>to receive</u> a better explanation rather than <u>to remain</u> confused. (The infinitive forms are parallel.)
Not parallel:	His raw intelligence was as important as working hard.
Parallel:	<u>His raw intelligence</u> was as important as <u>his hard work</u>. (The nouns are parallel.)

Two-Part Constructions

Use parallel structure when comparing or contrasting ideas using these constructions: *either . . . or, not . . . but, both . . . and,* or *neither . . . nor.*

Not parallel:	My experience was both exciting and a challenge.
Parallel:	My experience was both <u>exciting</u> and <u>challenging</u>. (The adjectives are parallel.)
Not parallel:	She decided either to publish her research or burning it.
Parallel:	She decided either <u>to publish</u> her research or <u>to burn</u> it. (The infinitives are parallel.)

Section 5
**COMMON
SENTENCE
ERRORS**

PRACTICE 3

Correct any errors in parallel construction. If the sentence is correct, write *C* in the blank.

EXAMPLE:

Our solar system not only includes the sun and planets but also
   consists
~~is consisting~~ of more than sixty moons, millions of asteroids, and

billions of comets.   _____

1. Not only do scientists divide the solar system into the inner part and outer part, but they are listing the celestial bodies in each. _____

2. Mercury, Venus, Earth, and the planet Mars are found in the inner solar system. _____

3. Jupiter, Saturn, Uranus, Neptune, and Pluto are in the outer solar system. _____

4. Pluto is the farthest planet from the sun and containing one moon called Charon. _____

5. The earth is revolving around the sun as well as to spin on its axis. _____

6. When a planet completes one journey around the sun, its path is called an orbit. _____

7. Earth's orbit lasts 365 days while the orbit of Mercury lasts 88 Earth days. _____

8. Earth takes 24 hours, or one Earth day, to complete its spin while Jupiter takes only 10 Earth hours finishing its spin. _____

9. The stars look smaller than the sun because they are farther away from us. _____

10. Astronomers have realized that some of those stars are both larger and more bright than our sun. _____

Section 5
**COMMON
SENTENCE
ERRORS**

PRACTICE 4

A. Fill in the blanks with parallel and logical words, phrases, or clauses.

EXAMPLE:
We studied _after class_ and _on weekends_.

1. At college, I am studying both _____ and

_____ .

2. To get to the college library, you must go _____,

_____, and _____.

3. My friend is _____, _____,

and _____.

4. As a child, I _____, _____,

and _____.

5. My instructor complained that _____, and

_____.

B. Compose three sentences that contain parallel structure. Try to use a variety of constructions. For example, you might use parallel nouns in one sentence and parallel verbs in another.

6. _____

_____

7. _____

_____

8. _____

_____

PRACTICE 5

Correct eight errors in parallel construction.

EXAMPLE:

Many people still believe that the history books ~~lie~~, *are lying* that the encyclopedias are lying, and that NASA engineers and astronauts are lying when they claim that human beings landed on the moon.

1.   According to conspiracy theorists, the U.S. government,

the space agencies, and engineers with aeronautical degrees

had two very good reasons to fake the moon landing. First, the government wanted to divert attention from the Vietnam War and instilling pride in the American people. Second, the space and research agencies wanted to keep the flow of money into their institutions.

Astronaut Edwin Aldrin, Jr. (1969)

2.   There are many theories about how the U.S. government engineered the space travel reports. One theory states that the military forces flew the rockets to the South Pole instead of to the moon. They carefully picked up the command module, and they sent the module to the South Pacific with speed. Those scientists and technicians who knew about the conspiracy were given money to keep silent.

3.   Some skeptics who are American, French, Japanese, and those who live in Germany post Internet messages about their theories. They believe that the U.S. government forced film director Stanley Kubrick to direct the moon-landing film and distributing it. Skeptics offer photos of the flag on the moon as evidence. They say that there is no wind on the moon; therefore, the flag could not wave.

4.   NASA officials deny any part in a conspiracy and are offering rebuttals. For example, NASA officials say that a pole held the flag out in the moon-landing photos. Therefore, it only appears that the flag is waving in the wind. Furthermore, the twelve astronauts who have walked on the moon are serious, professional, and act with honesty.

5.   Many people wonder why believers of conspiracy theories promote such ideas. Perhaps they do it because they believe it, because they want to be famous, or for money. The only thing that is certain is that there will always be believers in conspiracy theories.

FINAL REVIEW

Correct ten errors in parallel construction.

EXAMPLE:

Space travel is exciting and ~~a challenge~~ *challenging*.

1.   Space travel has changed a lot over four decades. In the past, only highly trained astronauts went to outer space, but today tourists who are rich can do it. For example, in April 2001, California millionaire Dennis Tito was the 415th person in orbit. Tito paid the Russian space agency about $30 million for a seat on a Russian flight and traveling to the International Space Station. He was clearly a man who had a plan, who worked hard, and made his dream come true.

Section 5
COMMON SENTENCE ERRORS

2.   Some analysts, people who are politicians, and scientists are strongly opposed to space tourism. They argue that space travel is expensive and has dangers. According to a member of Congress, it is unfair to expect taxpayers to contribute to space research, to have no say in how the funds are spent, and watch rich citizens take flights to space. Representative Ralph Hall argues that space travel should be reserved for trained astronauts or for scientists who have specific research goals to fulfill. Additionally, space travel is still very dangerous, so it is premature to spend time and wasting money on space tourism.

3.   However, former astronaut Buzz Aldrin believes that ordinary people should have the chance to orbit the earth. Perhaps space travel is dangerous and not easy, but fulfilling a lifelong desire is more important than to worry about the dangers of space flight. Tony Webb, organizer of a space lottery, believes in space tourism. He thinks it should be available for everyone, not just for people with money and famous people.

 ## The Writer's Room

Write a paragraph about one of the following topics. After you finish writing, make sure that you have no faulty parallel structure.

1. Explain why you would or would not travel to outer space.
2. How are space explorers comparable to other types of explorers? Compare space explorers with other explorers.

Section 5
COMMON SENTENCE ERRORS

 ### CHECKLIST: PARALLEL STRUCTURE

When you edit your writing, ask yourself the next questions.

Are my grammatical structures balanced? Check for errors in these cases:
  –when words or phrases are joined in a series
  –when independent clauses are joined by *and*, *but*, or *or*
  –in comparisons or contrasts

                                      the harshest weather
Mars has <u>the largest volcano</u>, <u>the deepest valley</u>, and ~~its weather is very harsh~~ of any planet in our solar system.

READING LINK

Science
To read more about space travel, see the following essay:
"What It Feels Like to Walk on the Moon" by Buzz Aldrin (page 449)

 ## The Writers' Circle

Form a team with two other students. Imagine that your team has won first-class seats on a space cruise. Each one of you can bring only five small items on the flight. Work together to create a paragraph explaining what items you would bring. You can share the items, so consider what items would be most useful for all of you.

When you finish writing, verify that your paragraph contains no fragments or run-ons. Also, make sure that your sentences have parallel structure.

 See Chapter 20 on the Visualizing Writing CD-ROM for an additional audio and animated mini-lecture on **Parallelism**.

Section 5
**COMMON
SENTENCE
ERRORS**

CHAPTER 21

Adjectives and Adverbs

Section Theme: **RELATIONSHIPS**

CONTENTS

- Adjectives
- Adverbs
- Comparative and Superlative Forms

In this chapter, you will read about famous couples in history and in literature, such as Antony and Cleopatra and John Lennon and Yoko Ono.

Grammar Snapshot

Looking at Adjectives and Adverbs

Comedian Bill Cosby describes a high school romance. Review the underlined adjectives and adverbs.

> During my <u>last</u> year of high school, I fell in love <u>so hard</u> with a girl that it made my love for Sarah McKinney seem like a <u>stupid</u> infatuation with a teacher. Charlene Gibson was the <u>real</u> thing, and she would be Mrs. Charlene Cosby, serving me hot dogs, watching me drive to the hoop, and giving me the <u>full-court</u> press for the rest of my life.

In this chapter, you will identify and use adjectives and adverbs.

Adjectives

Adjectives describe nouns (people, places, or things) and pronouns (words that replace nouns). In other words, adjectives add more information and detail to the words they are modifying. They add information explaining how many, what kind, or which one. They also describe how things look, smell, feel, taste, and sound.

> The **handsome** <u>Romeo</u> loved the **beautiful** <u>Juliet</u>.
>
> My English class studied **two** of Shakespeare's <u>plays</u>.
>
> William Shakespeare wrote the **fabulous** <u>play</u> called *Romeo and Juliet*.
>
> Romeo and Juliet are the **main** <u>characters</u> in the play. <u>They</u> are **impulsive** and **creative**.

PRACTICE I

Underline all of the adjectives in these sentences.

EXAMPLE:

Cleopatra was a <u>gorgeous</u> and <u>troubled</u> woman.

1. Cleopatra was the last Egyptian queen. She was beautiful and intelligent.

2. She was also a gifted linguist. She could speak nine languages.

3. When the Roman army invaded Egypt, Cleopatra became the mistress of the powerful Roman general, Julius Caesar.

4. Her true love was the brave soldier Marc Antony, who became an important general after Julius Caesar was killed.

5. Cleopatra and Marc Antony had a scandalous and passionate affair.

Section 6
MODIFIERS

Placement of Adjectives

You can place adjectives either before a noun or after a linking verb such as *be*, *look*, *appear*, or *become*.

Before the noun:	The **young** <u>Frida Kahlo</u> fell in love with a much older painter.
After a linking verb:	Their <u>relationship</u> was **passionate** and **volatile**.

> **Hint** **Problems with Adjective Placement**
>
> In some languages, adjectives can appear directly after nouns. However, in English, never place an adjective directly after the noun that it is describing.
>
> *very elegant lady.*
> Martha Dandridge Washington was a ~~lady very elegant.~~
>
> *forty and a half years.*
> She was married to George Washington for ~~forty years and half.~~

PRACTICE 2

Some of the following sentences have errors in adjective placement. Underline and correct each error. If a sentence is correct, write *C* in the blank.

EXAMPLE:

magnificent palace.
The young lovers lived in a ~~palace magnificent.~~ _____

1. Cleopatra and Marc Antony planned to conquer the powerful city of Rome. _____

2. After the fierce battle, Marc Antony heard the rumor false that the vivacious Cleopatra was dead. _____

3. The handsome and shrewd general, Marc Antony, became depressed and killed himself. _____

4. Cleopatra heard the horrible news about Marc Antony, and she committed suicide by allowing a snake poisonous to bite her. _____

5. With the death of Cleopatra, the rule of the pharaohs ended, and Egypt became a province Roman. _____

Section 6
MODIFIERS

Order of Adjectives

When using two or more adjectives together, place them in this order: number, quality, size, age, color, origin, and type. The following chart indicates the order of adjectives.

Determiner (number, etc.)	Quality	Size or Shape	Age	Color	Origin	Type	Noun
We bought two	beautiful		old	red		Persian	rugs.
Santa Fe is a	lovely	large			New Mexico	desert	town.

 **Punctuating Adjectives**

Place commas between adjectives of equal weight. In other words, if two adjectives describe a quality, place a comma between them.

Comma: Shah Jahan presented the <u>lovely, rare</u> sculpture to the princess.

Do not place commas between adjectives of unequal weight. For example, if one adjective describes a quality and another describes a place of origin or color, do not put a comma between them.

No comma: Shah Jahan presented the <u>rare Greek</u> sculpture to the princess.

PRACTICE 3

Complete these sentences by writing the adjectives in parentheses in the correct order. If any are already in the correct order, write *C*.

EXAMPLE:

The (young, handsome) _handsome young_ Shah Jahan became the Mughal emperor of seventeenth-century India.

1. A (Indian, 15-year-old, shy) _____ princess

   named Mumtaz married Shah Jahan in 1612 and became his favorite wife.

   They shared a (long, passionate) _____ love that

   lasted until she died in 1629.

2. Shah Jahan constructed the (white, beautiful) _____

   Taj Mahal as a symbol of their love. Around (skilled, 20,000)

   _____ workers and (Indian, gray, 1,000)

   _____ elephants took nearly twenty years to

   complete the Taj Mahal.

Section 6
MODIFIERS

3. The mausoleum is made of (smooth, white) _____

   marble and sits on a sandstone platform. The interior contains

   (intricate, Islamic) _____ designs made of

   semiprecious stones. Shah Jahan planned to build a (marble, black, stunning)

   _____ mausoleum for himself, but the

   project was never started. When he died, he was buried beside his

   (beloved, young) _____ queen in the Taj Mahal.

Problems with Adjectives

You can recognize many adjectives by their endings. Be particularly careful when you use the following adjective forms.

Adjectives Ending in *-ful* or *-less*

Some adjectives end in *-ful* or *-less*. Remember that *-ful* ends in one *l* and *-less* ends in two *s*'s.

> Diego Rivera, a **skillful** artist, created many **beautiful** paintings and murals. His work appeared **effortless** because he was so prolific.

Adjectives Ending in *-ed* and *-ing*

Some adjectives look like verbs because they end in *-ing* or *-ed*.

- When the adjective ends in *-ed*, it describes someone's expression or feeling.

> The **pleased** and **well-regarded** artist presented his mural to the public.

- When the adjective ends in *-ing*, it describes the quality of the person or thing.

> His **exciting, surprising** images are displayed on public buildings in Mexico.

Hint **Keep Adjectives in the Singular Form**

When a noun describes another noun, always make it singular, even if the noun following it is plural.

> year
> Juliet was a thirteen-~~years~~-old girl when she met Romeo.

> dollar
> We bought several ten-~~dollars~~ tickets to see the play *Romeo and Juliet*.

Section 6
MODIFIERS

PRACTICE 4

Correct nine adjective errors in the paragraphs. The adjectives may have the wrong form, or they may be misspelled.

EXAMPLE:

interesting
Frida Kahlo was one of the world's most ~~interested~~ painters.

1.　　Frida Kahlo was born in 1907 and was raised in an upper-class Mexican neighborhood. From an early age, she enjoyed wearing flamboyant, shocked clothing. She would appear in men's suits or long dresses, and she often wore beautifull flowers in her hair.

2.　　In high school, the restles young girl first met the great Mexican artist Diego Rivera when he painted a wonderfull mural for her school. At the age of twenty, Frida met Diego again when she showed him some of her colorfull paintings. Diego encouraged Frida and told her that her self-portraits were very originals.

3.   Even though Diego was much older than Frida, they fell in love and married in 1929. Their stormy relationship included many affairs. Diego was a skilfull womanizer and, after several years of marriage, he pursued Frida's younger sister, Cristina. Perhaps to retaliate, Frida also had extramarital relationships. She had a surprised romance with the Communist leader Leon Trotsky when he was a guest at her home.

4.   The scandalous, passionate relationship between Frida Kahlo and Diego Rivera remains one of Mexico's most publicizing love stories.

Adverbs

Adverbs add information to adjectives, verbs, or other adverbs. They give more specific information about how, when, where and to what extent an action or event occurred.

Robin Hood **often** robbed from the rich and gave to the poor.

Robin Hood learned archery **easily.**

Robin Hood fell in love with Maid Marian **quite quickly**.

Robin Hood and his merry men were **tremendously** intelligent.

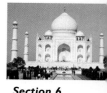

Adverb Forms

Adverbs often end in *-ly*. In fact, you can change many adjectives into adverbs by adding *-ly* endings.

Adjective: honest   **Adverb:**   honestly

- If you add *-ly* to a word that ends in *l*, then your new word will have a double *l*.

  joyful + -ly

  Eros watched **joyfully** as Psyche walked toward him.

- If you add *-ly* to a word that ends in *e*, keep the *e*. Exceptions to this rule are *true—truly* and *due—duly*.

  passionate + -ly

  In Greek mythology, Eros, the god of love, fell **passionately** in love with Psyche.

Hint **Some Adverbs and Adjectives Have the Same Form**

Some adverbs look exactly like adjectives. The only way to distinguish them is to see what they are modifying or describing.

Examples:	early	far	high	often	right
	fast	hard	late	past	soon

Adjective: In the **early** morning, Eros pierced the heart of a mortal.

Adverb: Psyche arrived **early** at the wedding.

PRACTICE 5

Change each adjective into an adverb. Make sure that you spell the adverb correctly.

EXAMPLE:

pure   _purely_____

1. beautiful   _____   6. extreme   _____

2. often   _____   7. delightful   _____

3. virtual   _____   8. heavy   _____

4. soon   _____   9. wonderful   _____

5. real   _____   10. entire   _____

Section 6
MODIFIERS

Placement of Frequency Adverbs

Frequency adverbs are words that indicate how often someone performs an action or when an event occurs. They are words such as *always*, *often*, *sometimes*, *usually*, and *ever.*

- Place frequency adverbs before regular present and past tense verbs.

  Zeus **usually** <u>lived</u> on Mount Olympus.

- Place frequency adverbs after the verb *be.*

  The bridegroom <u>is</u> **usually** very dependable.

- Place frequency adverbs after helping verbs.

  Michael <u>has</u> **never** <u>been</u> married before.

PRACTICE 6

Correct five errors with word order or adjective and adverb forms.

EXAMPLE:

Newspapers and magazines ~~contain often~~ *often contain* articles about the love affairs of the rich and famous.

1.   One of the most famous love stories of the twentieth century was the romance between John Lennon and Yoko Ono. In 1967, John met Yoko in a gallery where she was exhibiting her artwork. John climbed up a ladder and careful examined a tiny painting. On the painting was the word *yes*, and John liked the fact that the message was positive.

2.   When John and Yoko married, the press followed often them, and they usually were chased by photographers. The couple also had a truely difficult time because Beatles fans did not accept Yoko. In 1973, the couple broke up, but John eventualy realized that he wanted to be in New York with the love of his life. Unfortunately, when John was forty years old, he was killed by a deranged gunman.

Section 6
MODIFIERS

Problems with Adverbs

Sometimes people use an adjective instead of an adverb after a verb. Ensure that you always modify your verbs using an adverb.

Aphrodite waited ~~real quiet~~ *really quietly* for the celebrations to begin.

PRACTICE 7

Each sentence has one error with adverb or adjective forms or placement. Correct the errors.

EXAMPLE:

Some people ~~sincerelly~~ *sincerely* believe in arranged marriages.

1. Arranged marriages are commonly in many parts of the world.

2. Parents find often a mate for their son or daughter based on criteria such as level of education, job prospects, and family background.

3. Advocates of arranged marriages believe real strongly that love can come later in the relationship.

4. Love marriages happen regular in many countries.

5. In love marriages, people sometimes fall in love quick.

6. In some Western societies, common-law unions have gradualy become popular.

7. The Netherlands officialy recognizes common-law unions.

8. In your opinion, should common-law couples have the same legally rights as married couples?

Good and Well, Bad and Badly

Good is an adjective, and *well* is an adverb.

Adjective:	The pastry chef made a **good** wedding cake.
Adverb:	The pastry chef cooks **well.**

Exception: Use *well* to describe a person's health.

Adverb:	I do not feel **well.**

Bad is an adjective, and *badly* is an adverb.

Adjective:	I am a **bad** singer.
Adverb:	I sang **badly** at the wedding.

Section 6
MODIFIERS

PRACTICE 8

Underline the correct adjectives or adverbs.

EXAMPLE:

Generally, couples who communicate (good, <u>well</u>) have successful relationships.

1. Varied wedding traditions exist in the world. In Fiji, it is considered a (good, well) practice to give a whale tooth symbolizing wealth to the bride's father.

2. At Greek weddings, guests throw dishes on the floor for (good, well) luck.

3. In North American Christian weddings, it is (bad, badly) luck for the groom to see the bride's dress before the wedding. There is usually a big wedding feast, and sometimes the food is cooked (bad, badly).

4. At traditional Jewish weddings, an Israeli dance called the hora is performed. Some people dance (good, well) while others dance (bad, badly).

5. Many people consider a community center to be a (good, well) place to hold a wedding reception.

Comparative and Superlative Forms

Use the **comparative form** to compare two items.

Adjectives:	Romeo is <u>younger</u> than Mercutio.
	Juliet is <u>more romantic</u> than her nurse.
Adverbs:	Shakespeare wrote <u>more quickly</u> than most other playwrights.
	Romeo debated the issue <u>more convincingly</u> than Juliet.

Use the **superlative form** to compare three or more items.

Adjectives:	Juliet was one of the <u>youngest</u> characters in Shakespeare's plays.
	Shakespeare was the <u>most creative</u> playwright of his era.
Adverbs:	Benvolio reacted the <u>most swiftly</u> of all of Romeo's cousins.
	Romeo spoke the <u>most convincingly</u> of all of Juliet's suitors.

Section 6
MODIFIERS

How to Write Comparative and Superlative Forms

You can write comparative and superlative forms by remembering a few simple guidelines.

Using -er and -est Endings

Add *-er* and *-est* endings to one-syllable adjectives and adverbs.

	Comparative	**Superlative**
short	shorter than	the shortest
fast	faster than	the fastest
quick	quicker than	the quickest

Double the last letter when the adjective ends in one vowel + one consonant.

	Comparative	**Superlative**
hot	hotter than	the hottest

Using *More* and *The Most*

Generally add *more* and *the most* to adjectives and adverbs of two or more syllables.

	Comparative	**Superlative**
modern	more modern than	the most modern
clearly	more clearly than	the most clearly
worried	more worried than	the most worried

When a two-syllable adjective ends in *y*, change the *y* to *i* before you add the *-er* or *-est*.

	Comparative	**Superlative**
happy	happier than	the happiest

Using Irregular Comparative and Superlative Forms

Some adjectives and adverbs have unique comparative and superlative forms. Study this list to remember how to form some of the most common ones.

	Comparative	**Superlative**
good, well	better than	the best
bad, badly	worse than	the worst
some, much, many	more than	the most
little (a small amount)	less than	the least
far	farther, further	the farthest, the furthest

 **Farther versus Further**

- *Farther* indicates a physical distance.

    The wedding reception was **farther** from my home than it was from my fiancé's home.

- *Further* means "additional."

    I need **further** information before I can make a decision.

PRACTICE 9

Write the comparative and superlative forms of each adjective and adverb.

	Comparative	**Superlative**
EXAMPLE: famous	more famous	most famous
1. easy	_____	_____
2. easily	_____	_____
3. good	_____	_____

		Comparative	Superlative
4.	bad		
5.	happy		
6.	quickly		
7.	careful		
8.	fast		
9.	thin		
10.	lazy		
11.	red		
12.	decent		

PRACTICE 10

Underline the correct superlative or comparative form of each adjective or adverb.

EXAMPLE:

Lalita's wedding day was the (worse, <u>worst</u>) day of her life.

1. Two weeks before the big day, Lalita went to the (better, best) store in the city to buy her wedding sari.

2. The sari shop had the (worse, worst) selection that she had ever seen.

3. She went to another store that was much (further, farther) away.

4. The material of the wedding sari was much (heavier, heaviest) than she had expected it to be.

5. Lalita ordered the (better, best) traditional Indian food that money could buy.

6. However, the caterers made the (bigger, biggest) mistake they could possibly make when they got the date wrong.

7. On her wedding day, Lalita's brother offered to cook but wanted (farther, further) information about the type of food to prepare.

8. Her brother cooked the food because he was a (better, best) cook than Lalita.

9. At the reception, Lalita's cousin sang, but he was the (worse, worst) singer she had ever heard.

10. The guests had a (better, best) time than Lalita.

Section 6
MODIFIERS

PRACTICE 11

Fill in each blank with either the comparative or superlative form of the adjective in parentheses.

EXAMPLE:

Many people find love stories to be the (interesting) _most interesting_ form of literature.

1.   Some of the (great) _____ works of fiction are based on some of the (passionate) _____ relationships. Many of Shakespeare's plays were based on relationships, including *Antony and Cleopatra* and *Romeo and Juliet.* Shakespeare also wrote romantic sonnets. I think that love poetry is (good) _____ than love stories. I like to read horror stories the (little) _____ of all types of literature.

2.   Henry Wadsworth Longfellow wrote a poem in 1858 called *The Courtship of Miles Standish.* This poem was about one of the (early) _____ romances that took place in the American colonies.

3.   Miles Standish was an upstanding leader who fell in love with Priscilla Mullins, the (beautiful) _____ maiden in the colonies. Oddly, although he was one of the (respected) _____ men in the colony, he was also one of the (timid) _____. Because of his acute shyness, Standish could not bring himself to express his love for Priscilla. His friend John Alden, who was (outgoing) _____ than he, decided to tell Priscilla about Standish's feelings. Unfortunately, Priscilla fell in love with Alden, who was the (charming) _____ man she had ever met. The love triangle resolved itself, and Alden eventually married Priscilla with Miles Standish's blessing.

Section 6
MODIFIERS

Problems with Comparative and Superlative Forms

In the comparative form, never use *more* and *-er* to modify the same word. In the superlative form, never use *most* and *-est* to modify the same word.

His date with Jan was ~~more~~ *better* than his date with Catherine.

It was the ~~most~~ *best* date of his life.

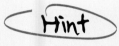 **Using "*the*" in the Comparative Form**

Although you would usually use *the* in superlative forms, you can use it in some two-part comparatives. In these expressions, the second part is the result of the first part.

    action   result

<u>The more</u> you work at a relationship, <u>the better</u> it will be.

PRACTICE 12

Correct twelve adjective and adverb errors.

EXAMPLE:

     most

One of the ~~more~~ famous relationships in the twentieth century was between Charles Lindbergh and Anne Morrow.

1.   Charles Lindberg was an all-American hero because, in 1927, he was the first person to fly safe across the Atlantic Ocean. Charles originaly pursued Anne Morrow's sister. However, when he saw the more younger Anne, he fell in love with her. She was real beautiful. They lived happy for a while. She wrote a memoir of their relationship that led to more greater celebrity status for the pair. The more Anne wrote, the happiest she became.

2.   In some respects, the couple had a perfect relationship. Anne worked tireless beside her husband, helping him navigate during his flights. In an era when most women did not work outside the home, Anne was more happier pursuing her writing and flying careers than being a housewife.

Section 6
MODIFIERS

3.   However, the relationship between Charles and Anne was not perfect. They both had affairs, and at one point, Anne fell in love with one of the most best writers of the era, Antoine de Saint-Exupéry. Charles and Anne also lived through the more tragic event of their lives. In 1932, their first child was kidnapped and murdered. About four years later, Bruno Richard Hauptmann was executed for the crime.

4.   The more Charles and Anne suffered, the strongest their relationship became. They went on to have more children, and they were together until the death of Charles in 1974.

FINAL REVIEW

Correct fifteen adjective or adverb errors.

EXAMPLE:

Oscar Wilde was one of the ~~most famousest~~ *famous* writers of the nineteenth century.

1.   Oscar Wilde wrote interesting short stories, poems, and plays. One of his more better short stories is "The Model Millionaire."

2.   Hughie, the main character, is not very intelligent, but he is real good-looking. He falls in love with Laura, a beautiful young woman. The more he pursues her, the most her father objects. Hughie proposes to Laura anyway, but her father continualy disapproves of him. To make matters worst than before, Laura's father does not want them to marry until Hughie finds himself in a more better financial situation.

3.   One day, Hughie goes to his friend Trevor's house. Trevor is an artist who paints really good. In Trevor's studio, Hughie meets a poor dressed man who is Trevor's model. The beggar's

Section 6
MODIFIERS

clothes are more older and dirtier than the artist's clothes. Hughie gives all of his money to the beggar because he pities the man. Then Hughie leaves the room quick.

4.   The next day, Trevor admits that he had told the beggar about Hughie's financial problem. Then, with a smile, Trevor tells Hughie that the beggar is actual one of the most richest men in the world. Hughie feels more sillier than ever before. How could he have given money to such a rich man?

5.   The next morning, a letter is delivered to Hughie's house containing a check for $10,000 and a very good-written note that says, "To Hughie and Laura, a wedding present from an old beggar." Soon after, the most happy day of Hughie's life occurs when he marries Laura.

 The Writer's Room

Section 6
MODIFIERS

Write a paragraph about one of the following topics. After you finish writing, underline any adjectives and adverbs. Decide whether your paragraph has enough descriptive words and phrases.

1. Describe your ideal partner. What characteristics should he or she have?
2. Narrate what happened on a funny, boring, or romantic date that you have had.

 CHECKLIST: ADJECTIVES AND ADVERBS
When you edit your writing, ask yourself the following questions.

Do I use adjectives correctly? Check for errors in these cases:
  –placement of adjectives
  –order of adjectives
  –spelling

Throughout history, ~~countles~~ countless people have enjoyed having ~~romances wonderfull~~ wonderful romances.

(continued)

Do I use adverbs correctly? Check for errors in these cases:

　—spelling of adverbs that end in -*ly*

　—placement of frequency adverbs

　　　　　　　often
　Many marriages take place ~~often~~ in places of worship.

Do I use the correct adverb form? Check for errors in these cases:

　—use of adjectives instead of adverbs to modify verbs

　—use of *good, well* and *bad, badly*

　　The Romantic poet Elizabeth Barrett Browning wrote ~~good~~ *well*
　　when she was a child.

　　　　　　　　　　　　　　　　　　　　　　　quickly
　　She and her husband, Robert Browning, eloped rather ~~quick~~ to
　　escape her father.

Do I use the correct comparative and superlative forms? Check for
errors in these cases:

　—*more* and -*er* comparisons

　—*the most* and -*est* comparisons

　　　　　　　　　　　　　　better
　　The more you write, the ~~more better~~ writer you become.

See Chapter 21 on the Visualizing Writing CD-ROM for
additional audio and animated mini-lectures on **Adjectives
and Adverbs**.

Section 6
MODIFIERS

Mistakes with Modifiers

Section Theme: **RELATIONSHIPS**

CONTENTS

- Misplaced Modifiers
- Dangling Modifiers

In this chapter, you will read about relationship issues such as Internet dating and workplace romances.

Grammar Snapshot

Looking at Modifiers

In an essay titled "Marriage Is an Outdated Institution," college student Winston Murray writes about the decline of marriage. In the following excerpt, some of the modifiers are underlined.

> Weddings are expensive and extravagant affairs <u>that indebt families for years to come</u>. Parents of the bride and groom <u>often</u> take out second mortgages to give their children the ideal wedding. <u>After paying for the wedding dress</u>, they must pay for the reception hall, flowers, music, catering, and limousines to have a one-night party.

In this chapter, you will identify and correct misplaced and dangling modifiers.

Misplaced Modifiers

A **modifier** is a word, phrase, or clause that describes or modifies nouns or verbs in a sentence. To use a modifier correctly, place it next to the word(s) that you want to modify.

modifier   modified noun

<u>Holding her hand</u>, **Charles** proposed.

A **misplaced modifier** is a word, phrase, or clause that is not placed next to the word that it modifies. When a modifier is too far from the word that it is describing, the meaning of the sentence can become confusing or unintentionally funny.

Confusing:	I saw the Golden Gate Bridge riding my bike.
	(How could a bridge ride a bike?)
Clear:	**Riding my bike,** I saw the Golden Gate Bridge.
Confusing:	Boring and silly, Amanda closed the fashion magazine.
	(What is boring and silly? Amanda or the magazine?)
Clear:	Amanda closed the **boring and silly** fashion magazine.

Commonly Misplaced Modifiers

Some writers have trouble placing certain types of modifiers close to the words they modify. As you read the sample sentences for each type, notice how they change meaning depending on where a writer places the modifiers. In the examples, the modifiers are underlined.

Prepositional Phrase Modifiers

A prepositional phrase is made of a preposition and its object.

Confusing:	Sheila talked to the man in the bar <u>with dirty hands</u>.
	(Can a bar have dirty hands?)
Clear:	When Sheila was in the bar, she talked to the man <u>with dirty hands</u>.

Section 6
MODIFIERS

> ### PRACTICE I
>
> In each sentence, underline the prepositional phrase modifier. Then draw an arrow from the modifier to the word that it modifies.
>
> **EXAMPLE:**
>
> <u>With anticipation</u>, Arianne contacted the dating service.
>
> 1. Arianne found Cupid Dating Service in a phone book.
>
> 2. On the table, a glossy pamphlet contained information.
>
> 3. Arianne, in a red dress, entered the dating service office.

4. With a kind expression, the interviewer asked Arianne personal

   questions.

5. Arianne, with direct eye contact, discussed her preferences.

Present Participle Modifiers

A present participle modifier is a phrase that begins with an *-ing* verb.

Confusing:	The young man proposed to his girlfriend <u>holding a diamond ring</u>.
	(Who is holding the diamond ring?)
Clear:	While <u>holding a diamond ring</u>, the young man proposed to his girlfriend.

PRACTICE 2

In each sentence, underline the present participle modifier. Then draw an arrow from the modifier to the word that it modifies.

EXAMPLE:

<u>Swallowing nervously</u>, Arianne explained her dating history.

1. Hoping to find a soul mate, Arianne described what she wanted.

2. Matching people with similar tastes, Cupid Dating Service is very

   successful.

3. Some customers using the service express satisfaction.

4. Feeling disappointed, customer Stephen Rooney has never met a suitable

   companion.

5. However, the owner of Cupid Dating, citing statistics, says that most

   clients are very satisfied.

Past Participle Modifiers

A past participle modifier is a phrase that begins with a past participle (*walked, gone, known,* and so on).

Confusing:	<u>Covered with dust</u>, my girlfriend wiped the windshield of her new car.
	(What was covered with dust? The girlfriend or the car?)
Clear:	My girlfriend wiped the windshield of the car that was <u>covered with dust</u>.

Section 6
MODIFIERS

In each sentence, underline the past participle modifier. Then draw an arrow from the modifier to the word that it modifies.

EXAMPLE:

Shocked, Arianne met her first blind date.

1. Covered in paint, Stephen sat at Arianne's table.

2. Torn between staying and leaving, Arianne smiled at Stephen.

3. Bored with life, Stephen talked for hours.

4. Trapped in a horrible date, Arianne longed to escape.

5. Stephen, surprised by her actions, watched Arianne stand up and leave.

Other Dependent-Clause Modifiers

Other dependent-clause modifiers can begin with a subordinator or a relative pronoun such as *who, whom, which,* or *that.*

Confusing: I presented Jeremy to my mother who is my boyfriend.
(How could "my mother" be "my boyfriend?")

Clear: I presented Jeremy, who is my boyfriend, to my mother.

In each sentence, underline the relative clause modifier. Then draw an arrow from the modifier to the word that it modifies.

EXAMPLE:

Arianne complained about the date that had gone horribly wrong.

Section 6
MODIFIERS

1. She discussed the date with her friend, Maggie, who was sympathetic.

2. Maggie knew about a place that had many single people.

3. The women went to a club where they met a new friend, Mel.

4. Maggie told Mel, who was also single, about her dating problems.

5. But Mel, whom Maggie really liked, asked Arianne out on a date instead.

Read each pair of sentences on the next page. Circle the letter of the correct sentence. Then, in the incorrect sentence, underline the misplaced modifier.

EXAMPLE:

    a. We read about the love lives of celebrities <u>with curiosity</u>.

    (b.) With curiosity, we read about the love lives of celebrities.

1. a. In the past, increasing their sales, tabloid newspapers focused on scandalous stories about celebrities.

    b. In the past, tabloid newspapers focused on scandalous stories about celebrities increasing their sales.

2. a. Today, many journalists publish stories about celebrities on the front page.

    b. Today, many journalists publish stories on the front page about celebrities.

3. a. Followed by paparazzi, celebrities such as Jude Law have no privacy.

    b. Celebrities such as Jude Law have no privacy followed by paparazzi.

4. a. In 2003, Kobe Bryant spoke to a female reporter with his wife.

    b. In 2003, with his wife, Kobe Bryant spoke to a female reporter.

5. a. I read an article saying that some celebrities are angry in the newspaper.

    b. I read an article in the newspaper saying that some celebrities are angry.

6. a. Celebrities should not complain about the curiosity of the public appearing on thousands of movie screens daily.

    b. Appearing on thousands of movie screens daily, celebrities should not complain about the curiosity of the public.

Section 6
MODIFIERS

 **Correcting Misplaced Modifiers**

To correct misplaced modifiers, do the following:

1. Identify the modifier.

    Ricardo and Alicia saw the beach <u>driving past Miami</u>.

2. Identify the word or words that are being modified.

    Ricardo and Alicia

3. Move the modifier next to the word(s) that are being modified.

    Driving past Miami, **Ricardo and Alicia** saw the beach.

| PRACTICE 6 |

Correct the misplaced modifiers in the following sentences.

EXAMPLE.

Sitting in my car,
I listened to the radio ~~sitting in my car~~.

1. The law professor spoke on the radio about marriage laws from Indiana.

2. Mixed-race couples were prohibited from marrying by legislators lacking their basic human rights.

3. Mixed-race couples felt angry who were prohibited from marrying legally.

4. In 1967, allowing interracial couples to marry, a decision was made by the U.S. Supreme Court.

5. The professor explained why these laws were morally wrong last week.

6. My sister married a man of another race who is my twin.

7. The wedding was in a beautiful garden photographed by a professional.

8. My parents welcomed the groom with champagne who supported my sister's choice.

Section 6
MODIFIERS

Dangling Modifiers

A **dangling modifier** opens a sentence but does not modify any words in the sentence. It "dangles," or hangs loosely, because it is not connected to any other part of the sentence. To avoid having a dangling modifier, make sure the modifier and the first noun that follows it have a logical connection.

Confusing:	<u>Phoning the company</u>, a limousine was booked in advance. (Can a limousine book itself?)
Clear:	<u>Phoning the company</u>, **the groom** booked the limousine in advance.
Confusing:	<u>Walking down the aisle</u>, many flower petals were on the ground. (Can flowers walk down an aisle?)
Clear:	<u>Walking down the aisle</u>, **the bride** noticed that many flower petals were on the ground.

PRACTICE 7

Read each pair of sentences. Circle the letter of each correct sentence, and underline the dangling modifiers.

EXAMPLE:

  a. On July 29, 1981, <u>in a beautiful white gown</u>, the royal wedding

  occurred.

  (b.) On July 29, 1981, in a beautiful white gown, Diana married Charles.

1. a. Falling in love with a prince, Diana Spencer was envied by many people.

  b. Falling in love with a prince, many people envied the royal couple.

2. a. Chased by members of the press, a high level of stress was experienced.

  b. Chased by members of the press, Diana experienced a high level of stress.

3. a. By ignoring his wife, the relationship was doomed.

  b. By ignoring his wife, Charles doomed the relationship.

4. a. Unhappy with the situation, Diana became increasingly depressed and

  lonely.

  b. Unhappy with the situation, there was an increasing sense of loneliness

  and depression.

5. a. By cheating, the marriage vows were broken.

  b. By cheating, Charles broke his marriage vows.

6. a. To get revenge, there were many extramarital affairs.

  b. To get revenge, Diana entered into many extramarital affairs.

7. a. Unhappy with their relationship, the couple separated.

  b. Unhappy with their relationship, a separation occurred.

8. a. To understand why the wedding took place, we must examine the rules

  regarding royal marriages.

  b. To understand why the wedding took place, rules regarding royal

  marriages must be examined.

Section 6
MODIFIERS

> **Hint** **Correcting Dangling Modifiers**
>
> To correct dangling modifiers, follow these steps.
>
> 1. Identify the modifier.
>
>   <u>Walking down the aisle</u>, many flower petals were on the ground.
>
> 2. Decide who or what should be modified.
>
>   the bride
>
> 3. Add the missing subject (and in some cases, also add or remove words) so that the sentence makes sense.
>
>   Walking down the aisle, **the bride noticed that** many flower petals were on the ground.

PRACTICE 8

Correct the dangling modifiers in the following sentences. Begin by underlining each dangling modifier. Then rewrite the sentence. You may have to add or remove words to give the sentence a logical meaning.

EXAMPLE:

<u>Always having to remain beautiful</u>, bodies are changed.

Always having to remain beautiful, movie stars change their bodies.

1. Reading through old magazines, ideas about beauty have changed over time.

   _____

   _____

2. In the past, seeing curvy movie stars, dieting was not very common.

   _____

   _____

3. Today, making their clients thinner, the bodies of famous people are altered.

   _____

   _____

4. Watching Jennifer Lopez, her natural beauty is envied.

   _____

   _____

5. While looking in the mirror, her puppy sat on her lap.

   _____

   _____

Section 6
MODIFIERS

6. Reading about Jennifer Lopez, her problems were like mine.

_____

_____

PRACTICE 9

Underline each dangling or misplaced modifier, and correct the mistakes. Remember that you may have to add or remove words to give some sentences a logical meaning. If a sentence does not have modifier errors, simply write _C_ to indicate it is correct.

EXAMPLE.

whom I like
I met a man at my workplace ~~whom I like~~.   _____

1. Some personnel department employees are debating the

    subject of workplace relationships in their meetings.   _____

2. Two employees can have a lot of problems with their

    superiors who fall in love.   _____

3. Some people believe that companies should develop

    policies prohibiting workplace romances.   _____

4. Debating sexual harassment, discussions have been

    heated.   _____

5. Couples can develop antagonistic feelings who work

    together.   _____

6. Perhaps employers have no right to forbid relationships

    between employees.   _____

7. Policies can cause problems in people's lives that prohibit

    workplace romances.   _____

8. Many couples have successfully worked together.   _____

9. Workplace romance in the future is a topic that will be

    debated.   _____

Section 6
MODIFIERS

FINAL REVIEW

Correct ten errors with dangling or misplaced modifiers.

EXAMPLE:

Divorcing her husband, ~~the public was scandalized~~. *she scandalized the public.*

1.   In the 1920s, Edward VIII was an eligible bachelor. One day, the prince met a married American woman named Wallis Simpson who was going to be king. Feeling very guilty, the relationship developed into love. Wallis sometimes stayed in a hotel near the palace wearing a wig.

2.   On January 30, 1936, people were pleased when King George V died with the news that Edward would be the next king. Soon after, Wallis got a divorce who was in love with the king. As the king, Edward VIII ruled England for 325 days. Edward gave interviews to the press who wanted to abdicate the throne. Edward had decided that his love for Wallis was more important than his role as the British monarch.

3.   Wallis ran off with Edward in high heels. Not caring about the monarchy, the marriage lasted for many years. Wallis Simpson appeared to love Edward in magazine interviews. Chasing after the couple, there were many articles written by prominent journalists.

Section 6
MODIFIERS

The Writer's Room

Write a paragraph about one of the following topics. Take care to avoid writing misplaced or dangling modifiers.

1. How are romance movies unrealistic? List examples of some movies or scenes that are not realistic.

2. What is the best way to break up with somebody? Give some steps that a person can take.

3. What causes people to search for love on the Internet? Explain why people visit online dating sites.

✓ CHECKLIST: Modifiers

When you edit your writing, ask yourself the following questions.

Are my modifiers in the correct position? Check for errors with the following:

–prepositional phrase modifiers

–present participle modifiers

–past participle modifiers

–*who, whom, which,* or *that* modifiers

Eating ice cream, the

~~The~~ young couple looked at the sportswear ~~eating ice cream~~.

Do my modifiers modify something in the sentence? Check for dangling modifiers.

my girlfriend created

Reading love poetry, a romantic atmosphere ~~was created~~.

READING LINK

Relationships
To read more about relationships, see the following essays:

"Birth" by Maya Angelou (page 432)

"For Marriage" by Kirsteen Macleod (page 435)

"Against Marriage" by Winston Murray (page 436)

The Writers' Circle

Work with a group of students on the following activity.

STEP 1 Choose one of the following topics. Brainstorm and come up with adjectives, adverbs, and phrases that describe each item in the pair.
a. A good date and a bad date
b. A great relationship and an unhappy relationship
c. A good romance movie and a bad romance movie

EXAMPLE: A good friend and a bad friend.

A good friend: smart, makes me laugh, good talker

A bad friend: ignores my calls, insults me, rude

STEP 2 For each item in the pair, rank the qualities from most important to least important.

STEP 3 As a team, write a paragraph about your topic. Compare the good with the bad.

STEP 4 When you finish writing, edit your paragraph. Ensure that you have written all adjectives and adverbs correctly Also, ensure that you have no dangling or misplaced modifiers.

Section 6
MODIFIERS

See Chapter 22 on the Visualizing Writing CD-ROM for an additional audio and animated mini-lecture on **Misplaced or Dangling Modifiers**.

CHAPTER 23

Spelling

Section Theme: **ZOOLOGY**

CONTENTS

- Improving Your Spelling
- Writing *ie* or *ei*
- Adding Prefixes and Suffixes
- Writing Two-Part Words
- 120 Commonly Misspelled Words

In this chapter, you will read about zoos and animal conservationists.

Grammar Snapshot

Looking at Spelling

In this excerpt from the novel *The Life of Pi*, writer Yann Martel discusses the characteristics of zoos. The underlined words are sometimes difficult to spell.

> A house is a <u>compressed</u> territory where our basic needs can be <u>fulfilled</u> close by and safely. Such an enclosure is <u>subjectively</u> neither better nor worse for an animal than its condition in the wild; so long as it <u>fulfills</u> the animal's needs, a territory, natural or constructed, simply *is*, without <u>judgment</u>, a given, like the spots on a leopard.

In this chapter, you will identify and correct misspelled words.

Improving Your Spelling

It is important to spell correctly. Spelling mistakes can detract from good ideas in your work. You can become a better speller if you always proofread your written work and if you check a dictionary for the meaning and spelling of words about which you are unsure.

 **Reminders About Vowels and Consonants**

When you review spelling rules, it is important to know the difference between a vowel and a consonant. The vowels are *a, e, i, o, u,* and sometimes *y.* The consonants are all of the other letters of the alphabet.

The letter *y* may be either a consonant or a vowel, depending on its pronunciation. In the word *happy,* the *y* is a vowel because it is pronounced as an *ee* sound. In the word *youth,* the *y* has a consonant sound.

PRACTICE I

Answer the following questions.

1. Write three words that begin with three consonants.

   EXAMPLE: strong   _____ _____ _____

2. Write three words that begin with *y* and contain at least two vowels.

   EXAMPLE: yellow   _____ _____ _____

3. Write three words that have double vowels.

   EXAMPLE: moon   _____ _____ _____

4. Write three words that end with three consonants.

   EXAMPLE: birth   _____ _____ _____

Section 7
WORD USE AND SPELLING

Writing *ie* or *ei*

Words that contain *ie* or *ei* can be tricky. Remember to write *i* before *e* except after *c* or when *ei* is pronounced *ay,* as in *neighbor* and *weigh.*

i before e:	chief	patient	priest
ei after c:	conceit	perceive	deceive
ei pronounced as *ay:*	weigh	neighbor	freight
Exceptions:	efficient	either	neither
	science	foreigner	seize
	society	height	their
	species	leisure	weird

PRACTICE 2

Underline the correct spelling of each word.

EXAMPLE:

<u>ceiling</u>, cieling

1. conceive	concieve	7. efficient	efficeint
2. field	feild	8. weird	wierd
3. receipt	reciept	9. deciet	deceit
4. hieght	height	10. acheive	achieve
5. vien	vein	11. weight	wieght
6. science	sceince	12. decieve	deceive

PRACTICE 3

Correct the spelling error with *ie* or *ei* in each sentence. If the sentence is correct, write *C* in the blank.

EXAMPLE:

species

Natural habitats of many ~~speceis~~ are being drastically reduced. _____

1. Western soceities have become increasingly aware of the need

   for wildlife conservation. _____

2. This awareness was hieghtened after Joy Adamson published

   her book *Born Free*. _____

3. In 1956, Joy Adamson took care of three lion cubs after her

   husband, George, killed their dangerous mother. _____

4. Zoos recieved two of the cubs, and the Adamsons kept the third

   cub, Elsa. _____

5. Joy Adamson concieved of a plan to teach Elsa survival skills. _____

6. Adamson believed that Elsa would learn how to hunt by practicing

   each day. _____

7. It took a long time, but niether Joy nor Elsa gave up, and,

   eventually, Elsa could hunt as well as a wild lion. _____

8. Adamson acheived a feat that had never been done before. _____

Section 7
**WORD USE
AND SPELLING**

Adding Prefixes and Suffixes

A **prefix** is added to the beginning of a word, and it changes the word's meaning.

<u>re</u>organize   <u>pre</u>mature   <u>un</u>fair   <u>mis</u>understand

A **suffix** is added to the ending of a word, and it changes the word's tense or meaning.

amuse<u>ment</u>   sure<u>ly</u>   offer<u>ing</u>   watch<u>ed</u>

When you add a prefix to a word, keep the last letter of the prefix and the first letter of the main word.

u**n** + **n**erve = u**nn**erve   di**s** + **s**imilar = di**ss**imilar

When you add the suffix -*ly* to a word that ends in *l*, keep the *l* of the root word. The new word will have two *l*'s.

beautiful + **l**y = beautifu**ll**y   real + **l**y = rea**ll**y

 **Words Ending in -*ful***

Although the word *full* ends in two *l*'s, when -*full* is added to another word as a suffix, it ends in one *l*.

wonder**ful**   peace**ful**

Notice the unusual spelling when *full* and *fill* are combined: *fulfill*.

PRACTICE 4

Underline the correct spelling of each word.

EXAMPLE:

<u>awful</u>, awfull

1. unecessary   unnecessary
2. dissolve   disolve
3. personally   personaly
4. irational   irrational
5. immature   imature
6. mispell   misspell
7. plentiful   plentifull

8. universaly   universally
9. fullfilled   fulfilled
10. usually   usualy
11. disrespectfull   disrespectful
12. joyfuly   joyfully
13. useful   usefull
14. ilogical   illogical

Section 7
**WORD USE
AND SPELLING**

Adding -*s* or -*es* Suffixes

Generally, add -*s* to nouns and to present tense verbs that are third-person singular. However, add -*es* to words in the following situations.

- When a word ends in *s, sh, ss, ch,* or *x,* add -*es.*

Noun:	porch	porch**es**
Verb:	mix	mix**es**

- When a word ends in the consonant *y,* change the *y* to *i* and add -*es.*

Noun:	lady	lad**ies**
Verb:	carry	carr**ies**

- Generally, when a word ends in *o,* add -*es.*

Noun:	tomato	tomato**es**		
Verb:	go	go**es**		
Exceptions:	piano	piano**s**	radio	radio**s**

- When a word ends in *f* or *fe,* change the *f* to a *v* and add -*es.*

Nouns:	calf	cal**ves**	wife	wi**ves**
Exceptions:	roof	roof**s**	belief	belief**s**

PRACTICE 5

Add an -*s* or -*es* ending to each word.

EXAMPLE:

reach   *reaches*

1. piano _____
2. watch _____
3. fax _____
4. leaf _____
5. marry _____
6. box _____

7. volcano _____
8. spy _____
9. kiss _____
10. baby _____
11. belief _____
12. vanish _____

Section 7
**WORD USE
AND SPELLING**

Adding Suffixes to Words Ending in -e

When you add a suffix to a word ending in *e,* make sure that you follow the next rules.

- If the suffix begins with a vowel, drop the *e* on the main word. Some common suffixes beginning with vowels are -*ed,* -*er,* -*est,* -*ing,* -*able,* -*ent,* and -*ist.*

  create–creating   mov**e**–movable

Exceptions: For some words that end in the letters *ge,* keep the *e* and add the suffix.

  courag**e**–courag**e**ous   chang**e**–chang**e**able

- If the suffix begins with a consonant, keep the *e.* Some common suffixes beginning with consonants are -*ly,* -*ment,* -*less,* and -*ful.*

  definit**e**–definit**e**ly   improv**e**–improv**e**ment

Exceptions: Some words lose the final *e* when you add a suffix that begins with a consonant.

argu**e**–argument   tru**e**–truly

PRACTICE 6

Rewrite each word by adding the suggested ending.

EXAMPLE:

use + ed   <u>used</u>

1. advertise + ment _____   7. produce + er _____
2. convince + ing   _____   8. judge + ment _____
3. complete + ly   _____   9. believe + ing _____
4. give + ing   _____   10. move + ing   _____
5. true + er   _____   11. use + able   _____
6. cure + able   _____   12. late + er   _____

PRACTICE 7

Correct the spelling mistakes in the underlined words.

EXAMPLE:

The story of the gray wolf in Yellowstone is <u>truely</u> *truly* amazing.

1.   Before the arrival of Europeans, gray <u>wolfs</u> were found in all

parts of North America. By the 1920s, these animals had been

almost <u>completly</u> eradicated in the United States. Early settlers

<u>unecessarily</u> shot large numbers of the animals. Biologists

from the Fisheries and Wildlife Department decided to try

<u>reintroduceing</u> the gray wolf into the wild in Yellowstone

National Park. In 1995, fifteen animals were transferred from

Alberta, Canada, to Yellowstone.

2.   The wolf reintroduction program has <u>definitly</u> been a

success. The animals have multiplied and the secondary effects

have <u>actualy</u> been very positive. For example, the elk population

Section 7
**WORD USE
AND SPELLING**

has been reduced. As a result, trees around the banks of lakes are <u>thriveing</u>. The numbers of <u>foxs</u> have increased in the area because they eat the carcasses of the elks.

3. Today, there are many wolf packs in the park, and it is <u>ilegal</u> to hunt them. Each wolf pack <u>flourishs</u> in Yellowstone National Park.

Adding Suffixes by Doubling the Final Consonant

Sometimes when you add a suffix to a word, you must double the final consonant. Remember these tips when spelling words of one or more syllables.

One-Syllable Words

■ Double the final consonant of one-syllable words ending in a consonant-vowel-consonant pattern.

  stop–sto**pp**ing   drag–dra**gg**ed

Exception: If the word ends in *w* or *x*, do not double the last letter.

  snow–snowing   fix–fixed

■ Do not double the final consonant if the word ends in a vowel and two consonants or if it ends with two vowels and a consonant.

  look–looking   list–listed

Words of Two or More Syllables

■ Double the final consonant of words ending in a stressed consonant-vowel-consonant pattern.

  confer–confe**rr**ing   omit–omi**tt**ed

■ If the word ends in a syllable that is not stressed, then do not double the last letter of the word.

  open–opening   focus–focused

Section 7
**WORD USE
AND SPELLING**

PRACTICE 8

Rewrite each word with the suggested ending.

	Add -*ed*		**Add -*ing***
EXAMPLE:		**EXAMPLE:**	
park	_parked_	open	_opening_
1. answer	_____	4. happen	_____
2. clean	_____	5. run	_____
3. prod	_____	6. drag	_____

Add -*ed*	**Add -*ing***

7. mention _____   9. refer _____

8. prefer _____   10. question _____

Adding Suffixes to Words Ending in -y

When you add a suffix to a word ending in *y*, follow the next rules.

- If a word has a consonant before the final *y*, change the *y* to an *i* before adding the suffix.

    heavy–heavily   angry–angrily   easy–easily

- If a word has a vowel before the final *y*, if it is a proper name, or if the suffix is -*ing*, do not change the *y* to an *i*.

    play–played   fry–frying   Binchy–Binchys

Exceptions: Some words do not follow the previous rule.

    day–daily   lay–laid   say–said   pay–paid

PRACTICE 9

Rewrite each word by adding the suggested ending.

EXAMPLES:

say + ing = ___saying_____

1. justify + able _____   6. lively + hood _____

2. fly + ing _____   7. day + ly _____

3. enjoy + ed _____   8. mercy + less _____

4. Kowalsky + s _____   9. duty + ful _____

5. beauty + ful _____   10. pretty + est _____

Section 7
**WORD USE
AND SPELLING**

PRACTICE 10

Correct six spelling mistakes in the next selection.

EXAMPLE:

                    stopped
Many tourists ~~stoped~~ at Yellowstone to see wolves.

1.   The wolf reintroduction program is a controversial subject.

    Farmers and ranchers are unhappy with it, and many feel that

    their livelyhood will be threatened. Sheep farmers in particular, refering to statistics of sheep that have already been killed by bears, eagles, and coyotes, are against this program.

2. Fortunatly, Defenders of Wildlife, a private group that has developed a compensation fund, is confering with farmers and ranchers. This group gives monetary compensation to farmers who lose animals to predators. Farmers get payed for each animal that is lost. The happyest supporters of the wolf program are the small businesses that make money from tourists who want to see the wolves.

Writing Two-Part Words

The following indefinite pronouns sound as if they should be two separate words, but each is a single word.

Words with *any:*	anything, anyone, anybody, anywhere
Words with *some:*	something, someone, somebody, somewhere
Words with *every:*	everything, everyone, everybody, everywhere

 **Writing *Another* and *A lot***

• *Another* is always one word.

    <u>Another</u> gorilla has escaped from the zoo.

• *A lot* is always two words.

    <u>A lot</u> of people are looking for the animal.

Section 7
**WORD USE
AND SPELLING**

PRACTICE 11

Correct ten spelling errors in the next paragraph.

EXAMPLE:

Everyone
~~Every one~~ should be concerned about the destruction of the Amazon rain forest.

1. One of the most amazeing and crucial ecosystems on the planet is the Amazon River basin. It is an immense area and contains 20 percent of the world's fresh water. This region

includes the rain forest, which houses unnusual species of plants and animals that are not found any where else in the world. For example, alot of giant river otters swim in the Amazon. An other unique species is the emerald tree boa.

2.   Naturaly, it is disheartening to hear that the Amazon jungle is being completly destroyed through logging, mineral extraction, and livestock grazing. It is in every one's interest to protect the fragile Amazon basin. Our planet depends on this ecosystem, and it is ilogical not to develop policies that will protect it. Stoping destruction of the rain forest is crucial.

120 Commonly Misspelled Words

The next list contains some of the most commonly misspelled words in English. Learn how to spell these words. You might try different strategies, such as writing down the word a few times or using flash cards to help you to memorize the spelling of each word.

absence	comparison	harassment	parallel
absorption	competent	height	performance
accommodate	conscience	immediately	perseverance
acquaintance	conscientious	independent	personality
address	convenient	jewelry	physically
aggressive	curriculum	judgment	possess
already	definite	laboratory	precious
aluminum	definitely	ledge	prejudice
analyze	desperate	legendary	privilege
appointment	developed	leisure	probably
approximate	dilemma	license	professor
argument	disappoint	loneliness	psychology
athlete	embarrass	maintenance	questionnaire
bargain	encouragement	mathematics	receive
beginning	environment	medicine	recommend
behavior	especially	millennium	reference
believable	exaggerate	mischievous	responsible
business	exercise	mortgage	rhythm
calendar	extraordinarily	necessary	schedule
campaign	familiar	ninety	scientific
careful	February	noticeable	separate
ceiling	finally	occasion	sincerely
cemetery	foreign	occurrence	spaghetti
clientele	government	opposite	strength
committee	grammar	outrageous	success

surprise	tomorrow	vacuum	wreckage
technique	truly	Wednesday	writer
thorough	Tuesday	weird	writing
tomato	until	woman	written
tomatoes	usually	women	zealous

 **Using a Spelling Checker**

Most word processing programs have spelling and grammar tools that will alert you about some common errors. They will also suggest ways to correct them. Be careful, however, because these tools are not 100 percent accurate. For example, a spelling checker cannot differentiate between *your* and *you're*.

PRACTICE 12

Underline the correctly spelled words in parentheses.

EXAMPLE:

Many interest groups (campaine, <u>campaign</u>) to raise public awareness.

1. Today, there is no lack of information about the need to protect the (environment, enviroment). Animals and humans must be able to (accomodate, accommodate) each other. However, as populations increase, there is growing competition between animals and humans for land resources.

2. In Africa, conservationists face a (dillema, dilemma) regarding the preservation of elephant habitats. Almost everybody loves the elephant and believes in the (necessity, neccesity) of protecting this magnificent creature. In fact, international lawmakers have tried (conscientiously, conscienciously) to protect elephants from illegal hunting by banning the sale of ivory. But as elephant herds increase, and the (absence, absense) of their habitat increases, they compete for space with those people who live beside them. As a result, elephants and humans are coming into more and more contact with each other. There have been (occurrances, occurrences) of elephants trampling villagers.

Section 7
WORD USE AND SPELLING

3.   African and Asian farmers often complain to their (goverments, governments) that elephants have trampled on or eaten their crops. When farmers lose their entire crops, they become (desperate, desparate.) However, conservation groups are (developping, developing) strategies to help the farmers and protect elephants. For example, Masai farmers in Kenya use simple (techniques, technics) such as banging drums or lighting fires to prevent elephants from coming into their fields. Also, farmers in Zimbabwe have found that elephants do not like chili, so they coat fences with chili sauces to deter the elephants. Moreover, farmers are having (sucess, success) by changing some traditional crops into chili production.

4.   Clearly, both farmers and conservationists have to show (perseverance, perserverence) to develop clever conservation strategies. After all, humans are very (priviledged, privileged) to share this planet with so many beautiful creatures.

 **Strategies to Become a Better Speller**

These are some useful strategies to improve your spelling.

- In your spelling log, which could be in a journal, binder, or computer file, keep a record of words that you commonly misspell. (See Appendix 5 for more on spelling logs.)
- Use memory cards or flash cards to help you memorize difficult words.
- Write down the spelling of difficult words at least ten times to help you remember how to spell them.
- Always check a dictionary to verify the spelling of difficult words.

Section 7
**WORD USE
AND SPELLING**

FINAL REVIEW

Correct twenty spelling errors in the following selection.

EXAMPLE:

their
Historically, zoos have displayed ~~thier~~ collections of wild animals for public entertainment and profit.

1.   Since the begining of civilization, human beings have always

enjoyed viewing animals. Originaly, wild animals were captured and displayed for the pleasure of the upper classes. By the early twentieth century, zoos were openned to the general public. For example, 98 percent of North Americans state that they have been to a zoo at least once in their lives. Today, the role of zoos is a hotly debated subject in our soceity.

2. Supporters of zoos argue that in the past two decades, zoos have tried to acheive different goals and objectives. They claim that in the past twenty years, zoos in the Western world have spent millions of dollars on upgrading facilities by creating truely naturalistic enviroments for the animals. Furthermore, supporters state that the role of zoos has become neccesary and educational. Zoos bring to the public's attention the threat of the extinction of many species, and zoo breeding programs have helped bring about a noticable increase in the population of alot of threatened species.

3. Zoo opponents from countrys around the world beleive that zoos are imoral prisons for wild animals, and they say that a zoo's only function is to entertain the public and run a profitable buisness. According to various animal rights groups, displaying animals in small cages is cruel, unatural, and unethical. Furthermore, zoo opponents have questionned the validity of breeding statistics released by zoos. Animal Aid, an animal rights group in the United Kingdom, argues that only 2 percent of endangered animals are bred in zoos.

4. Conservationist Gerald Durrell, who started the Jersey Zoological Park, has stated that a zoo is successfull if it can contribute to the conservation of forests and feilds. However, others think that zoos are archaic institutions that should be

Section 7
WORD USE
AND SPELLING

banned. Certainly, everyone should consider whether zoos are

helpfull or harmfull.

The Writer's Room

Write a paragraph about one of the following topics. After you finish writing, circle any words that you may have misspelled.

1. If you could live in a natural environment, what type of environment would you prefer: a forest, a seashore, a mountain, a desert, a lakefront, or a prairie? Explain your answer.

2. Do you do anything to help conserve the environment? For example, do you recycle or take public transit? What are some steps that you and others can take to help the environment?

3. Examine this photo. What are some terms that come to mind? Some ideas might be *zoo, captivity,* or *conservation.* Define a term or expression that relates to this photo.

Section 7
WORD USE
AND SPELLING

CHECKLIST: SPELLING RULES

When you edit your writing, ask yourself the next questions.

Do I have any spelling errors? Check for errors in words that contain these elements:

- –an *ie* or *ei* combination
- –prefixes
- –suffixes

(continued)

GRAMMAR LINK

Keep a list of words that you commonly misspell. See Appendix 5 for more about spelling logs.

species *disappearing*
Many ~~speices~~ of animals and plants are ~~dissappearing~~ from our planet.

Do I repeat spelling errors that I have made in previous assignments? (Each time you write, check previous assignments for errors or consult your spelling log.)

See Chapter 23 on the Visualizing Writing CD-ROM for an additional audio and animated mini-lecture on **Spelling**.

Section 7
**WORD USE
AND SPELLING**

Commonly Confused Words

CHAPTER 24

Section Theme: **ZOOLOGY**

CONTENTS

• Commonly Confused Words

In this chapter, you will read about pet ownership and exotic animals.

Grammar Snapshot

Looking at Commonly Confused Words

In his book *Animal Wonderland*, Frank W. Lane examines experiments with animals. In this excerpt, commonly confused words are underlined.

> A feeding apparatus was installed in a cage whereby a pellet of food fell <u>through</u> a slot when a lever was pressed. Lever and slot <u>were</u> side by side. Three rats were placed one at a time in the cage, and soon each learned <u>to</u> use the lever. <u>Then</u> Mowrer put the lever on the side of the cage opposite the food slot, thus making it necessary for a rat to run from one end of the cage to the other for every <u>piece</u> of food. Again the rats learned, separately, how to obtain <u>their</u> food.

In this chapter, you will identify and use words that sound the same but have different spellings and meanings.

Commonly Confused Words

Some English words can sound the same but are spelled differently and have different meanings. For example, two commonly confused words are *for*, which is a preposition that means "in exchange," and *four*, which is the number. Dictionaries will give you the exact meaning of unfamiliar words.

Here is a list of some commonly confused words.

Commonly Confused Words	Meaning	Examples
accept	to receive or to admit	Presently, the public <u>accepts</u> the need for wildlife preservation.
except	excluding or other than	Everyone in my family <u>except</u> my sister wants a pet.
affect	to influence	Pollution <u>affects</u> our environment in many ways.
effect	the result of something	Deforestation has bad <u>effects</u> on global climate.
been	past participle of the verb *be*	Joy Adamson has <u>been</u> a role model for conservationists.
being	present progressive form (the *-ing* form) of the verb *be*.	She was <u>being</u> very nice when she agreed to give a speech.
by	next to, on, or before	Gerald Durell sat <u>by</u> the rocks to film the iguana. He hoped to finish filming <u>by</u> next year.
buy	to purchase	Many people <u>buy</u> exotic animals for pets.
complement	to add to or to complete	The book will <u>complement</u> the library's zoology collection.
compliment	to say something nice about someone	Ann Struthers receives many <u>compliments</u> for her book on snakes.

Section 7
WORD USE AND SPELLING

PRACTICE I

Underline the appropriate word in each set of parentheses.

EXAMPLE:

Owners of exotic pets must (<u>accept</u>, except) responsibility for the behavior of these creatures.

1.   Many people (buy, by) exotic animals for pets. Stop (buy, by) any pet store these days, and you are sure to find at least a couple of unusual animals. For example, a sugar glider is (been, being) displayed at my local pet shop.

2.   Sugar gliders are very small marsupials that come from Indonesia. They are relatively easy to care (for, four); however, there are two important things owners need to know. First, people should (buy, by) sugar gliders in pairs because the animals need companionship. Also, owners should train them (by, buy) using kindness because they are badly (affected, effected) (buy, by) harsh treatment and will suffer negative (affects, effects) if punished.

3.   After considering all of the facts, I finally bought a pair of sugar gliders. Wherever I take them, people (complement, compliment) the animals because they are so cute. Everyone in my family, (accept, except) our dog Murphy, likes my sugar gliders.

Commonly Confused Words

	Meaning	**Examples**
conscience	a personal sense of right or wrong	Poachers have no <u>conscience</u>.
conscious	to be aware or to be awake	The poacher was <u>conscious</u> of his crime.
everyday	ordinary or common	Poaching is an <u>everyday</u> occurrence.
every day	during a single day or each day	Government officials search <u>every day</u> for poachers.
find	to locate	Biologists are trying to <u>find</u> the nesting grounds of parrots.
fine	of good quality; a penalty of money for a crime	A robin prepares a <u>fine</u> nest. Poachers must pay a <u>fine</u> when caught.
fun	an experience of amusement	In the past, many people had <u>fun</u> shooting passenger pigeons.
funny	comical or odd	Ostriches look very <u>funny</u>.
its	possessive case of the pronoun *it*	The baby elephant was separated from <u>its</u> herd.
it's	contraction for *it is*	<u>It's</u> known that elephants are very intelligent.
knew	past tense of *know*	We <u>knew</u> that the lioness had three cubs.
new	recent or unused	We used a <u>new</u> camera to film the cubs.
know	to have knowledge of	Photographers <u>know</u> that the public loves pictures of animals.
no	a negative	I have <u>no</u> photos of Bengal tigers.

Section 7
WORD USE AND SPELLING

PRACTICE 2

Underline the appropriate word in each set of parentheses.

EXAMPLE:

Did you (no, <u>know</u>) that snakes cannot hear?

1. Snakes can be dangerous creatures. Herpetologists, or people who study reptiles, (know, no) that not all snakes are dangerous. However, they are (conscience, conscious) that people, in general, fear snakes. (Its, It's) believed that there are around 2,700 species of snakes in the world today.

2. In the fashion industry, (new, knew) trends are an (everyday, every day) occurrence. Because many trends involve snakeskins, snakes are killed (everyday, every day). Poachers (fine, find) and kill snakes for money. These criminals have (know, no) (conscience, conscious) about their actions. They may receive a (find, fine) if they are caught.

3. I never (new, knew) that people could buy poisonous snakes, but my friend bought one two weeks ago. It ejects venom through (its, it's) fangs. Sometimes it makes (fun, funny) noises. I'm not too crazy about the creature, but my friend has a lot of (fun, funny) with his pet.

Section 7
**WORD USE
AND SPELLING**

Commonly Confused Words

	Meaning	Examples
lose	to misplace or forfeit something	If we <u>lose</u> a species to extinction, we will <u>lose</u> a part of our heritage.
loose	too big or too baggy; not fixed	They wear <u>loose</u> clothing at work.
loss	a decrease in an amount; a serious blow	The <u>loss</u> of forests is a serious problem.
past	previous time	In the <u>past</u>, people shot big game for fun.
passed	accepted or sanctioned; past tense of *to pass*	Recently, governments have <u>passed</u> laws forbidding the killing of endangered species.
peace	calm; to stop violence	I feel a sense of <u>peace</u> in the wilderness.
piece	a part of something else	I found a <u>piece</u> of deer antler in the woods.

	Meaning	**Examples**
personal	private	My professor showed us her <u>personal</u> collection of snake photographs.
personnel	employees or staff	The World Wildlife Fund hires a lot of <u>personnel</u>.
principal	main; director of a school	The <u>principal</u> researcher on snakes is Dr. Alain Leduc.
principle	rule or standard	I am studying the <u>principles</u> of ethical research techniques.

PRACTICE 3

Commonly confused words are underlined. Correct six word errors. If the word is correct, write *C* above it.

EXAMPLE:

Sometimes, a snake can regrow its tail if a _{piece}⌃ <u>peace</u> of it breaks off.

1. India has many species of snakes, and laws have been <u>past</u> to protect them. One of the best-known snakes in India is the cobra. It has been worshipped in the <u>past</u> and continues to play a <u>principle</u> role in the Hindu religion today.

2. Nagpanchami is a religious festival to honor the cobra. It is based on Hindu religious <u>principles</u> in which nature plays an important role. On that day, many people make a <u>personnel</u> offering of milk to the cobra. Snake charmers wearing <u>loose</u> clothing bring snakes into villages and cities. Everyone prays for <u>piece</u>, and it is customary to eat <u>pieces</u> of sweets during the holiday.

3. Snakes are vital to the Indian economy. Without snakes, Indian farmers would <u>loose</u> a large part of their crops to rodents. The farmers would not be able to withstand such a <u>lost</u>.

Section 7
WORD USE AND SPELLING

Commonly Confused Words

	Meaning	Example
quiet	silent	It was quiet in the woods.
quite	very	The herd was moving quite fast.
quit	stop	The zoo director quit after receiving a bad report.
sit	to seat oneself	I will sit on this rock to watch the birds.
set	to put or place down	He set his book about birds on the grass.
taught	past tense of *to teach*	Dr. Zavitz taught a class on sharks.
thought	past tense *to think*	His students thought that he was a good teacher.
than	word used in comparisons	Whales are larger than dolphins.
then	at a particular time or after a specific time	The grizzly entered the river, and then it caught some salmon.
that	word used to introduce a clause	Some people do not realize that grizzlies are extremely dangerous.
their	possessive form of *they*	Anita and Ram went to see their favorite documentary on bird migration.
there	a place; something exists	There are many birds in the park. The students went there by bus.
they're	contraction of *they are*	They're both very interested in falcons.

PRACTICE 4

Underline the appropriate word in each set of parentheses.

EXAMPLE:

(There, Their) are many types of venomous snakes.

Section 7
**WORD USE
AND SPELLING**

1. A few decades ago, snake charmers were (quiet, quit, quite) common in India. They used to (set, sit) at corners and (set, sit) (they're, their, there) baskets of snakes in front of them.

2. People (taught, thought) (than, that) snake charmers had some magical hold over the snake and that charmers (taught, thought) the snake to dance. Crowds would gather around the snake charmer and become very (quiet, quit, quite) as the charmer lifted the lid of the basket. (Then, Than) the snake charmer would play his flute, and the snake would slowly sway to the music.

3. (There, They're, Their) are fewer snake charmers today (then, than, that) ever before. Today, (there, they're, their) finding it hard to earn a living. (Their, There, They're)

profession is dying because of strict conservation laws passed by the Indian government. Many snake charmers have (quite, quiet, quit) the profession.

Commonly Confused Words

	Meaning	Examples
through	in one side and out the other; finished	The monkeys climbed <u>through</u> the trees. Although they were still active, we were <u>through</u> for the day.
threw	past tense of *throw*	The monkeys <u>threw</u> fruit down from the tree.
thorough	complete	The biologist did a <u>thorough</u> investigation of monkey behavior.
to	indicates direction or movement; part of an infinitive	I want <u>to</u> go <u>to</u> Africa.
too	*also* or *very*	Kenya is <u>too</u> hot in the summer. It is hot in Somalia, <u>too</u>.
two	the number after one	Africa and the Amazon are <u>two</u> places that intrigue me.
write	to draw symbols that represent words	I <u>write</u> about conservation issues for the newspaper.
right	correct; the opposite of *left*	Is this the <u>right</u> way to go to the village? The <u>right</u> turn signal of the jeep does not work.
where	question word indicating location	<u>Where</u> did the zoo keep the gorillas?
were	past tense of *be*	The gorillas <u>were</u> in the enclosure.
we're	contraction of *we are*	<u>We're</u> going to see a film about gorillas.
who's	contraction of *who is*	Makiko, <u>who's</u> a friend of mine, is doing research on lemurs.
whose	pronoun showing ownership	Animals <u>whose</u> habitat is disappearing need to be protected.
you're	contraction of *you are*	<u>You're</u> going on the field trip, aren't you?
your	possessive adjective	<u>Your</u> sister went to the pet store.

Section 7
**WORD USE
AND SPELLING**

PRACTICE 5

In the next sentences, write one of the words in parentheses in each blank.

EXAMPLE:

(We're, Were) ___*We're*___ going to watch a presentation about rat experiments.

1. (we're, were, where) _____ learning a lot about scientific experiments.

   In his book *Animal Wonderland*, Frank W. Lane describes how rats

   _____ put into a cage _____ they _____ observed

   by a zoologist.

2. (to, too, two) _____ rats had to press a lever _____ get some food. One rat pressed _____ hard and broke the lever.

3. (threw, through, thorough) We sat outside a lab and watched spider monkeys _____ a window. The zoologist _____ some food behind a door. The monkeys smelled the food and did a _____ search of their cage. Then one monkey noticed the door and reached _____ it to pick up the food. When the experiment was _____, the zoologist rewarded the monkeys with more food.

4. (right, write) We plan to _____ an article about the monkey experiment. At the _____ time, we will present our paper to our instructor.

5. (who's, whose) A zoologist _____ profession involves close contact with various species studies animal habitats. A friend of ours, _____ an excellent zoologist, will receive government funding.

6. (your, you're) _____ welcome to come with us to a presentation. You can bring _____ friend with you. If _____ late, the presentation will start without you.

FINAL REVIEW
Correct fifteen errors in word choice.

EXAMPLE:

People often learn different sides of controversial issues ~~thorough~~ *through* discussions.

1.   Recently, more and more pet owners have tried to purchase exotic animals. In many shops, people can by a variety of rats, snakes, and lizards. Ownership of exotic animals has become a passionately debated subject.

2.   Some people believe that it is wrong to keep exotic animals as pets. They argue than exotic animals need to be kept in

Section 7
**WORD USE
AND SPELLING**

there natural environment. If they're caged, they will suffer. Furthermore, exotic animals have diseases that can be transmitted to humans. For example, scientists believe that Gambian pouch rats where responsible for the monkeypox virus. Additionally, exotic animals are often released into the wild when they're owners become tired of them. For example, Thomas Sawland, whose a fisherman, found the Chinese snakehead fish thriving in some lakes and killing native fish species. Unfortunately, many owners of exotic pets do not really no how to take care of their animals because they have never been thought. For example, 90 percent of pet snakes die within the first year of captivity because they have been mistreated.

3.   Owners of exotic pets state that its perfectly reasonable to keep such animals. Proponents say that accept for the occasional case, most exotic pet owners are very responsible and have strong principals. Owners with a strong conscious would never neglect their pets. Moreover, the sale of exotic pets is a huge and profitable business, and many business owners would loose their income if the sale of exotic pets were prohibited. Also, everyday some people abuse dogs and cats, but few people pressure the government to ban the ownership of such pets.

4.   Lawmakers are hoping to past laws that limit the exotic animal market. However, many pet owners are opposed to such legislation because they say it infringes on their rights. Clearly, this subject will continue to be debated.

Section 7
**WORD USE
AND SPELLING**

The Writer's Room

Write a short paragraph about one of the following topics. After you finish writing, circle any words that you might have misspelled.

1. What are some reasons that people own pets? How can pet ownership affect a person's life? Write about the causes or effects of pet ownership.

2. Would you ever own an exotic pet such as a snake, an alligator, or a tiger? Should people have the right to own exotic pets?

CHECKLIST: COMMONLY CONFUSED WORDS

When you edit your writing, ask yourself whether you have used the correct words. Check for errors with commonly confused words.

My friend Patricia, ~~whose~~ *who's* a veterinarian, believes ~~than~~ *that* pet owners should take courses on how to take care of ~~they're~~ *their* pets.

The Writers' Circle

This activity is similar to the spelling bees we participated in as children. As a team, you will try to spell words from the list of commonly misspelled words on page 353 in Chapter 23.

1. In a team of five students, appoint a leader to write answers and then spell words out loud.

2. Listen carefully to the word your instructor or another student asks your team to spell.

3. Consult with your team members, and, when you come to an agreement, ask the team leader to spell it aloud.

4. If your team spells the word correctly, you get a point. If your team spells the word incorrectly, you lose your turn, and the next team has a chance to spell it. The team with the most points wins.

Section 7
**WORD USE
AND SPELLING**

READING LINK

Zoology
To read more about zoology, see the following essay:
"The Zoo Life" by Yann Martel
(page 452)

See Chapter 24 on the Visualizing Writing CD-ROM for an additional audio and animated mini-lecture on **Commonly Confused Words**.

Commas

CHAPTER 25

Section Theme: **THE BUSINESS WORLD**

CONTENTS

- Understanding Commas
- Commas in a Series
- Commas After Introductory Words and Phrases
- Commas Around Interrupting Words and Phrases
- Commas in Compound Sentences
- Commas in Complex Sentences
- Commas in Business Letters

In this chapter, you will read about business-related topics, including job searching and unusual jobs.

Grammar Snapshot

Looking at Commas

Jeff Kemp is a former NFL quarterback. In his article "Sports and Life: Lessons to Be Learned," Kemp narrates his experiences as a professional athlete. Notice the use of commas in this excerpt from his article.

> In 1988₂ I was playing for the Seattle Seahawks against my old team₂ the 49ers₂ when I learned firsthand that there are two competing value systems. I wasn't bitter that my old team had traded me₂ but I wanted to beat them all the same. Quarterback Dave Krieg had been injured₂ and I was to start.

In this chapter, you will learn how to use commas correctly.

Understanding Commas

A **comma (,)** is a punctuation mark that helps keep distinct ideas separate. Commas are especially important in series, after introductory words and phrases, around interrupting words and phrases, and in compound and complex sentences.

Some jobs, especially those in the service industry, pay minimum wage.

Commas in a Series

Use a comma to separate items in a series of three or more items. Remember to put a comma before the final *and* or *or*.

Item 1	,	item 2	,	and or	item 3	.

Series of nouns: The conference will be in Dallas, Houston, Galveston, or Austin.

Series of verbs: During the conference, guests will eat, drink, and network.

Series of phrases: She dressed well, kept her head up, and maintained eye contact.

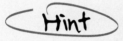 **Punctuating a Series**

In a series of three or more items, do not place a comma after the last item in the series (unless the series is part of an interrupting phrase).

His mother, father, and sister/were at the ceremony.

Do not use commas to separate items if each item is joined by *and* or *or*.

The audience clapped <u>and</u> cheered <u>and</u> stood up after the speech.

Section 8
PUNCTUATION AND MECHANICS

PRACTICE I

Each sentence contains a series of items. Add the missing commas.

EXAMPLE:
John L. Holland, a psychology professor from Johns Hopkins University, has taught students, done research, and published books.

1. According to John L. Holland, the six basic types of jobs include realistic jobs conventional jobs investigative jobs artistic jobs social jobs and leadership jobs.

2. When trying to choose a career, you should try a variety of jobs work in different places and volunteer for various tasks.

3. Realistic jobs involve working with tools large machines or other types of equipment.

4. People who work with tools or machines are usually strong competitive and physically healthy.

5. Bank tellers secretaries office managers and accountants have conventional jobs.

6. People who describe themselves as outgoing cooperative helpful and responsible have social jobs.

7. Eric Townsend wants to be a teacher nurse or social worker.

8. Investigative workers often do market surveys develop military strategies or tackle economic problems.

9. Adela Sanchez is energetic self-confident and ambitious.

10. Sanchez hopes to get a leadership job in sales politics or business.

Commas After Introductory Words and Phrases

Place a comma after an **introductory word**. The word could be an interjection such as *yes* or *no*, an adverb such as *usually*, or a transitional word such as *therefore*.

| Introductory word(s) | , | sentence | . |

<u>Yes</u>, I will help you finish the project.

<u>Honestly</u>, you should reconsider your promise.

<u>However</u>, the job includes a lot of overtime.

Introductory phrases of two or more words should be set off with a comma. The phrase could be a transitional expression such as *of course* or a prepositional phrase such as *in the morning*.

<u>As a matter of fact</u>, the manager explained the new policy.

<u>In the middle of the meeting</u>, Nancy decided to leave.

<u>After his speech</u>, the employees asked questions.

Section 8
**PUNCTUATION
AND MECHANICS**

PRACTICE 2

Underline the introductory word or phrase in each sentence. Add fifteen missing commas.

EXAMPLE:

Honestly, interviews can be very stressful.

1. Before a job interview you should do certain tasks. After contacting the company take some time to prepare for the interview. First of all do some research about the company. As soon as possible you could go on the Internet and find out about the company's performance. Certainly you can impress the hiring committee if you appear knowledgeable about the business.

2. Undoubtedly talking to new people adds to the stress of a job interview. Nonetheless you can do well if you act confident. In fact try to make direct eye contact with the interviewer. After a difficult question take the time you need to think about it. Of course it is important to answer questions honestly. However try to find a positive spin. For example the interviewer may ask why you left a previous job. At that moment do not criticize your former boss or complain about your former job. Instead simply say that you needed new challenges. Clearly it is important to be positive.

Commas Around Interrupting Words and Phrases

Interrupting words or phrases appear in the middle of sentences. Such interrupters are often asides that break the sentence's flow but do not really affect the meaning.

| Noun | , | interrupting word(s) | , | rest of sentence. |

My co-worker, for example, has never taken a sick day.

Kyle, frankly, should never drink during business lunches.

The company, in the middle of an economic boom, went bankrupt!

 **Using Commas with Appositives**

An appositive comes before or after a noun or pronoun and adds further information about the noun or pronoun. The appositive can appear at the beginning, in the middle, or at the end of the sentence. Set off appositives with commas.

beginning
An ambitious man, Donald has done well in real estate.

middle
Cancun, a coastal city, depends on tourism.

end
The hotel is next to Alicia's, a local restaurant.

PRACTICE 3

Underline any interrupting phrases, and ensure that the necessary commas are there. If the sentence needs commas, add them. If the sentence is correct, write *C* in the blank.

EXAMPLE:

Some talk show hosts, for example, earn very high salaries.

_____ 1. Oprah Winfrey, a talk-show host is a successful entrepreneur.

_____ 2. Winfrey a media icon, grew up in an impoverished rural area in Mississippi.

_____ 3. Her childhood in fact was extremely dysfunctional.

_____ 4. She knew, deep in her heart that she would be successful one day.

_____ 5. She moved to Nashville, Tennessee, to live with her father.

_____ 6. Vernon, a barber and businessman proved to be a guiding influence in Winfrey's life.

_____ 7. Oprah Winfrey at age nineteen, became an anchor at a television station.

_____ 8. Her career, of course, escalated.

_____ 9. In 1985, her nationally syndicated television talk show became extremely successful.

_____ 10. She also appeared in a Steven Spielberg movie, *The Color Purple* that same year.

_____ 11. Having a keen business sense, Winfrey decided to produce her show herself.

_____ 12. Harpo, the word *Oprah* spelled backwards became the name of her production company.

_____ 13. Winfrey a generous person, uses her enormous wealth to support numerous charities.

_____ 14. *Fortune 500* a business magazine, consistently lists Oprah Winfrey as one of the most successful women in America.

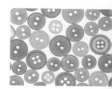

Section 8
PUNCTUATION AND MECHANICS

PRACTICE 4

The following sentences contain a few series of items, introductory words, and interrupting words. Add ten missing commas.

EXAMPLE:

Oprah, a successful talk-show host, may help others deal with problems.

1. According to Dr. Howard Garrell talk shows are extremely important in many people's lives. Garrell a psychoanalyst, did a comprehensive study of talk-show viewers. In his opinion viewers look to hosts like Oprah or Dr. Phil for guidance on personal, financial or health problems. On television, they hear experts discuss job loss, marital infidelity, financial problems and health issues.

2. This reliance on talk shows, according to Garrell is not negative. In fact talk-show viewers are often more informed about physical, emotional and financial issues than others. Such programming basically helps some viewers live fulfilled healthy and rewarding lives.

Commas in Compound Sentences

A compound sentence contains two or more complete sentences joined by a coordinating conjunction (*for, and, nor, but, or, yet, so*).

| Sentence | , and | sentence. |

The job is interesting, **and** the pay is decent.

The job requires fluency in Spanish, **so** maybe I will be hired.

Michael works as a bank teller, **but** he is looking for a better position.

**Section 8
PUNCTUATION
AND MECHANICS**

 **Commas and Coordinators**

You do not always have to put a comma before coordinating conjunctions such as *and, but,* or *or*. To ensure that a sentence is truly compound, cover the conjunction with your finger and read the two parts of the sentence.

• If each part of the sentence contains a complete idea, then you need to add a comma.

Comma: Anna does marketing surveys, and she sells products.

• If one part is incomplete, then no comma is necessary.

No comma: Anna does marketing surveys and sells products.

PRACTICE 5

Add six missing commas to the following letter.

EXAMPLE:

I am honest, and I am hardworking.
     ^

Dear Mr. Yamasaki,

I am looking for work and I saw an ad in the <u>Boston Globe</u> stating that your clinic needs a nurse. I am a nursing student and have just completed my studies. I am interested in the job so I have enclosed a résumé highlighting my skills in this field.

Your advertised position mentions shift work but this would not be a problem for me. I have no children and am able to work the day or night shift. I also know that nursing requires both physical strength and emotional stability and I have both of those qualities.

I am available for an interview at any time so please do not hesitate to contact me. Thank you for your consideration and I look forward to hearing from you.

Yours truly,

Jamilla Shabbaz

Jamilla Shabbaz

Commas in Complex Sentences

A **complex sentence** contains one or more dependent clauses (or incomplete ideas). When a **subordinating conjunction**—a word such as *because*, *although*, or *unless*—is added to a clause, it makes the clause dependent.

<u>**When** opportunity knocks</u>, you should embrace it.
    dependent clause   independent clause

Use a Comma After a Dependent Clause

If a sentence begins with a dependent clause, place a comma after the clause. Remember that a dependent clause has a subject and a verb, but it cannot stand alone. When the subordinating conjunction comes in the middle of the sentence, it is not necessary to use a comma.

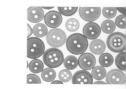

Section 8
**PUNCTUATION
AND MECHANICS**

Dependent clause	**,**	main clause.

Comma: <u>Because she loves helping people</u>, she is studying nursing.

Main clause	**dependent clause.**

No comma: She is studying nursing <u>because she loves helping people</u>.

PRACTICE 6

Edit the following sentences by adding or deleting commas. If a sentence is correct, write *C* in the blank.

EXAMPLE:

Before she went to the interview, Ellen removed her eyebrow ring.   _____

1. Because first impressions count, it is important to dress well for an interview.   _____

2. Before you leave the house review your wardrobe.   _____

3. Although your current boss may accept casual clothing, your future boss may object.   _____

4. Monica Zacharias wants to work as a restaurant manager, because she is ambitious.   _____

5. Although she loves her tattoos she will cover them with clothing during the interview.   _____

6. After she gets the job Zacharias will dress to show her personality.   _____

7. When Clayton Townsend wore a T-shirt and baggy pants to the interview he was not hired.   _____

8. Because Townsend wanted to be hired, he should have tried to make a better impression.   _____

9. After she left her job as a personnel director Amy Rowen started an employment consulting business.   _____

10. According to Rowen, unless job applicants want to work in an artistic milieu they should wear conservative clothing to interviews.   _____

Section 8
PUNCTUATION AND MECHANICS

Use Commas with Nonrestrictive Clauses

Clauses beginning with *who*, *that*, and *which* can be restrictive or nonrestrictive. A **restrictive clause** contains essential information about the subject. Do not place commas around restrictive clauses.

No commas: The woman <u>who invented the windshield wiper</u> never became wealthy.

(The clause is essential to understand the sentence.)

A **nonrestrictive clause** gives nonessential information. In such sentences, the clause gives additional information about the noun, but it does not restrict or define the noun. Place commas around nonrestrictive clauses.

Commas: The restaurant, <u>which is on Labelle Boulevard,</u> has excellent seafood.

(The clause contains extra information. If you removed it, the sentence would still have a clear meaning.)

 **Which, That, Who**

which
Use commas to set off clauses that begin with *which*.

> Apple Computer, **<u>which</u> started in 1976,** was co-founded by Steve Wozniak and Steve Jobs.

that
Do not use commas to set off clauses that begin with *that*.

> One product **<u>that</u> changed the world** was the personal computer.

who
When a clause begins with *who*, you may or may not need a comma. If the clause contains nonessential information, put commas around it. If the clause is essential to the meaning of the sentence, then it does not require commas.

> **Essential:** The man **<u>who</u> employs me** uses Apple computers.
> **Not essential:** Steve Jobs, **<u>who</u> has four children,** is a billionaire.

PRACTICE 7

Each sentence contains a clause beginning with *who*, *which*, or *that*. Underline the clause, and then set it off with commas, if necessary.

EXAMPLE:

People <u>who do not want mainstream jobs</u> can work in various fields.

1. Jobs that are unusual can provide people with entertaining stories.

2. Lyle Baker who lived in Vancouver worked for the police department.

3. The department which had several police dogs trained the animals to find criminals.

4. Lyle who was a student acted as prey for the police dogs.

5. A piece of clothing that Lyle had worn would be shown to the dogs.

6. The job which required quick reflexes involved hiding from the animals.

7. Lyle who was young and agile would hide in the nearby woods.

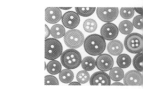

Section 8
**PUNCTUATION
AND MECHANICS**

8. Lyle's protective gear which included a plastic bat and a padded leather armpiece usually kept him safe.

9. One experience that left a scar on his leg occurred during the training.

10. A dog that found Lyle tried to pull him out of a tree.

11. Today, the scar which appears on Lyle's ankle is a souvenir from his summer job.

12. People who have scars usually have interesting stories to tell.

Commas in Business Letters

When you write or type formal correspondence, ensure that you use commas correctly in all parts of the letter.

Addresses

In the address at the top of a business letter, put a comma between these elements.

- The street and apartment number
- The city and state or country

Do not put a comma before the zip code.

> Anita Buchinsky
>
> XYZ Company
>
> 11 Maple Lane, Suite 450
>
> Brownfield, Texas 79316

If you include an address inside a complete sentence, use commas to separate the street address from the city as well as the city from the state or country. If you include only the street address, do not put a comma after it.

Commas: The building at 1600 Pennsylvania Avenue, Washington, D.C., is called the White House.

No comma: The building at 1600 Pennsylvania Avenue is called the White House.

Section 8
PUNCTUATION AND MECHANICS

Dates

In the date at the top of the letter, put a comma between the full date and the year.

January 28, 2006

If you write just the month and the year, then no comma is necessary.

January 2006

If you include a date inside a complete sentence, put commas after the day of the week, the day of the month, and the year.

On Monday, July 26, 2005, we flew to New York.

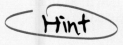 **Writing Numbers**

In business letters, do not write ordinals, which are numbers such as *first* (1st), *second* (2nd), *third* (3rd), and *fourth* (4th). Instead, write just the number *1, 2, 3, 4,* and so on.

May 13, 2004   September 25, 1954

Salutations

Salutations are formal letter greetings. The form "To Whom It May Concern" is no longer used regularly. The best way to address someone is to use the recipient's name followed by a comma.

Dear Ms. Weinberg,   Dear Mrs. Bertolucci,   Dear Sir or Madam,
Dear Miss Wayne,   Dear Mr. Rahim,   Dear Claims Department,

Complimentary Closings

Capitalize the first word of a complimentary closing, and place a comma after the closing. Here are some formal complimentary closings.

Respectfully,   Sincerely,   Yours truly,
Respectfully yours,   Yours sincerely,   Many thanks,

Section 8
**PUNCTUATION
AND MECHANICS**

PRACTICE 8

Add nine missing commas to the following business letter.

Amanda Sitlali
33 Green Avenue
Las Vegas NV 89101

September 4 2005

Elwood River Rafting
1771 Center Street
Redwood Falls MN 56283

Dear Mr. Elwood

On Tuesday August 2 2005 I went on a river rafting expedition with your company. When I returned home, I realized that I had lost a bracelet. It may have dropped inside the raft. The bracelet is made of gold, and it has great sentimental value.

If you have found it, please contact my parents. They live at 34 Reed Avenue Redwood Falls. Their phone number is 309-555-3933.

Yours truly

Amanda Sitlali

Amanda Sitlali

FINAL REVIEW

Edit the following essay by adding or removing commas. There are seventeen missing commas and three unnecessary commas.

EXAMPLE:

Some workers, especially those in sales, travel on a regular basis.
                                      ^

1. On March 11, 2005 when I went to the airport for a winter vacation I saw several passengers in business suits with laptop computers. The passenger who was sitting beside me typed on his laptop during most of the flight. After we had spoken for a few minutes this man, Antonio Morales, told me about his travel fatigue. Morales who has a job at Anderson Plastics, spends over 180 days a year on the road. On the day we met, he had to fly to Los Angeles drive to San Diego and return to Los Angeles within twenty-four hours. Many people think that workplace travel is glamorous, because business travelers visit exotic places.

Section 8
**PUNCTUATION
AND MECHANICS**

Those who travel on a regular basis, however can have physical and psychological problems.

2.   Alina Tugend, a writer for the *New York Times* has written about the stressed business traveler. According to Tugend business travel is not as exciting as it appears. Frequent travel which is defined as six or more business trips each year can cause eating, sleeping and breathing disorders. It can also cause serious heart problems, that require hospitalization. Executive Ted Burke, for example had a stroke that may have been linked to his long hours spent on airliners.

3.   The World Bank, which conducted a study in 1997 looked at health-care claim forms that were filed by workers. According to the study, male workers who traveled extensively filed 80 percent more forms than their colleagues, who did not travel. My travel companion, for example suffers from stress-related ailments.

4.   Businesses should reconsider the travel schedules of employees. Perhaps frequent travelers should be given days off to recuperate after trips and they should also be given fewer responsibilities after returning to work. If corporate culture does not change, good employees will leave their jobs. For example, although he loves working in sales Morales is looking for a new job that requires less travel.

 The Writer's Room

Write a paragraph about one of the following topics. After you finish writing, make sure that you have used commas correctly.

1. Would you like to have a job that includes a lot of travel? List some reasons for your answer.

2. Have you, or has someone you know, ever had an interesting or unusual job? Describe the job.

(continued)

Section 8
**PUNCTUATION
AND MECHANICS**

CHECKLIST: COMMAS

When you edit your writing, ask yourself the following questions.

Do I use commas correctly in series of items?

The store sells bikes, inline skates, and skateboards.

Do I use commas correctly after introductory words or phrases?

In fact, many sportswear companies hire athletes to promote their products.

Do I use commas correctly around interrupting words and phrases?

The campaign, in my opinion, is extremely creative.

Do I use commas correctly in compound sentences?

The advertisement is unusual, and it is quite shocking.

Do I use commas correctly in complex sentences?

When the commercial airs, the company will track viewer responses.

The company, which was founded in 1998, is very successful.

See Chapter 25 on the Visualizing Writing CD-ROM for an additional audio and animated mini-lecture on **Commas**.

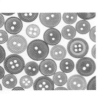

Section 8
PUNCTUATION AND MECHANICS

The Apostrophe

CHAPTER 26

Section Theme: **THE BUSINESS WORLD**

CONTENTS

- Understanding Apostrophes
- Using Apostrophes in Contractions
- Using Apostrophes to Show Ownership
- Using Apostrophes in Expressions of Time

In this chapter, you will read about controversies in the business world.

Grammar Snapshot

Looking at Apostrophes

This excerpt is taken from the article "How to Handle Conflict" by P. Gregory Smith. Review the underlined words.

> "I <u>don't</u> mind doing my fair share of the dirty jobs around here," Ramon continued, "but I feel like <u>I'm</u> getting a lot more mop time than anyone else." By using a statement that began with "I," Ramon was able to state his feelings honestly, without accusing Mr. Jefferson. "I" statements usually <u>can't</u> be considered false or cause an argument because <u>they're</u> a simple statement of feelings.

In this chapter, you will learn to use apostrophes correctly.

Understanding Apostrophes

An **apostrophe** (') is a punctuation mark. It shows that two words have been contracted into one word, or it shows ownership.

> **Richard's** business is new, but **it's** growing.

Using Apostrophes in Contractions

A **contraction** is two words joined into one. When you contract two words, the apostrophe generally indicates the location of the omitted letter(s).

> is + not = isn't   I + am = I'm

Hint ⟩ **Formal Writing**

Do not use contractions when you write a formal academic paper. For example, in a literary analysis, you would not use contractions.

Common Contractions

There are two types of common contractions. You can join a verb with *not;* you can also join a subject and a verb.

Verb + *not*

When a verb joins with *not*, the apostrophe replaces the letter *o* in *not*.

Common Contractions

is + not = isn't	does + not = doesn't
are + not = aren't	has + not = hasn't
can + not = can't	have + not = haven't
could + not = couldn't	should + not = shouldn't
do + not = don't	would + not = wouldn't

Exception: will + not = won't

PRACTICE I

Write contractions for the underlined words in the next sentences.

EXAMPLE:

don't

Many American companies <u>do not</u> think twice about outsourcing to other countries.

1. If you plan to get information about a credit card, chances are great that

   you <u>will not</u> speak to an American customer service representative.

2. It <u>is not</u> unusual to speak with a person from another part of the world.

3. You <u>would not</u> even know that he or she <u>is not</u> an American.

4. He or she <u>does not</u> have an accent when speaking English.

5. Also, you <u>should not</u> be surprised that the person at the call center knows everything about American culture.

6. Companies outsource because they <u>do not</u> have to pay high salaries in other nations.

Subject + Verb

When you join a subject and a verb, you must remove one or more letters to form the contraction.

Contractions with *be*
I + am = I'm
he + is = he's
it + is = it's
she + is = she's
they + are = they're
we + are = we're
you + are = you're
who + is = who's

Contractions with *will*
I + will = I'll
he + will = he'll
it + will = it'll
she + will = she'll
they + will = they'll
we + will = we'll
you + will = you'll
who + will = who'll

Contractions with *have*
I + have = I've
he + has = he's
it + has = it's
she + has = she's
they + have = they've
we + have = we've
who + has = who's

Contractions with *had* or *would*
I + had *or* would = I'd
he + had *or* would = he'd
it + had *or* would = it'd
she + had *or* would = she'd
they + had *or* would = they'd
we + had *or* would = we'd
you + had *or* would = you'd
who + had *or* would = who'd

Exception: Do not contract a subject with the past tense of *be*. For example, do not contract *he + was* or *they + were*.

When you asked her about the product, ~~she's~~ *she was* not helpful.

The sales staff were in a meeting. ~~They're~~ *They were* discussing new products.

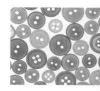

Hint > **Contractions with Proper Nouns**

You can contract a proper noun with the verb *be* or *have*.

Shania's late for work. **Deiter's** been waiting for her since 9 a.m.
Shania is   *Deiter has*

PRACTICE 2

Add the missing apostrophes to the underlined words in this selection.

EXAMPLE:

                                    who's
Daniel Pink is a journalist <u>whos</u> written articles for *Wired* magazine.

1.   In his article "The New Face of the Silicon Age," Daniel

Pink describes Americans who are losing their jobs because of

outsourcing. He mentions Aparna Jairam, a computer programmer

<u>whos</u> thirty-three years old. <u>Shes</u> worked in various jobs in

the software industry. Currently, <u>shes</u> working for Hexaware

Technologies in Mumbai, India. Compared to U.S. programmers,

she <u>doesnt</u> earn a high salary. However, <u>shes</u> happy with her job,

and <u>shed</u> like to keep it.

2.   According to Pink, many Americans are worried that people

like Jairam are "stealing" their jobs. For example, Scott Kirwin, a

Delaware programmer, says that <u>hes</u> angry about the situation. In

2003, he lost his job when his employer outsourced the work

of his entire department. <u>Hes</u> been trying to get members of

Congress to do something about outsourcing.

3.   Executives know that <u>theyre</u> cutting costs by outsourcing.

Highly qualified Indian or Chinese workers can do the same jobs

as Americans for a fraction of the cost. For U.S. companies, <u>its</u>

about the bottom line, or profit maximization. On the other

hand, massive changes in the agricultural and manufacturing

sectors have occurred before, and the workplace has adjusted

with jobs opening up in entirely new sectors. Perhaps <u>its</u> difficult

right now, but the job situation may improve in the future.

Section 8
**PUNCTUATION
AND MECHANICS**

 Contractions with Two Meanings

Sometimes one contraction can have two different meanings.

   I'd = I had *or* I would   **he's** = he is *or* he has

When you read, you can usually figure out the meaning of the contraction by looking at the words in context.

   He is   He has
   He's starting up a new company. **He's** had three successful businesses.

PRACTICE 3

Look at each underlined contraction, and then write out the complete word.

EXAMPLE:

They <u>weren't</u> ready to start a business.   *were not*

1. <u>Yusef's</u> working for a large bank.   _____

2. <u>He's</u> been an investment counselor for two years.   _____

3. <u>He's</u> a very intelligent man.   _____

4. When we met last year, I was impressed because <u>I'd</u> never seen such a hardworking person before.   _____

5. <u>I'd</u> like to work with him.   _____

Using Apostrophes to Show Ownership

Possession means that someone or something owns something else. Nouns and indefinite pronouns such as *anyone* and *everyone* use an apostrophe to show ownership.

   the office of the businessman = the businessman's office

Singular Nouns: To show possession of singular nouns, add -'s to the end of the singular noun.

   Sheila's mother works as a dispatcher.

   Everyone's computer was upgraded.

Even if the noun ends in *s*, you must still add -'s.

   Dennis's dad helped him find a job.

   My **boss's** assistant arranges her schedule.

Plural Nouns: To show possession when a plural noun ends in *s*, add just an apostrophe.

Section 8
**PUNCTUATION
AND MECHANICS**

Many **employees'** savings are in pension plans.

Taxi drivers' licenses are regulated.

Add -*'s* to irregular plural nouns to indicate ownership.

That **men's** magazine is very successful.

The **children's** toy department is on the main floor.

Compound Nouns: When two people have joint ownership, add the apostrophe to the second name only.

joint ownership
Mason and **Muhammad's** restaurant is successful.
(They share ownership of a restaurant.)

When two people have separate ownership, add apostrophes to both names.

separate ownership
Mason's and **Muhammad's** cars are parked in the garage.
(They each own a car.)

PRACTICE 4

Write the possessive forms using apostrophes.

EXAMPLE:

the office of Nicolas   *Nicolas's office*

1. the bank account of James   _____
2. the committee of the ladies   _____
3. the company of Matt and Harrison   _____
4. the promotion of the manager   _____
5. the desks of Marcia and Lewis   _____
6. the building of the company   _____
7. the investment club of the women   _____
8. the accounting book of Dolores   _____
9. the work force of China   _____
10. the lawyers of the Smiths   _____

Section 8
**PUNCTUATION
AND MECHANICS**

PRACTICE 5

Correct nine errors in possessive forms.

EXAMPLE:

company's
The ~~companys~~ profits are very high this year.

1.   Nike has become synonymous with Americas corporate success. Nikes' beginnings are very interesting. The business started from the back of Phil Knights car in the early 1960s. In 1963, Knight went to Japan. By chance, he met with Japanese businessmen who manufactured running shoes. At the businessmens' meeting, Knight asked to import Japanese running shoes to America.

2.   Back in the United States, Knight taught an accounting class at Portland State University. In the departments hallway, he saw several design student's work. He commissioned student Carolyn Davidson to come up with a design. Davidsons swoosh symbol became Nikes logo. At the time, she was paid only $35 for her design. However, several years later, Knight presented her with an envelope containing some of the companys stock. Davidson says that she has been adequately compensated for her design.

Using Apostrophes in Expressions of Time

If an expression of time (year, week, month, or day) appears to possess something, you can add an apostrophe plus -*s*.

My mother won a **month's** supply of groceries.

Eve Sinclair gave **three weeks'** notice before she left her job.

When you write out a year in numerals, you can use an apostrophe to replace the missing numbers.

The graduates of the class of **'04** often networked with each other.

However, if you are writing the numeral of a decade or century, do not put an apostrophe before the final *s*.

In the **1800s,** many farmers took factory jobs in nearby towns.

Many investors lost money in the **1990s.**

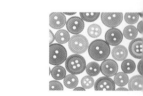

Section 8
PUNCTUATION AND MECHANICS

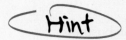 **Common Apostrophe Errors**

• Do not use apostrophes before the final *s* of a verb.

        wants
    Zaid ~~want's~~ to start a new business.

• Do not confuse contractions with possessive pronouns that have a similar sound. For example, the contraction *you're* sounds like the pronoun *your*. Remember that possessive pronouns never have apostrophes.

                      Its
    The corner store is new. ~~It's~~ owner is very nice.

                        theirs
    That is our account. It is not ~~their's~~.

PRACTICE 6

Correct the apostrophe mistakes in each sentence.

EXAMPLE:

      your
I saw ~~you're~~ friend at the meeting.

1. Its well known that many clothing manufacturers receive criticism for poor working conditions of employees in Third World countries.

2. Theres documented evidence that these workers are usually underpaid.

3. For example, Nikes directors have admitted that there was a problem in Indonesia in the late 1990's.

4. In 2001, Nike realized that its' Indonesian plant managers were abusing workers.

5. Kathie Lee Giffords clothing line for Wal-Mart was manufactured in Honduras.

6. In 1995, reports revealed that the plants employees were working under terrible conditions.

7. Gifford publicly acknowledged that working condition's had to be improved.

8. Mitsumi work's as a buyer for an internationally known clothing company.

Section 8
PUNCTUATION AND MECHANICS

9. Her companys official policy is to buy clothing from manufacturers who

   pay fair wages.

10. As a consumer, Ill always try to be well informed about the things that I buy.

FINAL REVIEW

Correct fifteen apostrophe errors. Apostrophes may be used incorrectly, or there
may be errors with possessive nouns.

EXAMPLE:

don't   *shouldn't*
If you ~~dont~~ like the product, you ~~should'nt~~ buy it.

1.   The worlds largest company is Wal-Mart. Its larger than

      Exxon, Microsoft, or General Electric. In the 1990's, Wal-Mart's

      expansion into Mexico, Canada, and many other nations

      occurred. Mexico City and Toronto's stores have been

      extremely successful.

2.   Wal-Mart's company policy is to supply it's customers with

      the cheapest prices possible. Customers are happy because theyre

      getting good deals. However, some Wal-Mart suppliers are'nt as

      thrilled.

3.   In an article for *Fast Company* magazine, Charles Fishman

      examines Wal-Marts pricing policies. According to Fishman,

      suppliers for Wal-Mart are pressured to reduce prices. When

      prices are too low, it force's them out of business. For example,

      Fisher mentions the Loveable Company, which used to supply

      lingerie to Wal-Mart. Executives at Wal-Mart asked the

      company to lower its prices. Loveable refused. Within three

      year's, the company went out of business.

4.   On the other hand, some suppliers say that theres a positive

      outcome when they supply to Wal-Mart. Most companies

Section 8
**PUNCTUATION
AND MECHANICS**

manufacturing practices must become very efficient in order to supply Wal-Mart with low-cost products. Also, many suppliers want to do business with Wal-Mart because they can get huge boosts in their sales.

5.   Consumer's also benefit from pricing policies at Wal-Mart. Families' with low incomes can afford to shop there for quality products. Many consumers budgets are helped by the low cost of goods at Wal-Mart.

The Writer's Room

Write a paragraph about one of the following topics. After you finish writing, underline any words with apostrophes, and verify that you have correctly used the apostrophes.

1. Describe your ideal job.
2. Do you enjoy shopping, or do you consider it to be a tedious chore? Describe your shopping personality.

CHECKLIST: PRONOUNS

When you edit your writing, ask yourself the next questions.

☐ Do I use the apostrophe correctly in contractions? Check for errors in these cases:
   –contractions of verbs + *not*
   –contractions with subjects and verbs

   > shouldn't   weston's
   > You ~~should'nt~~ be surprised that ~~Westons'~~ going to be a consultant in China.

☐ Do I use the apostrophe correctly to show possession? Check for errors in these possessives:
   –singular nouns (*the student's*)
   –plural nouns (*the students'*)
   –irregular plural nouns (*the women's*)
   –compound nouns (*Joe's and Mike's motorcycles*)

   > Chris's
   > ~~Chris'~~ company gave him the use of a car.

(continued)

Section 8
PUNCTUATION AND MECHANICS

Do I place apostrophes where they do not belong? Check for errors in these cases:

–possessive pronouns

–spelling of third-person singular present tense verbs

It ~~look's~~ *looks* like my company is moving ~~it's~~ *its* headquarters to Tokyo.

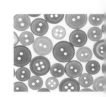
See Chapter 26 on the Visualizing Writing CD-ROM for an additional audio and animated mini-lecture on **Apostrophes**.

Section 8
**PUNCTUATION
AND MECHANICS**

Quotation Marks and Capitalization

Section Theme: **THE BUSINESS WORLD**

CONTENT

- Direct and Indirect Quotations
- Quotation Marks
- Capitalization
- Titles

In this chapter, you will read about business success stories.

Grammar Snapshot

Looking at Quotation Marks

This excerpt is taken from Ben Carson's autobiography, *Gifted Hands*. The quotation marks and associated capital letters are underlined.

> One of the counselors at our high school, Alma Whittley, knew my predicament and was very understanding. One day I poured out my story, and she listened with obvious concern. "I've got a few connections with the Ford Motor Company," she said. While I sat next to her desk, she phoned their world headquarters. I particularly remember her saying, "Look, we have this young fellow here named Ben Carson. He's very bright and already has a scholarship to go to Yale in September. Right now the boy needs a job to save money for this fall." She paused to listen, and I heard her add, "You have to give him a job."

In this chapter, you will learn how to use direct quotations correctly. You will also learn about capitalization and punctuation of titles.

Direct and Indirect Quotations

A **direct quotation** reproduces the exact words of a speaker or writer. An **indirect quotation,** however, simply summarizes someone's words. Indirect quotations often begin with *that*.

Direct quotation:	Mrs. Delaware said, "I'm moving to a new office."
Indirect quotation:	Mrs. Delaware said **that** she was moving to a new office.

The next sections discuss proper capitalization and punctuation of direct quotations.

Quotation Marks

Use **quotation marks** (" ") to set off the exact words of a speaker or writer. If the quotation is a complete sentence, there are some standard ways that it should be punctuated.

- Capitalize the first word of the quotation.
- Place quotation marks around the complete quotation.
- Place the end punctuation inside the closing quotation marks.

Generally, attach the name of the speaker or writer to the quotation in some way.

> **. . . said,**   **"Complete sentence."**

Mrs. Delaware said, "You are hired."

Using Quotation Marks with an Introductory Phrase

When the quotation is introduced by a phrase, place a comma after the introductory phrase.

> **. . . says,**   "_____."

Miguel Lanthier says, "You should feel passionate about your work."

PRACTICE 1

Place quotation marks around the direct quotations in the following sentences. Add capitals and other punctuation where necessary.

EXAMPLE:

Beverly Sills stated ~~You~~ ,"You may be disappointed if you fail, but you are doomed if you don't try."

1. According to businessman J. C. Penney   every business is built on friendship.

2. Mahatma Gandhi once said   you must be the change you wish to see in

   the world.

Section 8
**PUNCTUATION
AND MECHANICS**

3. Booker T. Washington, a political pundit, stated   success is to be measured not so much by the position that one has reached in life as by the obstacles one has overcome.

4. Senator Dianne Feinstein said   toughness doesn't have to come in a pinstripe suit.

5. General Norman Schwarzkopf declared   when placed in command, take charge.

Using Quotation Marks with an Interrupting Phrase

When the quotation is interrupted, do the following:

■ Place a comma after the first part of the quotation.
■ Place a comma after the interrupting phrase.

"_____," . . . **says,** "_____."

"To cultivate kindness," said essayist Samuel Johnson, "is a valuable part of business life."

PRACTICE 2

Place quotation marks around the direct quotations in the following sentences. Add capital letters and other punctuation marks where necessary.

EXAMPLE:

One chance' said Jessie Owens' is all you need.

1. Hard work without talent is a shame said entrepreneur Robert Half but talent without hard work is a tragedy.

2. I like Mr. Gorbachev remarked former British Prime Minister Margaret Thatcher so we can do business together.

3. Whether you think you can said famous automaker Henry Ford or whether you think you can't, you're right!

4. When you're riding declared jockey Bill Shoemaker only the race in which you're riding is important.

Section 8
**PUNCTUATION
AND MECHANICS**

5. Singleness of purpose is one of the chief essentials for success in life said

   millionaire John D. Rockefeller no matter what may be one's aim.

Using Quotation Marks with an End Phrase

When you place a phrase at the end of a quotation, end the quotation with a comma instead of a period.

"_____," **says** . . . .

"There's no business like show business," said Irving Berlin.

If your quotation ends with another punctuation mark, put it inside the ending quotation mark.

"_____?" **says** . . . .

"Don't do that!" he yelled.
"Why did you hire her?" she asked.

PRACTICE 3

Place quotation marks around the direct quotations in the following sentences. Add capital letters and other punctuation marks where necessary.

EXAMPLE:

"You're never beaten until you admit it" said General George S. Patton.

1. To succeed in business or to reach the top, an individual must know all it is

   possible to know about that business stated businessman John Paul Getty.

2. The first one gets the oyster and the second one gets the shell! said steel

   magnate Andrew Carnegie.

3. We fall forward to succeed declared Mary Kay Ash, the founder of Mary

   Kay Cosmetics.

4. Power is the ability to do good things for others said philanthropist

   Brooke Astor.

5. What I do best is share my enthusiasm stated Bill Gates, the founder of

   Microsoft.

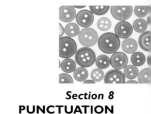

Section 8
**PUNCTUATION
AND MECHANICS**

Using Quotation Marks with an Introductory Sentence

You can introduce a quotation with a complete sentence. Place a colon (:) after the introductory sentence.

He explains his views: "_____."

Writer William Feather explains his views on parenthood: "Setting a good example for children takes all the fun out of middle^age."

PRACTICE 4

Place quotation marks around the direct quotations in the following sentences. Add capital letters and other punctuation marks where necessary.

EXAMPLE:

The philosopher Friedrich Nietzsche explained perseverance : "What ~~what~~ doesn't kill us makes us stronger."

1. Entrepreneur P. D. Armour expressed his views anybody can cut prices, but it takes a brain to produce a better article.

2. Malcolm Forbes, a magazine publisher, discusses how to succeed try hard enough.

3. Spanish writer Miguel Cervantes referred to his success to be prepared is half the victory.

4. We discussed the words of Norman Vincent Peale it's always too soon to quit.

5. Philanthropist Thomas Dewar discusses human minds they only function when open.

6. Ayn Rand, a philosopher and writer, ponders success the ladder of success is best climbed by stepping on the rungs of opportunity.

Section 8
PUNCTUATION AND MECHANICS

PRACTICE 5

Place quotation marks around the direct quotations in bold print. Add capital letters and punctuation marks to the direct quotations.

EXAMPLE:

My supervisor Lisa said ,"Learn **~~learn~~ from the words of Henry ~~Ford.~~** "

1.   Henry Ford often said **an idealist is a person who helps other people to prosper.** Ford's innovations changed the American way of life. Before his Model T, only two out of ten Americans lived in a city. By World War II, that number had changed significantly.

2.   Ford was born in 1863, on a farm near Dearborn, Michigan. Since his childhood, Ford experimented with mechanical objects. He was determined to manufacture cars. **You can't build a reputation on what you are going to do** he once stated. In 1903, he became the vice president of the Ford Motor Company and started to build cars.

3.   Ford was a risk taker. His contemporaries thought that his company would be successful if he built expensive cars for the rich, but he was against that idea. **There is one rule for the industrialist** Ford often said **and that is make the best quality of goods possible, at the lowest cost possible, and pay the highest wages possible.**

4.   In 1908, he introduced the Model T, which was affordable for a large number of people. Some customers asked for the car in other colors, to which Ford said **people can have the Model T in any color so long as it's black.** To meet the growing demand for the car, Ford introduced the assembly line in 1913.

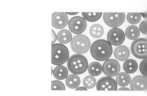

Section 8
**PUNCTUATION
AND MECHANICS**

Ford explained **nothing is particularly hard if you divide it into small jobs.** The assembly line made car production quick and efficient. By 1913, the Ford Motor Company had become the largest car manufacturing company in the world. Ford summed up his life philosophy **you can do anything if you have enthusiasm.**

Capitalization

Remember to always capitalize the following:

- The pronoun *I*
- The first word of every sentence

   My co-workers and **I** share an office.

There are many other instances in which you must use capital letters. Always capitalize the following:

- **Days of the week, months, and holidays**

   Wednesday   **J**anuary 1   **N**ew **Y**ear's **E**ve

   Do not capitalize the seasons: summer, fall, winter, spring.

- **Titles of specific institutions, departments, companies, and schools**

   IBM   U.S. **D**epartment   **P**inewood
                     of **D**efense   **E**lementary **S**chool

   Do not capitalize general references.

   the company   the department   the school

- **Names of specific places, such as buildings, streets, parks, cities, states, and bodies of water**

   Dale **S**treet   **T**imes **S**quare   **L**os **A**ngeles, **C**alifornia
   Central **P**ark   **M**ississippi   **L**ake **E**rie

   Do not capitalize general references.

   the street   the state   the lake

- **Names of specific languages, nationalities, tribes, races, and religions**

   Portuguese   **N**avaho   **B**uddhist   an **I**talian restaurant

- **Titles of specific individuals**

   General **E**isenhower   **P**resident **K**ennedy   **D**r. **M**arcos
   Professor **W**ong   **P**rime **M**inister **B**lair   **M**rs. **E**leanor **R**oosevelt

   If you are referring to the profession in general, or if the title follows the name, do not use capital letters.

   a senator   my professor   the doctors

Section 8
**PUNCTUATION
AND MECHANICS**

- **Specific course and program titles**

    Mathematics 201   Civil Engineering 100   Beginner's Spanish

    If you refer to a course but do not mention the course title, then it is not necessary to use capitals.

    He is in economics.   I study hard for my civil engineering class.

- **The major words in titles of literary or artistic works**

    The Lord of the Rings   *The Matrix*   *War and Peace*

- **Historical events, eras, and movements**

    the Korean War   Impressionism   the Industrial Revolution

 **Capitalizing Computer Terms**

Always capitalize the following computer terms.

        Internet   World Wide Web

Capitalize software titles as you would any other published work.

        Netscape   Microsoft Office

PRACTICE 6

Add any necessary capital letters to the following sentences.

EXAMPLE:

$$\overset{F\quad\ D}{\text{I often forget to call my father on father's day.}}$$

1. Samuel Gompers founded the American federation of Labor.

2. He believed that Labor day was created to recognize the achievements of the american worker.

3. It is generally believed that Matthew McGuire, from paterson, new jersey, proposed a workers' holiday.

4. McGuire was the secretary of the Central Labor union in New york.

5. The first Labor Day holiday was actually on Tuesday, september 5, 1882.

6. Eventually, in 1884, the first monday of September was proposed as the holiday.

Section 8
**PUNCTUATION
AND MECHANICS**

7. On february 21, 1887, oregon became the first state to legislate Labor Day as a legal holiday.

8. I work for a company called golden flowers, which is a flower wholesaler.

9. Each year, my company has a picnic and golf tournament near lake ambrosia to celebrate Labor Day.

10. The president of our company, ms. Kahn, gives a speech.

11. We raise money for the United way.

12. Our annual Labor Day event is reported in our daily newspaper, *The Phoenix mail.*

Titles
Punctuating Titles

Place the title of a short work in quotation marks. Underline (or italicize, if you are using a computer) the title of a longer document.

Short Works		Long Works	
Short story:	"The Bear"	**Novel:**	The Da Vinci Code
Chapter:	"Abbreviations"	**Book:**	MLA Handbook for Writers of Research Papers
Newspaper article:	"Missing in Action"	**Newspaper:**	New York Times
Magazine article:	"History's Fools"	**Magazine:**	Newsweek
Web article:	"Music Artists Lose Out"	**Web site:**	Blackbeat.com
Essay:	"Neighborhoods of the Globe"	**Textbook:**	Essentials of Sociology
TV episode:	"Shrunk"	**TV series:**	Lost
Song:	"Naughty Girl"	**CD:**	Dangerously in Love
Poem:	"The List of Famous Hats"	**Collection:**	Reckoner

Section 8
**PUNCTUATION
AND MECHANICS**

Capitalizing Titles

When you write a title, capitalize the first letter of the first word and all the major words. Do not capitalize the letters *.com* in a Web address.

This Side of Paradise   Monster.com   "Lucy in the Sky with Diamonds"

Also, do not capitalize the following words, except as the first or last word in a title.

Articles:	a, an, the
Coordinators:	but, and, or, nor, for, so, yet
Short prepositions:	of, to, in, off, out, up, by

PRACTICE 7

Add ten capital letters to the next paragraph. Also, add quotation marks or underlining to six titles.

EXAMPLE:

Ayn Rand's book ~~anthem~~ <u>Anthem</u> begins with strong words: "It was a sin to write this."

Ayn Rand, a writer and philosopher, was born in 1905 in st. petersburg, Russia. Her most famous novel, The fountainhead, was published in 1943. Her next novel was Atlas shrugged. Rand proposed that self-interest should guide people, and her views have been widely debated. Michael Shermer criticized Rand in a magazine called skeptics. He compares her followers to sheep in the article The Unlikeliest cult in history. Rand also has numerous supporters, and her philosophy, objectivism, has been analyzed by many distinguished thinkers. Peter St. Andre, for example, wrote the essay Why I Am a libertarian, which appeared in the magazine full context. Rand's books continue to sell millions of copies, and her supporters have created numerous Web sites to promote her work and philosophy.

FINAL REVIEW

A. Add three missing capital letters, and properly punctuate the two quotations in bold point.

EXAMPLE:

Graham Lopez was born in Seattle, ~~w~~ashington.

The labor movement has an interesting history in the united states. There are many proponents and opponents of unionization. Graham Lopez is a member of the United Auto

Section 8
PUNCTUATION AND MECHANICS

workers Union. He believes that unions help workers get better pay and social and health benefits. Neela Subramanyam works for a small car parts company. There is no union at her company. **None of the workers want one** she says **because they believe that unions create disharmony between managers and workers.** Subramanyam also believes that unions support mediocrity. **It is hard to remove union members who do not do their jobs** she argues.

B. Add seven missing capital letters, and properly punctuate three titles.

EXAMPLE:

There was an article about unions in the magazine called ~~f~~^Fortune 500.

I read about the history of the union movement in a book called Working Detroit: The Making of a union town. The United auto Workers Union started in 1935, in Detroit, michigan. One of the most famous union strikes was at the Ford motor company. Henry Ford was against unionization. In the magazine The Industry standard, Kevin Baker wrote an article called Ford's Paradox. Baker discussed how Ford increased car sales by raising the wages of his workers. However, Baker also stated that Ford was so powerful that he could cut workers' wages at a whim. Nowadays, no president of a large company can arbitrarily cut wages.

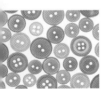

Section 8
PUNCTUATION AND MECHANICS

The Writer's Room

Write a paragraph about one of the following topics. After you finish writing, circle any words that you have capitalized or directly quoted.

1. Have you, or has anyone you know, ever worked in a unionized workplace? Compare or contrast a unionized and a nonunionized workplace.

2. What are some things that you should do to get your dream job? List at least five steps that you should take.

CHECKLIST: QUOTATION MARKS AND CAPITALIZATION

When you edit your writing, ask yourself the next questions.

Are there any direct quotations in my writing? Check for errors with these elements:

–punctuation before or after quotations

–capital letters

–placement of quotation marks

"You're fired," said Donald Trump to his latest apprentice.

Do my sentences have all the necessary capital letters?

               I   War
About two years ago, ~~i~~ saw a movie about World ~~war~~ II.

Are the titles of artistic works properly punctuated?

                                    Saving Private
Steven Spielberg directed the award-winning movie ~~Saving private~~
Ryan
~~ryan~~.

READING LINK

The Business World
To read more about the business world, see the next essays:
"How to Handle Conflict" by P. Gregory Smith (page 457)
"The Rewards of Dirty Work" by Linda L. Lindsey and Stephen Beach (page 459)

 The Writers' Circle

Work with a partner. Take turns reading a dialogue from an essay at the back of this book. Write down everything that your partner says. When you are both finished, exchange papers, compare them with the original essays, and mark any misspelled words or incorrectly placed punctuation or quotations marks. Here are some suggested readings.

"Birth" (page 432), paragraphs 3 to 8 (stop at the word *condemnation*)

"The Appalling Truth" (page 438), paragraphs 3 to 9 (stop at the words *Mr. Ed*.)

In a dialogue, begin a new paragraph every time the speaker changes.

 See Chapter 27 on the Visualizing Writing CD-ROM for additional audio and animated mini-lectures on **Quotation Marks** and **Capitalization**.

Section 8
PUNCTUATION AND MECHANICS

Editing Practice

In this chapter, you will practice editing different types of writing, including a memo and a letter.

After you finish writing the first draft of a paragraph or essay, it is important to edit your work. When you edit, carefully review your writing to verify that your grammar, punctuation, sentence structure, and capitalization are correct. In this chapter, you can practice editing written pieces that you see every day, including e-mail, paragraphs, essays, and business correspondence.

PRACTICE I

Correct the underlined errors. An editing symbol appears above each error. To understand the meaning of each symbol, refer to the revising and editing symbols on the inside front cover of this book.

Some <u>argues</u> *(agr)* that television <u>contribute</u> *(agr)* to the decline of

values in our society and that viewers become addicted to <u>there</u> *(sp)*

TV screens. However, television cannot be blamed for all of the

problems in the world. In fact, television has a positive role in

our ~~life~~ [pl]. First, television ~~teach~~ [agr] us important things about politics,

religion, science, and human relations. For example, during

the last election, my brother and ~~me~~ [pro] learned ~~alot~~ [sp] about the

presidential candidates. We watched the debates and ~~examine~~ [shift]

how each candidate spoke to the viewers. Furthermore, if

negative images appear on our screens, it is because television

~~reflect~~ [agr] what is going on in society. It ~~do~~ [agr] not create what happens

in society. Television also ~~have~~ [agr] another important role. It ~~make~~ [agr]

us smile. When we watch TV, we no longer worry about

personal ~~problems, we~~ [ro] simply relax and get carried away by

the funny and entertaining programs. Jib Fowles, in an article

titled "Whipping Boy," says_"The attack on television violence is, [p]

at least in part, an attack by the upper classes and their partisans

on popular culture." Television plays an important role in our

lives_and we should not blame it for problems in our society. [p]

PRACTICE 2

Correct the underlined errors. An editing symbol appears above each error.

Television undoubtedly has a negative influence on people.

First, the lives of a normal children have changed a lot. They

no longer spend time outside playing, and such inactivity

contributes to childhood obesity. Additionally, children watch

too much violent images on TV. Theses images affects the way

that children see the world. In a psychological study did at the

University of Pennsylvania, fifty preschool children were expose

to violent images and fifty were not. The children who had seen

violent programs were more likelier to show aggressive behavior.

Also, the average American waste too much time staring at the

television. All that time could be use for other activities such

as reading, doing sports, and simply to communicate with

others. On a weekday evening, visit a typical American home.

Family members will likely be sitting in front of their

television sets.

PRACTICE 3

There are no editing symbols in the next paragraph. Proofread it as you would your own writing, and correct ten errors.

People often wonder what do motivational speakers do. In fact, they inspire audience members to achieve particular goals. Many companies hire motivational speakers to encourage its employees and to give keynote speeches at conferences. Companies look for speakers who has a positive message and who are engaging. Much people who have achieved success have become motivational speakers, including General Norman Schwarzkopf and former New York City mayor Rudolph Giuliani. Actors, former presidents, and sports heroes also inspires audiences. Some times, a motivational speaker can earn more than fifty-thousands dollars for an appearance. The best motivational speakers encourages the audience members to analyze their own beliefs, and goals.

PRACTICE 4

In the next memo, there are no editing symbols. Identify and correct ten errors.

Memo: Summer Party

This year, Winston and me are in charge of organizing the company party that is gonna take place on July 12. The summer partys theme is baseball. Please dress appropriate. Any body who plays baseball really good or who just wants to play is invited. Everyone is welcome to bring their friends. There is baseball equipments in the supply room. Let's make this party, the most best event of the year.

Uma Kamarchung, Party Organizer

Section 9
EDITING

PRACTICE 5

Identify and correct fifteen errors in the next letter.

Dear Maya,

I have being at the police training center for two weeks. It is real hard. Every day, we have to get up at 5:30 and go for a ten-mile run in the dark. It is very likely than I will get into great shape by the end of my training.

Each morning, we receive our schedule. For the rest of the day. We don't have no time to relax. Their is no time for leisure activities. The older students have said that there used to the long hours.

Last week, we visited a police department and learned some investigative techniques. In one workshop, we pretended to arrest thiefs. I prefered target shooting to any other activity on our visit. I am more better at shooting than the other students in my class.

I imagine that your busy this summer. Did you go to Puerto Rico last april? Did your mother go to? I hear that your brother and his friend are local heroes, they rescued a boy. Who was drowning.

I have to go, but I will write again. I am looking forward to coming home.

Your friend,

Christine

Section 9
EDITING

PRACTICE 6

Identify and correct ten errors.

Its understandable that American consumers want to get the lowest price possible for products. However, low prices may actually come at a high cost. For example, many Americans desire for clean air and water is actually being threatened by low prices. If a companys profits are reduced because it's forced to lower prices, then the company cant spend money on enviromental protection programs. Americans want to live in a healthy environment but dont want to pay for it. Furthermore, the demand for lower prices drive's manufacturers to build plants in other parts of the world. Workers in countries such as China, India, and Vietnam get real low salaries. For instance, Shanon Nguyen, whos Vietamese, earns a very low daily wage. While people like Mrs. Nguyen struggle those in wealthier countries expect to buy inexpensive products. Perhaps we need to reconsider whether a bargain is worth it.

PRACTICE 7

Identify and correct twelve errors.

There is several things you should do to avoid credit card fraud. First, make sure that you sign your credit card as soon as it arrive. Keep a record of your card number, the expiration date, and the phone number of the credit card company. When you give your credit card to a cashier, watch the transaction, then get your card back immediatly. Keep your receipt untill you get your credit card bill. Check each months bill carefully, and report any suspicious transactions. Do not throw old receipts in the garbage because it contain your credit card information. Criminals go often through recycling bins and garbage cans to find old receipts. With just your name and number, a criminals can run up huge credit card bills. Therefore, it is adviseable to burn receipts or tear it into very small peaces.

Section 9
EDITING

PRACTICE 8

Correct ten punctuation and capitalization errors in this formal business letter.

80 Riverside avenue
Fort Lauderdale, FL 33051

September 4, 2005

Dr. Robert Graham
144 Oceanview boulevard
Miami, FL 33111

Dear Dr. Graham

We had a telephone conversation on tuesday, August 6,

regarding the graduation ceremony at Seneca college. I

asked if you could give a speech to our graduating class,

and you accepted. Here are some details about the event.

The ceremony is on october 25. For your speech, we will provide

you with a projector, a tape recorder, and a podium. We will

make arrangements, to pick you up at your hotel and take you

to the college for the ceremony.

Please confirm these arrangements with Professor Cuomos

secretary. If you have any further questions please call me

at (305) 555-2221. Thank you very much.

Yours Truly,

Monice Richard

Monice Richard

Section 9
EDITING

PRACTICE 9

Identify and correct fifteen errors.

1.　　Bats has acquired a bad reputation and are associated with sinister creatures such as vampires. Some people think that bats will drink their blood or be flying into their hair. However, bats are actualy interesting, useful animals.

2.　　Even though both types of creatures can fly bats are not related to birds. In fact, bats are mammals. The bone structure of a bat's wing is similar to the bone structure of a human arm, therefore, a bat's wing has more maneuverability then a bird's wing. For example, bats use their wings to climb trees. The design of the bat's wing also allow the bat to change directions quickly while flying.

3.　　Furthermore, bats had another interesting feature that makes them good hunters. Because bats primarily hunt at night, they rely on sound and vibrations to help them track their prey. While it is hunting. A bat emits a high sound that bounce off objects in it's way. The bat echo helps to determine the exact location of an object.

4.　　Moreover, bats are a necesary part of a balanced ecosystem. Many bats are insectivores, and they can eat over 1,000 mosquitoes in an hour. For instance, Bracken Cave in Texas have about 20 million bats. They consumes around 200 tons of insects each night. Bats in tropical areas also pollinate mango and banana crops.

Section 9
EDITING

5.   Bats are more than just interesting animals. They demonstrate how sound can be used in navigation, and they help control the numbers of pests. The next time you see a bat, do not be repulsed or feeling frightened. Be appreciative.

PRACTICE 10

Identify and correct twenty editing errors in this student essay.

1.   Many people and events has influenced my life and changed my way of thinking. For exemple, sports were important to me when I was a child. I tried various types of sports, but I never stay with one sport in particular. At the age of seventeen, I had problems with my back, so my doctor recomended that I start weight lifting. Weight lifting has changed my life in a profound way. In fact, if I would have known the benefits of exercise, I would have started weight lifting sooner.

2.   Before becoming a weight lifter, I did not like how I looked physicaly. When I started lifting weights, I learned to like my appearance and to respect my body. I realized that I only have one body, so I gotta take care of it. Now that I am more conscience of my health, I make an effort to eat good. As a result, I am more stronger and more energetic. I am finally treating my body with the respect he deserves.

3.   Furthermore, weight lifting has taught me to persevere. At the beginning of my fitness program, I consulted my cousin who showed me how to do the exercises correctly, the more I trained, the better the effects were. I could lift heavy weights more easy than before. Now I no longer wonder how can I do something. I make goals and stay with them.

Section 9
EDITING

4.   Moreover, weight lifting it has also changed my personallity
and helped me be more confident. I am more at peace with
myself, and I am able to accept each success and failures with
grace. I am also more focused, and I do not loose my temper as
easily as I used to.

5.   Fitness training clearly has both physical and psychological
benefits. It has improved my body, my health, and my self-
esteem. I have been practicing this sport since ten years, and
I will continue to do so. People should choose activities. That
motivate them.

Section 9
EDITING

PART III

Reading Strategies and Selections

SOCIAL SCIENCES

- "Fish Cheeks," Amy Tan, page 421
- "A Conversation with John E. Smelcer," Dale E. Seeds (interview), page 425
- "The Point Is?" John G. Tufts, page 428

I n Chapter 29, you will learn strategies that can help you improve your reading skills. Then, you will read a number of thought-provoking essays that present a wide range of viewpoints about topics related to the social sciences, entertainment and culture, beliefs, politics, science, relationships, zoology, and the business world.

As you read each essay, think about how the writer achieves his or her purpose using one or a combination of these writing patterns.

- Illustration
- Narration
- Description
- Process
- Definition
- Comparison and contrast
- Cause and effect
- Argument

ENTERTAINMENT AND CULTURE

- "The Appalling Truth," Dorothy Nixon, page 438
- "The New Addiction," Josh Freed, page 442
- "The Culture War," Linda Chavez, page 444
- "Going Thin in Fiji," Ellen Goodman, page 447
- "Sports and Life: Lessons to Be Learned," Jeff Kemp, page 430

BELIEFS

- "Fish Cheeks," Amy Tan, page 421
- "A Conversation with John E. Smelcer," Dale E. Seeds (interview), page 425
- "The Point Is?" John G. Tufts, page 428
- "For Marriage," Kirsteen Macleod, page 435
- "Against Marriage," Winston Murray, page 436
- "Going Thin in Fiji," Ellen Goodman, page 447

POLITICS

- "Political Activism," Craig Stern, page 454
- "How to Handle Conflict," P. Gregory Smith, page 457
- "The Hijab," Naheed Mustafa, page 423

SCIENCE

- "What It Feels Like to Walk on the Moon," Buzz Aldrin, page 449
- "The Zoo Life," Yann Martel, page 452

RELATIONSHIPS

- "Birth," Maya Angelou, page 432
- "For Marriage," Kirsteen Macleod, page 435
- "Against Marriage," Winston Murray, page 436

ZOOLOGY

- "The Zoo Life," Yann Martel, page 452

THE BUSINESS WORLD

- "How to Handle Conflict," P. Gregory Smith, page 457
- "The Rewards of Dirty Work," Linda L. Lindsey and Stephen Beach, page 459

Reading Strategies and Selections

CONTENTS

- Reading Strategies
- Reading Selections

The essays in this chapter have been categorized according to theme just as a library classifies books according to subject matter. As you read each selection, consider the writing patterns that have been used.

Reading Strategies

Reading helps you develop your writing skills. Each time you read, you accomplish these goals.

- Expand your vocabulary.
- Learn how other writers develop topics.
- Learn to recognize and use different writing patterns.
- Find ideas for your own paragraphs and essays.

The strategies discussed in this chapter can help you become a more successful reader and writer.

Previewing

When you **preview** a passage, you quickly look at key points. You can get a general sense of a passage's topic and main ideas by checking visual clues.

- Read the title and the main headings.
- Look at the first and last sentence of the introduction.
- Look at the first sentence of each paragraph.

- Look at the concluding sentences in the essay.
- Review any photos, graphs, or charts, and read the captions that accompany them.

Previewing helps you prepare for the next step, which is reading the essay.

Taking Notes

To help you remember and quickly find the important points in a text, you can highlight key ideas and make annotations. An **annotation** is a comment, question, or reaction that you write in the margin of a passage.

Highlighting and Making Annotations

Each time you read a passage, do the following:

- Look at the introductory and concluding paragraphs, and underline sentences that sum up the main idea.
- Using your own words, write the main idea in the margin.
- Underline or highlight supporting ideas. You might even want to number the arguments or ideas. This will allow you to understand the essay's development.
- Circle words that you do not understand.
- Write questions in the margin if you do not understand the author's meaning.
- Write notes beside passages that are interesting or that relate to your own experiences.
- Jot down possible writing topics.

If you are reading a library book, or if you have borrowed a book from somebody else, use sticky notes to make annotations. Do not write in the book!

A Highlighted and Annotated Passage

Is this true?

How could racism be a cause of death?

Main point is that police harassment causes stress for minorities.

Who is Norman Podhoretz?

What is vantage?

1   <u>Black Americans live shorter lives than whites and are more likely to suffer stress-related maladies like high blood pressure, which contributes to stroke and heart attack.</u> The medical profession has yet to list "racism" as a cause of death. But some social scientists now see tension related to discrimination as a health hazard on par with smoking and a high-fat diet. Among the day-to-day acts of discrimination that shadow African-Americans, none are more stressful or dangerous than those committed by police, some of whom treat black people as criminals until proved otherwise.

2   The situation is largely invisible to whites, many of whom see the complaints as a function of what the writer (Norman Podhoretz) once described as "paranoid touchiness" among black people. Not all whites hold the Podhoretz view, of course, and the current police scandals in New York City and New Jersey are broadening the (vantage) point on this problem. When these sagas are over, millions of white people who thought black people paranoid will have substantial insight into a nightmarish reality that whites barely glimpse but that black people live through day after day.

—Brent Staples, "When the Paranoids Turn Out to Be Right"

Understanding Unfamiliar Words

When you read, you will sometimes come across an unfamiliar word. You can try to guess the word's meaning, or you can circle it and look it up later.

Use Context Clues

Context clues are hints in the text that help define a word. To find a word's meaning, try the next steps.

1. **Determine the word's function.** For example, is it a noun, a verb, or an adjective? Sometimes you can understand a word if you know how it functions in the sentence.

2. **Look at surrounding words.** Try to find a relation between the difficult word and the words that surround it. Maybe there is a **synonym** (a word that means the same thing) or an **antonym** (a word that means the opposite). Maybe other words in the sentence help define the word.

3. **Look at surrounding sentences.** Look at the sentences, paragraphs, and punctuation surrounding the word. If you use logic, you may understand what the word means.

PRACTICE I

Can you define the word *heed?*   ____ Yes   ____ No

Can you define *yearn?*   ____ Yes   ____ No

If you do not understand the meaning of those two words, then read the words in context in the next example. You will notice that it is much easier to guess their meanings in context.

> Travel makes it impossible to pay no **heed** to the suffering of others, simply because they are far away. It erases distance, and makes you a more sensitive citizen of the world, **yearning** for peace everywhere.
> —Arthur Frommer, "How Travel Changed My Life"

Now write your own definitions of the words.

1. heed: _____

2. yearn: _____

 **Word Twins**

Word twins are English words that may look and sound like words in another language. For example, the English word *graduation* is similar to the Spanish word *graduacion,* but it is spelled differently.

If English is not your first language, and you see an English word that looks similar to a word in your language, check how the word is being used in context. It may, or may not, mean the same thing in English that it means in your language.

For example, in English, *deception* means "to deliberately mislead someone." In Spanish, *decepcion* means "disappointment." If you are not sure of a word's meaning, consult a dictionary.

Use a Dictionary

If you are unable to understand the meaning of an unfamiliar word by using context clues, then you should look up the word in a dictionary. Review the following tips for proper dictionary usage.

- Look at the preface and notes in your dictionary. The preface contains explanations about the various symbols and abbreviations. Find out what your dictionary has to offer.
- Some words have many definitions. When you are looking up a word, *do not stop after you read the first meaning!* Keep reading, and look for the meaning that best fits the context of your sentence.
- If the difficult word has a prefix such as *un-* or *mis-*, you may have to look up the root word.

For example, the word *sensible* has the following definitions.

Word-Break Divisions
Your dictionary may use heavy black dots to indicate places for dividing words.

Stress Symbol (ʹ) and Pronunciation
Some dictionaries provide the phonetic pronunciation of words. The stress symbol (ʹ) lets you know which syllable is stressed.

Parts of Speech
This means that *sensible* is an adjective. If you don't understand the "parts of speech" symbol, look in the front or the back of your dictionary for a list of symbols and their meanings.

sen′si•ble /(senʹsə-bəl)/ *adj* 1. reasonable. 2. aware; cognizant. 3. perceptible through the senses. 4. capable of sensation.

From *The New American Webster Handy College Dictionary,*
New York: Signet, 2000 (606)

Writing About the Reading

After you finish reading a text, you may have to answer questions about it or write about it. There are several steps you can take to help you better understand a reading passage.

- **Summarize** the reading. When you summarize, you use your own words to write a condensed version of the reading. You leave out all information except for the main points.
- **Outline** the reading. An outline is a visual plan of the reading. First, write the main idea of the essay, and then write the most important idea from each paragraph. Under each idea, you can include a detail or an example.

Respond to the Reading

Before you make a written response to the reading, ask yourself the next questions.

- What is the writer's main point?
- What is the author's purpose: to entertain, to persuade, or to inform?

- Who is the intended reader? Is the writer directing the message at someone like me?
- What is my opinion of the reading?
- What aspects of the topic can I relate to?

Reading Selections

READING 1

Fish Cheeks
Amy Tan

> Amy Tan, the author of the best-selling novel *The Joy Luck Club*, wrote this essay for an issue of *Seventeen* magazine. Using vivid detail, Tan describes a family dinner. As you read, notice how the author uses mainly description but also elements of narration and illustration.

1   I fell in love with the minister's son the winter I turned fourteen. He was not Chinese, but as white as Mary in the manger. For Christmas I prayed for this blond-haired boy, Robert, and a slim new American nose.

2   When I found out that my parents had invited the minister's family over for Christmas Eve dinner, I cried. What would Robert think of our shabby Chinese Christmas? What would he think of our noisy Chinese relatives who lacked proper American manners? What terrible disappointment would he feel upon seeing not a roasted turkey and sweet potatoes but Chinese food?

3   On Christmas Eve, I saw that my mother had outdone herself in creating a strange menu. She was pulling black veins out of the backs of fleshy prawns. The kitchen was littered with appalling mounds of raw food: a slimy rock cod with bulging eyes that pleaded not to be thrown into a pan of hot oil; tofu, which looked like stacked wedges of rubbery white sponges; a bowl soaking dried fungus back to life; and a plate of squid, their backs crisscrossed with knife markings so they resembled bicycle tires.

4   And then they arrived—the minister's family and all my relatives in a clamor of doorbells and rumpled Christmas packages. Robert grunted hello, and I pretended he was not worthy of existence.

5   Dinner threw me deeper into despair. My relatives licked the ends of their chopsticks and reached across the table, dipping them into the dozen or so plates of food. Robert and his family waited patiently for platters to be passed to them. My relatives murmured with pleasure when my mother brought out the whole steamed fish. Robert grimaced. Then my father poked his chopsticks just below the fish eye and plucked out the soft meat. "Amy, your favorite," he said, offering me the tender fish cheek. I wanted to disappear.

6   At the end of the meal, my father leaned back and belched loudly, thanking my mother for her fine cooking. "It's a polite Chinese custom to show you are satisfied," explained my father to our astonished guests. Robert was looking down at his plate with a reddened face.

The minister managed to muster up a quiet burp. I was stunned into silence for the rest of the night.

7   After everyone had gone, my mother said to me, "You want to be the same as American girls on the outside." She handed me an early gift. It was a miniskirt in beige tweed. "But inside you must always be Chinese. You must be proud you are different. Your only shame is to have shame."

8   And even though I didn't agree with her then, I knew that she understood how much I had suffered during the evening's dinner. It wasn't until many years later—long after I had gotten over my crush on Robert—that I was able to fully appreciate her lesson and the true purpose behind our particular menu. For Christmas Eve that year, she had chosen all my favorite foods.

VOCABULARY AND COMPREHENSION

1. What is the meaning of *muster* in paragraph 6?
   a. To summon up or create   b. To gather
   c. A yellow sauce

2. What three reasons does Tan give for her embarrassment when Robert comes for dinner? Use your own words.

   _____

   _____

   _____

3. What lesson was the author's mother trying to teach her?

   _____

   _____

4. On the surface, Tan's purpose is to entertain, but what is her deeper purpose?

   _____

   _____

5. Tan uses descriptive imagery. Imagery includes active verbs, adjectives, and other words that appeal to the senses (sight, smell, touch, sound, taste). Highlight at least five examples of imagery.

GRAMMAR LINK

6. Underline six adjectives in paragraph 3. Then circle the nouns that the adjectives modify. Discuss how the adjectives make the writing more vivid.

7. Identify six irregular past tense verbs not including the verb *be*. Write the present- and past-tense forms of each verb on the lines provided.

   _____   _____

   _____   _____

   _____   _____

DISCUSSION AND WRITING

8. Think about a time when you felt different from others. Explain what happened. Try to use some descriptive vocabulary.

9. What are the possible causes for a person to give up his or her own cultural traditions (language, dress, food, ceremonies, etc.)? What are the effects when people lose their cultural distinctiveness? Discuss the causes or effects of losing cultural traditions.

READING 2

The Hijab

Naheed Mustafa

Naheed Mustafa, a North America–born Muslim woman, has taken to wearing the traditional hijab scarf. While studying in a Canadian university, she wrote about her reasons for wearing the hijab. As you read this definition essay, notice how the author also uses argument.

1   I often wonder whether people see me as a radical fundamentalist Muslim terrorist packing an AK-47 assault rifle inside my jean jacket. Or maybe they see me as the poster girl for oppressed womanhood everywhere. I am not sure which it is. I get the whole **gamut** of strange looks, stares, and covert glances. You see, I wear the hijab, a scarf that covers my head, neck, and throat. I do this because I am a Muslim woman who believes her body is her own private concern.

gamut: the whole range

2   Young Muslim women are reclaiming the hijab, reinterpreting it in light of its original purpose—to give back to women ultimate control of their own bodies. The Qur'an teaches us that men and women are equal, and that individuals should not be judged according to gender, beauty, wealth, or privilege. The only thing that makes one person better than another is her or his character.

3   Nonetheless, people have a difficult time relating to me. After all, I'm young, Canadian born and raised, and university-educated. Why would I do this to myself, they ask. Strangers speak to me in loud, slow English and often appear to be playing charades. They politely inquire how I like living in Canada and whether or not the cold bothers me. If I am in the right mood, it can be very amusing. But, why would I, a woman with all the advantages of a North American upbringing, suddenly, at 21, want to cover myself so that only my face and hands show?

4   Women are taught from early childhood that their worth is proportional to their attractiveness. Women feel compelled to pursue abstract notions of beauty, half realizing that such a pursuit is futile. When they reject this form of oppression, they face ridicule and contempt. Whether it is women who refuse to wear makeup, to shave their legs, or to expose their bodies, others have trouble dealing with them.

5   In the Western world, the hijab has come to symbolize either forced silence or radical, unconscionable militancy. Actually, it is

neither. It is simply a woman's assertion that judgment of her physical person is to play no role whatsoever in social interaction. Wearing the hijab has given me freedom from constant attention to my physical self. Because my appearance is not subjected to public scrutiny, my beauty, or perhaps lack of it, has been removed from the realm of what can legitimately be discussed. No one knows whether my hair looks as if I just stepped out of a salon, whether or not I can pinch an inch, or even if I have unsightly stretch marks. And because no one knows, no one cares.

6   Feeling that one has to meet the impossible male standards of beauty is tiring and often humiliating. I should know; I spent my entire teenage years trying to do it. I was a borderline bulimic and spent a lot of money I did not have on potions and lotions in hopes of becoming the next Cindy Crawford. The definition of beauty is ever-changing; waifish is good, waifish is bad, athletic is good—sorry, athletic is bad.

7   Women are not going to achieve equality with the right to bare their breasts in public, as some people would like to have you believe. That would only make us **party to** our own objectification. True equality will be had only when women don't need to display themselves to get attention and won't need to defend their decision to keep their bodies to themselves.

party to: a part of

VOCABULARY AND COMPREHENSION

1.   Find a word in paragraph 4 that means *pressured*.

    _____

2.   What do you know about the author?

    _____

3.   Why does Mustafa choose to wear the hijab?

    _____

    _____

4.   According to Mustafa, what does the hijab symbolize to non-Muslim North Americans?

    _____

5.   How does Mustafa define *hijab*? Give both the literal and symbolic meanings.

    _____

    _____

GRAMMAR LINK

6.   In paragraph 4, the first sentence uses the passive voice. Rewrite the sentence using the active voice.

    _____

    _____

7. In the last sentence of paragraph 5, highlight the verbs that follow *no one*. Why does each verb end in *s?*

_____

_____

DISCUSSION AND WRITING

8. In paragraph 4, the author claims, "Women are taught from early childhood that their worth is proportional to their attractiveness." Do you agree or disagree with this statement? Explain your answer.

9. In the introductory paragraph, the author says she thinks that people judge her because she is wearing the hijab. What are some stereotypes that people might have about your city, state, nation, or culture? Describe those stereotypes, and give examples showing that the stereotypes are or are not based on reality.

10. Think of a term that could describe your nationality or your generation. Define the term, and give examples.

READING 3

A Conversation with John E. Smelcer
Dale E. Seeds

John E. Smelcer is a writer of Ahtna Athabaskan, Cherokee, and German ancestry. Today, he is the author of over 250 publications in such periodicals as *The Atlantic Monthly*, and he is publisher of the literary quarterly *Rosebud*. Dale E. Seeds, the author of a book about indigenous theater, compiled this interview after having various conversations with Smelcer.

1   SEEDS: What was it like to grow up in Alaska in a culturally mixed background? Looking back, who or what influenced you?

2   SMELCER: Growing up, I only knew my father's side of the family. None of my mother's family lived within 3,000 miles of Alaska. Because my mom's side is essentially white, I look pretty damn white. In public school I wasn't mistreated like most Indian kids. I remember in eighth grade being part of a group of Fairbanks students who were flown into the small village of Nulato on the Yukon River. We arrived in the middle of winter to participate in that village's annual Stick Dance, a weeklong ceremony for the dead that culminates in a traditional **potlatch.** At first, other Indians were skeptical (they still are) about my physical appearance, but once they got to know me, they knew I was Indian.

potlatch: a ceremonial exchange of gifts

3   SEEDS: You trace your Ahtna heritage through your father. What can you tell us about him?

4   SMELCER: My father was taken from his family and shipped to a boarding school in Valdez where he was taught to discard all things Indian. Most people don't realize this, but federal law allowed for such forced removal and relocation of Indian children in Alaska up until the 1960s. Consequently, I believe my father has since resented being Indian. Today, he is socially more distant from his Ahtna heritage than

BIA: Bureau of Indian Affairs

his brothers and sisters who were not relocated by the government. I remember something he told me years ago while driving down the main road of our village one summer. He stopped our yellow van before a perfectly aligned row of **BIA**-subsidized Indian houses, stared down the street for a long time, and turned to me and said, quite matter-of-factly, "Don't ever live like this." I took it to mean not to embrace my Indianness. But, as is the case with many teenagers, his advice was lost on me. After all, most of my relatives were Indian.

5   SEEDS: Since your father distanced himself from his "Indianness," as you say, how did you connect with your traditional culture?

6   SMELCER: In much of our mythologies, a young man's uncle played a larger role in his life. It was often the uncle who taught the boy about hunting, for instance. At 37 years, it is still my uncle, Herbert Smelcer, my father's youngest brother, who teaches me such things. We've hunted together for most of my life. In addition to being the elected president of our tribal organization, it is he who teaches me most what it means to be Indian.

rancorous: bitter; showing resentment

7   SEEDS: The question over who is termed a "Native American" author is a difficult and even **rancorous** issue. What are your observations and experiences with this?

8   SMELCER: At some point, I believe, every major writer claiming Indian identity has felt such pressures to some degree or another. A couple of years ago, I had a book publisher who wanted me to change my name on the cover to an "Indian-sounding" name like Johnny Running Deer or Johnny Two-Dogs-in-Heat (it might as well have been Johnny Fakes-His-Name). I refused and ended up finding a publisher with integrity. I'm always a little suspicious of Indian writers, musicians, or artists with such names—though some are no doubt genuine. From my own experience, I have learned that the question of authenticity, or "How Indian are you really," undermines the credibility of many Native authors. Such unmerited accusations often result in very spiteful attacks levied against a person of whom the attacker has no real personal knowledge.

9   SEEDS: How do you discuss these identity issues with your students?

10   SMELCER: I ask my Native American literature students during the first class to come up with a working definition of what or who they think is Indian. The discussions always begin with stereotypes: Indians are red-skinned (I've never seen a red-skinned person in my life except for extreme sunburn victims); they lived (yes, past tense) on reservations; they have long black hair and dark eyes; they are spiritually attuned to nature, and so forth. Truth be told, Indians don't all have black hair, and indeed, some full-blood Eskimos (Yup'ik and Inupiaq) and Indians have blue eyes, and some even have blond hair. Most of the Indian authors I know have never even been alone in the forest and find nature alien and frightening. It's a complex issue.

VOCABULARY AND COMPREHENSION

1.   Find a word in paragraph 2 that means *ends* or *finishes.*

2. Why does Smelcer's father resent being Native American?

    _____

    _____

3. How is his uncle important in Smelcer's life?

    _____

    _____

4. Why does Smelcer ask his students to define "Indian" on the first day of class?

    _____

    _____

5. Smelcer has a mixed heritage, yet he firmly identifies himself as Native American. Why does he mainly identify with one part of his background?

    _____

    _____

    _____

    _____

    _____

GRAMMAR LINK

6. In paragraph 9, the question contains the word *these*. What does *these* refer to? What is the difference between *this* and *these?*

    _____

    _____

7. In paragraph 10, underline all capitalized words except those at the beginning of each sentence. What rule could you make about the use of capital letters?

    _____

    _____

DISCUSSION AND WRITING

8. Smelcer has a mixed heritage, yet he chooses to identify most closely with his Native American heritage. Why do many people need to know their roots and identify with that background?

9. Conduct a short taped interview with someone you think is very interesting. You might choose someone who is much older than you are. (Remember to ask the person for permission to do the taping.) Ask questions to discover what major lessons the person has learned in life. Then write a paragraph or essay about the person.

READING 4

The Point Is?

John G. Tufts

John G. Tufts wrote the next article for the *ASU Ram Page*, Angelo State University's student newspaper. As you read, notice how the author uses mainly definition and some argument to explain why he has gone to college.

1   On May 15, I, like many of my fellow seniors, will be walking across the stage to receive a single sheet of paper—a document that proudly proclaims to the world that I am a survivor of the educational system. I graduated from college—thank God! However, as May draws closer, I've caught myself wondering, "Why did I do it? Why has going to college been so important? What's the point?" Perhaps a college education should be valued for how it changes us, and not for what it will give us.

2   There are misconceptions about the value of a college education. A college degree does not guarantee that we will receive an awesome salary. A higher education only provides the possibility of such a future. For example, compare the salary of your average Harvard graduate with that of, say, Bill Gates, a college dropout who is a multibillionaire. Furthermore, college doesn't necessarily make us more well rounded. University life certainly provides opportunities in which we are exposed to diversity and other people's opinions and ideas, but it doesn't guarantee we will become more knowledgeable.

3   The ultimate benefit of going to college is the development of human curiosity. A college education allows us to become curious about a whole range of topics. It does not mean that we sit in a classroom, get information, and **regurgitate** that information. It took me nearly four years to understand this—curiosity and self-motivation are what it's all about. And yet, I'm continually surprised by the looks and comments I get while walking through the University Center with an armload of books from the library. "What class is that for!?" other students ask in mock horror.

regurgitate: give back

4   "I'm only curious," I tell them—much to their bewilderment.

5   On graduation day, as I walk across the stage in cap and gown, I will know the full value of what my college experience has given me, and it won't be contained in the little sheet of paper I'm about to be handed. My diploma, my proclamation to the world that I'm a survivor, will only represent one part of my education. The real value will be in the classes that taught me how to look up information for myself and in the teachers that inspired me to do so.

6   The movie *Higher Learning* follows the lives of three first-year college students at a fictitious university. There's a great scene between Ice Cube, playing the part of a six-year senior "professional student," and Omar Epps, a freshman. In the scene, Epps enters Ice Cube's room and asks if he can borrow a certain book. Cube smiles and hands it over.

7 Epps says, "Thanks. I need this for an essay in my political science class."

8 The smile on Ice Cube instantly fades, and he yanks the book away: "I thought you said you needed this book."

9 Epps replies, "Yeah, I said it's for a class; why else would I need it?"

10 Ice Cube responds, "To feed yo' brain, fool."

VOCABULARY AND COMPREHENSION

1. Find a word in paragraph 2 that means *false impressions*.

    _____

2. What is the author's main point? Underline the thesis statement.

3. According to Tufts, what do most people generally believe a college education will provide?

    _____

4. How does Tufts define a college education?

    _____

    _____

5. The author ends the essay with an example of a scene from a movie. How does it support the author's main point?

    _____

    _____

    _____

GRAMMAR LINK

6. How valid is the author's argument? Explain your answer.

    _____

    _____

7. What other benefits does a college education provide?

    _____

    _____

8. Circle five contractions in the text. Then write out the long form of each contraction. For example, in paragraph 1, the contraction *I've* is written out as *I have*.

    _____

9. In the first sentence of paragraph 2, why does Tufts write *There are* instead of *There is*?

    _____

    _____

DISCUSSION AND WRITING

10. Define *education*. Give examples to support your definition.

11. Poll five students. Ask them why they have chosen to go to college. Write about your poll results, and mention the names and approximate ages of the people that you have polled.

READING 5

Sports and Life: Lessons to Be Learned
Jeff Kemp

Jeff Kemp was a National Football League quarterback for the Los Angeles Rams, the San Francisco 49ers, the Seattle Seahawks, and the Philadelphia Eagles. Kemp describes a lesson that he learned during his football years. As you read this narrative essay, notice how the author also uses elements of illustration, description, and cause and effect writing.

1   Sports are elevated life. They are noble and ignoble, beautiful and ugly. They reveal the best and worst of human nature in an action-packed arena dominated by intense emotion. When sports commentators repeat the old cliché about "the thrill of victory and the agony of defeat," we all know exactly what they are talking about. As players or spectators, we have experienced both. Yet, underneath the adrenaline rush is something even more powerful: our value system. Sports, in other words, reveal what we treasure most.

2   In 1988, I was playing for the Seattle Seahawks against my old team, the 49ers, when I learned firsthand that there are two competing value systems. I wasn't bitter that my old team had traded me, but I wanted to beat them all the same. Quarterback Dave Krieg had been injured, and I was to start. I had a great week of practice and felt totally prepared. I entered the Kingdome in Seattle **brimming** with excitement. I envisioned leading my team to victory and establishing myself as the Seahawks' starter.

brimming: filled; overflowing

3   Coming out of the pre-game meal, one of the offensive coaches put his arm around me and strongly affirmed his faith in me: "I want you to know how happy I am that you are the Seahawk quarterback. I've been waiting for this day." I felt honored, valued, and esteemed. This was going to be a great day!

4   Well, we ran the ball on our first two plays, and we did not gain much. On third down and eight, I threw to Hall of Famer wide receiver Steve Largent, who split two defenders. The pass hit him right in the hands, yet he dropped the ball. Next to Jerry Rice, Largent is, statistically speaking, the greatest receiver in history. He also is one of my best friends. All I could do at that moment was chuckle and moan, "Steve, what's the matter? You never drop the ball. Why are you doing this to me?"

5   After that, he did not make any mistakes, but I did. In fact, I played the worst game of my life. At the end of the first half, the 49ers were ahead 28–0. Every person in the Kingdome, with the exception of my wife (and there isn't even a witness to vouch for her), was booing me. Have you ever heard nearly 60,000 people booing you? It's quite an experience.

6   As I came off the field at halftime, I knew that I might be benched, but I wasn't defeated. Ever since I was a small boy, my father had been drumming into my head British Prime Minister Winston Churchill's brave words to the students at Harrow School in the dark days of 1941: "Never give in, never give in, never, never, never, never—in nothing, great or small, large or petty—never give in except to convictions of honor and good sense."

7   I waded through the players to find the coach who had been so supportive before the game. I wanted to discuss some offensive strategies that might turn things around in the second half. As I approached him and began, "Coach . . ." he turned his back on me without a word. Then he called to another quarterback, put his arm around him, and began to discuss plays that player would run in the second half.

8   Now, I understood that I was being taken out of the game. That made sense. I was hoping it would not happen, but I understood. However, that coach did not say one word to me for the rest of the game even though we stood next to each other on the sidelines. Nor did he say anything on Monday when we watched the game films. For about a month, there was complete rejection. He simply couldn't deal with the fact that I had not lived up to his hopes and that I had not helped the team to succeed. He rejected me relationally because my performance had fallen short.

9   I discovered during this painful episode a faulty value system that is conditional and performance-based. It rejects relationships and dishonors the diverse yet equal value of every person. My coach, as well as other coaches and even team owners, was not only exerting but also feeling the pressure of this value system that has been adopted by so many in business and the culture at large.

10   My career slowly, steadily had been rising, and now, all of a sudden, it seemed it was on a speedy downward course. The fifth-stringer had made it to first string only to be benched, booed by the crowd, and shunned by his own coach. It looked like my last chance to succeed had come and gone.

11   Eventually, though, I found renewed hope and confidence through a **transcendent** value system, which is quite different. It is an unconditional, relational, and character-based value system. It leads us to treat others as we wish to be treated. Of course, performance and competition are important, as are rewards and incentives, but none of these things enhances or **demeans** the value of an individual.

transcendent: inspirational

demeans: degrades; lowers

VOCABULARY AND COMPREHENSION

1.   In paragraph 6, the author says, "As I came off the field at halftime, I knew that I might be benched." What does he mean by *benched?*

_____

2.   In paragraph 6, why does the author quote Winston Churchill?

_____

_____

3.   Explain how the coach's attitude toward Kemp changes during the Seattle Seahawks game.

_____

_____

_____

4. Why does Kemp reject the value system of his coach?

_____

_____

5. Kemp tells a story about a specific event in his life. Retell the story in two or three sentences.

_____

_____

_____

_____

GRAMMAR LINK

6. Look at the quotation in paragraph 3. Why is there a colon before the quotation? Explain the punctuation rule.

_____

_____

7. Underline an example of a simple sentence, a compound sentence, and a complex sentence. Why does the author use different types of sentences?

_____

DISCUSSION AND WRITING

8. Kemp describes an experience that changed his outlook on life. What life-changing experiences have you had? Choose one, and describe what happened.
9. What lessons can people learn when they play team sports?

READING 6

Birth

Maya Angelou

> Maya Angelou is an award-winning author. In this selection from her best-known autobiographical work, _I Know Why the Caged Bird Sings_, Angelou writes about the birth of her son. As you read, notice how the author uses mainly narration but also elements of description and cause and effect writing.

1   Two days after V-Day, I stood with the San Francisco Summer School class at Mission High School and received my diploma. That evening, in the bosom of the now-dear family home, I uncoiled my fearful secret, and in a brave gesture left a note on Daddy Clidell's bed. It read, "Dear Parents, I am sorry to bring this disgrace upon the family, but I am pregnant. Marguerite."

2   The confusion that ensued when I explained to my stepfather that I expected to deliver the baby in three weeks, more or less, was

reminiscent of a **Molière** comedy. Daddy Clidell told Mother that I was "three weeks gone." Mother, regarding me as a woman for the first time, said indignantly, "She's more than any three weeks." They both accepted the fact that I was further along than they had first been told but found it nearly impossible to believe that I had carried a baby, eight months and one week, without their being any the wiser.

3   Mother asked, "Who is the boy?" I told her. She recalled him, faintly.

4   "Do you want to marry him?"

5   "No."

6   "Does he want to marry you?" The father had stopped speaking to me during my fourth month.

7   "No."

8   "Well, that's that. No use ruining three lives." There was no **overt** or subtle **condemnation.**

9   Daddy Clidell assured me that I had nothing to worry about. He sent one of his waitresses to I. Magnin's to buy maternity dresses for me. For the next two weeks I whirled around the city going to doctors, taking vitamin shots and pills, buying clothes for the baby, and except for the rare moments alone, enjoying the **imminent** blessed event.

10   After a short labor, and without too much pain (I decided that the pain of delivery was overrated), my son was born. Just as gratefulness was confused in my mind with love, so possession became mixed up with motherhood. I had a baby. He was beautiful and mine. No one had bought him for me. No one had helped me endure the sickly gray months. I had had help in the child's conception, but no one could deny that I had had an immaculate pregnancy.

11   I was afraid to touch him. Home from the hospital, I sat for hours by his bassinet and absorbed his mysterious perfection. His extremities were so dainty they appeared unfinished. Mother handled him easily with the casual confidence of a baby nurse, but I dreaded being forced to change his diapers. Wasn't I famous for awkwardness? Suppose I let him slip, or put my fingers on that throbbing pulse on the top of his head?

12   Mother came to my bed one night bringing my three-week-old baby. She pulled the cover back and told me to get up and hold him while she put rubber sheets on my bed. She explained that he was going to sleep with me.

13   I begged in vain. I was sure to roll over and crush out his life or break those fragile bones. She wouldn't hear of it, and within minutes the pretty golden baby was lying on his back in the center of my bed, laughing at me.

14   I lay on the edge of the bed, stiff with fear, and vowed not to sleep all night long. But the eat-sleep routine I had begun in the hospital, and kept up under Mother's dictatorial command, got the better of me. I dropped off.

15   My shoulder was shaken gently. Mother whispered, "Maya, wake up. But don't move."

16   I knew immediately that the awakening had to do with the baby. I tensed. "I'm awake."

17   She turned the light on and said, "Look at the baby." My fears were so powerful I couldn't move to look at the center of the bed. She

reminiscent: similar to

Molière: a French playwright (1622–1673)

overt: evident, open

condemnation: criticism; disapproval

imminent: forthcoming, soon to arrive

said again, "Look at the baby." I didn't hear sadness in her voice, and that helped me to break the bonds of terror. The baby was no longer in the center of the bed. At first I thought he had moved. But after closer investigation, I found that I was lying on my stomach with my arm bent at a right angle. Under the tent of blanket, which was poled by my elbow and forearm, the baby slept touching my side.

18   Mother whispered, "See, you don't have to think about doing the right thing. If you're for the right thing, then you do it without thinking."

19   She turned out the light, and I patted my son's body lightly and went back to sleep.

VOCABULARY AND COMPREHENSION

1. In paragraph 10, Angelou says, "I had had help in the child's conception, but no one could deny that I had had an immaculate pregnancy." Why does she call her pregnancy *immaculate?*

   _____

   _____

2. How does Angelou's family react to the pregnancy?

   _____

3. In paragraph 11, the author says that she was afraid to touch her own baby. Why did she feel this way?

   _____

4. Were her fears well-founded? Why or why not?

   _____

   _____

5. What does the reading suggest about becoming a parent?

   _____

   _____

GRAMMAR LINK

6. The author uses quotations in her narration. How do the quotations enhance the story?

   _____

   _____

7. Angelou uses the following vivid verbs. Write two or three synonyms next to each verb.

   whirled (paragraph 9) _____

   handled (paragraph 11) _____

   dreaded (paragraph 11) _____

   begged (paragraph 13) _____

DISCUSSION AND WRITING

8. In paragraph 18, the author's mother says, "See, you don't have to think about doing the right thing." Do you agree that people instinctively know how to become parents? Explain your answer.

9. The author acted impulsively when she was an adolescent. Write about an impulsive act that you did when you were an adolescent. What happened, and what were the consequences? Try to use some descriptive language in your writing.

Readings 7 and 8: Two Views About Marriage

The next two essays provide opposing viewpoints about the institution of marriage. Read both essays, and then answer the questions that follow.

READING 7

For Marriage
Kirsteen Macleod

> British medical student Kirsten Macleod is a member of the Cambridge debating team. She wrote this argument essay as part of a debating competition in which she had to defend the institution of marriage.

1   Marriage is arguably losing its appeal, claim many social scientists and tabloid journalists. With one out of every three marriages ending in divorce, the institution of marriage as a religious and legal bond may be considered outdated in today's society. Cohabitation is no longer unacceptable; indeed, it is commonplace among the youth of today, and illegitimacy no longer carries a social stigma. However, the marital bond helps maintain a stable family environment.

2   Just because some marriages may fail does not mean that we should give up on an ideal. Marriage statistics show that one out of three marriages is a remarriage; therefore, such statistics actually suggest that people continue to have faith in marriage as an institution. We are frequently disillusioned by the criminal justice system when it fails, but we support principles it upholds in society. The same can be said for marriage.

3   Furthermore, marriage is still important because it presents a rational view of what a loving and committed relationship is. Passionate love is **transient,** so it is important to have a foundation that holds couples together. True love includes friendship, support, trust, and commitment, and it is more lasting than feelings of passionate love.

transient: temporary; of short duration

4   Legally, marriage represents a solid and protected base for both parties, whereas cohabitation does not. Marital laws provide financial protection for a surviving spouse after the death of the partner. In addition, if a couple does decide to separate, each partner gets a fair share of the marital property and access to the children. Most importantly, spouses may decide to work harder at the relationship because they are bound together by a legal as well as an emotional contract.

5   Marriage as an institution still retains its validity. It provides families with stability, especially regarding the children's welfare. Spouses are more protected financially when they are legally married than when they simply live together. Because marriage is a socially recognized symbol of love and commitment, we should continue to support it.

READING 8

Against Marriage

Winston Murray

> College student Winston Murray attacks the institution of marriage in the next argument essay.

1   My friends Donna and Doug want a fairy-tale wedding. They believe that marriage will provide them with a lifelong partner. They hope to live happily ever after in their dream home with their two children and their dog. However, it is not necessary to get married to have a committed, long-term relationship.

2   A marriage certificate does not guarantee that a relationship will be happy and long lasting. One out of three marriages ends up in divorce, and married partners often take each other for granted and feel trapped. Cohabitating partners, on the other hand, choose to be together. Indeed, many cohabitating couples have stronger and longer-lasting relationships than married couples. If one partner does not hold up his or her end of the relationship, the other partner can simply leave. Thus, cohabitating partners often treat each other better than married partners do. Ultimately, if people want to be together, they do not need a piece of paper to unite them. If they want to split up, the formal bond of matrimony simply creates a longer and more painful separation process.

3   Couples do not need marriage in order to provide children with a stable home environment. Actors Goldie Hawn and Kurt Russell have had a common-law relationship for over twenty years. Together, they have raised Goldie's two children, Kate and Oliver, and they have had one child together. They claim that they are as devoted to each other and to their children as any married couple would be.

4   Moreover, there are laws that protect couples who live together. If a separated couple has children, for example, both partners are legally responsible for the financial support of the children. Also, many jurisdictions have laws protecting the property rights of common-law spouses. In fact, fifteen states recognize common-law relationships and accord them the same rights and obligations as legal marriages.

5   Finally, weddings are expensive and extravagant affairs that indebt families for years to come. Parents of the bride and groom often take out second mortgages in order to give their children the ideal wedding. After paying for the wedding dress, they must pay for the reception hall, flowers, music, catering, and limousines to have a one-night party. Common-law couples are under no obligation to have an expensive

ceremony. They can, if they choose, celebrate their partnership, but they do not have societal pressure to put on an elaborate affair.

6　　Marriage is an old-fashioned institution that no longer needs to be protected or supported. It is extremely expensive to have a wedding, and it is also costly to get a divorce. Common-law relationships are now socially acceptable and popular. Therefore, if you plan to have a long-term relationship, consider having a common-law relationship.

VOCABULARY AND COMPREHENSION

1.　What introduction style does Macleod use in Reading 7?
　　a. Anecdote　　　　　　b. General
　　c. Historical　　　　　　d. Contrasting position
2.　What introduction style does Murray use in Reading 8?
　　a. Anecdote　　　　　　b. General
　　c. Historical　　　　　　d. Contrasting position
3.　Underline the thesis statement in each essay.
4.　Write two different terms that mean the same thing as "living together without marriage."

_____

5.　In Reading 7, paragraph 1, the author says that "illegitimacy no longer carries a social stigma." What does the author mean? Rewrite the sentence using your own words.

_____

_____

6.　Make two columns, and list the main arguments in each essay.

"For Marriage"	"Against Marriage"
_____	_____
_____	_____
_____	_____
_____	_____
_____	_____
_____	_____
_____	_____
_____	_____

7.　In your opinion, which essay argues more convincingly? Why?

_____

_____

_____

8. At one point, both authors use the same point to justify one of their arguments. Which point is it? How does each author interpret the information?

_____

_____

_____

_____

GRAMMAR LINK

9. Underline at least five transitional words or expressions in Reading 8. Look for words that appear at the beginning of sentences. For example, in paragraph 1, *However* is a transitional expression.
   a. How are the transitional expressions punctuated?

   _____

   b. What purpose do transitional expressions serve?

   _____

DISCUSSION AND WRITING

10. Add one more argument for each side of the marriage debate.
11. Argue for or against large, extravagant weddings. Support your point of view with many examples.
12. Describe your first infatuation. Give a detailed description of the person that you had a crush on.

READING 9

The Appalling Truth
by Dorothy Nixon

Dorothy Nixon, a freelance writer, has written for *Salon.com*, *Chatelaine*, and *Today's Parent* magazine. In the next reading, she discusses the issue of television addiction. As you read this illustration essay, notice how the writer also uses elements of narration, description, and comparison and contrast.

Pavlovian: refers to Russian behavior psychologist Ivan Pavlov

oracle: a prophet who gives advice and answers questions

McCluhan: Marshall McCluhan, an academic and media commentator who developed theories about the influences of the electronic media on popular culture

1 Technology changes us. With the invention of the clock we have lost the ability to live in the present. The telephone has made us slaves, in the **Pavlovian** sense, to a ringing bell. With the advent of television we all moved indoors, leaving the streets empty and clear for the criminal element, and we left our minds open and susceptible to the mash served up on the screens.

2 As a mother and very serious media watcher, I am as troubled as anyone about the violent and sexist content on television. But were television wall-to-wall PBS type programming, without commercials, I would be just as concerned. I just don't like what it is doing to my family. It has become some kind of **oracle**—never mind **McCluhan's** "electronic fireplace"—it commands all of our attention and we don't

listen to each other: husband to wife, parents to kids, or kids to parents. It is with this in mind that I suggest to my husband that we ban the tube from the house, on an experimental basis, for, say, about a year.

3   "No way!" he says.

4   "Why not?" I ask.

5   "Because it would be hypocritical," he deftly answers. "We both work in the TV industry."

6   "You work in TV. I don't," I counter.

7   "Well, you like to criticize TV for the local paper. How can you criticize something you don't watch?"

8   "Good point. I just don't like what that thing is doing to our family," I continue. "It's noisy. It jangles the nerves. It's like a drug. It's addictive. With satellite TV we watch anything, even those stupid reality shows and retro shows like *Mr. Ed.* That show is about a talking horse, for heaven's sake. It was my favorite show when I was 8! We used to read thoughtful books like *1984;* now we watch *24.* Besides, the stupid contraption keeps us from doing what human beings are really supposed to be doing."

foraging: searching

9   "What's that? **Foraging** for nuts and berries?" My husband, the TV junkie, sees nothing wrong with the boob tube: "I grew up on TV, and I'm no psycho."

10   If my husband had his way, there would be a TV in every room. And they would all be tuned into *24,* twenty-four hours a day. And, I must admit, there are times when I have felt that the only interests we have in common are the *Sopranos* or *CSI.* In the early months of my first pregnancy we would cuddle together on the couch like two spoons and I would fall asleep, head cradled in his lap, eyes on the tube. Togetherness.

11   But now we are like two channel-zapping zombies. "You know, *they* say that spending time together in front of the television does nothing to enhance a relationship," I tell my now bleary-eyed husband, trying to make him feel guilty. It's a war of **attrition** and it is working, sort of.

attrition: gradual wearing away of resistance

12   "OK. Two weeks," my husband relents. "We'll try no TV for two weeks. That's all. But *you* tell the kids." We have two boys, Andrew and Mark, seven and four. They kick up a huge fuss when I tell them that our tiny bungalow has been unilaterally declared a TV free zone. Now it is their turn to try to make me feel guilty. They hang their pathetic little heads in genuine mourning as they watch their dad reluctantly disconnect the enormous tangle of wires enabling the miracle of modern home theater in our suburban castle. And am I feeling guilty? No way! I stand tall and victorious in our living room, the protector of my children.

13   That evening, we read our children books, sing them songs, and tuck them in for the night. I go to bed with that Margaret Drabble I have been using as a giant paperweight for the past year and my husband snuggles up with Stephen King.

14   Two days pass. The kids have finally stopped complaining about their terrible loss. In fact, they do not appear to care at all, anymore. They have found other more interesting things to do. I, on the other hand, am suffering from a mean case of withdrawal.

15   "It's *Will and Grace* night, and it's the *only* show I like. Do you think maybe you can bring the TV up for just this show?" I ask my husband, who happens to be down in his workroom drilling a hole into a six foot piece of plywood for no apparent reason. "We'll keep the sound really low" (because kids can hear hypocrisy even in their sleep).

16   "Why don't you read, Ms. Literature Freak? You haven't exactly been burning up the library shelves," my husband sneers, rather condescendingly as he stops to wipe some sawdust from his nosehairs.

17   "Well, that's because I only read the best, and my brain's too fried at the end of the day to read the best," I answer, convincing even myself. (That has been my pat excuse for my intellectual lethargy since becoming a mother.)

18   My husband rolls his eyes and puts down the drill. There is no further argument from him. He happily carries the TV upstairs and reconnects the myriad wires in no time. We sit back and laugh at the antics of Will, Grace, Jack, and Karen. The problem is, we do the same for *Everybody Loves Raymond* a few days later. And for *Six Feet Under*, each night my husband clambering up the basement stairs with a 20-inch Sony stuck to his face, and then stumbling down again thirty-something minutes later, trailing his wires behind him.

19   Then there is the true test. Indeed, it is a real dilemma for us. A brand new episode of *Desperate Housewives* is airing, and the kids are still awake. What can we do? There is clearly no sleazy hypocritical way around this.

20   "I can always get a tape and watch it at work," my husband, the news editor, smiles, taunting me once again. "You, on the other hand, will have to do without."

21   It is a real dilemma. The HOTTEST show on TV features four fortyish suburban women at various stages of freak out. Have I died and gone to heaven? My friends tell me the show is better than marriage therapy because their husbands love to watch it too.

Stepford wife: submissive, domestic, married woman (from the Ira Levin novel *The Stepford Wives*)

22   So here are **Stepford wife** Bree, timid Susan, wacked out Lynette, and sexy Gabrielle who are forcing me to face a very real truth. It is not my kids. I am the real TV addict in my family.

VOCABULARY AND COMPREHENSION

1.   Television "has become some kind of oracle" (paragraph 2). What does Nixon mean?

_____

_____

_____

2.   Compare the author's attitude toward television with that of her children.

_____

_____

_____

_____

_____

_____

3. What does Nixon learn about herself?

4. What is the significance of the title?

5. The author gives many examples to illustrate how hypocritical she is. List some of those examples.

GRAMMAR LINK

6. Choose five present tense verbs from the essay. Choose verbs that have irregular past forms. Then write the past and past participle of each verb.

7. Underline all of the television show titles in the essay. Write a rule explaining how to write the titles of television shows.

DISCUSSION AND WRITING

8. Originally, the television was intended to provide us with a pleasurable leisure-time activity. However, the author complains that television is addictive. Do you agree that someone can be seriously addicted to television? Explain your answer by giving specific examples.

9. What harmful or harmless products or activities can be addictive? List them.

10. Why do people become addicted to things? What are they looking for, or what are they trying to escape? Describe how the pursuit of pleasure can become a full-blown addiction.

READING 10

The New Addiction

Josh Freed

Josh Freed is an award-winning columnist for the *Montreal Gazette*. Freed has published many books, including *Fear of Frying and Other Fax of Life*. In the next comparison and contrast essay, Freed makes an interesting comparison. As you read, notice how the author also uses definition writing.

scourge: affliction; serious problem

1   Is the cell phone the cigarette of our times? That is what I have been asking myself lately as the **scourge** of smokers slowly disappears from city life, and a scourge of cell-phone users takes their place. Everywhere I look, people hold cell phones up to their mouths instead of cigarettes, and non-users react as intolerantly as nonsmokers ever did. How does the cell phone resemble the cigarette? Let me count the ways.

2   It is an oral habit. For many users, the cell phone is an obvious substitute for smoking. It is a nervous habit that gives them something to do with their hands—whether they are dialing, checking their messages, or just fondling the buttons. Just like cigarettes, the phone sits in a person's breast pocket or on a restaurant table, ready to bring quickly to his or her mouth. Often, it is in a fliptop case that pops opens as easily as a cigarette pack.

3   It pollutes. Instead of filling the air with smoke, cell-phone users fill it with words. For those nearby, the cell is just as annoying as the cigarette because instead of secondhand smoke, they get secondhand conversation. It is voice pollution. One phone can pollute a room quicker than a cigarette, especially on a bus, or in a checkout line, when others hear someone hollering about his or her cousin's prostate operation or planning the night's dinner menu.

4   "Honey! The veal chops were expensive so I got lamb chops instead. Whaddya think we should serve with them? Do we need potatoes?"

5   Many people feel they must yell to be heard, and there is usually only one way to shut them up. Join into their conversation and say, "You know, I don't really feel like lamb chops tonight—how about turkey and wild rice?"

6   Cell-phone users do not blow smoke rings from the next restaurant table, like smokers. But cell-phone rings can be just as annoying, whether they play the "William Tell Overture" or yodeling sounds or Christmas tunes like "Sleigh Bells Ringing." Phone users are even more oblivious to their own noise than smokers are to their wisps of smoke.

7   Furthermore, there is an anti-cell lobby. Cell-phone users are the target of a growing intolerance that is almost as zealous as the anti-smoking movement's. Go to a movie, play, or concert and no one bothers to tell you not to smoke anymore. They know your seatmates will take care of that. Instead, movie ads and other warnings are all about shutting off your cell, the new public enemy No. 1. Anti-cell rage is so extreme that if you forget to shut off your phone in a movie, there is only one safe strategy to avoid a lynching when your phone goes off. Look around for the culprit accusingly, like everyone else in the place, and bluff your way out until your phone stops ringing.

8   Lately, "No Cell Phone" signs are getting even bigger than "No Smoking" signs. I was in San Francisco recently, where half the shops were plastered with warnings like "Don't even think about it. Cell-phone users will be escorted out and made to feel extremely embarrassed." On the train from Washington to New York there is now a special "quiet" car where cell phones are banned. How long before the whole train is divided into cell and noncell sections, in a new version of smoking **apartheid?** If they ever find the slightest link between cell phones and any illness, you can expect to see cell-free hotel rooms, cell-free rest rooms, and a growing number of cell-free cities.

9   Cell phones may be addictive. Just like cigarettes, the cell phone spreads by targeting the young. The Big Phone companies keep offering teenagers dirt-cheap plans, trying to hook them for life. The cell has become the cool teen status symbol, as powerful as the cigarette, though less lethal. How long before we see class actions against the big phone companies for deliberately addicting our kids to the nicotine of words? How long will it be before the first cell-phone pollution settlement?

10   I suspect cell-phone makers will eventually be forced to come up with special filters, like cigarettes. All phones will be sold with a soundproof helmet or at least a mask-and-muffler to protect others from the noise. Get ready for the cell-phone snorkel.

apartheid: former political system in South Africa that separated the privileged whites from people of other races

VOCABULARY AND COMPREHENSION

1.   What is the meaning of *zealous* in paragraph 7? Try to guess the meaning using context clues.

2.   What is Freed's main point?

3.   List five examples the author uses to support his main point.

4.   What is the author's tone (his attitude toward the subject)?
     a. Serious   b. Cynical
     c. Lighthearted   d. Detached
     Give examples to support your answer.

5. What can you infer, or guess, about the author?

_____

_____

_____

_____

GRAMMAR LINK

6. In paragraph 4, the author writes "Whaddya." What does this word mean? Why does the author include an invented word in his text?

_____

_____

7. Why does the author use dialogue in paragraphs 4 and 5?

_____

_____

_____

DISCUSSION AND WRITING

8. Choose two addictive items and compare them, just as Freed did in this essay. Do not compare cell phones and cigarettes.

9. Should cell phones be banned or restricted? Explain your answer. If you think cell phones should be restricted, what types of restrictions should be placed on them?

READING 11

The Culture War
Linda Chavez

Linda Chavez, a regular contributor to _Jewish World Review_, is also president of the Center for Equal Opportunity. In the next cause and effect essay, Chavez discusses her unhappiness with shock radio.

1   The culture war came home in a very personal way this week when I innocently gave my granddaughter her first radio. It never occurred to me that I was doing anything **subversive** until I saw the look on her father's face when she came running up the porch brandishing her new gift. "Look, Daddy," she said, holding the tiny red transistor in her hands, "it even has earphones."

2   The radio was one of those logo-bearing giveaways I'd picked up at a talk-show convention where I'd been broadcasting my own daily radio show earlier in the week. Rather than tossing it in a drawer, I'd passed it on to my 7-year-old granddaughter, thinking she'd enjoy listening to her own music when the family went on outings.

3   I remember getting my own radio for my ninth birthday, a pink plastic job powered by four "D" batteries that weighed at least five

subversive: revolutionary

pounds, despite being billed as "portable." I discovered classical music on my own thanks to that radio, tuning in to Denver's one classical station each night before I went to sleep. But that was the 1950s, when the cultural terrain was far different than today.

4   I should have known better than to try to give my granddaughter the same experience.

5   So much of what comes over the public airwaves these days is unsuitable for children that it is simply dangerous to give a child his or her own radio or television. Tune in to Howard Stern by accident and you'll hear every manner of sexual perversion discussed. Tune in to a rap station and you'll hear not only sex but also glorified violence and **misogyny.** In fact, it is almost impossible not to hear something objectionable if you move up or down the AM and FM dials, even during the early morning hours or after school.

misogyny: hatred of women

6   Those who'd like to keep the filth on the air claim that cleaning up the airwaves infringes on the First Amendment rights of all Americans. Howard Stern, Opie and Anthony (who broadcast descriptions of an actual couple having sex in New York's St. Patrick's Cathedral as part of an on-air contest), Bubba the Love Sponge, and all the other shock-jocks out there aren't forcing you to listen, after all.

7   That's like saying that the company that dumps raw sewage into the reservoir isn't forcing you to drink polluted water. These programs are toxic; they have degraded our culture and threaten the well-being of an entire generation of young people. And so pervasive is their influence that there is almost no way to shelter the young entirely.

8   Even when parents try to protect their children, they can't do so 24 hours a day. What happens when the kids are at school or playing at friends' houses? What happens when they're in the back seat of the family station wagon stopped at a red light and the guy in the next car is blaring Fifty Cent or the Greaseman?

9   Children are bombarded on a daily basis by disturbing and overtly sexualized images in **omnipresent** advertising. You can't watch the evening news without advertisements for erectile dysfunction, or walk into a mall without lewd images from Victoria's Secret or Abercrombie and Fitch leaping out at you from every turn.

omnipresent: present in all times and places

10   Last week, Clear Channel, the nation's largest radio network, suspended Howard Stern's show just in time for its CEO to testify before Congress about the company's new zero tolerance policy on indecency. Perhaps these companies are finally getting the message.

11   Sure there's an audience for trash—and if adults want to buy this smut, the Supreme Court has ruled they have that right. But why not force those who want to buy obscene and indecent products to be the ones inconvenienced rather than the rest of us? With all the various methods of delivering images and sounds, why use the public airwaves to present the likes of Howard Stern? You've always been able to buy pornography, only it used to be sold under the counter and in brown wrapping paper; it didn't come into your home uninvited.

12   Maybe if we put the onus on those who want this garbage by insisting it be available only through direct purchase and not on the public airwaves, it would be safe again to give a child a simple radio.

VOCABULARY AND COMPREHENSION

1. What is the meaning of *brandishing* in paragraph 1?
   a. Waving   b. Polishing
   c. Burning

2. What does *onus* mean, in paragraph 12?

   _____

3. In paragraph 6, what is the meaning of the slang term *shock-jocks?*

   _____

   _____

   _____

4. Why does the author think that she should not have given a radio as a present to her granddaughter?

   _____

5. Reread paragraphs 6 and 7. What comparison does the author make? How valid is the comparison?

   _____

   _____

   _____

   _____

6. Chavez calls radio shows "trash." What other emotionally charged words does she use to describe radio shows?

   _____

7. How does the emotional language help or hurt Chavez's argument?

   _____

GRAMMAR LINK

8. In the last sentence of paragraph 2, there are two different contractions ending in *'d.* Write out the complete form of each contraction.

   _____

9. In the second sentence of paragraph 8, the word *friends'* ends in an apostrophe. Explain the difference between *friend's* and *friends'.*

   _____

   _____

   _____

DISCUSSION AND WRITING

10. In paragraph 3, the author says that "the cultural terrain" in the 1950s was very different than it is today. Compare another era with the current one, and explain how the cultural terrain is different.
11. The author suggests that there should be stricter censorship of radio programming. What are some possible effects of stricter censorship?
12. Argue against Chavez, and explain why there is no need for stricter censorship.

READING 12

Going Thin in Fiji
Ellen Goodman

Ellen Goodman is a Pulitzer Prize–winning columnist for the *Boston Globe*. Her column is syndicated in over 400 newspapers. In the next essay, Goodman examines how television changed the women of Fiji. As you read the selection, notice how the author mainly uses the cause and effect writing pattern but also uses elements of comparison and contrast.

1   First of all, imagine a place where women greet one another at the market with open arms, loving smiles, and a cheerful exchange of ritual compliments: "You look wonderful! You have put on weight!"

2   Does that sound like dialogue from Fat Fantasyland? Or a skit from fat-is-a-feminist-issue satire? Well, this Western fantasy was a South Pacific fact of life. In Fiji, before 1995, big was beautiful and bigger was more beautiful—and people really did flatter one another with exclamations about weight gain.

3   In this island paradise, food was not only love; it was a cultural **imperative.** Eating and overeating were **rites** of mutual hospitality. Everyone worried about losing weight—but not the way we do. "Going thin" was considered to be a sign of some social problem, a worrisome indication the person wasn't getting enough to eat.

imperative: necessity

rites: rituals; traditions

4   The Fijians were, to be sure, a bit obsessed with food; they prescribed herbs to stimulate the appetite. They were a reverse image of our culture. And that turns out to be the point.

5   Something happened in 1995. A Western mirror was shoved into the face of the Fijians. Television came to the island. Suddenly, the girls of rural coastal villages were watching the girls of *Melrose Place* and *Beverly Hills 90210*. Within 38 months, the number of teenagers at risk for eating disorders more than doubled to 29 percent. The number of high school girls who vomited for weight control went up five times to 15 percent. Worse yet, 74 percent of the Fiji teens in the study said they felt "too big or fat" at least some of the time and 62 percent said they had dieted in the past month.

6   This before-and-after television portrait of a body image takeover was drawn by Anne Becker, an anthropologist and psychiatrist who directs research at the Harvard Eating Disorders Center. She presented her research at the American Psychiatric Association last week with

subsistence: just enough to provide the necessities of life

robust: strong and healthy

acute: intense

Calista Flockhart: extremely thin actress who played the lead role in the 1990s television series *Allie McBeal*

all the usual caveats. No, you cannot prove a direct causal link between television and eating disorders. Heather Locklear doesn't cause anorexia.

7   Fiji is not just a Fat Paradise Lost. It's an economy in transition from **subsistence** agriculture to tourism, and its entry into the global economy has threatened many old values. Nevertheless, you don't get a much better lab experiment than this. In just 38 months, and with only one channel, a television-free culture that defined a fat person as **robust** has become a television culture that sees robust as, well, repulsive.

8   "Going thin" is no longer a social disease but the perceived requirement for getting a good job, nice clothes, and fancy cars. As Becker says carefully, "The **acute** and constant bombardment of certain images in the media are apparently quite influential in how teens experience their bodies."

9   Speaking of Fiji teenagers in a way that sounds all too familiar, she adds, "We have a set of vulnerable teens consuming television. There's a huge disparity between what they see on television and what they look like themselves—that goes not only to clothing, hairstyles, and skin color, but size of bodies."

10   In short, the sum of Western culture, the big success story of our entertainment industry, is our ability to export insecurity. We can make any woman anywhere feel perfectly rotten about her shape. I'm not surprised by research showing that eating disorders are a cultural byproduct. We have watched the female image shrink down to **Calista Flockhart** at the same time we have seen eating problems grow. But Hollywood hasn't been exactly eager to acknowledge the connection between image and illness.

11   Since the Columbine High massacre, we have broken through some denial about violence as a teaching tool. It's pretty clear that boys are literally learning how to hate and harm others. Maybe we ought to worry a little more about what girls learn: to hate and harm themselves.

VOCABULARY AND COMPREHENSION

1.   Using context clues, define *disparity* as it is used in paragraph 9.

_____

2.   In paragraph 4, Goodman says that Fiji was a "reverse image of our culture." What does the author mean?

_____

_____

3.   In paragraph 7, Goodman writes, "You don't get a much better lab experiment than this." What does she mean?

_____

_____

_____

_____

4.   Why does Goodman refer to the Columbine High massacre?

_____

_____

_____

_____

5.   Whom does Goodman blame for eating disorders in Fiji?

_____

_____

_____

GRAMMAR LINK

6.   The past participle is the third form in most verb lists. For example, _gone_ and _watched_ are the past participles of _go_ and _watch_. Past participles always follow helping verbs. Underline at least five past participles and circle the helping verbs. Then discuss which verbs are regular and which are irregular.

7.   In the first sentence of paragraph 11, the author uses the present perfect form of the verb: _have broken_. Why does she use the present perfect instead of the simple past (_broke_)?

_____

_____

DISCUSSION AND WRITING

8.   How does the entertainment industry reinforce unrealistic or negative body images? Give examples to support your point.

9.   Goodman suggests that media images have contributed to the rise in eating disorders. What other things cause people to develop eating disorders?

10. What can the media do to provide viewers with more positive body images? Give examples to support your point.

READING 13

What It Feels Like to Walk on the Moon
Buzz Aldrin

On July 20, 1969, _Apollo 11_ landed on the moon. Astronauts Neil Armstrong, Michael Collins, and Edwin E. Aldrin, Jr., (also known as Buzz Aldrin) spent two and a half hours walking on the moon's surface. In the next essay, Aldrin describes that experience. As you read, notice how the author mainly uses description but also elements of process writing.

1   The surface of the moon is like fine talcum powder. It is very loose at the top. At a deeper level, a half inch or so, it becomes much more compact, almost as if it were cemented together. It seems that way because there are no air molecules between the molecules of dust.

2   When I put my foot down in the powder, the boot print preserved itself exquisitely. When I would take a step, a little semicircle of dust would spray out before me. It was odd, because the dust did not

behave at all the way it behaves here on Earth. On Earth, dust is sometimes puffy or sandy. On the moon, the powdery dust travels through no air at all, so the dust is kicked up, and then it all falls at the same time in a perfect semicircle.

3   I am trying the best I can to put it into words, but being on the moon is just different—different from anything I have ever seen. To use the word *alien* would mislead people. *Surreal* is probably as good a word as I have. When I looked out the window of the lunar lander as we touched down, the sun was out, the sky was velvety black, the engine was shut down, and everything was silent. That was surreal.

4   When I was on the moon, there was very little audio around, only the sounds of my suit—the hum of pumps circulating fluid. But I didn't hear any amplified breathing inside my mask; that is a Hollywood **contrivance.** The name of the game on the moon was staying cool and not exerting too much so that I would never be out of breath.

contrivance: deceitful invention

5   If you remember the television images we sent back, you know that I was attempting to demonstrate different walking motions, going back and forth in front of the camera. I tried what you might call a kangaroo hop, and then I demonstrated how I needed a few steps to change direction because of the **inertia** that was up there. I found that the best way to move around at a fairly good clip was not by using a jogging motion—one foot, then the other—but rather by moving more the way a horse gallops: one-two, one-two, two steps in rapid succession, followed by a lope, followed by two more rapid steps.

inertia: inability to move with ease; sluggish movement

6   And then there is the picture where I was standing next to the flag. I was leaning forward a good bit because of the center of gravity of the backpack that I was wearing. On the moon, it was sometimes hard to tell when I might be on the verge of losing my balance. As I leaned a little bit to one side or the other, I came in danger of falling. But it was easy to right myself by pushing down on the surface with my feet. The lunar surface is so easy, so natural, and so readily adapted to by any human being. The low gravity makes it very convenient to get around. It is really a very nice environment.

7   While we were on the moon, there was not time to savor the moment. It seemed as though what we were doing was so significant that to pause for a moment and reflect **metaphysically** was really contrary to our mission. We were not trained to smell the roses. We were not hired to utter philosophical truisms on the spur of the moment. We had a job to do.

metaphysically: refers to abstract, philosophical thinking

8   I do remember that one realization **wafted** through my mind when I was up there. I noted that here were two guys farther away from anything than two guys had ever been before. That is what I thought about. And yet, at the same time, I was very conscious that everything was being closely scrutinized a quarter of a million miles away.

wafted: floated

9   Everything and anything we did would be recorded, remembered, and studied for ages. It felt a little like being the young kid in the third or fourth grade who is all of a sudden asked to go up on stage in front of the whole school and recite the Gettysburg Address. And as he tries to remember the words, he has got gun-barrel vision. He does not see what is going on around him; he is focused on that particular task,

conscious only of his performance. It was like that but even more so. The eyes of the world were on us, and if we made a mistake, we would regret it for quite a while.

10   I guess, if I look back on things, there was one little moment of **levity,** a bit of unusual **extemporaneousness.** When the countdown came to lift off from the moon, when it got to twenty seconds, Houston said, "Tranquility Base, you're cleared for liftoff." And I said in response, "Roger, we're number one on the runway." Now comedy is the absurd put into a natural position. There was no runway up there. And there certainly wasn't anyone else waiting in line to lift off. I was conscious of that, being first.

levity: lightness; humor

extemporaneousness: improvised or unplanned action

VOCABULARY AND COMPREHENSION

1. Find a word in paragraph 7 that means "to say."

    _____

2. In the introduction, Aldrin uses an analogy, or comparison of two things, to make the reader understand the situation. What is this analogy, and how effective is it?

    _____

    _____

3. In paragraph 3, Adrin describes the moonscape as *surreal*. What does he mean? You might try dividing *surreal* into the prefix and the main word.

    _____

4. What does Aldrin mean when he writes in paragraph 7 that astronauts "were not trained to smell the roses"?

    _____

    _____

5. Underline five descriptive phrases that best describe what it feels like to walk on the moon.

6. What can you infer, or guess, about the author's character?

    _____

    _____

    _____

GRAMMAR LINK

7. Highlight five adjectives. Then circle the nouns that the adjectives modify. Discuss how the adjectives make the writing more vivid.

    _____

    _____

8. Why does the author use a semicolon in the second sentence of paragraph 4?

_____

_____

DISCUSSION AND WRITING

9. Go for a walk in a new place. Use your senses and give details about what you see, hear, smell, and touch.
10. In the future, it may be possible for ordinary citizens to travel to outer space. Would you like to go on a space flight? Why or why not?
11. Buzz Aldrin does not introduce his topic. Instead, he immediately describes his sensations when he walked on the moon. Write an introduction for this essay.

READING 14

The Zoo Life
Yann Martel

Yann Martel, the son of diplomats, was born in Spain but has lived in various countries throughout the world. In 2002, he won the prestigious Man Booker Prize for his novel *The Life of Pi*, from which this excerpt is taken. As you read the selection, notice how the author mainly uses comparison and contrast writing as well as elements of argument.

1   If you went to a home, kicked down the front door, chased the people who lived there out into the street and said, "Go! You are free! Free as a bird! Go! Go!"—do you think they would shout and dance for joy? They wouldn't. The people you've just evicted would sputter, "With what right do you throw us out? This is our home. We own it. We have lived here for years. We're calling the police, you scoundrel."

2   Don't we say, "There's no place like home"? That's certainly what animals feel. Animals are territorial. That is the key to their minds. Only a familiar territory will allow them to fulfill the two relentless imperatives of the wild: the avoidance of enemies and the getting of food and water. A biologically sound zoo enclosure—whether cage, pit, moated island, corral, terrarium, **aviary,** or aquarium—is just another territory, peculiar only in its size and in its proximity to human territory. That it is so much smaller than what it would be in nature stands to reason.

aviary: enclosure for birds

3   Territories in the wild are large not as a matter of taste but of necessity. In a zoo, we do for animals what we have done for ourselves with houses: we bring together in a small space what in the wild is spread out. Whereas before for us the cave was here, the river over there, the hunting grounds a mile that way, the lookout next to it, the berries somewhere else—all of them **infested** with lions, snakes, ants, leeches and poison ivy—now the river flows through taps at hand's reach and we can wash next to where we sleep, we can eat where we

infested: invaded by

have cooked, and we can surround the whole with a protective wall and keep it clean and warm.

4   A house is a compressed territory where our basic needs can be fulfilled close by and safely. A sound zoo enclosure is the equivalent for an animal (with the noteworthy absence of a fireplace or the like, present in every human habitation). Finding within it all the places it needs—a lookout, a place for resting, for eating and drinking, for bathing, for grooming, etc. and finding that there is no need to go hunting, food appearing six days a week, an animal will take possession of its zoo space in the same way it would lay claim to a new space in the wild, exploring it and marking it out in the normal ways of its species, with sprays of urine perhaps. Once this moving-in ritual is done and the animal has settled, it will not feel like a nervous tenant, and even less like a prisoner, but rather like a landholder, and it will behave in the same way within its enclosure as it would in its territory in the wild, including defending it tooth and nail should it be invaded.

5   Such an enclosure is neither better nor worse for an animal than its condition in the wild; so long as it fulfills the animal's needs, a territory, natural or constructed, simply *is*, without judgment, a given, like the spots on a leopard. One might even argue that if an animal could choose with intelligence, it would opt for living in a zoo, since the major difference between a zoo and the wild is the absence of parasites and enemies and the abundance of food in the first, and their respective abundance and scarcity in the second. Think about it yourself. Would you rather be put up at the Ritz with free room service and unlimited access to a doctor or be homeless without a soul to care for you? But animals are incapable of such **discernment.** Within the limits of their nature, they make do with what they have.

discernment: judgment

6   A good zoo is a place of carefully worked-out coincidence: exactly where an animal says to us, "Stay out!" with its urine or other secretion, we say to it, "Stay in!" with our barriers. Under such conditions of diplomatic peace, all animals are content and we can relax and have a look at each other.

VOCABULARY AND COMPREHENSION

1. Find a word in paragraph 5 that means the opposite of *abundance*.

    _____

2. What is Martel's main argument?

    _____

    _____

3. Martel compares a house and an animal's enclosure. What are the similarities?

    _____

    _____

    _____

4. Reread paragraph 1. The author suggests that people would not want to be kicked out of their homes. He then goes on to suggest that a zoo enclosure is an animal's home. Do you think this is a fair comparison? Explain your answer.

_____

_____

_____

5. In paragraph 5, the author asks, "Would you rather be put up at the Ritz with free room service and unlimited access to a doctor or be homeless without a soul to care for you?" How would you answer the question? Explain why.

_____

_____

_____

GRAMMAR LINK

6. The next-to-last sentence in paragraph 2, beginning with "A biologically sound," has many commas. What rule could you write about the use of commas with a series of items?

_____

_____

7. The first sentence in paragraph 6 contains the word _carefully_. Why do you have to spell _carefully_ with two _l_'s? Try to remember the rule.

_____

_____

DISCUSSION AND WRITING

8. The author mentions that animals mark their territories in some way, perhaps with a spray of urine. What are ways that humans mark or identify their territory?
9. Compare and contrast a zoo enclosure and life in the wild. What are some similarities and differences?
10. Develop arguments that oppose Martel's main points.

READING 15
Political Activism
Craig Stern

Craig Stern wrote the next article for _The Daily Trojan_, the student newspaper at the University of Southern California. In this process essay, he explains how to become more politically active. As you read, notice how the author also uses elements of argument writing.

1   Let's discuss the things you can do on your own to make this world a better place. Actually, that is a bit misleading. You can't do all that much on your own. Almost everything worth doing in this country requires the cooperation of other people. You can register to vote, which is a good first step. You can actually vote, which is even better. But as Senator Larry Craig once said, "Simply voting is not enough." Democracy hinges on the exchange of ideas, and that means networking and organizing.

2   The truth is that this is an exciting time to be young and to get involved in politics. The means to organize on a grassroots level have expanded drastically in the past four years, thanks largely to the Internet.

3   Countless organizations based upon the **infrastructure** of the Internet have made politics more accessible than ever. *Truthout.org* is a newsletter that collects the seven or eight most important news stories each day and delivers them to your inbox. Congress.org provides a free searchable database with the contact information of practically every elected official in the United States. The **nonpartisan** site OpenSecrets.org provides free access to information on fundraising broken down by the socioeconomic status of the contributors, available for both party and candidate. Where else would you find out that "women without an income-earning occupation tend to send most of their contributions to Republicans, while women with incomes separate from their spouses tend to give most of their money to Democrats"—and see it backed up with hard numbers?

infrastructure: the fundamental features

nonpartisan: unbiased; impartial

4   E-mail alone, with its ease of use and capacity for near-instant communication, has revolutionized letter-writing campaigns. I have casually participated in e-mail campaigns that end up crashing government e-mail systems within minutes of beginning. It is truly an empowering phenomenon. As computers become an increasingly cheap commodity, access to the Internet can only increase, and the power to network across social groups, races, and geographical distances will grow more relevant than ever.

5   Of course, the bigger issue is likely to revolve not around how many people are connected to the Internet, but rather how many of them are convinced of the need to mobilize and commit themselves to action. Face-to-face interaction is still the most effective way to change someone's mind about an issue, to transmit energy and enthusiasm, and to win his or her dedication to a cause. This continues to be the most important justification for canvassing, even as more cost-effective fundraising options present themselves.

6   People interested in really making a difference on the ground should go looking for canvassing positions at organizations. These jobs are out there—just take a look in the classifieds section of your local alternative newspaper. Turnover rates are high in canvassing, so there is always a need for enthusiastic applicants.

7   In a political landscape littered with **blowhards** and **impotent posturing,** there remains more room than ever for the young, the dedicated, and the sincere to perform the groundwork that political change is built upon. We are the real deal. Let us now make something of ourselves.

blowhards: loudmouths

impotent posturing: powerless and empty attitudes and gestures

VOCABULARY AND COMPREHENSION

1. Define *canvassing* as it is used in paragraph 5.

    _____

    _____

2. Who is the audience for this essay?

    _____

    _____

3. What is Stern's main point? Look in the first few paragraphs and underline the thesis statement.

4. In the author's opinion, what three steps can people take to become politically active?

    _____

    _____

    _____

    _____

5. How does Stern conclude the essay? Choose the best answer.
    a. With a suggestion   b. With a prediction
    c. With a quotation

GRAMMAR LINK

6. In paragraph 1, underline five sentences with commas. Then write three different rules about comma usage. (Do not include the one given here.)
    Example: Actually, that is a bit misleading.(Second sentence)
    Rule: Place a comma after an introductory word or phrase.

    _____

    _____

    _____

    _____

    _____

7. In the middle of paragraph 5, the author writes *his or her.* What is the antecedent for those pronouns?

    _____

DISCUSSION AND WRITING

8. Are you politically active? Explain why or why not.

9. Explain what steps people can follow to avoid being politically active.

READING 16

How to Handle Conflict

P. Gregory Smith

> P. Gregory Smith writes for *Career World*. In the next essay, he describes some steps a person can take to avoid conflict. As you read this process essay, notice how the author also uses elements of argument writing.

1   "Hey, college boy," Mr. Jefferson smirked as Ramon walked into the supermarket, "a lady just dropped a bottle of grape juice in aisle six. Do you think you could lower yourself enough to mop it up?" Ramon was seething inside as he grabbed the mop and headed off to clean up the spill. Ever since he told some of his co-workers that he had applied to the state university, Mr. Jefferson, the night manager, had teased and taunted him. As Ramon returned to the front of the store, he remembered the presentation his guidance counselor, Mrs. Chang, gave last week on something called assertiveness. It is a way of standing up for one's rights without creating conflict. As Ramon walked toward Mr. Jefferson, the main points of the presentation started to come back to him.

2   Find the right time and place. Mr. Jefferson was talking with a customer when Ramon reached the front of the supermarket. Ramon waited until Mr. Jefferson was finished and then asked, "Can I talk with you in your office when you have a moment?" By waiting for the right time, Ramon was likely to have Mr. Jefferson's attention. Also, by asking to speak with him in private, Ramon reduced the chances that Mr. Jefferson would feel that he had to impress others, protect his reputation, or save face.

3   Maintain good posture, eye contact, and a relaxed **stance.** Before Ramon said the first word, he reminded himself of a few important things. If he wanted to stand up for himself, he would need to stand up straight! He knew that it was important to make eye contact. Ramon also knew the importance of relaxing his hands and keeping a comfortable distance from Mr. Jefferson. He did not want to appear hostile or threatening. Even though he was angry, Ramon reminded himself that he must speak calmly, clearly, and slowly in order to get his point across. If he let his anger creep in, he would probably get an angry or defensive response from Mr. Jefferson. Even worse, if he hid his feelings behind a quiet tone or rapid speech, then Mr. Jefferson would probably doubt his seriousness.

stance: manner; position

4   Use *I* statements. Mr. Jefferson closed the office door, folded his arms, and looked at Ramon questioningly. Ramon took a deep breath and began, "Mr. Jefferson, I really feel embarrassed when you call me 'college boy.' I like it a lot better when people call me Ramon. I don't mind doing my fair share of the dirty jobs around here," Ramon continued, "but I feel like I'm getting a lot more mop time than anyone else." By using a statement that began with *I*, Ramon was able to state his feelings honestly, without accusing Mr. Jefferson. *I* statements usually can't be considered false or cause an argument because they're simple statements of feelings.

5   Then introduce cooperative statements. Ramon said, "We used to get along fine until everybody started talking about me going to

college next year. I haven't changed, and I'd like to go back to the way things were." Cooperative statements—or statements that connect you with the other person—create common ground for further discussion. They also serve as a subtle reminder that you share experiences and values with the other person.

6   "Remember that standing up for your personal rights, or being assertive, is very important," explains Betty Kelman of the Seattle University School of Nursing. "Standing up for your rights involves self-respect—respect for your rights and the other person's rights. Respecting yourself is the ability to make your own decisions involving relationships, how you spend your time, and whom you spend it with." Kelman also explains what assertiveness is not. "Standing up for yourself does not mean that you express yourself in an aggressive, angry, or mean way." She sums it up this way: "Think of standing up for yourself as being in a win-win situation. You win and they win."

VOCABULARY AND COMPREHENSION

1.   What are *cooperative statements* (paragraph 5)?

_____

2.   What introduction style does the author use?
     a. Anecdote   b. General
     c. Historical   d. Contrasting position

3.   What is Smith's main point?

_____

4.   List the steps in the process that Smith describes.

_____

_____

_____

_____

5.   How does the quotation from Betty Kelman (paragraph 6) support the author's point of view?

_____

_____

_____

GRAMMAR LINK

6.   Underline the verbs in the first sentences of paragraphs 2 through 5. Who or what is the subject in each sentence?

_____

7. In paragraph 5, the author says, "I haven't changed, and I'd like to go back to the way things were." Write out the long form of each contraction.

_____

_____

DISCUSSION AND WRITING

8. Can you think of a time when you should have been more assertive? Describe what happened.
9. Explain the steps that you take when you are faced with a major problem. What do you usually do?

READING 17

The Rewards of Dirty Work
Linda L. Lindsey and Stephen Beach

Linda L. Lindsey teaches sociology at Maryville University of St. Louis, and Stephen Beach teaches at Kentucky Wesleyan College. In the next essay, they list some surprising rewards of dirty work. As you read, notice how the authors mainly use the illustration writing pattern but also use elements of description and argument.

1   As sociologist Everett Hughes once pointed out, in order for some members of society to be clean and pure, someone else must take care of unclean, often taboo work, such as handling dead bodies and filth. In India and Japan, such jobs were, and to some extent still are, relegated to the Dalits (or Untouchables) and the Eta, respectively. Both groups were regarded as ritually impure. Our society does not have formal taboos against dirty work, but some jobs are rated near the bottom of the scale of occupational prestige and are viewed as not quite respectable and certainly not something to brag about. Garbage collection is a good example. Why would anyone choose to become a garbage collector? Stewart Perry asked this question to sanitation workers for the Sunset Scavenger Business in San Francisco. For a job that requires little training or education, the pay is relatively good. But pay was not what drew men to the job.

2   One attraction of becoming a garbage collector was variety. The job involves many different activities. Collecting garbage also means being outdoors and moving around. On another level, variety means the unexpected. For the sanitation workers, every day brought something different: witnessing a robbery, calling in a fire alarm and getting residents out of the building before the fire truck arrived, and responding to FBI requests to save all the rubbish from a house under surveillance.

3   Also, the garbage itself was full of surprises. Almost every day the men found something of interest, whether a good book, a child's toy, or a fixable radio. Almost inevitably, garbage men became collectors. In

the course of his research, Perry himself acquired a rare seventeenth-century book of sermons and a sheepskin rug.

4   Garbage men got to know intimately the neighborhoods in which they worked. Watching children grow up, couples marry or separate, or one house or block deteriorating while another was being renovated had the appeal of an ongoing story, not unlike a soap opera on TV. They witnessed not just public performances, but also what Erving Goffman called the "backstage" of life. The respectable facades in affluent neighborhoods cannot hide the alcoholism a garbage man detects from cans full of empty liquor bottles or the sexual longings symbolized by bundles of pornographic magazines.

5   Another attraction of garbage collection was a sense of camaraderie among workers. The friendships people make on the job are a major source of satisfaction in any occupation. Many Sunset workers came from the same ethnic background (Italian) and in some cases from the same neighborhood. All of the men hoped that their own sons would go to college and make something better of themselves. But at least thirty were following in their fathers' footsteps. These intergenerational family ties and friendships made the company a familiar and welcome place and a stronghold of tradition for members of ethnic communities that were beginning to break apart.

6   The garbage collectors liked working at their own pace, scheduling their own breaks, deciding when to do their paperwork—in short, being their own bosses. Collecting garbage may be "dirty work" in many peoples' eyes, but these men were proud of what they did for a living.

VOCABULARY AND COMPREHENSION

1.   What is a *taboo?* See paragraph 1 for clues.

_____

_____

2.   How is Western society different from other societies regarding garbage collecting or other dirty work?

_____

_____

_____

_____

3.   According to the authors, how do Western societies judge the profession of garbage collecting?

_____

_____

_____

_____

4. The authors give a positive spin on garbage collecting. List the main points.

_____

_____

_____

_____

_____

_____

5. How do garbage collectors see the "backstage" of life?

_____

_____

_____

GRAMMAR LINK

6. Underline five irregular past tense verbs in paragraphs 3 and 4. Then write the present and past forms of each verb.

_____

_____

7. In paragraph 5, who does the word *themselves* refer to?

_____

DISCUSSION AND WRITING

8. List some jobs that might be considered dirty. What do the jobs have in common?
9. What are some stereotypes that we have about other professions? These professions could be prestigious or nonprestigious. Give some examples.
10. Think of another job that lacks prestige. Explain why that job has value and is rewarding.

Appendix 1
Grammar Glossary

Term	Meaning	Examples
Active voice	• Form of the verb when the subject does the action	Maria <u>will mail</u> the letter.
Adjective	• Adds information about the noun	quiet, clear, decent
Adverb	• Adds information about the verb; expresses time, place, or frequency	quietly, clearly, decently; sometimes, usually, never
Base form of verb	• The main form in a dictionary (like the infinitive but without *to*)	go, rent, discuss, meet, rely
Clause	• An independent clause has a subject and verb and expresses a complete idea.	The athlete was thrilled.
	• A dependent clause has a subject and verb but cannot stand alone. It "depends" on another clause to be complete.	Because she won a gold medal
Conditional sentence	• Explains possible, imaginary, or impossible situations. Each type of conditional sentence has a condition clause and a result clause.	Possible future: If I win, I will fly to Morocco. Unlikely present: If I won, I would fly to Morocco. Impossible past: If I had won, I would have flown to Morocco.
Conjunctive adverb	• Shows a relationship between two ideas	also, consequently, finally, however, furthermore, moreover, therefore, thus
Coordinating conjunction	• Connects two ideas of equal importance	for, and, nor, but, or, yet, so
Determiner	• Identifies or determines whether a noun is specific or general	a, an, the; this, that, these, those; any, all, each, every, many, some, one, two, three
Indirect speech	• Reports what someone said without using the person's exact words	Mr. Simpson said that he would never find a better job.
Infinitive	• *To* plus the base form of the verb	He wants <u>to think</u> about it.
Interjection	• A word expressing an emotion that is added to a sentence	ouch, yikes, wow, yeah, oh
Irregular verb	• A verb that does not have an *ed* ending in the past forms	broke, ate, had, swam
Modal	• A type of helping verb that indicates willingness, possibility, advice, and so on	<u>may</u> help, <u>can</u> go, <u>should</u> deliver
Noun	• A person, place, or thing	Singular: man, dog, person Plural: men, dogs, people
Passive voice	• Form of the verb when the subject does not perform the action (*be* + past participle)	The letter <u>will be mailed</u> shortly.
Preposition	• Shows a relationship between words (source, direction, location, etc.)	at, to, for, from, behind, above
Pronoun	• Replaces one or more nouns	he, she, it, us, ours, themselves

Term	Meaning	Examples
Sentence types	• Simple sentences have one independent clause that expresses a complete idea.	Some food is unhealthy.
	• Compound sentences have two or more independent clauses joined together.	Some restaurants serve junk food, and others serve healthy meals.
	• Complex sentences have at least one dependent and one independent clause joined together.	Although the food is not healthy, it is very tasty.
	• Compound-complex sentences have at least two independent clauses joined with at least one dependent clause.	Although the food is not healthy, it is very tasty, and I enjoy eating it.
Transitional word or expression	• Linking words or phrases that show the reader the connections between ideas	in addition, however, furthermore, in fact, moreover, for example

Appendix 2
Verb Tenses

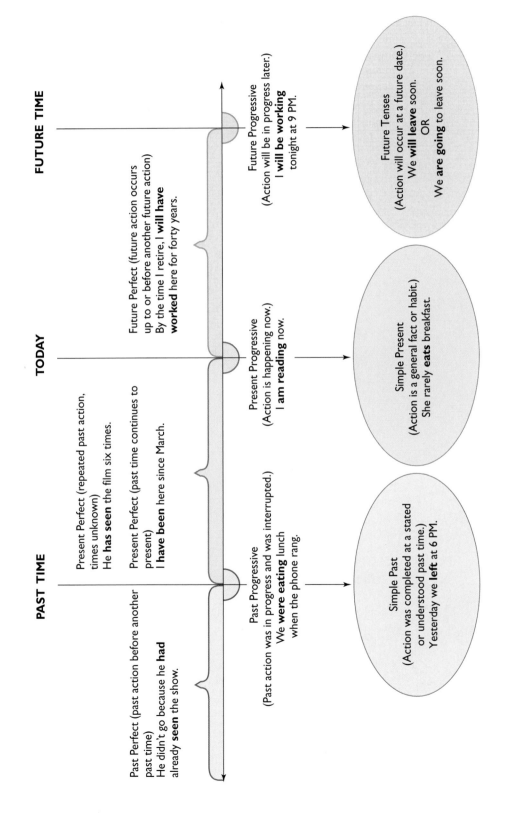

PAST TIME

TODAY

FUTURE TIME

Past Perfect (past action before another past time)
He didn't go because he **had** already **seen** the show.

Present Perfect (repeated past action, times unknown)
He **has seen** the film six times.

Present Perfect (past time continues to present)
I **have been** here since March.

Future Perfect (future action occurs up to or before another future action)
By the time I retire, I **will have worked** here for forty years.

Past Progressive
(Past action was in progress and was interrupted.)
We **were eating** lunch when the phone rang.

Present Progressive
(Action is happening now.)
I **am reading** now.

Future Progressive
(Action will be in progress later.)
I **will be working** tonight at 9 PM.

Simple Past
(Action was completed at a stated or understood past time.)
Yesterday we **left** at 6 PM.

Simple Present
(Action is a general fact or habit.)
She rarely **eats** breakfast.

Future Tenses
(Action will occur at a future date.)
We **will leave** soon.
OR
We **are going** to leave soon.

Appendix 3
Combining Ideas in Sentences

Making Compound Sentences

A.

Complete idea

, coordinator
, but
, or
, yet
, so
, for
, and
, nor

complete idea.

B.

Complete idea

;

complete idea.

C.

Complete idea

; transitional expression,
; however,
; in fact,
; moreover,
; therefore,
; furthermore,

complete idea.

Making Complex Sentences

D.

Complete idea

subordinator
although
because
before
even though
unless
when

incomplete idea.

E.

Subordinator
Although
Because
Before
Even though
Unless
When

incomplete idea

,

complete idea.

Apostrophe (')

Use an apostrophe for the following reasons.

- To join a subject and verb

    She's tired.

- To join an auxiliary with *not*

    You **shouldn't** smoke.

- To indicate possession

    Mike's camera is new.

Comma (,)

Use a comma in the following cases.

- To separate words in a series of more than two things

    Everyone needs food, water, and shelter.

- After an introductory word or phrase

    After the election, the candidate rested.

- Around interrupting phrases that give additional information about the subject

    Isabelle, an artist, makes astonishing paintings.

- In compound sentences before the coordinator

    The job is easy, but it does not pay well.

- Around relative clauses containing *which*

    The files, which are in my office, contain important information.

- In quotations, after an introductory phrase or before an end phrase

    Durrell said, "Personality is an illusion."

    "Personality is an illusion," Durrell said.

Note: Do not join two complete sentences with a comma.

Colon (:)

Use a colon in the following cases.

- After a complete sentence that introduces a list or after *the following*

    An essay has the following parts: an introduction, a body, and a conclusion.

- After a complete sentence that introduces a quotation

> Durrell's point was clear: "Personality is an illusion."

Semicolon (;)

Use a semicolon to join two independent and related clauses.

> Many Brazilian tribes are isolated; they do not interact with the outside world.

Quotation Marks (" ")

Use quotation marks around direct speech. When a quotation is a complete sentence, do the following:

- Capitalize the first word in the quotation.
- Place the end punctuation mark inside the closing quotation marks.

> In her essay, Dorothy Nixon said, "**I** am the television addict."

Integrated Quotation

If you integrate a quotation into your sentence, just add quotation marks.

> Dorothy Nixon calls herself a "television addict."

"Inside" Quotation

If one quotation is inside another quotation, use single quotation marks (' ') around the inside quotation.

> Maya Angelou describes the moment: "She turned on the light and said, 'Look at the baby.'"

Citing Page or Paragraph Numbers

Put the page or paragraph number in parentheses. Place the final period *after* the parentheses.

> In her novel, Maya Angelou says, "I didn't feel lonely or abandoned" (127).

Capitalization

Always capitalize the following:

- The pronoun *I* and the first word of every sentence
- The names of days of the week, months, and holidays

> **W**ednesday   **A**pril 14   **L**abor **D**ay

- The names of specific places, such as buildings, streets, parks, public squares, lakes, rivers, cities, states, and countries

> **E**lm **S**treet   **M**ississippi **R**iver   **M**iami, **F**lorida

- The names of languages, nationalities, tribes, races, and religions

> **G**reek   **M**ohawk   **C**hristian

- The titles of specific individuals

    General Smith   **President Bush**   **Mrs. Sloan**

- The major words in titles of literary or artistic works

    War and Peace   *The Last Supper*   *The Godfather*

Punctuating Titles

Capitalize all of the major words in a title. Place quotation marks around the titles of short works (songs, essays, short stories, poems, newspaper articles, magazine articles, etc.).

> Chopin's most famous story was called "The Storm."

Underline (or italicize, if you are using a computer) the titles of longer works (television series, movies, plays, books, works of art, magazines, newspapers, etc.).

> I read the classic novel <u>The Awakening</u>.
> I read the classic novel *The Awakening*.

Appendix 5

Spelling, Grammar, and Vocabulary Logs

The goal of keeping spelling and grammar logs is to help you stop repeating errors. When you do new writing assignments, you can consult the lists and hopefully break some ingrained bad habits. The vocabulary log can provide you with interesting new terms that you can incorporate into your writing.

Spelling Log

Every time you misspell a word, record both the mistake and the correction in your spelling log. Then, before you hand in a writing assignment, consult your list of misspelled words. The goal is to stop repeating the same spelling errors.

EXAMPLE:

Incorrect	Correct
alot	a lot
responsable	responsible

Grammar Log

Each time a writing assignment is returned to you, identify one or two repeated errors and add them to your grammar log. Then, consult the grammar log before you hand in writing assignments to avoid making the same errors. For each type of grammar error, follow these steps.

- Identify the assignment, and write down the type of error.
- In your own words, write a rule about the error.
- Include an example from your writing assignment.

EXAMPLE: <u>Narration Paragraph</u> (Sept. 28): Run-on

Do not connect two complete sentences with a comma.

We hit a telephone ~~pole, the~~ pole. The airbags exploded.

Vocabulary Log

As you read, you will learn new vocabulary words and expressions. Keep a record of the most interesting and useful vocabulary words and their meanings. Write a synonym or definition next to each new word.

EXAMPLE:

Term	Meaning
reminisce	to recollect in an enjoyable way

Spelling Log

Grammar Log

Vocabulary Log

Credits

Index

A

a, an
  as determiners, 116–18
  singular noun after, 112
abstract nouns, 115
academic writing
  avoiding contractions in, 384
  avoiding slang in, 283
  if clause in, 215
accept/except, 360
action verb, 153–54
active voice, 191, 462
addresses, 378
  Web, 402
adjective(s), 316, 317–21, 462
  comparative form, 325–26
  -ed and *-ing* ending, 320
  -ful or *-less* ending, 320
  good/bad, 324–25
  order of, 318
  parallel, 306, 309
  past participle as, 190
  placement of, 317–18
  possessive, 135, 136–37
  punctuating, 319
  with same form as adverbs, 322
  singular form, 320
  superlative form, 325–26
adverb(s), 321–25, 462
  adjectives with same form as, 322
  beginning sentence with, 277
  comparative form, 325
  conjunctive, 249, 255, 462
  forms of, 321–22
  frequency, 322–23
  introductory word, 371
  -ly ending, 277, 321–22
  negative, 174
  parallel, 307
  problems with, 323–25
  superlative form, 326
  well and *badly*, 324–25
affect/effect, 78, 360
affirmative forms
  past progressive, 201
  present progressive, 198
agreement
  pronoun-antecedent, 128–34
  subject-verb, 161, 224–39
all, plural noun after, 112
a lot, 352
and
  compound antecedents joined by, 128
  as coordinating conjunction, 250
  multiple subjects joined by, 149, 231
  parallel structure with, 307
  pronouns joined by, 138–39
anecdote, 85
  in introduction, 98–100
annotations, making, 418

another, 112, 352
antecedent, 128
  compound, 128
  pronoun-antecedent agreement, 128–34
  to reflexive pronouns, 143
  vague pronouns referring to, 132–33
antonym, 419
any, spelling two-part words with, 352
apostrophe, 383–93, 466
  common errors, 390
  in contractions, 384–87
  defined, 384
  in expressions of time, 389–91
  possessive pronouns and, 136–37
  to show ownership, 387
appealing to readers' senses, 54
appositive, commas with, 372
argument paragraph, 44, 81–88
  circular reasoning, avoiding, 85
  plan/outline, 85
  supporting ideas, 84–85
  topic sentences, 83–84
articles
  as determiners, 116
  in titles, 403
as, comparisons with, 138
assignment, understanding, 4
at vs. *to*, 121
audience, 4, 92
  instructor as, 4

B

background information in introduction, 98–100
bad/good, 324–25
badly/well, 324–25
base form of verb, 462
  after *did*, 172
  after *to* (infinitive form), 219
  past participle of, 179, 180–83
  simple present tense, 160
been/being, 360
be verb
  common errors with, 172–74
  contractions with, 385
  frequency adverbs after all forms of, 323
  linking verb, 154
  passive voice formed with, 190–93
  past tense (*was* and *were*), 170–74, 228
  present tense forms, 161–62, 226–27
  in progressive form, 198, 200, 202
  before subject in questions, 229
body of paragraph, 90
body sentences, 13. *See also* supporting details
both...and, parallel structure using, 309
both, plural noun after, 112
brainstorming, 7
  to generate ideas, 21
  to generate supporting details, 96
  to narrow topic, 14, 92

business letters, 378–81
    editing, 412
but
    as coordinating conjunction, 250
    parallel structure with, 307
by... phrase in passive sentences, 192
by/buy, 360

C
capitalization, 400–404, 405, 467–68
    of computer terms, 401
    of days of week, months, holidays, 467
    of first word of quotation, 395
    of first word of sentence, 400, 467
    of historical events/eras/movements, 401
    of names of languages/nationalities/tribes/races and
        religions, 400, 467
    of place names, 400, 467
    of pronoun *I*, 400, 467
    of titles of course/program, 401
    of titles of institutions/companies, 400
    of titles of literary/artistic works, 401, 468
    of titles of people, 400, 468
case, pronoun, 134–36, 138–39
    objective, 135, 138–39
    possessive, 135–37
    subjective, 135, 138
category, definition by, 66
cause and effect paragraph, 44, 75–81
    plan/ outline, 79
    supporting ideas, 79
    topic sentences, 76, 78
checklists
    adjectives and adverbs, 331–32
    apostrophes, 392–93
    argument paragraph, 88
    capitalization, 405
    cause and effect paragraph, 81
    commas, 382
    commonly confused words, 368
    comparison and contrast paragraph, 75
    complex sentences, 274
    compound sentences, 260
    definition paragraph, 69
    descriptive paragraph, 60
    developing paragraph, 31
    exact language, 286
    exploring topics, 11
    illustration paragraph, 49
    modifiers, 343
    narrative paragraph, 54
    nouns, determiners, and prepositions, 125–26
    parallel structure, 314
    past participles, 196
    present and past tenses, 177
    process paragraph, 65
    progressive tenses, 207
    pronouns, 145
    quotation marks, 405
    revising and editing, 42

run-ons, 304
sentence fragments, 295
sentence variety, 286
spelling rules, 357–58
subjects, 158
subject-verb agreement, 239
tense consistency, 246
verb forms, 223
verbs, 158
writing essay, 104–5
chronological order. *See* time/chronological order
circular reasoning, 35, 85
clause(s), 462. *See also* sentence(s)
    dependent, 262–64, 267–70, 292, 337–38, 375–76, 462
    essential vs. nonessential, 376–77
    if, 214, 215, 217
    independent, 262–64, 307, 462
    paired, 307
    relative, modifiers beginning with, 336
    restrictive vs. nonrestrictive, 376–77
clichés, 281–83
closing of letter, complimentary, 379
clustering, 8–9
    to generate ideas, 21
    to generate supporting details, 96
    to narrow topic, 14
coherence, revising for, 32, 36–37, 103
collective nouns, 233–34
colon, 466–67
    after introductory sentence, 398
comma(s), 369–82, 466
    with appositives, 372
    around interrupting words/phrases, 372–74
    in business letters, 378–81
    in clauses beginning with relative pronouns, 268
    in complex sentences, 375–78
    in compound sentences, 374–75
    before coordinating conjunction, 249
    defined, 370
    after dependent clause, 375–76
    ending quotation with, 397
    after introductory words or phrases, 278, 371–72,
        395
    in quotation with interrupting phrase, 396
    in series, 370–71
    to set off nonrestrictive clauses, 377–78
    with subordinator, 263, 264
    after transitional expression, 256
    which clause set off by, 140, 142, 376–78
commands, 150
comma splice, 299
common nouns, 109
comparative forms, 325–30
    -er ending, 325–26, 328–29
    irregular forms, 326
    more, 326, 328–29
    problems with, 328–29
    using *the* in, 329
comparison and contrast, 70
    comparisons with *than* or *as*, 138

parallel structure in comparisons, 309
comparison and contrast paragraph, 44, 70–75
plan/outline, 73
supporting ideas, 73
topic sentences, 72
complement/compliment, 360
complete subject, 148–49
complex sentences, 261–74, 463
combining simple sentences to make, 276, 465
commas in, 375–78
defined, 262
punctuating, 263, 264
subordinating conjunctions in, 262–67, 375
using embedded questions, 271–72
using relative pronouns, 267–70
compound antecedent, 128
compound-complex sentence, 262, 463
compound nouns, 110
possessive forms of, 388
compound sentence(s), 248–60, 374, 463
combining simple sentences to make, 276, 465
commas in, 374–75
comparing simple and, 249
recognizing, 249
using coordinating conjunctions, 249–53, 374
using semicolons, 249, 253–55
using transitional expressions, 249, 255–58
compound subjects, 149
compound verb, 153
computer(s)
capitalizing computer terms, 401
spelling checker, 354
concluding paragraph, 100–102
concluding sentence of paragraph, 13, 30, 90
conclusion of essay, 90, 100–102
problems, 101
conditional sentences, 214–15, 462
conditional verb forms, 214–18
conjunction. *See* coordinating conjunctions; subordinating conjunctions
conjunctive adverbs, 249, 255, 462
conscience/conscious, 361
consonants, 345
constructive criticism from peers, 39
context clues, using, 419
contractions
apostrophe in, 384–87
common, 384
negative verb forms, 164, 210, 384
possessive adjectives sounding like, 136–37
with two meanings, 387
contrast. *See* comparison and contrast
controlling idea, 15–16, 72. *See also* thesis statement; topics; topic sentence
coordinating conjunctions, 249–53, 462, 465
chart of, 250–51
comma before, 249
in compound sentence, 249–53, 374
meanings of, 250–51
in titles, 403

could, 210, 242
past tense, 211–12
could of (nonstandard form), 217
count nouns, 114–16
determiners before, 116

D
dangling modifiers, 338–41
correcting, 340
dates
in letters, 379
numerals of decade or century, writing, 389
definition, 65
by category, 66
by negation, 66
by synonym, 66
definition paragraph, 44, 65–69
plan/outline, 67–68
supporting ideas, 67–68
topic sentences, 66–67
demonstratives, as determiners, 116
dependent-clause fragments, 292–94
dependent clause modifiers, 337–38
dependent clauses, 262–64, 267–70, 292, 375–76, 462
descriptive paragraph, 43, 54–60
plan/outline, 58
supporting details, 56–57
topic sentence, 55–56
details. *See* supporting details
determiners, 116–20, 462
developing stage of writing process, 12–31
first draft of paragraph, 29–30
narrowing topic, 14–15
plan/outline of paragraph ideas, 28–29
supporting details, 20–28
topic sentence, 13, 15–20
development of supporting details, 73
dictionary, using, 419–20
direct quotation, 395
dominant impression, creating, 55, 56
double negatives, 174–75
do verb
base form of verb after *did*, 172
negative past forms, 171, 172
negative present forms, 164–65
present tense forms, 226–27
question forms, 163–65, 171, 172
drafts. *See* final draft; first draft
during vs. *for*, 122

E
each, single noun after, 112
editing, 32
for errors, 33, 38–39
essay, 103
editing practice, 406–15
essay, 413–15
formal letter, 412
letters, 410, 412

editing practice (*cont.*)
    paragraph, 406–9, 410–11
    workplace memo, 409–10
effect/affect, 78, 360
effects. *See* cause and effect paragraph
either...or, parallel structure using, 309
embedded questions, 271–72
emphatic order, 24–25, 79, 97
    in process paragraph, 63
end phrase after quotation, 397
English, nonstandard vs. standard American, 160, 283–84
entertaining writing, 5
errors
    with apostrophes, 390
    with *be* verb, 172–74
    editing for, 33, 38–39
    fragments, 288–96
    with *have* verb, 173–74
    with progressive tense, 200, 202
ESL teaching tips (AIE), 109, 159
    adjectives, 318, 320
    apostrophes, 384, 385, 390
    argument paragraph, 81, 85
    business letters, 378, 379
    capitalization rules, 400
    circular reasoning, 35
    clichés, 282
    commonly confused words, 361, 364
    comparative forms, 329
    contractions, 385
    coordinating conjunctions chart, 250
    determiners, 116, 117, 118
    double negatives, 174
    double subjects, 132
    exploring strategies, 5
    frequency adverbs, 322
    gerunds and infinitives, 218
    group work, 37, 255
    helping verbs, 229
    his and *her*, 137
    interrupters, 156
    irregular verb *be*, 162
    main verbs, 155, 213
    modals, 209
    negative forms of modals, 210
    negative verbs, 164, 165
    noncount nouns, 115
    nonprogressive verbs, 204
    paragraph form, 14
    past participles, 180
    past vs. *passed*, 167
    plural nouns, 110, 113
    prepositions, 120, 121, 122, 151
    present perfect tense, 183, 184
    question forms, 229
    reading selections, 429
    reflexive pronouns, 143
    relative pronouns, 140
    simple and progressive verb forms, 160
    spelling, 345, 347, 350
    subject after subordinator, 266

    subject-verb agreement, 227, 229
    subordinating conjunctions, 263
    supporting details, 85
    than and *that*, 364
    there, sentences beginning with, 229
    third-person singular verb form, 161
    topic sentences, 17
    transitional words, 255
    verbs, 155, 225
    vivid vocabulary, 57
    word twins, 420
    would and *could*, 242
    writing about reading, 420
essay(s), 89–104
    conclusion, 90, 100–102
    defined, 89
    editing, 102, 103
    editing, practice at, 413–15
    final draft, 103
    first draft, 102
    introduction, 90
    length, 90
    narrowing topic of, 92–93
    plan/outline, 97–98
    pronoun shifts in, avoiding, 133
    revising, 102–3
    supporting ideas, 94, 96–97
    thesis statement, 90, 93–95
    title, 402
essay links, 12
    coherence, 36
    concluding paragraph, 30
    exploring steps, 3
    organizational methods, 23
    revising and editing, 33, 34
    style, 38
    supporting ideas, 20
    thesis statements, 16, 20
every
    single noun after, 112
    spelling two-part words with, 352
everyday/every day, 361
evidence. *See* supporting details
exact language, 279–81
examples
    to avoid circular reasoning, 85
    in cause and effect paragraph, 79
    in illustration paragraph, 46–47
    supporting details, 46–47
except/accept, 360
explanatory fragments, 290–92
exploring stage of writing process, 3–11, 92
exploring strategies (prewriting strategies), 5–9
    to generate ideas, 21
    to narrow topic, 14

F
facts, 85
farther/further, 326
feedback, peer, 39–40
few, 112, 118–19

final draft
  of essay, 103
  of paragraph, 41
find/fine, 361
first draft
  of essay, 102
  of paragraph, 29–30
Florida Exit Test competencies
  capitalization, 395, 400, 400–404, 402–3, 405
  effectively using coordination, 249–53, 374, 403, 462, 465
  effectively using irregular verbs, 161–62, 168–74, 180–83
  effectively using semicolons, 249, 253–55
  effectively using subordination, 262–67, 292, 375, 465
  effectively using transitions, 23, 25, 26, 37, 103, 249, 255–58, 371
  effectively using verb tense, 156, 159–77, 183–89, 197–207, 214–18, 225–29, 306, 322
  effectively using verb tense/consistency, 240–47
  look-alike words, 359–68
  parallel structure, 305–15
  prefixes and suffixes, 347
  pronoun case, 134–36, 138–39
  pronoun consistency, 133–34
  pronoun reference, 128–34
  recognizing comma splices, 299
  recognizing fused sentences, 299
  recognizing misplaced modifiers, 334–38
  recognizing sentence fragments, 288–96
  recognizing unclear pronoun reference, 132–33
  sound-alike words, 359–68
  spelling, 344–58
  subject-verb agreement, 161, 224–39
  understanding adjectives/adverbs, 135, 136–37, 174, 190, 277, 306, 309, 316–32, 371
  understanding apostrophes/possessives, 136–37, 383–93
  understanding comparatives/ superlatives, 325–30
  understanding topic sentences, 13, 15–20, 45–46, 55–56, 61–62, 66–67, 72, 76, 78, 83–84, 90, 96
  understanding word choice/vocabulary, 279–81, 419–20
for, as coordinating conjunction, 250
for/four, 360
formal letter, 412
for vs. *during,* 122
fragments, sentence, 288–96
  dependent-clause fragments, 292–94
  explanatory fragments, 290–92
  with *-ing* and *to,* 218–22
  phrase fragments, 289–90
freewriting, 5–6
  to generate ideas, 21
  to generate supporting details, 96
  to narrow topic, 14
frequency adverbs, 322–23
fun/funny, 361
further/farther, 326
fused sentence, 299
future conditional, 214
future perfect tense, 464
future progressive tense, 198, 203, 464

G
gender of possessive adjective, 137
gerunds, 148, 218–22
  common verbs and expressions followed by, 219
  progressive tense (noncompared to, 218
gonna, gotta (nonstandard form), 213–14
good/bad, 324–25
grammar glossary, 462–63
grammar links, 357
  apostrophes, 136
  editing, 103
  present perfect, 228
  punctuating relative clauses, 268
  spelling, 166
  subject-verb agreement, 161
  which clause set off with commas, 140
grammar log, 38, 469, 471

H
have verb
  common errors with, 173–74
  contractions with, 385
  past perfect tense, 187–89
  present perfect tense, 183–87
  present tense forms, 161–62, 173, 226–27
helping verb(s), 155–58, 289
  embedded questions and, 271
  frequency adverbs after, 323
  modals, 156, 191, 209–13, 462
  in negative forms, 164–65
  past participle with, 179
  in progressive form, 198, 200, 202
  in questions, 156, 163–64, 165, 229
here, sentence beginning with, 229
here/there, 150
highlighting your reading, 418
his or *her,* choosing, 137
hisself (nonstandard form), 143
hyphenated compound nouns, 110

I
I, capitalizing, 400, 467
if clause, 214, 215, 217
illustration, 44
illustration paragraph(s), 43, 44–49
  plan/outline, 46–47
  supporting ideas in, 46–47
  topic sentence of, 45–46
incomplete verbs, 289
indefinite pronouns, 130–32, 232–33
  as determiners, 116
  one-word, spelling, 352
  plural, 232–33
  singular, 232–33
independent clause, 262–64, 462
  parallel structure of joined, 307
indirect quotation, 395

indirect speech, 462
infinitives, 155, 219–22, 462
    fragment beginning with, 218, 219–22
    parallel, 307, 309
informational writing, 5
-ing verbs, 197–207
-ing words
    gerunds, 148, 218–22
    present participles, 198, 199, 202
integrated quotation, 467
interjection, 462
interrupting words and phrases
    commas around, 372–74
    in quotation, commas around, 396
    subject-verb agreement and, 234–36
    between verbs, 156
introduction to essay, 90, 98–100
introductory paragraph, 98–100
    styles, 98–100
    thesis statement placement in, 99
introductory phrase, 371
    comma to set off, 278, 371–72, 395
    introducing quotation, comma after, 395
introductory sentence, 398
introductory word, 277–79, 371–72
    comma after, 278, 371–72, 395
irregular comparative and superlative forms, 326
irregular plural nouns, 109
irregular verbs, 462
    be (*was* or *were*), 170–74
    past participles of, 180–83
    past tense, 168–74
    present tense, 161–63
it, as vague pronoun, 132
italicizing title, 402, 468
its/it's, 361

J
journal, 10

K
knew/new, 361
know/no, 361

L
language
    clichés, 281–83
    exact, 279–81
    slang vs. standard English, 283–84
    vivid, 57, 279–81
letter(s)
    addresses, 378
    business, 378–81, 412
    complimentary closings, 379
    dates, 379
    editing, 410, 412
    formal, editing, 412
    salutations, 379
linking verb, 154
    adjectives after, 317
little, 118–19

look-alike words, 359–68
lose/loose/loss, 362

M
main verb, 155, 156–58, 209
    following modal, 213
    gerunds following, 218–22
    infinitives following, 219–22
many, 112, 118–19
memo, workplace, 409
misplaced modifiers, 334–38
    correcting, 337
misspelled words, commonly, 353–54
modals, 156, 209–13, 462
    active and passive voice, 191
    common forms, 209
    negative forms, 210
    present and past forms, 209, 210–13
    subject-verb agreement and, 228
modes, paragraph, 43. *See also specific types of paragraphs*
modifiers, 333–43
    creating vivid language with, 279–80
    dangling, 338–41
    defined, 334
    introductory phrase, 371
    misplaced, 334–38
more, 326, 328–29
most, 326, 329
much, 118–19

N
names
    capitalizing, 400, 401, 467
    historical events, eras, and movements, 401
    languages, nationalities, tribes, races, and religions, 400, 467
    places, 400, 467
narration
    first-person, 49
    tense consistency in, 243–44
    third-person, 49
narrative paragraph, 43, 49–54
    first-person narration, 49
    plan/outline, 52
    supporting details, 51
    third-person narration, 49
    topic sentence, 51
narrowing topic, 14–15, 92–93
negation, definition by, 66
negatives, double, 174–75
negative verb forms
    contractions, 164, 210, 384
    modals, 210
    past progressive, 201
    past tense, 171
    present progressive, 198
    present tense, 164–65
neither...nor, parallel structure using, 309
new/knew, 361
no/know, 361
noncount nouns, 114–16
    determiners before, 118

nonprogressive verbs, 204–5
nonrestrictive clause, comma to set off, 377–78
nonstandard English, 160
    gonna, gotta, wanna, 213–14
    verb forms, 212–13, 213–14, 217
    would of, could of, should of, 212–13, 217
nor
    as coordinating conjunction, 250
    multiple subjects joined by, 231
    neither...nor, 309
not...but, parallel structure using, 309
not, contractions with, 164, 384
notes, taking, 418
nouns, 109–16, 462. *See also* pronouns
    collective, 233–34
    common, 109
    compound, 110, 388
    count, 114–16, 116, 118
    determiners and, 116–20, 462
    irregular, 109
    modifying for specificity, 279–80
    noncount, 114–16, 118
    object of preposition, 151
    parallel, 306, 307, 309
    plural, 109–14, 387–88
    possessive, 387–89
    proper, 109, 385
    regular, 109
    singular, 109–14, 387
    -s or *-es* endings, 109
number(s)
    as determiners, 116
    numerals of decade or century, writing, 389
    pronouns consistent in, 133–34
    writing, 379

O

object, 135
    in prepositional phrase, 151
objective case, 135, 138
of the expressions
    indefinite pronouns with, 131
    in interrupting phrases, 234
    plural nouns following, 113
one, singular noun after, 112
opposing position in introduction, 98–100
opposition, answers to, 85
or
    compound antecedents joined by, 128
    as coordinating conjunction, 250
    multiple subjects joined by, 231
    parallel structure with, 307
    pronouns joined by, 138–39
order
    emphatic, 24–25, 63, 79, 97
    space, 25–27, 97
    time, 23–24, 52, 58, 60, 62, 97
    word, 229, 271, 318
organization of supporting details, 23–28, 97
outline
    of argument paragraph, 85

    of cause and effect paragraph, 79
    of comparison and contrast paragraph, 73
    of definition paragraph, 67–68
    of descriptive paragraph, 58
    essay, 97–98
    of illustration paragraph, 46–47
    of narrative paragraph, 52
    paragraph, 28–29
    of process paragraph, 63
    as reading strategy, 420

P

paired clauses, 307
paragraph(s), 13. *See also types of paragraphs*
    body, 90
    coherence of, 32, 36–37
    concluding, 100–102
    concluding sentence, 13, 30, 90
    controlling idea, 15–16
    development, 12–31
    editing, 32, 33, 38–40
    editing, practice at, 406–9, 410–11
    emphatic order, 24–25
    final draft, 41
    first draft, 29–30
    form, 14
    introductory, 98–100
    patterns (modes), 43. *See also specific types of paragraphs*
    peer feedback on, 39–40
    plan/outline, 28–29
    pronoun shifts in, avoiding, 133
    revising, 32–38
    space order, 25–27
    structure, 13
    supporting details, 20–28, 32, 34–36
    time order, 23–24
    topic, 14–15
    topic sentence, 13, 15–20, 90
    unity, 22, 32, 33–34
paragraph plan, 28–29
parallel structure, 305–15
    in comparisons, 309
    faulty, 307–14
    in paired clauses, 307
    in series of words or phrases, 307
    in two-part construction, 309
parentheses, page or paragraph number of quotation in, 467
passive voice, 190–93, 462
    by... phrase understood in, 192
    overuse of, 191
    verb *be* suggested but not written, 193
past conditional, 215, 216, 217
past participle(s), 178–96, 212
    as adjective, 190
    of irregular verbs, 180–83
    modifiers, 335–36
    passive voice and, 190–93
    past perfect tense, 187–89, 228, 464
    present perfect tense, 183–87, 188, 191, 228–29, 464
    of regular verbs, 179–80
past/passed, 167, 362

past perfect tense, 187–89, 464
   in past condition *if* clause, 217
   subject-verb agreement and, 228
past progressive tense, 198, 200–202, 464
past tense
   agreement, 227–28
   be verb, 170–74
   frequency adverbs before, 322
   irregular verbs, 168–74
   modals, 209, 210–13
   narration in, 243
   regular, 166–68
   simple, 166–74, 184, 185, 191, 227–28, 464
peace/piece, 362
peer feedback, 39–40
perception verbs, 204
perfect tense
   past, 187–89, 217, 228, 464
   present, 183–87, 188, 191, 228–29, 464
   present perfect progressive, 198, 204
person, pronouns consistent in, 133–34
personal/personnel, 363
persons vs. *people*, 110
persuasive writing, 5. *See also* argument paragraph
phrase, 151. *See also* prepositional phrase(s); transitional words and expressions
   interrupting, 156, 234–36, 372–74, 396
   introductory, 278, 371–72, 395–96
phrase fragments, 289–90
piece/peace, 362
plan. *See* outline
plural nouns, 109–14
   irregular, 109
   key words for, 112
   possessive forms of, 387–88
plural subject, 148
plural verbs. *See* subject-verb agreement
point-by-point development, 73
portfolio, writing, 10
possession verbs, 204
possessive case, 135–37
   adjectives, 135, 136–37
   pronouns, 136–40, 390
possessive nouns, 387–89
   -'s to show ownership, 387–89
prediction, ending conclusion with, 100
preference verbs, 204
prefixes, 347
preposition(s), 120–25, 126, 462
   common, 151
   commonly confused, 122
   common prepositional expressions, 122–24
   of place, 120–22
   plus gerunds, 219
   of time, 120–22
   in titles, 403
prepositional phrase(s), 151–53
   as interrupting phrase, 234, 372
   as introductory phrase, 371
   modifiers, 334–35

object in, 151
   parallel, 306
   pronouns in, 138
   sentence beginning with, 277–78
present conditional, 214–15
present participle
   modifiers, 335
   in progressive tenses, 198, 202
   spelling of, 199
present perfect progressive, 198, 204
present perfect tense, 183–87, 188, 464
   active and passive voice, 191
   agreement, 228–29
present progressive tense, 198–200, 464
   active and passive voice, 191
   simple present tense compared to, 199–200
present tense
   agreement, 225–27
   be verb, 161–62, 226–27
   do verb, 226–27
   frequency adverbs before, 322
   have verb, 161–62, 173, 183–87, 188, 226–27
   modals, 209, 210–13
   narration in, 243
   negative, 164–65
   question forms, 163–64, 165
   simple, 160–66, 191, 199–200, 225–27, 464
previewing, 417–18
prewriting strategies (exploring strategies), 5–9, 14, 21
principal/principle, 363
process, 60
   steps vs. examples of, 62
process paragraph, 43, 60–65
   plan/outline, 63
   supporting details, 62
   topic sentence, 61–62
progressive tense, 197–207
   common errors with, 200, 202
   future, 198, 203
   gerund compared to, 218
   past, 198, 200–202
   present, 191, 198–200, 464
pronoun-antecedent agreement, 128–34
   consistency in number, 133–34
   consistency in person, 133–34
   indefinite pronouns, 130–32
   vague pronouns, 132–33
pronouns, 127–46, 462
   with *and* or *or*, 138–39
   case, 134–36, 138–39
   in comparisons with *than* or *as*, 138
   defined, 128
   demonstrative, 116
   I, capitalizing, 400, 467
   indefinite, 116, 130–32, 232–33, 352
   objective case, 135, 138
   object of preposition, 151
   possessive, 136–40, 390
   in prepositional phrases, 138

pronoun-antecedent agreement, 128–34, 133–34
pronoun shifts, 133–34
reflexive, 142–44
relative, 140–42, 267–70, 292, 336
subject, 148
subjective case, 135, 138
vague, 132–33
pronoun shifts, 133–34
proofreading, 41. *See also* editing
essay, 103
proper nouns, 109
contractions with, 385
punctuation, 369–405, 466–68. *See also* capitalization
between adjectives, 319
apostrophe, 136–37, 383–93, 466
colon, 398, 466-67
commas, 140, 142, 249, 256, 263, 264, 268, 278, 319, 369–82, 395, 396, 397, 466
of complex sentences, 263, 264
of compound sentences, 249, 253–55
hyphen, 110
after opening words/phrase, 278
quotation marks, 394–400, 467, 468
of quotations, 395–400, 467
with relative pronouns, 268
in run-on sentences, 299–303
semicolons, 249, 253–55, 467
of series, 370–71
in titles, 402, 468
before and after transitional expressions, 256
purpose for writing, 5, 92

Q

questioning (strategy), 9
to narrow topic, 92
questions
embedded, 270–72
helping verbs in, 156, 163–64, 165, 229
word order in, 229
question verb forms, 163–64, 165, 229
past progressive, 201
past tense, 171–72
present progressive, 198
present tense, 163–64, 165
quiet/quite/quit, 364
quotation(s)
inside another quotation, 467
citing page or paragraph numbers for, 467
commas in or ending, 396, 397
direct, 395
ending conclusion with, 100
indirect, 395
introducing or integrating, 467
punctuating, 395–400, 467
quotation marks, 394–400, 467
around title of short works, 402, 468
with ending phrase, 397
with interrupting phrase, 396–97
with introductory phrase, 395–96
with introductory sentence, 398

R

reading links
argument readings, 87
beliefs, 247
business world, 405
cause and effect readings, 81
comparison and contrast readings, 75
definition essays, 69
descriptive readings, 59
entertainment and culture, 223
illustration readings, 48
narrative essays, 53
politics, 287
process readings, 64
relationships, 343
science, 314
social sciences, 146
zoology, 368
reading selections, 416, 421–61
"Appalling Truth, The" (Nixon), 438–41
"Birth" (Angelou), 432–35
"Conversation with John E. Smelcer, A" (Seeds), 425–27
"Culture War, The" (Chavez), 444–47
"Fish Cheeks" (Tan), 421–23
"Going Thin in Fiji" (Goodman), 447–49
"Hijab, The" (Mustafa), 423–25
"How to Handle Conflict" (Smith), 457–59
"For Marriage" (Macleod), 435–36
"Against Marriage" (Murray), 436–38
"New Addiction, The" (Freed), 442–44
"Point Is?, The" (Tufts), 428–29
"Political Activism" (Stern), 454–56
"Rewards of Dirty Work, The" (Lindsey & Beach), 459–61
"Sports and Life: Lessons to Be Learned" (Kemp), 430–32
"What It Feels Like to Walk on the Moon" (Aldrin), 449–52
"Zoo Life, The" (Martel), 452–54
reading strategies, 417–21
highlighting and making annotations, 418
making written response, 420–21
outlining, 420
previewing, 417–18
summarizing, 420
unfamiliar words, understanding, 419–20
reflexive pronouns, 142–44
regular verbs
past participles of, 179–80
past tense, 166–68
relative clause, modifiers beginning with, 336
relative pronouns, 140–42, 267–70
dependent-clause modifiers beginning with, 336
dependent clauses beginning with, 292
punctuation with, 268
repeated subject, 132
restrictive clause, 376–77
revising, 32–38. *See also* editing
for adequate support, 32, 34–36, 103
for coherence, 32, 36–37, 103

revising (*cont.*)
  essay, 102–3
  for style, 33, 38
  for unity, 32, 33–34, 103
right/write, 365
root words, looking up, 420
run-on sentences, 298–304
  correcting, 300–303
  punctuation in, 299–303

S

salutations, 379
-self/-selves, 142–44
semicolons, 467
  in compound sentences, 249, 253–55
  joining related ideas, 254–55
  before transitional expression, 256
senses, description appealing to, 54
sensory details, listing, 56
sentence(s), 147–58. *See also* topic sentence
  body, 13
  capitalizing first word of, 400, 467
  combining, 276, 465
  complex, 261–74, 276, 375–78, 463, 465
  compound, 248–60, 276, 374–75, 463, 465
  compound-complex, 262, 463
  concluding, 13, 30, 90
  conditional, 214–15, 462
  defined, 89
  fragments, 288–96
  fused, 299
  introductory, 398
  length, 276–77
  opening words of, 277–79
  parallel structure in, 305–15
  run-on, 298–304
  simple, 276, 463
  style, 38
  subject of, 147, 148–51
  variety, 275–79
  verb in, 153–58
series
  comma in, 370–71
  of words or phrases, parallel structure in, 307
several, plural noun after, 112
should of (nonstandard form), 212–13, 217
simple past tense, 166–74, 464
  active and passive voice, 191
  agreement, 227–28
  irregular, 168–74
  past perfect tense compared to, 188
  past progressive, 198, 200, 464
  present perfect tense compared to, 184, 185, 188
  regular, 166–68
simple present tense, 160–66, 464
  active and passive voice, 191
  agreement, 225–27
  forms of, 160
  irregular verbs, 161–62
  negative and question forms, 163–65
  present progressive tense compared to, 199–200

simple sentence(s), 463
  combining, 276
  comparing compound and, 249
simple subject, 148–49
singular nouns, 109–14
  key words for, 112
  possessive forms of, 387
singular subject, 148
sit/set, 364
slang vs. standard English, 283–84
so, as coordinating conjunction, 251
some
  plural noun after, 112
  spelling two-part words with, 352
sound-alike words, 359–68
space order, 25–27, 97
Spanish speakers, words misused by, 420
spelling, 344–58
  adding prefixes, 347
  adding *-s* or *-es*, 347–48
  adding suffixes, 347–52
  changing *y* to *i*, 351
  commonly misspelled words, 353–54
  doubling final consonant, 350–51
  dropping final *e*, 348–49
  -ful, words ending in, 347
  ie or *ei*, 345–46
  look-alike and sound-alike words, 359–68
  of present participle, 199
  regular past tense verbs, 166
  rules, 345–53
  strategies, 355
spelling checker, computer, 354
spelling log, 38, 469, 470
standard American English, 160, 283–84
state verbs, 204
statistics, 85
storytelling. *See* narration
style, introduction, 98–100
style, revising for
  paragraph, 33
  sentence, 38
subjective case, 135, 138
subject(s) of sentence, 135, 147, 148–51
  asking *who* or *what* to determine, 150
  complete, 148–49
  compound, 149
  contraction joining verb and, 385
  following verb, 150
  indefinite pronouns, 232–33
  multiple, 149, 231
  plural, 148
  repeated, 132
  in sentence fragment, 289, 290
  simple sentence, 249
  simple subject, 148–49
  singular, 148
  special problems, 150–51
  after subordinator, 266
  unstated, 150
  verb before, 229–30

subject pronoun, 148
subject-verb agreement, 161, 224–39
  basic rules, 225–29
  collective nouns, 233–34
  future tense, 228
  indefinite pronouns, 232–33
  interrupting words and phrases, 234–36
  modals, 228
  more than one subject, 231
  past perfect tense, 228
  present perfect tense agreement, 228–29
  simple past tense agreement, 227–28
  simple present tense agreement, 225–27
  verb before subject, 229–30
subordinating conjunctions, 262–67, 465
  comma usage with, 263, 264
  common, 263
  in complex sentences, 262–67, 375
  dependent clauses beginning with, 292
  subject after, 266
suffixes, 347–52
suggestion, ending conclusion with, 100
summarizing, as reading strategy, 420
superlative forms, 325–30
  -est ending, 325–26, 329
  irregular forms, 326
  most, 326, 329
  problems with, 328–29
supporting details, 20–28
  adding specific, 28
  in argument paragraph, 84–85
  to avoid circular reasoning, 35
  in cause and effect paragraph, 79
  choosing best, 22
  in comparison and contrast paragraph, 73
  in definition paragraph, 67–68
  in descriptive paragraph, 56–57
  developing, 73
  for essay, 94, 96–97
  generating, 21
  identifying best, 22
  in illustration paragraph, 46–47
  in narrative paragraph, 51
  organizing, 23–28, 97
  point-by-point development, 73
  in process paragraph, 62
  revising for adequate, 32, 34–36, 103
  sensory details, 56
  topic-by-topic development, 73
synonyms, 419
  definition by, 66

T

taught/thought, 364
teaching tips (AIE). *See also* ESL teaching tips
  adjectives, 316
  adverbs, 316, 321
  appositives, 372
  argument paragraph, 82, 83, 85, 86
  brainstorming, 441, 456
  business letters, 380

cause and effect paragraph, 76, 78, 79
checklists, 30
class work, 16
clichés, 282
clue words for present progressive, 200
clustering, 9
colons, 398
commas, 369, 370
comma splices, 299
comparison and contrast paragraph, 71, 72, 73
complex sentence, 261, 262, 263, 271
compound sentences, 248, 249, 252, 257, 272
concluding sentence, 30
constructive criticism, 39
contractions, 164
controlling idea, 45, 51, 55, 61, 83, 93
coordinating conjunctions, 252
definition, 66
definition paragraph, 66
descriptive paragraph, 55, 58
determiners, 108
editing, 406
embedded questions, 271
engaging students in discussion, 44
essays, 92, 94, 100, 101
essay topics, 92, 93
essential vs. nonessential clauses, 377
exploring strategies, 5, 6
"finger" technique, 249
first draft, 29
fragments, 288
grammar, 108
group work, 100, 311
helping verbs, 198
if clause, 215
illustration paragraph, 45, 46, 47, 48
indefinite pronouns, 130
independent and dependent clauses, 262
-ing form, 148
look- or sound-alike words, 359, 360, 365
models, 208
modifiers, 337, 339, 340, 341, 342
narrative paragraph, 50, 51, 52
narrowed topics, 14
nonstandard verb forms, 217
nouns, 108, 146
pair readings, 435
pair work, 17, 33, 34, 94, 101, 188, 243, 257, 272, 276, 278, 281, 283, 337, 339, 340, 341, 342, 345, 365, 366, 456
paragraph plan, 46
paragraph structure, 13
parallel structure, 305, 306, 311
past participles, 178, 182, 188
peer editing form, 48
prepositions, 108
process paragraph, 61, 62
progressive tense, 197
pronoun case, 138
pronouns, 127, 146, 267
punctuation, 402, 405
questioning strategy, 9

teaching tips (*cont.*)
  quotation marks, 394, 395
  for reading selections, 421, 425, 427, 435, 438, 441, 446, 447, 454, 456
  revising and editing, 39
  run-on sentences, 298, 299
  sentence variety, 275, 276, 278
  slang or nonstandard English, 283
  spelling, 344, 345, 353, 368
  spelling, grammar, and vocabulary logs, 469
  steps in vs. examples of process, 62
  subjects, 147, 148
  subject-verb agreement, 225
  subordinating conjunctions, 263
  supporting details/ideas, 29, 47, 52, 58, 68, 73, 79, 86
  tense shifts, 240
  test materials, 124, 144, 157, 175, 194, 205, 221, 237, 244, 258, 272, 284, 294, 302, 313, 330, 342, 355, 366, 380, 391, 403
  topics, 4, 45, 51, 55, 61, 66, 71, 76, 83
  topic sentences, 19, 33, 61, 82, 83
  transitional words, 37
  types of errors, 39
  verbs, 155, 223, 224
  verb tense, 159
  vivid language, 280
  whose vs. *who's*, 140
  word order, 271
  Writer's Desk activities, 45, 50
technology links
  cutting and pasting, 22
  spelling and grammar checkers, 39
  topic sentences, 21
tense, verb, 156, 159–77, 464
  active vs. passive voice, 191
  conditional forms, 214–18
  consistency, 240–47
  future, 228, 464
  future perfect, 464
  future progressive, 198, 203, 464
  modals, 209, 210–13
  parallel, 306, 307
  past. *See* past tense
  past perfect, 187–89, 228, 464
  past progressive, 198, 200–202, 464
  present. *See* present tense
  present perfect, 183–87, 188, 191, 228–29, 464
  present perfect progressive, 198, 204
  present progressive, 198–200, 464
  progressive forms, 197–207
  simple past, 166–74, 184, 185, 188, 191, 227–28, 464
  simple present, 160–66, 225–27, 464
tense shift, 241–47
Texas Higher Education Assessment
  adjectives and adverbs, 135, 136–37, 174, 249, 255, 277, 306, 309, 316–32, 326, 371
  comparatives/superlatives, 325–30
  concrete examples, 46–47
  coordinators, 249–53, 374, 403, 462, 465
  development, 12–31
  introductions and conclusions, 90, 98–102

  look-alike words, 359–68
  organization, 23–28, 97
  parallel structure, 305–15
  prefixes and suffixes, 347–52
  prewriting skills, 5–9, 14, 21
  pronoun-antecedent agreement, 128–34
  recognizing dangling modifiers, 338–41
  recognizing effective organization, 23–28
  recognizing effective sentences, 147–58
  recognizing fragments, 288–96
  recognizing ineffective word choice, 279–81, 419–20
  recognizing purpose and audience, 4–5, 92
  recognizing run-on sentences, 298–304
  recognizing standard American English, 160, 283–84
  recognizing unity, focus and development, 12–31, 32, 33–34, 96, 103
  rough outline of essay, 97–98. *See also* outline
  sound-alike words, 359–68
  subject-verb agreement, 161, 224–39
  subordinators, 262–67, 292, 375, 465
  thesis statements, 90, 93–95, 99, 100, 103
  unity and focus, 22, 32, 33–34, 96, 103
  verb forms, 160–66, 166–74, 178–223, 225–29
than, comparisons with, 138
than/then/that, 364
that
  indirect quotation beginning with, 395
  as vague pronoun, 132
that, those, 118–19
that clause, 140, 268–70, 376–78
  dependent-clause modifiers beginning with, 336
  subject-verb agreement and, 236
the
  in comparative forms, 329
  as determiner, 116–18
  overuse of, 117
theirselves (nonstandard form), 143
their/there/they're, 364
there, sentence beginning with, 229
there/here, 150
thesis statement, 90, 93–95
  characteristics of good, 93
  placement of, 99
  rephrased in conclusion, 100
  specific details in, 94
  support for, 103
  writing effective, 93–95
they, as vague pronoun, 132
third-person singular form, 225, 232
  negative and question forms, 163, 164, 165
  of simple present tense, 160
this, as vague pronoun, 132
this, these, 118–19
thought/taught, 364
through/threw/thorough, 365
time, apostrophes in expressions of, 389–91
time/chronological order, 23–24, 97
  descriptive paragraph, 58
  narrative paragraph, 52
  process in, 60
  process paragraph, 62

time markers, 185
titles
    articles in, 403
    capitalizing, 400, 401, 402–3, 468
    of courses and programs, 401
    essay, 402
    of individuals, 400, 468
    of institutions, departments, companies, and schools, 400
    of literary or artistic works, 401, 468
    prepositions in, 403
    punctuation of, 402, 468
    underlining or italicizing, 402, 468
to, sentence fragments with, 218, 219–22
to be. See be verb
to do. See do verb
to have. See have verb
topic-by-topic development, 73
topics, 4
    clustering ideas related to, 8–9
    essay, 92–93
    exploring, 4
    exploring/prewriting strategies, 5–9
    generating ideas about, 5–7, 9
    illustration paragraphs, 48
    journal writing, 10
    narrowing, 14–15, 92–93
    paragraph, 14–15
    process paragraph, 64
topic sentence, 13, 15–20, 90
    in argument paragraph, 83–84
    in cause and effect paragraph, 76, 78
    characteristics, 15
    in comparison and contrast paragraph, 72
    debatable, 83, 84
    in definition paragraph, 66–67
    in descriptive paragraph, 55–56
    in illustration paragraph, 45–46
    interesting, 19
    in narrative paragraph, 51
    placement, 18
    in process paragraph, 61–62
    thesis statement and, 96
    writing effective, 16–17
to/too/two, 365
to vs. *at*, 121
transitional words and expressions, 23, 463
    for coherence, 36–37, 103
    common, 36–37
    with complete sentences, 37
    in compound sentences, 249, 255–58, 465
    in emphatic-order paragraphs, 25
    introductory phrase/word, 371
    punctuation before and after, 256
    in space-order paragraphs, 26
    in time-order paragraph, 23
two, plural noun after, 112
two-part constructions, parallel structure for, 309

U

underlining title, 402, 468
unity
    in essay, 96, 103
    in paragraph, 22, 32, 33–34
    revising for, 32, 33–34, 103
used to, 220

V

vague words, 279
    pronouns, 132–33
verb(s), 147, 148. *See also* helping verb(s); subject-verb agreement; tense, verb
    action, 153–54
    adjectives looking like, 320
    base form of. *See* base form of verb
    with both regular and irregular past forms, 169
    compound, 153
    conditional forms, 214–18
    contraction joining subject and, 385
    -d or *-ed* ending, 166–67
    gerunds, 148, 218–22
    incomplete, 289
    infinitives, 155, 218, 219–22
    interrupting words between, 156
    irregular, 161–63, 168–74, 180–83, 462
    linking, 154, 317
    main, 155, 156–58, 209, 213
    modals, 156, 209–13, 462
    modifying for specificity, 279–80
    negative forms, 164–65, 384
    nonprogressive, 204–5
    nonstandard forms, 212–13, 213–14, 217
    past participles, 178–96, 212
    progressive forms, 197–207
    question form, 163–64, 229
    regular, 166–68, 179–80
    in sentence fragment, 289, 290
    simple past tense, 166–74
    simple present tense, 160–66
    in simple sentences, 153–58, 249
    -s or *-es* ending, 160, 161, 165, 225
    spelling, 166
    standard English forms, 160
    before subject, 229–30
vivid language, 57, 279–81
vocabulary. *See also* word(s)
    interesting descriptive, 57
    specific and detailed, 279–81
    unfamiliar words, understanding, 419–20
vocabulary log, 469, 472
voice
    active, 191, 462
    passive, 190–93, 462
vowels, 345

W

wanna (nonstandard form), 213–14
Web addresses, 402
well/badly, 324–25
were, in *if* clause, 215
were/we're/where, 365
which, as vague pronoun, 132
which clause, 140, 268–70
    comma to set off, 140, 142, 376–78

which clause (*cont.*)
    dependent-clause modifiers beginning with, 140
    subject-verb agreement and, 236
who clause(s)
    comma to set off, 376–78
    parallel, 306
    subject-verb agreement and, 236
who or *whom*, choosing, 140
who's/whose, 140–41, 365
who (*whom, whoever, whomever, whose*) clauses, 140, 268–70
    dependent-clause modifiers beginning with, 336
will, contractions with, 385
word(s)
    commonly confused, 359–68
    commonly misspelled, 353–54
    interrupting, 372–74
    introductory/opening, 277–79, 371–72, 395
    look-alike and sound-alike, 359–68
    opening, 277–79
    understanding unfamiliar, 419–20
    vague, 132–33, 279
    vivid, 279–81
word order
    adjectives, 318
    embedded questions and, 271
    in questions, 229
word twins, 420
workplace memo, 409
would, 210, 242
    contractions with, 385
    past tense, 211–12
would of (nonstandard form), 217
write/right, 365
Writers' Circle activities, 146, 223, 246–47, 286–87, 314–15, 343, 368, 405
Writer's Desk exercises
    brainstorming, 7
    cause and effect paragraph, 80
    clustering, 8–9
    comparison and contrast paragraphs, 74
    conclusion, 102
    definition paragraph, 68
    descriptive paragraph, 59
    essay plan, 98
    exploring, 45, 50, 55, 61, 66, 71, 76–77
    final drafts, 41, 103
    first drafts, 30
    freewriting, 6
    illustration paragraph, 47
    images and impressions, 57
    introductions, 100
    narrative paragraph, 53
    narrowing topics, 14–15, 92–93
    organizing ideas, 28

paragraph plans, 29
process paragraph, 64
revising and editing essay, 103
revising and editing paragraph, 39
supporting details/ideas, 21, 47, 52, 58, 63, 68, 73, 79–80, 96–97
thesis statements, 95
topic sentences, 20, 46, 51, 56, 62, 67, 72, 78
Writer's Room activities, 223
    argument paragraph, 86
    essay topics, 104
    paragraph topics, 41
    supporting details, 86
    topics, 10–11, 30–31
    topics for argument paragraphs, 87
    topics for cause and effect paragraphs, 80–81
    topics for comparison and contrast paragraphs, 74–75
    topics for definition paragraphs, 69
    topics for descriptive paragraphs, 59
    topics for illustration paragraph, 48
    topics for narrative paragraph, 53
    topics for process paragraphs, 64
    topics for writing, 125, 145, 158, 176, 195–96, 206, 222, 238, 246, 259–60, 273–74, 286, 295, 303, 314, 331, 342, 357, 368, 381, 392, 404–5
writing from reading. *See also* reading selections
    outlining reading, 420
    summarizing reading, 420
    written response, 420–21
writing links, 52, 58, 97
    argument writing topics, 87
    cause and effect writing topics, 80
    comparison and contrast writing topics, 74
    definition writing topics, 69
    descriptive writing topics, 59
    illustration writing topics, 49
    narrative writing topics, 53
    process writing topics, 64
    revising for unity and support, 103
writing portfolio, 10
writing process, 2–11
    audience, 4
    developing stage in, 12–31
    exploring stage of, 3–11, 92
    exploring strategies, 5–9
    journal, 10
    portfolio, 10
    purpose, 5, 92
    revising and editing, 32–42
    topic, 4

Y

yet, as coordinating conjunction, 251
you're/your, 365

Notes

Notes

Notes

Notes

SINGLE PC LICENSE AGREEMENT AND LIMITED WARRANTY

READ THIS LICENSE CAREFULLY BEFORE OPENING THIS PACKAGE. BY OPENING THE CD PACKAGE IN THE MIDDLE OF THIS BOOK, YOU ARE AGREEING TO THE TERMS AND CONDITIONS OF THIS LICENSE. IF YOU DO NOT AGREE, DO NOT OPEN THE PACKAGE. PROMPTLY RETURN THE UNOPENED PACKAGE AND ALL ACCOMPANYING ITEMS TO THE PLACE YOU OBTAINED THEM.

1. GRANT OF LICENSE and OWNERSHIP: The enclosed computer programs ("Software") are licensed, not sold, to you by Pearson Education, Inc. ("We" or the "Company") and in consideration of your purchase or adoption of the accompanying Company textbooks and/or other materials, and your agreement to these terms. We reserve any rights not granted to you. You own only the disk(s) but we and/or our licensors own the Software itself. This license allows you to use and display your copy of the Software on a single computer (i.e., with a single CPU) at a single location for academic use only, so long as you comply with the terms of this Agreement. You may make one copy for back up, or transfer your copy to another CPU, provided that the Software is usable on only one computer.

2. RESTRICTIONS: You may not transfer or distribute the Software or documentation to anyone else. Except for backup, you may not copy the documentation or the Software. You may not network the Software or otherwise use it on more than one computer or computer terminal at the same time. You may not reverse engineer, disassemble, decompile, modify, adapt, translate, or create derivative works based on the Software or the Documentation. You may be held legally responsible for any copying or copyright infringement which is caused by your failure to abide by the terms of these restrictions.

3. TERMINATION: This license is effective until terminated. This license will terminate automatically without notice from the Company if you fail to comply with any provisions or limitations of this license. Upon termination, you shall destroy the Documentation and all copies of the Software. All provisions of this Agreement as to limitation and disclaimer of warranties, limitation of liability, remedies or damages, and our ownership rights shall survive termination.

4. LIMITED WARRANTY and DISCLAIMER OF WARRANTY: Company warrants that for a period of 60 days from the date you purchase this SOFTWARE (or purchase or adopt the accompanying textbook), the Software, when properly installed and used in accordance with the Documentation, will operate in substantial conformity with the description of the Software set forth in the Documentation, and that for a period of 30 days the disk(s) on which the Software is delivered shall be free from defects in materials and workmanship under normal use. The Company does not warrant that the Software will meet your requirements or that the operation of the Software will be uninterrupted or error-free. Your only remedy and the Company's only obligation under these limited warranties is, at the Company's option, return of the disk for a refund of any amounts paid for it by you or replacement of the disk. THIS LIMITED WARRANTY IS THE ONLY WARRANTY PROVIDED BY THE COMPANY AND ITS LICENSORS, AND THE COMPANY AND ITS LICENSORS DISCLAIM ALL OTHER WARRANTIES, EXPRESS OR IMPLIED, INCLUDING WITHOUT LIMITATION, THE IMPLIED WARRANTIES OF MERCHANTABILITY AND FITNESS FOR A PARTICULAR PURPOSE. THE COMPANY DOES NOT WARRANT, GUARANTEE OR MAKE ANY REPRESENTATION REGARDING THE ACCURACY, RELIABILITY, CURRENTNESS, USE, OR RESULTS OF USE, OF THE SOFTWARE.

5. LIMITATION OF REMEDIES and DAMAGES: IN NO EVENT, SHALL THE COMPANY OR ITS EMPLOYEES, AGENTS, LICENSORS, OR CONTRACTORS BE LIABLE FOR ANY INCIDENTAL, INDIRECT, SPECIAL, OR CONSEQUENTIAL DAMAGES ARISING OUT OF OR IN CONNECTION WITH THIS LICENSE OR THE SOFTWARE, INCLUDING FOR LOSS OF USE, LOSS OF DATA, LOSS OF INCOME OR PROFIT, OR OTHER LOSSES, SUSTAINED AS A RESULT OF INJURY TO ANY PERSON, OR LOSS OF OR DAMAGE TO PROPERTY, OR CLAIMS OF THIRD PARTIES, EVEN IF THE COMPANY OR AN AUTHORIZED REPRESENTATIVE OF THE COMPANY HAS BEEN ADVISED OF THE POSSIBILITY OF SUCH DAMAGES. IN NO EVENT SHALL THE LIABILITY OF THE COMPANY FOR DAMAGES WITH RESPECT TO THE SOFTWARE EXCEED THE AMOUNTS ACTUALLY PAID BY YOU, IF ANY, FOR THE SOFTWARE OR THE ACCOMPANYING TEXTBOOK. BECAUSE SOME JURISDICTIONS DO NOT ALLOW THE LIMITATION OF LIABILITY IN CERTAIN CIRCUMSTANCES, THE ABOVE LIMITATIONS MAY NOT ALWAYS APPLY TO YOU.

6. GENERAL: THIS AGREEMENT SHALL BE CONSTRUED IN ACCORDANCE WITH THE LAWS OF THE UNITED STATES OF AMERICA AND THE STATE OF NEW YORK, APPLICABLE TO CONTRACTS MADE IN NEW YORK, AND SHALL BENEFIT THE COMPANY, ITS AFFILIATES AND ASSIGNEES. THIS AGREEMENT IS THE COMPLETE AND EXCLUSIVE STATEMENT OF THE AGREEMENT BETWEEN YOU AND THE COMPANY AND SUPERSEDES ALL PROPOSALS OR PRIOR AGREEMENTS, ORAL, OR WRITTEN, AND ANY OTHER COMMUNICATIONS BETWEEN YOU AND THE COMPANY OR ANY REPRESENTATIVE OF THE COMPANY RELATING TO THE SUBJECT MATTER OF THIS AGREEMENT. If you are a U.S. Government user, this Software is licensed with "restricted rights" as set forth in subparagraphs (a)-(d) of the Commercial Computer-Restricted Rights clause at FAR 52.227-19 or in subparagraphs (c)(1)(ii) of the Rights in Technical Data and Computer Software clause at DFARS 252.227-7013, and similar clauses, as applicable.

Should you have any questions concerning this agreement, please contact in writing: Legal Department, Prentice Hall, One Lake Street, Upper Saddle River, NJ 07458. If you need assistance with technical difficulties, call: 1-800-677-6337. If you wish to contact the Company for any reason, please contact in writing: English Media Editor for Humanities and Social Sciences, Prentice Hall, One Lake Street, Upper Saddle River, NJ 07458.